CAMBRIDGE LIBRARY COLLECTION

Books of enduring scholarly value

Medieval History

This series includes pioneering editions of medieval historical accounts by eye-witnesses and contemporaries, collections of source materials such as charters and letters, and works that applied new historiographical methods to the interpretation of the European middle ages. The nineteenth century saw an upsurge of interest in medieval manuscripts, texts and artefacts, and the enthusiastic efforts of scholars and antiquaries made a large body of material available in print for the first time. Although many of the analyses have been superseded, they provide fascinating evidence of the academic practices of their time, while a considerable number of texts have still not been re-edited and are still widely consulted.

Abstracts of the Chartularies of the Priory of Monkbretton

The priory of St Mary Magdalene, Monkbretton, was founded around 1154 as a daughter house of Pontefract, and became Benedictine in 1281 following disputes with the Cluniac order. The chartulary, abstracted and published in 1924, is unusually late, written after 1529, shortly before the priory's dissolution. It comprises 352 folios, arranged by location, with a table of contents. Also included are lists made in 1558 of books belonging to the prior and monks, by then dispersed among several owners. An earlier Latin chartulary exists in the British Library and an English abstract of this forms an appendix to the present volume, along with other items that do not appear in the later document. Although the priory was relatively small, the monks were careful stewards of their property. Most of its possessions were in the near vicinity, and it escaped the first round of dissolutions, with fourteen monks receiving pensions.

T0382613

Cambridge University Press has long been a pioneer in the reissuing of out-of-print titles from its own backlist, producing digital reprints of books that are still sought after by scholars and students but could not be reprinted economically using traditional technology. The Cambridge Library Collection extends this activity to a wider range of books which are still of importance to researchers and professionals, either for the source material they contain, or as landmarks in the history of their academic discipline.

Drawing from the world-renowned collections in the Cambridge University Library and other partner libraries, and guided by the advice of experts in each subject area, Cambridge University Press is using state-of-the-art scanning machines in its own Printing House to capture the content of each book selected for inclusion. The files are processed to give a consistently clear, crisp image, and the books finished to the high quality standard for which the Press is recognised around the world. The latest print-on-demand technology ensures that the books will remain available indefinitely, and that orders for single or multiple copies can quickly be supplied.

The Cambridge Library Collection brings back to life books of enduring scholarly value (including out-of-copyright works originally issued by other publishers) across a wide range of disciplines in the humanities and social sciences and in science and technology.

Abstracts of the Chartularies of the Priory of Monkbretton

EDITED BY JOHN WILLIAM WALKER

CAMBRIDGE
UNIVERSITY PRESS

CAMBRIDGE UNIVERSITY PRESS

Cambridge, New York, Melbourne, Madrid, Cape Town,
Singapore, São Paolo, Delhi, Mexico City

Published in the United States of America by Cambridge University Press, New York

www.cambridge.org
Information on this title: www.cambridge.org/9781108058537

© in this compilation Cambridge University Press 2013

This edition first published 1924
This digitally printed version 2013

ISBN 978-1-108-05853-7 Paperback

The Anniversary Reissue of Volumes from the Record Series of the Yorkshire Archaeological Society

To celebrate the 150th anniversary of the foundation of the leading society for the study of the archaeology and history of England's largest historic county, Cambridge University Press has reissued a selection of the most notable of the publications in the Record Series of the Yorkshire Archaeological Society. Founded in 1863, the Society soon established itself as the major publisher in its field, and has remained so ever since. The *Yorkshire Archaeological Journal* has been published annually since 1869, and in 1885 the Society launched the Record Series, a succession of volumes containing transcriptions of diverse original records relating to the history of Yorkshire, edited by numerous distinguished scholars. In 1932 a special division of the Record Series was created which, up to 1965, published a considerable number of early medieval charters relating to Yorkshire. The vast majority of these publications have never been superseded, remaining an important primary source for historical scholarship.

Current volumes in the Record Series are published for the Society by Boydell and Brewer. The Society also publishes parish register transcripts; since 1897, over 180 volumes have appeared in print. In 1974, the Society established a programme to publish calendars of over 650 court rolls of the manor of Wakefield, the originals of which, dating from 1274 to 1925, have been in the safekeeping of the Society's archives since 1943; by the end of 2012, fifteen volumes had appeared. In 2011, the importance of the Wakefield court rolls was formally acknowledged by the UK committee of UNESCO, which entered them on its National Register of the Memory of the World.

The Society possesses a library and archives which constitute a major resource for the study of the county; they are housed in its headquarters, a Georgian villa in Leeds. These facilities, initially provided solely for members, are now available to all researchers. Lists of the full range of the Society's scholarly resources and publications can be found on its website, www.yas.org.uk.

Abstracts of the Chartularies
of the Priory of Monkbretton
(Record Series volume 66)

When this edition was originally prepared, the manuscript of the cartulary was in the ownership of the Wentworth family of Woolley, who subsequently deposited it with the Yorkshire Archaeological Society. It was sold by the owner at an auction on 11 April 1961 at Sotheby's saleroom, where it formed Lot 143 and was acquired by the British Library. It now has the reference BL Additional Manuscript 50755. It is number 675 in G.R.C. Davies, *Medieval Cartularies of Great Britain: A Short Catalogue*, (London, 1958) and in the revised edition, *Medieval Cartularies of Great Britain and Ireland*, edited by C. Breary, J. Harrison and D.M. Smith (London, 2010). Further information may be found in J.R. Purvis, 'New light on the chartularies of Monkbretton Priory', *Yorkshire Archaeological Journal*, 37 (1948), 67–71, and G.R.C. Davies, 'Two chartularies from the West Riding', *British Museum Quarterly*, 24, no. 3/4 (December 1961), 67–70 and plates XXI–XXII. Lot 142 in the same sale, which is now Additional Manuscript 50754 of the British Library, was the cartulary of the Priory of St John of Pontefract, which forms Record Series volumes 25 and 30 (also reissued in the Cambridge Library Collection).

J.W. Walker, the editor of this volume, was president of the Yorkshire Archaeological Society from 1938 to 1948, and an obituary and bibliography appear in the *Yorkshire Archaeological Journal*, 38 (1951–5), 416–18. He edited volume 5 of the Wakefield Court Rolls for the Record Series, and was the author of *An Historical and Architectural Description of the Priory of St Mary Magdalene of Monk Bretton*, published by the Society as volume 5 of the Extra Series in 1926.

ABSTRACTS OF THE

CHARTULARIES

OF THE

PRIORY OF MONKBRETTON

THE YORKSHIRE
ARCHÆOLOGICAL SOCIETY

FOUNDED 1863.   INCORPORATED 1893.

RECORD SERIES.

VOL. LXVI.

FOR THE YEAR 1924.

ABSTRACTS OF THE

CHARTULARIES

OF THE

PRIORY OF MONKBRETTON

EDITED BY

J. W. WALKER, O.B E., F.S.A.,

*Honorary Secretary
Yorkshire Archæological Society Record Series.*

PRINTED FOR THE SOCIETY.

1924.

PREFACE.

A Priory in the wood of Lund, about one-and-three-quarter miles east of the town of Barnsley in the West Riding of the county of York, was founded by Adam Fitz-Swane about the year 1153–4,[1] for monks of the Cluniac order, and was dedicated to St. Mary Magdalene.

The founder died about Midsummer, 1159.[2]

This priory was a daughter house of the Cluniac priory of St. John of Pontefract; Adam, the fourth prior of that house, was chosen as the first prior of the new foundation, taking with him certain monks from Pontefract. Within a hundred years of the foundation dissensions arose as to the subjection of Monkbretton (or, as it was then called, Bretton) priory to the mother house, and the election of a prior. An adjudication of the dispute was made in 1269,[3] whereby the daughter house was to be " free and absolute of all subjection or obedience to Pontefract," and were to have " a free election or creation of the prior of their own will and pleasure whenever a vacancy occurs," but " they shall send to Pontefract for the prior of Pontefract to install him upon his election and creation." This judgment failed to satisfy the conflicting parties, and the monks of Bretton decided that their independence could only be secured by a complete severance of their house from Pontefract and also from the Cluniac order. On 8 September, 1279, a visitation was made by the priors of Montdidier and Lenton in the chapter house at Monkbretton, by order of Ives de Chassant, abbot of Cluni, when the prior of Montacute passed sentence of excommunication upon William de Rihale the prior, the subprior and the whole contumacious community; he also revoked the compact between the two priories and declared it null and void.[4]

On 4 January of the following year, 1280–1, William Wickwane, archbishop of York, visited Monkbretton priory, to whom, in their chapter house, the prior, subprior and the whole community pro-

---

[1] *Early Yorkshire Charters*, vol. iii, No. 1475, pp. 168–170.

[2] *Ibid.*, p. 319.

[3] *Monasticon Anglicanum*, vol. v, p. 123.

[4] *Visitations of English Cluniac Foundations*, p. 32. Sir G. F. Duckett.

mised canonical obedience,[1] and for the future were to be recognised as a Benedictine house.

The priory was surrendered on 21 November, 1538, by the prior and thirteen monks.

The Chartulary, now at Woolley Hall, must have been written between the years 1529 and 1538, as it contains several grants in the reign of Henry VIII, the latest dated 6 July, 1529, only nine years before the priory was dissolved.

This Woolley copy of the chartulary is a third volume of 352 pages of vellum, the leaves measuring 11 inches long by 8 inches broad, and (inclusive of its covers) 3¾ inches thick. Early in the nineteenth century it was bound in brown calf by its then owner, Godfrey Wentworth Wentworth, Esquire, whose bookplate it bears. Unfortunately the leaves were then cut down, and in the process some letters of the inscriptions on the margins were thus removed, and at the same time gilt was applied to the edges of the leaves.

The handwriting is large and clear, the vermilion ink, used in the titles and in the ornamentation of the initial letters, is very bright. The black ink used in the text is still unfaded. The initial letters, of which a few specimens are reproduced, are finely drawn, and in some cases very large; many of them include masks drawn with much humour, red, black and yellow inks being used for illuminating purposes. Towards the middle of the volume the initial letters are larger and more elaborate, but rarely bear faces; those on folios 269d to 278d are of a composite character. Quaint outline drawings of human heads have been made on the lower margins of folios 72 and 136. At folio 207 the handwriting changes, but the titles in vermilion continue to be in the same hand throughout.

The charters are grouped under vills, of which a consecutive list is given at the commencement of the volume. Following, and on the dexter side of the last leaf of this index, there has been inserted a list of books belonging to the priory, or rather to the prior and two of the monks, which was made by them 21 July, 1558 (twenty years after the dissolution of the priory), when they were living at Worsborough, a village near their old house. The inserted catalogue is in quite a different style of writing, and the ink has partially faded. It occupies four pages of double columns, and contains a list of 148 books, 31 of which are stated to be in the house

---

[1] Reg. Wm. Wickwane, Abp. of York, fo. 135d (Surtees Soc., vol. 114, p. 138).

of William Brown, formerly prior of Monkebretton; 28 in the house
of Thomas Wylkynson and Richard Hinchclyf at Worsburghe, given
to them by Thomas Frobyscer formerly subprior of the monastery;
15 belonged to Thomas Wylkynson, *alias* Bolton, in the same house;
54 were acquired or copied by Richard Hynchclyff, who also possessed 13 books on physic and 7 on grammar.

When the brethren left the priory they must have taken this
chartulary with them to Worsborough, and inserted the catalogue
of their books in it in 1558.

Worsborough is a village only three miles from Wortley Hall,
the next resting-place of this volume, so it is most probable that it
was acquired from the deposed monks residing at Worsborough,
either in their lifetime or on the death of the survivor, by Sir Richard
Wortley, of Wortley Hall, who died 25 July, 1603, or by his son,
Sir Francis, in whose possession it was on 30 December, 1629, when
Mr. Francis Burdett, of Birthwaite, lent to Roger Dodsworth some
notes " taken out of a Cowcher belonging to the priory of Monkbretton in the custody of Sʳ Francis Worteley, Knight, baronet."[1]
In August, 1630, Roger Dodsworth copied a large portion of it,
which copy is now in the Bodleian Library,[2] and states that it was
then in the possession of Sir Francis Wortley.   Extracts were taken
from this book in 1648, which was then in the possession of Sir George
Wentworth, of Woolley.[3]

How the chartulary passed from the library at Wortley Hall to
that at Woolley, between the years 1630 and 1648, is not known.
Dr. John Burton took extracts from this book when preparing his
Monasticon Eboracense, published in 1758, and records that the
owner was Sir Godfrey Wentworth, of Hickelton (and Woolley).[4]
Since that date it has remained the property of his descendants at
Woolley Hall.

There is an earlier chartulary in the British Museum (Landsowne
MS. 405).   It is smaller than the Woolley MS., having only 65 leaves
on vellum.   This MS. contains 262 charters, many of them not being
included in the Woolley copy.   Probably the lands to which they
referred had been sold or exchanged before the compilation of the
later chartulary, thus the deeds had passed out of the possession of,
and were of no further use to the priory.

[1] Dodsworth MS., vol. 155, fo. 67*d*.
[2] *Ibid.*, fo. 25.
[3] Lansdowne MS. 207, fo. 289 (old), 283 (new).
[4] *Mon. Ebor.*, p. 92, note *a*.

The Lansdowne chartulary once consisted of 10 small pages and 90 greater pages, according to a note made at the end of the book by a former owner, Sir William Armyne, 6 May, 1633, but is now reduced to 65 folios, 55 large and 10 small, The folios are of vellum, and measure the smaller 10½ by 6¼ inches, the larger 11 by 7¼ inches. It is now bound in brown leather, the binding measuring 11⅜ by 7¾ inches, and it is ⅝ inch thick.

The first two folios are on paper and contain a brief but inaccurate note on the chartulary by Dr. Ducarel, who examined it 18 April, 1763. The manuscript commences in the thirteenth and continues into the fourteenth century, the latter having only three deeds, of which the latest is dated 1336, the remaining 259 belong to the thirteenth century.

On folio 56 is a curious charm or curse in old French against worms, cancers, festerings, whitlows, scurvy, etc.

This chartulary came into the possession of William Blitheman when the site of the monastery with its buildings was granted to him in 1540. He died in 1543. His grandson, Jasper Blitheman, sold the site of the monastery and the buildings that had not been pulled down, and presumably the chartulary, in 1580, to George, sixth earl of Shrewsbury, who settled the Monkbretton property upon his fourth son, Henry Talbot, on his marriage with Elizabeth, daughter and heiress of Sir William Rayner, of Overton Longville, co. Huntingdon. Henry Talbot died in 1595, aged 33, leaving a widow and two daughters. The widow married, for her second husband, Thomas Holcroft, of Vale Royal, co. Chester, whom Dodsworth mentions as the custodian of this chartulary in 1614.[1] Henry Talbot's second daughter, Mary, married Sir William Armyne, of Osgodby, co. Lincoln, bart., and in the partition of her father's estate Monkbretton priory fell to her share. Dodsworth took extracts from this chartulary in 1634, which he states was then " in the possession of Sir William Ayrmin, Knight, of Osgodby."[2] In 1704 Peter le Neve saw it in the hands of the heir of Millington, the bookseller, of London.[3] Walter Clavell, Esq., had it in 1709, at whose sale it was purchased by James West, Esq., who was the owner on 18 April, 1763, when it was examined by Dr. Ducarel. At some period unknown it passed into the library of William, first Marquess of Lansdowne, who died 7 May, 1805. His manuscripts, including

---

[1] Dodsworth MS. 159, fo. 34.

[2] *Ibid.* 147, fo. 76; 155, fo. 61; 159, fo. 34.

[3] Harleian MS. 4757, p. 98.

the chartulary of Monkbretton, were purchased in 1807, by a vote of Parliament, for the sum of £4,925, from his representatives, and now form the Lansdowne collection in the British Museum. This chartulary is numbered 405.

A transcript of the Woolley MS. had been made by our late honorary librarian, Mr. W. T. Lancaster, F.S.A., but I have gone carefully through every deed in the original, making fairly complete abstracts of all the charters in English. For the sake of brevity I have omitted the warranty and sealing clauses. Christian names are usually given in a modern form, but surnames and place-names (except in a few cases of the former denoting a tradé or occupation) are printed as they appear in the original. The lists of witnesses, fortunately very complete, are always given, and it is hoped that they may be of use to Yorkshire genealogists, especially for fourteenth and fifteenth century pedigrees.

The Monkbretton Chartulary in the British Museum (Lansdowne MS. 405) was transcribed and abstracts in English made from it by the editor. When the same deed occurs in both the Woolley and Lansdowne chartularies it is printed in the Woolley copy, and its reference number is given in the Lansdowne copy, thus: Fo. 3*d*. 1, No. 6. W. MS. (Woolley MS.). The abstracts from the Lansdowne copy are generally summarised, only the bare facts are given, but all the witnesses' names are given.

When in 1634 Roger Dodsworth copied the chartulary, now Lansdowne MS. 405, it was complete and contained the ninety pages mentioned by Sir William Armyne in the previous year. Dodsworth's MS. 8, 147, 155, and 159 supply the deeds now missing in the original. To make this volume complete I have transcribed all those not contained in the Lansdowne copy, and added them as a supplement.

Where the name of the grantee is not mentioned in these transcripts it should be understood that the grant is always made to the prior and convent of Monkbretton.

The seal of the priory was a vesica, showing the patron saint, St. Mary Magdalene, full length, wearing a long open cloak, with the legend, *Marie*. This seal, 2¾ inches long by 2 inches, was attached to a deed of 1420.

My own and the thanks of the Society are specially due to Major Wentworth, of Woolley Hall, for his kindness in entrusting the chartulary and many other early deeds to me for the purposes of transcription and publication. I must also express the great obligation which I am under to my friend, Mr. Charles Clay, F.S.A., for his invaluable help in reading the proof sheets and for many suggestions; to Professor Hamilton Thompson, F.S.A., for help with the witnesses to the papal bulls, and to my daughter, Ethel W. Walker, for copying out the transcript of the Woolley chartulary for the printers, for preparing the index, and for copying the quaint drawings.

J. W. WALKER.

EAST HAGBOURNE,
        October, 1924.

THE
CHARTULARY OF MONKBRETTON PRIORY.

In this volume are inscribed all the charters, feoffments, confirmations, and also the quitclaims of all the lands and tenements
which belong to the Monastery of the Blessed Mary Magdalene
of Monkbretton and the monks serving God there, by whatever
title they are held according as they are found fully disclosed in
their places.

A LIST OF THE CONTENTS OF THE BOOK.

In primis of the original foundation of the monastery, the churches
of Roreston and Carleton with other donations.

Fasham.

In primis of the donations of Henry the Almoner and Roger
Montbegon. Item of a certain pasture in Brereley.

Cudworth.

In primis of the concessions of Robert Stapylton. Item of the
donation of Peter de Byrthwayt of that vill afterwards fully shown.

Monkbretton.

In primis of the lands and tenements formerly William Bretton's
and Richard Bretton's. Item of one messuage of four acres of land
formerly William Ruston's. Item of one messuage with its appurtenances formerly William Westall's. Item of the lands and tenements formerly Robert Dyconson's. Item of the lands and tenements of John Frere. Item of a rent of 16*d.* receivable from the
lands and tenements formerly Thomas Wroo's. Item of the lands
and tenements formerly Henry Staynton's. Item of certain lands
and tenements and rents in Monkbretton, Carleton, and Cudworth.
Item of the licence of our Lord the King for 14 shillings in Penyston,
Thoriston, and Oxspring. Item of the lands and tenements of
William Wylde, formerly Robert Heron's. Item of certain controversies for the aforesaid lands and tenements formerly Wilde's
and the attachment of the mill of Barnysley.

Carleton.

In primis of the lands and tenements formerly Richard Ricroft's.
Item of a rent of 8½*d.* for land in the territory of the said vill. Item
of lands and tenements formerly John Watman's.

Cudworth.

In primis of lands and tenements formerly John Sparke's. Item
of lands and tenements formerly Richard Bayard's. Item of lands

A

and rents in the said vill. Item of lands and tenements formerly
John Haywarde's. Item of lands and tenements formerly John
Phayrom's. Item of lands and tenements formerly William Carlyll's.
Item of a parcel of lands called Whyteleghes. Item of one acre
of land in William Roide. Item of three roods of land formerly
Nicholas Ruston's. Item of lands and tenements formerly John
Boyne's. Item of lands and tenements formerly William Depyng's.
Item of lands and tenements formerly Thomas Humbeloke's.

Erdysley.

In primis of the lands and tenements formerly William Scott's.
Item of certain lands of the same. Item of one assart called Wete-
royde. Item of the lands and tenements formerly Henry Brome's.
Item of certain lands and rents in the said vill. Item of one assart
called Normanroide. Item of certain controversies between the
prior of the above Monastery and William Bosewill. Item of
certain lands and rents formerly belonging to Alexander Drax.
Item of the attachments of the fulling mill. Item of a controversy
about the waste and wood in the aforesaid vill of Erdysley. Item
of the lands and tenements formerly John Daude's. Item of certain
lands and closes called Thomas Roide formerly Thomas Wode's.

Darffelde.

In primis of the lands and tenements formerly Richard Mauger's.

Mylnehows.

In primis of the mill of Millnehous. Item of a parcel of land
there called Pyknonyerde. Item of the lands formerly Richard
Woodhall's.

Hyll.

Item of lands in Hyll.

Howland.

Item of a rent of 4s. receivable from an assart called Gylbert-
royde. Item of two acres of land formerly Thomas Oxspryng's
in the said vill of Mylnehous.

Halton Minor.

Item of one messuage and croft with their appurtenances.

Halton Major.

In primis of certain lands and tenements in the said vill. Item
of a rent of 2s. 8d.

Byllyngley.

In primis of certain rents receivable from lands and tenements
in the said vill.

Thyrscho.

In primis of two tofts with six acres of land there.

Hykylton.

In primis of certain lands and tenements with other liberties
of the aforesaid vill formerly belonging to Randulph de Novomercato. Item of lands and tenements formerly Robert Palden's.
Item of lands and tenements formerly John Smyth's.

Cadby.

In primis of one bovate of land with the liberties of the said vill formerly belonging to William de Novomercato.

Adwyke super Stratum.

In primis of certain services and rents in the aforesaid vill.

Doncaster.

In primis of one messuage with its appurtenances in the said vill.

Wranbrok.

In primis of certain lands and tenements in the aforesaid vill formerly belonging to Roger Montbegon. Item of one parcel of land called Ravenescroft. Item of certain lands in the territory of that vill. Item of lands and tenements formerly John Pullen's. Item of lands and tenements formerly John Adamson's.

Newhall Brampton.

In primis of six and a half acres of land. Item of certain rents in Brampton and certain lands in Newhall. Item of lands formerly belonging to William Cressy. Item of lands and tenements formerly Thomas Chambers'. Item of two acres of land formerly William Lounde's.

Wyntworth.

In primis of lands and tenements called Swine in that vill. Item of a rent of 6d. receivable from one tenement formerly Robert Wodehall's. Item of eleven acres of land formerly Hugh Wyntworth's.

Mekysburgh.

In primis of lands and tenements formerly belonging to Thomas Plowrygth.

Wyrkysburghdalle (Worsboro dale).

In primis of lands called Blaberoxgang. Item of lands in the territory of the said vill called Wardeffeldys. Item of certain rents and services in the territory of the said vill. Item of lands and tenements called Wellehows. Item of certain lands and rents in the territory of the said vill. Item of lands and tenements called Wygfall. Item of lands and tenements formerly Thomas Gawde's in Worsburgth. Item of lands and tenements formerly belonging to John Frankyshe called Darleycliff. Item of lands and tenements called Spynkhowse.

Smythley.

Item of a rent of 4s. receivable from certain lands in the said vill.

Barneby.

Item of a rent of 16d. receivable from certain lands and tenements there.

Barghe.

Item of one culture in the territory of the said vill called Roger Royde.

Swalohyll.

Item of certain lands, rents and services there.

Dartton.

Item of two acres of land in the territory of that vill.

Cubley.

Item of lands and tenements there called Cubley.

Brokhows.

In primis of lands and tenements there called Brokhows.

Oxspryng.

Item of certain lands and rents in Oxspryng, Penyston, Thurleston and Cudworth.

Wakeffelde.

In primis of lands and tenements formerly Robert Mason's. Item of lands and tenements formerly John Royde's.

Ardyslaw.

Item of a rent of 6*d*. receivable from lands in the territory of that vill.

Roston.

In primis of one tenement with an orchard next the church of that vill. Item of one rood (*pertico*) of land belonging to the vicar of the Church of Roston.

Aboldehagh.

Item of four acres of land in the aforesaid place.

> [*Two entries have been erased here, only two or three of the words are legible.*]

Notton.

In primis of certain lands and rents in the said vill.

Dartton and Mapilwell.

In primis of a certain pasture there.

Morehows.

Item of a rent of 6*d*. receivable from certain lands there.

Wolley.

In primis of certain rents and lands in the said vill. Item of lands and tenements formerly Thomlynson Lande.

East Marcham.

In primis of lands, tenements and rents and services in the said vill. Item of the abundance of the said lands in the aforesaid vill.

Beghton.

In primis of the lands, tenements, rents and services in the aforesaid vill. Item of the connection between the prior of the aforesaid Monastery and the nuns of Wallandwells. Item of the connection between the aforesaid prior and the prior of Blida (Blyth). Item of certain rents there.

Finis.

These books with the following titles are in the house of William Brown, formerly prior of Monkbretton, 21 day of July, 1558, bought at his own expense.

In primis Vetus et Novum Testamentum translatore Hieronimo.

Item Opera Hugonis Cardinalis super totam Bibliam, in sex voluminibus distincta.

Ludulphus de vita Christi cum Expositione Evangeliorum totius anni.

Divus Augustinus super Epistolas Paulinas. Collectore venerabili Beda.

Jacobus de Valentia super Psalterium.

Sermones Thesauri novi de tempore.

S. Meffreth, alias Hortulus regia de tempore.

S. Joh'is Nider, tam de tempore quam de Sanctis.

Sermones parati.

S. Vincentii de Valentia, de tempore, in ii voluminibus.

Sermones de Societati de Sanctis.

Sermones Pomerii Phelberti de Sanctis.

Destructorium vitiorum.

Preceptorium Joh'is Nider, cum expositione.

Historia Scolastica et historia ecclesiastica ambo in uno volumine.

Summa angelica.

Hemetarius doctorum, tam de tempore quam de Sanctis, opus valde notabile.

Cathena Aurea Sancti Thome Aquinatis super evangelia.

Opus Regale de persecutionibus ecclesie, etcetera.

Sermones Meillardi dominicales et quadragesimales.

Anima fidelis, Sermones quadragesimales.

Revelationes Brigitte Virginis.

Figure Biblie.

Gerson de Imitatione Christi.

Legenda Anglicana.

Legenda Aurea in englysche.

Flowr of Comawndments.

Ye pylgramage of perfeccyon.

Gesta romanorum cum Moralationibus.

Methodius et Mawndewall.

Cronica cronicarum.

The following books are in the chamber of Thomas Wylkynson and Richard Hinchclyf at Worsburgh, the year and day above written, and were of the gift and at the expense of Thomas Frobyscer, formerly subprior of the aforesaid monastery.

In primis Nicolaus de Lyra super totum Vetus Testamentum in quatuor libros distinctos cum glosulario ordinario et additionibus.

Opera divi Chrisostomi, duo volumina preclara.

Dictionarius per Fratrem Petrum Baxcharii editus in tres libros distinctos ordine alphabetico.

Divi Augustini de civitate dei libri duo et viginti cum commentariis et additionibus necnon theologicis veritatibus Francisci Maronis in uno volumine.

Idem Augustinus super Johannem Evangelistam.
Tercia pars operum Sancti Ambrosii.
Nicolaus de Gorran super epistolas Paulinas.
Bruno super eadem Paulinas epistolas.
Ludulphus super psalterium.
Expositio D. Johannis Hyspani de terre ex psalter.
Sermones discipuli.
Sermones dicti Biga salutis perutiles.
Sermones Nicolai Denusie de dominicis et Sanctis.
Magister Sententiarum cum conclusionibus et commentariis.
Rationale divinorum.
Opera Augustini. Notata.
Tractatus de reparacione Humani generis.
Casus Longi Bernardi super decretales.
Regula beati Benedicti cum commentario.
Alius liber introductorius pro novitiis de ritu et ceremoniis
Religionis collectore Thoma Frobiscer scriptus R. Tyckyll.
Tractatus de profectu Religiosorum.
Reformaciones monastici vindicie.
Clementis P.P. v. cum extravagantiis Johannis P.P.
Lavacrum conscientie.
Benedictina sive constitiones Benedict. xii.
Boetii de consolatione philosophie. v. libros.
Scala perfectionis.
Schepard Kalendare.

The following books are (the property of) Thomas Wylkynson
alias Bolton, and remain in the same chamber at Worsburghe the
day and year above written.

In primis Domini Hugonis Cardinalis postilla in iiii^{or} evangeliorum apices.

Thomas tertius, collectanea venerabilis Bede presbyteri epistolas
Divi Pauli continens.
Eximii Johannis Damasceni de fide orthodoxa.
Explanationes Roberti Holcot in Proverbia Salomonis.
Nicolai de Orbellis super sententias compendium.
Guillelmus Worringtonii super sententiarum libros 4.
Sermones Gabrielis Berleti tum xll^{es} tum de sanctis.
Postillaciones super evangelia et epistolas per universum annum.
Novum Testamentum Erasmo translatore.
Quodlibetales questiones sancti Thome Aquinatis.
Albini Caroli magni in Genesi questiones.
Gramatica Johannis Dispanterii.
Gramatica Petri Pontarie.
Walgaria viri doctissimi Horman.
Colloquia Erasmi.

The books which are described on the following page are (the
property of) Richard Hynchclyff alias Wollay, acquired at his own
expense and by his hand, and are now at Worsburg in the aforesaid
chamber. In the year of the Birth of Christ, 1558, 21 July.

In primis Vita Christi ex medullis evangelicis collecta per Ludulphum ex saxonia.

Historiarum Domini Antonini Archipresulis Florentini, totam seriem veteris et Novi Testamenti necnon omnium fere sanctorum vitas breviter illucidant.

Onus ecclesie, Autore Johanne Clemens de vii ecclesie statibus abusibusque eisdem gravissimis et futuris calamitatibus eidem ingruentibus, ex Sanctorum Propheciis solidissimisque scripturis luce clarius enerrans.

Opuscula divi Augustini Hyponis episcopi.

Opera melluflui doctoris Bernerdi.

Rosetum exerticiorum spiritualium per venerabilem presbyter John Manburnum.

Decretum Gratiani.

Scolastica historia.

Omelia beate Gregorii pape super ezechielem prophetam et Libri officiorum sapientissimi Ambrosii; ambo in uno volumine.

Manipulus Florum.

Polleantheon opus suavissimis floribus exornatum, tam de Novo quam Vetere Testamento, et dicta doctorum.

Epistole beati Hieronimi.

Sermones Nicolai de Blouis de tempore et Sanctis multas hereses confutantes.

Opus aureum Antonii de Gislandis, expositiones evangeliorum in quadriplici sensu continens cum octo millibus questionibus.

Postille sive expositiones evangeliorum ac epistolarum totius anni.

Elucidissima in divi pauli commentaria Dionisii Carthusiani. Et vita auctoris simul, et operum ejus Cathologus.

Sermones parati.

Stellarium corone benedicte Marie virginis.

Dictionarius Pauperum. Et Figura Biblie; ambo in uno libro.

Enchyridion pietatis Amatorum, ex variis sanctorum patrum scriptis confectum.

Compendium theologice veritatis; paradisus anime Alberti Magni; et transitus beati Hieronimi; ac liber cure pastoralis Gregorii pape. Hii iiii tractatus in uno volumine.

Summa angelica.

Margareta Philosopica, vii artium liberalium precipua elucidans.

Speculum vite humane, videlicet statuum commoda et pericula exactissime describens.

Vetus et Novum [Testamentum] translatore Hieronimo in duobus voluminibus manualibis.

Magister Sententiarum.

Sanctus Thomas de Aquino super Magistrum sententiarum iiii^{or} volumina.

Aliud opus super sententias egregium, quod Resolutio Theologorum merite dicitur.

Libri Ethimologiarum Isidori Spalensis episcopi.

Ambrosius Calepinus, latinarum et grecarum dictionarium interpres perspicacissimus.

Mammotrectus totius Biblie et aliarum que in ecclesia recitatio partium difficilium significantias accentia per genera insinuans.

Consolatorium Theologicum Johannis de Tambaco.

Opus aureum de veritate contritionis per Johannis Ludovicum vivaldum de monte regali.

Lavacrum conscientie, cum tractatu de arte beati vivendi et bene moriendi.

Manuale Confessorum Johannis Nider, et libellus de morali liberti eiusdem Nider; ac libellus de regimine rusticorum; hii tres tractatus in uno volumine.

Libellus in quo continentur sex, videlicet, de justitia concomitativa; Consolatorium Conscientie; Tractatus de corpore Christi; de juditiis; Confessionale Sancti Thome; Et Elegantiarum xx^{ti} precepta, hii omnes in uno volumine.

Alius liber in quo continentur hii tres, 1° super psalmum Miserere explanatio; Secundo Horologium devocionis; Tertio de Castitate sacerdotum.

Flores evangeliorum Dominicalium Odonis cat'.

Alius liber in quo continentur hii tres, primo unius articuli dissolubilitate matrimonii contingentis; Secundo Pia exhortatio Rome ad Germaniam per Johannem Cochleum; Tertio Johannis Ditembergii de votis monasticis contra Lutherum.

Preceptorium Nicolai de Lira.

Soliloquium Bonaventure de iiii^{or} exercitiis.

Epistole Marsilii Sicini Florentini. Et Lactantii Firmiani de divinis institutionibus. Hi vii omnes in uno volumine.

Illustrium virorum Epistole, videlicet Angeli politiani Johannis pici miranduli et aliorum plurimorum.

Libellus epistolarum quas correctoria vocant.

Gesta Romanorum.

Opusculum de doctoribus et eorum privilegiis.

Aurora, tota ferme bibliam menitiarum usibus complectens.

Proverbia Solomonis.

Summa Johannis Bellet.

Regula Sancti Augustini.

Due Regule Sancti Benedicti cum diologo beati Gregorii, ambo portionales.

Venerabilis Bede presbiteri de temporibus.

Musica monachorum Johannis Norton Prior de Monte Gratie.

Likewise the following books on physic are (the property of) the same Richard Hinchclyfe.

In primis liber canonis quem princeps Abohali edidit, translatus a magistro Girardo Tremanensi.

Ortus Sanitatis, de Herboribus et Plantis de Animalibus et Piscibus.

Luminare maius medicis et aromaticariis necessarius.

Regimen Sanitatis magnimi mediolanensis medici. Secreta Hypochratis et Tractatus de vivis a magistro Arnaldo de Media villa editus. Omnes hii in uno libello.

Macer de herbarum viribus.
Regimen Sanitatis Salarnitatum.
Lumen apoticorum.
Diete universales et particulare Isaac.
Constantius de medendis egritudinibus.
Alii iiii°ʳ libelli propria manu exarati quorum unus extractus verbatim ex Johanne de Vigo exavatione; alii vero ex Mess et aliis.

Libri grammaticales et ad idem spectantes sunt hii.
In primis Roberti Whitintoni editio.
Johannis de Garlandia, tam Synonima et Equivoca.
Epistole et Oratii.
Colloquium Erasmi.
Elegantie terminorum; et Cato cum commentario.
Et Seneca moralissimus cum commentario; etcetera plurimis.

(*Folio* 1)¹ (1) Decree of the lord pope for the confirmation of the first foundation. Innocent, bishop, servant of the servants of God, to his chosen sons the prior of the church of St. Marie Magdalene of Bretton and the brethren of the same, who now or in the future profess the rule. I.N.P.P.M. Therefore beloved sons in the Lord we mercifully grant your just demands, and we take the aforesaid church of St. Marie Magdalene of Bretton, in which Divine worship is to be observed, under our protection and that of St. Peter. First, the statutes of the monastic order and the rules of St. Benedict must be inviolably observed for all time. Moreover whatever possessions or goods the said church possesses justly and canonically, or in a future pontificate by concession, by the gift of kings or princes, or the offerings of the faithful, or by any other just ways obtained, they are to remain fast and unimpaired to you and your successors for ever. We have caused them to be described under their particular designations. (*Fo.* 1d) The place where the said church is situated; by the gift of Adam son of Swane, the founder, Bretton with its appurtenances; Lunda, the mills of Dirna, Carleton with its appurtenances; the church of Roreston (which the Pope grants to the proper uses of the donees) with its appurtenances; a carucate of land in Derneshart with its appurtenances. By the gift of Henry the almoner (*elemosinarii*) Phasam. By the gift of Gilbert de Norton eighteen acres of land and a toft (*toftum*) in the same place. By the gift of Adam son of Horm six bovates of land in Cudewrda. By the gift of Robert de Stapelton twelve acres of land.² By the gift of Aibert³ four acres in the same place. By the gift of W. de Nevill and Roger de Monte Begon' one carucate of land in Wrainbroc. By the gift of Henry son of Swane 8s. yearly in the same vill. By the gift of Adam son of Peter the fish-pond (*vivarium*) between Roreston and Carletun, five acres of meadow in Sinedahalis, a moiety of the mill of Milnehous. By the gift of John son of Essolf the service of

¹ The previous folios are not numbered.

² The town is not stated. According to Pope Urban's confirmation (page 11 *post*) it was Cudworth.

³ *Sic*; according to Pope Urban's confirmations the donor was Adam de Flinthil (page 11 *post*).

Hugh de Witewrda. By the gift of Swane de Holanda the service of William (*fo.* 2) the smith (*fabri*) of Swalewehil; and all other possessions which the said founders of the church reasonably conveyed. Confirmation of liberties and immunities granted by founders and hitherto observed. Free clerks and laity "fleeing from the world" (*e seculo fugientes*) may be received into religion (*ad conversionem*) and retained. Prohibition against any brother, after profession, leaving the monastery except for a more strict religion, without the licence of the abbot, and against anyone keeping back such a seceder without letters of the monks.

Prohibition against anyone promulgating a sentence of excommunication, suspension, or interdict against the brethren or the monastery without manifest or reasonable cause. When there is a general interdict on the land, the brethren may celebrate divine offices in their monastery with low voice, doors being closed, excommunicate persons excluded, bells not being rung. The diocesan bishop to grant them the consecrated oil, consecration[1] of altars or churches, and ordination of their clerks or monks promoted to orders. (*Fo.* 2d) Sepulture at the house to be free so that no one may oppose the devotion and last wish of those who have resolved to be buried there, unless they be under excommunication or interdict, saving nevertheless the right of those churches from which bodies of dead are taken away. On the death of a prior, let no one, by cunning or violence, be appointed, except him who shall be chosen by common consent of the brethren, or of the majority of the wiser brethren according to God and the rule of St. Benedict.

Decree against disturbance of the house, deprival of possessions, or annoyance, but all things to be conserved wholly for the use of those for whose governance and support they were granted; saving always the authority of the Holy See and the canonical right of the diocesan. Denunciation of those, cleric or lay, who contravene this decree, unless after due warning satisfaction be made, and benediction of all preserving the rights of the house.[2]

I Innocent, the Pope (*Catholice Ecclesie Episcopus*).

✠ I Peter, Bishop of Porto and Sancta Rufina.

✠ I John, Bishop of Albano.

(*Fo.* 3d) ✠ I Guido, Bishop of Praeneste (Palestrina).

✠ I Pandolf, Cardinal Priest of the basilica of the XII Apostles.

✠ I Peter, Cardinal Priest of St. Cecilia.

✠ I Jordan, Cardinal Priest of St. Pudenziana.

✠ I Hugh, Cardinal Priest of St. Martin in Equitio.

✠ I Goffrid, Cardinal Priest of St. Praxede.

✠ I Bernard, Cardinal Priest of St. Peter ad Vincula tituli Eudoxiae.

✠ I Gregory, Cardinal Deacon of St. Mary in Porticu.

✠ I Gregory, Cardinal Deacon of St. George ad Velum aureum (Velabro).

---

[1] Written *consecrationis*.

[2] A sketch of the papal seal follows.

✠ I Peter, Cardinal Deacon of St. Mary in Via Lata.
✠ I Hugh, Cardinal Deacon of St. Eustachius.
✠ I Matthew, Cardinal Deacon of St. Theodore.

Given at the Lateran, by the hand of Blasius sub-deacon of the Holy Roman Church and Notary. 6 Id. December, Indic. iv, the year of the Divine Incarnation 1200; in the 3rd year of the Pontificate of Innocent III.

(Monkbretton Chartulary, Lansdowne MS. 405, fo. 62d.)

(Fo. 4) (2) Letters[1] of Pope Urban III with protection to the Priory of St. Mary Magdalene of Lunda with regulations as follows. The rule of St. Benedict established therein to be observed. Confirmation of possessions present and future reciting the following—the place in which the said church is situated with the appurtenances; (fo. 4d) by the gift of Adam son of Swane, Bretton with all its appurtenances and the mills of Derna and Lunda of his father and Karletona with the appurtenances, the church of Roriston with its appurtenances, and Newhale, and Raineberga and Luthewait[2] and whatever he had in Braton, and the mill of Neuhale, and all things belonging to the said lands, and in Halethun half a carucate of land, and the mill of Chinnkishahe, and 12d. in Wdehusun; by the gift of Robert the knight of Stapelton the land of Chudewrda; by the gift of Adam de Flinthil four acres in the same vill; by the gift of Swane de Derfeld eight acres in Erdesleia. By the gift of Henry son of Swane 8s. from half a carucate of land in Wrangebrok. By the gift of the noble man W. de Nesvilla and Amabel his wife the mill of Langedenedale. (Clauses as to receiving entrants, and prohibition of those having professed leaving the priory without licence, similar to those in Pope Innocent's letters, page 10 ante.) Lands newly cultivated by the canons or at their expense or forage of animals not to be subject to tithes,(fo. 5) liberties and immunities granted by ecclesiastic or secular persons to the canons or their men, and reasonable customs observed in the church confirmed and to remain unimpaired in future (clause of prohibition of excommunication or interdict without due cause (with prohibition from levying new or undue exactions on them or their men) as in Pope Innocent's letters, page 10 ante), also licence for modified service in time of interdict as in the same letter. No one to build churches within the parishes of the canons' churches without their consent and the bishop's (saving the privileges of the Roman Church). (Sepulture clause as before.) Prohibition against violence, rapine, or theft within the precincts of houses (fo. 5d) or granges of the canons. No one to demand money from them for the sacred oil, consecration of altars or churches, and other ecclesiastical sacraments. General prohibition against disturbance and seizure of their property, but all things are to be fully conserved for the general uses of those for whose governance and support they were granted; saving the authority of the Apostolic See and rights of the diocesan bishop. Denunciation of anyone attempting to contravene

---

[1] The document is partly printed in Mon. Ang., v, 139.

[2] Lintwait in Adam's charter.

this ordinance, after warning, unless satisfaction be made, as in the previous letter. The peace of our Lord Jesus Christ to all those who preserve the rights of the house, so that both here they may receive the reward of their good deeds, and before the strict Judge may find the reward of everlasting salvation.[1]

(*Fo.* 6) I Urban, the Pope (*Catholice Ecclesie Episcopus*).

✠ I Henry, Bishop of Albano.
✠ I Paul, Bishop of Praeneste (Palestrina).
✠ I Theobald, Bishop of Ostia and Velletri.
✠ I John, Cardinal Priest of St. Martin.
✠ I Peter de Bononia, Cardinal Priest of St. Susanna.
✠ I Laborans, Cardinal Priest of St. Mary's Transtiberi tituli Calixti.
✠ I Pandolf, Cardinal Priest of the XII Apostles.
✠ I Albinus, Cardinal Priest of the Holy Cross in Jerusalem.
✠ I Agelier, Cardinal Priest of St. John and St. Paul tituli Pammachii.
✠ I Adelard, Cardinal Priest of St. Marcellus.
✠ I Jacinthus, Cardinal Deacon of St. Mary in Cosmedin.
✠ I Gratian, Cardinal Deacon of St. Cosma and St. Damian.
✠ I Bobo, Cardinal Deacon of St. Angelo.
✠ I Octavian, Cardinal Deacon of St. Sergius and St. Bachus.
✠ I Geoffrey, Cardinal Deacon of St. Mary's in Via Lata.
✠ I Roland, Cardinal Deacon of St. Mary's in Porticu.
✠ I Peter, Cardinal Deacon of St. Nicholas in Carcere Pulliano.

(*Fo.6d*) ✠ I Ralph, Cardinal Deacon of St. George ad Velum aureum (Velabro).

Given at Verona by the hand of Albert, Cardinal Priest of the Holy Roman Church and Chancellor. 5 Kal. June, Indic. iv, in the year of the incarnation of our Lord 1186, the first year of the Pontificate of Urban III.

(Monkbretton Chart., Lansdowne MS. 405, fo. 62d.)

(*Fo.* 7) (3) General protection by Pope Innocent [IV] for the Canons, their house, and goods acquired or to be acquired, and confirmation of possessions. At Perugia, 10 Kal. Jan., in the first year of the Pontificate (1243-4).

(*Fo.* 7d) (4) Protection by Pope Honorius [III] for the canons and their house and possessions acquired or to be acquired; mentioning specially the vills of Bretton and Carleton with all their appurtenances and the wood called Londa; with confirmation of all possessions and liberties justly held by the canons. At Rieti, 10 Kal. Aug., the third year of the Pontificate (1227).

(Monkbretton Chart., Lansdowne MS. 405, fo. 63d.)

(*Fo.* 8) (5) Urban [IV] servant of the servants of God, to his beloved son the Abbot of Selby. It has come to our hearing that the prior and convent of the priory of Monkbretton and their predecessors have granted to certain clerks and laymen certain possessions of the house, to the grave damage thereof, for life, for

[1] A sketch of the papal seal follows.

a considerable term, or at perpetual farm or annual rent, whereof some have asked for Papal confirmation: We command you that what you find of the properties of the priory so unlawfully granted you procure the return of to the right and ownership of the priory. Any letters, instruments, renunciations or confirmations notwithstanding; (*fo. 8d*) restraining those gainsaying, by ecclesiastical censure, appeal being waived, witnesses who from regard, dislike or fear have withdrawn themselves, being compelled under the same penalty to testify to the truth. Dated the 16th Kal. May, the second year of the Pontificate (1262).

(*Fo.* 9) (6) Grant[1] by Adam son of Swane to God and St. Mary Magdalene of Lunda and Adam then prior of Brettona and to the monks serving God there, in pure and perpetual alms, of Brettona with all things to it belonging, and the mills of Derna and Lunda of his father and whatsoever is contained (*habetur*) between Dirne and Stainclyff as far as Meresbrook, Newhall and Rainesberga and Lintwait and whatever he had in Brampton. All these he confirms and grants, under the witness of the present charter, that they (the canons) may hold and possess quietly and freely, from the grantor and his heirs, in pure alms, for ever. Of this gift the witnesses are Alexander and Richard his (the donor's) sons, Esuuard de Alemaneburi and Robert his brother, Dolfin de Aluelai and William and Henry his sons and Siward his brother, Herbert the priest, Thomas de Dertona, Barnard de Silkestona and Richard his son, Alan de Brettona and Adam and Richard his brothers, Richard son of Herding and his brother, Matthew de Oxspring, Swane de Holand, Aelsi Bacun.

(Monkbretton Chart., Lansdowne MS. 405, fo. 3d. and 24.)

(*Fo.* 9d)[2] (7) Grant by Adam son of Swane to God and St. Mary Magdalene of Lunda and the monks serving God there, of Carletuina with its appurtenances and the church of Rorestune as far as belongs to him, in pure and perpetual alms, with the other alms he has given to the same house in wood and plain, in meadows, waters and pastures. Witnesses, Henry his brother, Rainald, prior of Wederhale, Walter his (Adam's) nephew, Gospatric son of Orm, Alan his (Adam's) nephew, and many others.

(Monkbretton Chart., Lansdowne MS. 405, fo. 4.)

(8) Grant by Adam son of Peter to God and St. Mary Magdelene of Brettona and the monks serving God there, of the fish-pond (*vivarium*) between Rorestun and Karleton, and the toft on which one man dwells at the head of the orchard at the west; in pure and perpetual alms, free and quit of all secular exaction, specially for the soul of Robert the donor's son. Witnesses, William de Rorestun, Richard de Laceles, Robert son of Adam, William de Winthewrtha, John de Rostun, and others.

(*Fo.* 10) (9) Confirmation by Roger de Montbegon to the church of St. Mary Magdelene of Bretton and the monks serving God there of whatever Adam son of Swane, his grandfather, gave

---

[1] Printed in *Mon. Ang.*, v, 136.

[2] Headed " Prima Fundacio."

them and by his charters confirmed, in pure alms, in wood and plain, in mills and waters, as Adam granted, in everything which belongs to him (Roger). He has likewise confirmed to them a full moiety of the vill of Karlet' with whatsoever belongs to it, and a mediety of the church of Roreston with all its appurtenances. And by way of addition he (Roger) has given them four bovates of land in Wrangebroc with all liberties and appurtenances in pure and perpetual alms. These confirmations and donations he has made for the health of his soul and the souls of Adam son of Swane, his grandfather; and of his father and mother, and his ancestors and heirs, free and quit of secular service, as pure alms should be. Witnesses, William son of Adam, Gilbert de Notton, Adam de Biri, Henry his brother, Adam[1] de Claipole, William de Penigeston, John Tirell, William Bacun, Hugh and Thomas his brothers, and others.

(Fo. 10d)   *Monkbretton.*

(10) Confirmation of Adam de Montbegon[2] and Matilda his spouse to the church of St. Mary Magdelene of Lunda and the monks serving God there of whatsoever Adam son of Swane granted and confirmed to them; namely in wood and plain, mills and waters, and everything which belongs to his (the present confirmor's) portion, in the hereditary right of (Adam Fitz Swane's) younger daughter,[3] whom the present confirmor has married. They confirm also to the monks for the soul of Adam son of Swane and of their own souls, their share of Carleton, namely a full moiety of the vill and whatsoever belongs to it, and the mediety of the church of Rorestun which falls to their share, as far as it appertains to them in free, pure, and perpetual alms. Witnesses, Rainer son of Swane, Walter Fleming (*Flandrensis*), Adam son of Peter and Roger his brother, Richard son of Herding, Henry son of Dolfin, Thomas son of Swane, Adam Brun, Richard de Reulent, Roger de Locceclat,[4] Uctred son of Suenebern, Ailsi Bacun, Hubert de Ckiu, and others.

(Fo. 11) (11) Confirmation by Geoffrey de Nevill and Mabel his wife to the church and monks as above of whatever Adam son of Swane granted and confirmed to them; namely in wood and plain, etc., and everything which belongs to them (the confirmors). They also confirm to the monks Carletona and the church of Roreston, with all appurtenances, as much as belongs to them, and they renounce all the right which they alleged they had in the said church, as well respecting the last presentation as other things, and they have by this deed confirmed the right to the monks. Witnesses, Robert de Skeknes, Peter de Nevill, Robert son of Adam, Roger de

---

[1] Written *Ade*.

[2] Written Mumbegon in text, but heading as above.

[3] *Junioris filie.* Adam Fitz Swain left two daughters, coheiresses, Amabel and Matilda. In view of the above statement it is difficult to account for Hunter's remark (*South Yorkshire*, ii, 228) that Amabel was the younger daughter. See also the confirmation by John Malherbe, Matilda's second husband, page 15 *post.* For correct pedigree see *Early Yorkshire Charters*, iii, 319.

[4] Farrar, *Early Yorkshire Charters*, has "Loccedal."

THE CHARTULARY OF MONKBRETTON PRIORY.

Notton, John parson of Felekirke, William son of John, William de Grimesthorpe, Richard Brasard, Ralph de Rupe, Robert de Deneby, and others.

(*Fo. 11d*)[1] (12) Confirmation by William de Nevill and Amabil his wife to the church of St. Mary Magdelene of Lunda and the monks serving God there of whatsoever Adam son of Swane granted and confirmed to them; namely in wood, in plain, in mills and waters, and in everything which belongs to William by hereditary right of his wife. They have confirmed also to the monks for the souls of Adam, their own souls, and those of their ancestors and successors, their share of Carleton, namely a full moiety of the vill with whatever belongs to it; and by way of additions they have granted the monks four bovates of land from their demesne in Wrangebroc in pure and perpetual alms, with all liberties and appurtenances; this grant they have made to the monks for their sustenance. Witnesses, Rainer the clerk of Derefeld, Serlo the clerk of Mirefeld and Hugh his brother, William de Nosmarche, Adam son of Horm, and many others.

(*Fo. 12*) (13) Confirmation by Thomas de Burgo and Sarra his wife to God and the church of St. Mary Magdelene of Lunda and the monks serving God there of all donations and confirmations which Adam son of Swane made to them (the monks) by his charters, and all donations and confirmations which William de Nevill and Amabil his wife made to them, to wit, of a moiety of the vill of Carleton with all appurtenances and liberties and of four bovates of land in Wrangebroc from their demesne with all appurtenances and of a mediety of the church of Roreston with the chapel and all appurtenances in pure and perpetual alms, as their charters witness. Witnesses, William de Nevill, Adam son of Orm, Richard son of Barnard, Nicholas de Gerdestune, Hugh son of Alan, Simon de Curs, Hugh de Elm, and many others.

(14) Confirmation by John (*fo. 12d*) Malherbe and Matilda his spouse to the church of St. Mary Magdelene of Lunda and the monks serving God there of whatsoever Adam son of Swane granted and confirmed to them, in wood, in plain, in mills and waters, and in everything which belongs to his (John's) portion by hereditary right of the younger daughter[2] (i.e. Adam's) whom he has taken to wife. They have likewise confirmed to the monks, for the souls of Adam, themselves, and their ancestors, their share of Carleton, namely a full moiety of the vill and whatever belongs to it, and also the mediety of the church of Roreston which falls to the share of himself (John) and his wife, as far as to them belongs, in free, pure and perpetual alms. Witnesses, Richard the chaplain, Ranulf de Morles, William de Lambervilla, Geoffrey Gerner, Ranulf Malherbe, William son of Adam, Roger Tirel, Roger de Mundbegun, William de Rorestun, Eustace son of John son of Esscolf, and others.

---

[1] This folio and folio 12d headed " Prima Fundacio."

[2] See note 3, page 14.

(*Fo.* 13) (15) Grant by Roger de Montbegun to the church of St. Mary Magdelene of Bretton and the monks there for the souls of Adam son of Swane, his father and mother, and all his predecessors, of all his land in Wrangebroc, namely four bovates with the appurtenances in wood and plain, etc., quit and free from all secular service and exaction, in pure and perpetual alms. Witnesses, William the priest, William de Peningeston and Simon his brother, John Tirel, Henry de Biri, Gilbert de Notton, William son of Richard, Richard de Tohleston, Robert Branchard, Adam the serjeant (*serviente*), and many others.[1]

Fasham.

(16) Grant by Henry son of William the almoner (*elemosinarii*) to God and St. Mary Magdelene of Bretton and the monks there of all his land of Fasham with all its appurtenances without retention (*fo.* 13*d*) and with all easements and liberties belonging to the land, in pure and perpetual alms. And in addition he has given the monks a penny yearly from a toft in Pontefract at Easter, from the service of Hervey son of Kaskil and from the service of William de Colna, 6*d*. at Martinmas from a toft in Pontefract. This gift he has made to the monks in pure alms, saving the service of his lord, Roger de Montebegon, rendering thence yearly to him (Roger) and his heirs from the land of Fasham, two pairs of hose (*hosarum*) of Pontefract for all service at Martinmas. Witnesses, William de Stapelton, Moses de Hoderode, John Tirell, Gilbert de Notton, Ernald Pigace, Ralph Tirel, William de Roreston, Hugh de Bretton, Peter de Erdesley, and many others.

(17) Grant by Roger de Montebegon to God and St. Mary Magdelene of Bretton and the monks there of the service of Henry the almoner from the land of Fasham which he held of right, namely two pairs of hose of Pontefract or 4*s*. yearly at Martinmas; for the health of his (Roger's) soul and the souls of his father and mother and of Adam son of Swane, his grandfather, (*fo.* 14) in pure and perpetual alms. Witnesses, Gilbert de Notton, Robert de Bretton, William and Adam and John his brothers, William son of Gilbert de Notton, Alexander the cook, Thomas de Tanelebi, Rainer the chamberlain (*camerario*), William son of Adam, Hugh de Bretton, and many others.

(18) Grant by Roger de Montebegon for the health of his soul and that of his grandfather, Adam son of Swane, to the men (*hominibus*) of St. Mary Magdelene of Lunda, dwelling in the vill of Fasham, of free common of pasture in the territory of Brerlay, in wood, in plain, in meadows and pastures with all other easements to the said common pertaining. So that they may have a common for their own animals without annoyance or molestation from him or his heirs. But the said men are not to receive the cattle of others to the damage of the said pasture. Warranty, as pure and perpetual

---

[1] See folio 179, page 102.

alms. Witnesses, Gilbert de Notton, William de Stapelton, Robert son of Adam, John de Hoderode, and others.

(*Fo.* 14*d*) (19) Confirmation and quitclaim by John son of Richard the parson of Hoderode to the men of St. Mary Magdelene of Bretton, and of the monks there, dwelling in the vill of Fasham, of free common of pasture in the territory of Schafton, whereof there was dispute between them; so that they may common in the pasture with the men of Schafton with their own animals, without disturbance by him or his heirs, but the said men shall not receive the animals of their lords or of others to the damage of the said pasture. Warranty, as far as appertains to the quitclaimor or his heirs. Witnesses, Roger de Montebegon, Gilbert de Notton, Robert Birthwait, Henry de Tancisleia, John de Rokeleia, William de Sotil, William de Grimestorp, Richard Brasard, John son of Hugh de Bretton, and many others.

(*Fo.* 15) (20) Grant by John son of Richard de Felekirke to God and the church of St. Mary Magdelene of Bretton and the monks there, in pure and perpetual alms, of three acres of land with the appurtenances, in the territory of Safton,[1] namely two acres on Gresilandes, and half an acre on Cunegeshaccroftes at Blindewelle, and half an acre at Kyrkeker, with the appurtenances. To hold freely and quietly, etc., in wood and plain, in pastures and meadows, with all easements, liberties and commons of the said vill of Safton. Warranty. Witnesses, Robert son of Adam, Roger de Notton, Jordan de Nunleswithe, William de Bosco, Robert de Holande, Alan de Rihil, Matthew de Notton, and many others.

Cudworthe.

(21) Grant by Sir Robert de Stapilton (*fo.* 15*d*) to God and St. Mary Magdelene of Bretton and the monks there of a bovate of land, of the two bovates which Peter the shepherd (*barcarius*) of Cutheworthe formerly held of him, with all the appurtenances: that one namely which lies to the north in the territory of Cutheworthe. To hold and to have freely and quietly, etc., in wood, in plain, etc., with all other easements and liberties and free commons to the said land belonging: rendering to the donor during his life 3*s.* of silver yearly for all service and demand save foreign service, as belongs to so much land of that fee in the said vill. And after the donor's death the said rent shall remain to the monks, free and quit, without claim or hindrance by his heirs, to make a corrody to the convent for ever on the day of his death. Warranty. These being [witnesses],[2] Sir John de Hoderode, William de Wenervile, Sir William de Bretton, and many others.

---

[1] The word here and again later in the charters seems to be written " Salton," but it is very plainly " Safton " in the heading—meaning doubtless Shafton.

[2] Word omitted in the manuscript.

B

(*Fo.* 16) (22) Grant by Robert son of William de Stapilton to God and the church of St. Mary Magdelene of Bretton and the monks there, in pure and free and perpetual alms, for the souls of himself, his wife and his ancestors, and for a yearly anniversary for him after his death, of that land in Cuthewortha which Robert de Brekere held, to wit, six acres of land and the toft and meadow belonging to the said land, and the essart of Moseleia which Robert son of Raven held, with all things appertaining to it, and with all liberties of the vill, without reserve. Witnesses, Rainer (*Renerius*) the clerk of Derfeld, Adam son of Orm, William son of Hervey, Hugh son of William de Stapelton, Gilbert de Notton, Richard son of Harding, Matthew son of Robert, and many others.

(23) Grant by Peter de Birkethwait son of Adam son of Orm to God and St. Mary Magdelene of Bretton and the monks there, of six bovates of land in Cudeworthe, to wit, five bovates which Robert de Pull and Henry de Stainton held and one bovate which Ralph son of Wlbern held, with all the appurtenances without retention, (*fo.* 16*d*) in wood, in plain, etc., within the vill and without, with free common of the same vill, in exchange for a moiety of the mill of the moor which his father gave the said monks in pure and perpetual alms, and for one bovate of land in Langeside with the pasture which his father had similarly given them in pure alms, and for a quitclaim of the service of Robert de Pul, brother of the present donor, from a carucate of land in Ailsitorp by Cudeworthe, namely 3*s*. yearly, whereof they had the charter and confirmation of his (Peter's) father, in perpetual alms. Warranty. Witnesses, William son of Everard then bailiff, William de Peningeston, Jeremiah de Tornhil, John Tyres, John the chaplain of Silkeston, Robert Walais, and many others.

(*Fo.* 17)[1]   *Monke Bretton.*

(24) Grant by William Bretton to Thomas Haryngton, esquire, Richard Pekke, William Bradforth and Thomas Dodworth, of two messuages, two crofts, eighteen and a half acres of land, wood, meadow and pasture, and six butts of land and a parcel of meadow with certain assarts called Emrode, Okecroft, Waterbutts, and two pighills (*pighellez*)[2] with appurtenances in Monkbretton, and similarly all lands and tenements lying in the same vill in a certain place called Hesilhirst; whereof of the said eighteen and a half acres of land, parcel of meadow and six butts, one rood lies on Snaperode between the land of John Shortlyng on the east and the land of the Prior of Monkbretton on the west abutting on Gamilwelrodhede, and four butts of curtilage land and meadow abutting on the croft of John Auty, etc., as more fully appears in the charter of the said William Bretton. He has also given to

---

[1] " Monkebretton " written in the margin. The dorses are headed " Monk-bretton " to 23*d*.

[2] Pightel, pightle, pighill, etc., a small field or enclosure, especially one near a house, a corner of a field, a long narrow slip of ground: see Wright's *Eng. Dialect Dict.*, iv, 489.

the said Thomas, Richard, William and Thomas, all other messuages, crofts, lands, tenements, woods, meadows and pastures,
with their appurtenances, which he has in the said vill and territory, excepting two essarts called Sixtrode and Turneng. To have
and to hold all the aforesaid to the grantees, their heirs and assigns,
from the chief lords of those fees, by the services (fo. 17d) thence
due and accustomed, for ever. Warranty. Appointment of Robert
Toye and John Grenwode as attorneys to deliver seisin. Witnesses, Nicholas Wortley junior, Hugh Brerelay, John Keresford,
and others. At Monkbretton aforesaid, 1 November, 23 Hen. VI
(1444).

(25) Release and quitclaim by Thomas Haryngton, Richard
Pekke, William Bradford and Thomas Dodworth (fo. 18) to Richard,[1]
prior of the monastery of Blessed Mary Magdelene of Monkbretton
and the convent thereof and their successors for ever, of all right,
title, and claim in two messuages, two crofts, eighteen and a half
acres of land, wood, meadow and pasture and six butts of land
and a parcel of meadow, with certain essarts called Emrode, Okecroft, Waterbuttes, and two pighills with their appurtenances, in
Monkbretton, and similarly all lands and tenements lying in the
same vill in a certain place called Hesilhirst; which they the grantors had by the grant of William Bretton. Dated 4 December,
23 Hen. VI (1444).

(26) Release and quitclaim by William Bretton, son and heir
of John Bretton, to the prior and convent of Blessed Mary Magdelen of Monkbretton and their successors of all right and claim in
certain lands and tenements, with the appurtenances, in Monkbretton, to wit, an essart called Emrode, an essart called Okecroft,
an essart called Waterbutts, and two pighills with the appurtenances,
which the prior and convent have and hold for a term of years by
demise of Richard Bretton his grandfather and the said John Bretton
his father. (Fo. 18d) Dated 20 September, 23 Hen. VI (1444).

(27) Grant by Richard de Bretton of Monkbretton, junior,
to William del Cotes of the same, and Matilda his wife and their
heirs or assigns, of a messuage with garden[2] adjoining and the
appurtenances, in the vill of Monkbretton, as situated between
the tenement of Richard Bretton the donor's father on the west,
and the tenement of Richard Hayron on the east. To have and to
hold to the grantees, their heirs and assigns, freely, quietly, (fo. 19)
and in peace, of the chief lords of that fee, by the services due
and accustomed. Warranty.[3] Witnesses, Richard Birton senior,
Richard Hairon, and others. Dated at Monkbretton, the feast of
Michaelmas, 3 Hen. IV (1401).

[1] In the heading called Richard Ledes.

[2] *cardino.*

[3] In this and other documents the warranty clause is cut down to "et
ego et heredes mei, etc.," or a nearly similar abbreviation.

(28) Grant[1] by William Cotes of Monkbretton to Richard Oxspryng of Cudworth and Thomas Dodworth of Bargh, their heirs and assigns, of a messuage with garden adjoining, which the grantor lately had by the gift of Richard Bretton junior, in the vill of Monkbretton. To have and to hold to the said grantees, their heirs and assigns, freely, quietly and in peace, from the chief lord of that fee, by the services due and accustomed. Warranty (abbreviated). Witnesses, John Keresforth, John Ruston, and others. Dated at Monkbretton, the feast of St. John of Beverley, 1430.

(29) Release and quitclaim (*fo.* 19*d*) by Richard Oxspryng and Thomas Dodworth to Richard,[2] prior of the monastery of the blessed Mary Magdelene of Monkbretton and the convent thereof and their successors for ever of all right, title, and claim in a messuage and garden adjoining,[3] with all the appurtenances in Monkbretton, which the grantors had by the gift of William Cotes. Dated at Monkbretton, 20 June, 16 Hen. VI (1438).

(30) Grant[4] by William Birtton[5] of Acworth to Thomas Boton, John Thomson, chaplains, and Thomas Robynson of a close called Sighrode lying beside the bridge of Barnyslay and also all his messuages, lands and tenements, meadows, woods and pastures within the parishes of Ruston and South Kyrkby, with all the appurtenances. To have and to hold to the grantees, their heirs and assigns, from the chief lords of those fees, by the services due and accustomed. (*Fo.* 20) Warranty. Appointment of John Walkar of Ruston and Richard Wilde of Barnysley as attorneys to deliver seisin. Witnesses, John Clyfe, John Person, William Raynald, and others. Dated at Ackworth, 5 January, 6 Edw. IV (1467).

(31) Demise and delivery by John Thomson, chaplain, and Thomas Robynson to Richard Ledes, prior of the house of blessed Mary Magdelene of Monkbretton, of a close called Sighroyde and a parcel of meadow called Turneyng, lying beside the bridge of Barnysley, with their appurtenances in Monkbretton, which the grantors, together with Thomas Boton now deceased, lately had, amongst (*fo.* 20*d*) other things, by the gift of William Birton. To have and to hold to the said prior and his successors for ever from the chief lords of those fees, by the services thence due and accustomed. Witnesses, William Dodworth, Richard Kersforth, Richard Symmes, and others. Dated at Monkbretton, 20 May, 7 Edw. IV (1467).

(32) Grant by William Ruston of Schafton, son and heir of John Ruston junior of Codworth to Thurston[6] Banyster and William

---

[1] Headed " Carta Willelmi Cotes, Ricardo Oxspryng et Thome Dodworth de predictis mesuagio et gardino."

[2] Styled Richard Ledes in the heading.

[3] In the heading, " In the aforesaid messuage and garden."

[4] Written opposite in the margin are the words " . . . . . yrrode and twrniug," the first letters of the former cut off in binding. ·

[5] Bretton in the heading.

[6] Thrustane.

Bradfforth, of a messuage and four acres of land and meadow with all the appurtenances in Monkbretton. To have and to hold to the grantees, their heirs and assigns, freely, quietly, etc., from the chief lord of that fee, by the services thence due and accustomed. Warranty. Witnesses, Thomas Dodworth, Hugh Brierley and Richard Wilde, and others. Dated at Monkbretton, the feast of St. Mathias, apostle, 1444.

(*Fo.* 21) (33) Release and quitclaim by Thirstan Banaster and William Bradforth to the prior of the Monastery of the blessed Mary Magdelene of Monkbretton and the convent thereof and their successors for ever of all right, title, claim and demand of and in a messuage and four acres of land with their appurtenances in Monkbretton, which they had by the gift of William Roston. At Monkbretton, 20 June, 1445.

(34) Grant by William Grubber of Monkbretton to Richard Ledes, prior of the Monastery of blessed Mary Magdelene of Monkbretton and the convent there, of all that messuage with the buildings thereon, with the toft and croft and an acre of land to the said messuage belonging, with the appurtenances, in the vill and within the bounds (*fo.* 21*d*) of Monkbretton ; whereof half an acre lies on Hesilwelrode between the land of the said prior and convent on either side, and a rood and a half lie together in Le Fall, one head abutting on the land of the prior and the other on Gamulrodewellesike between the land of John de Bretton on the north and the land of the said prior and convent on the south; and half a rood lies on Lynghill and abuts at one head on Shepeyngesike, and at the other on Constablebutts: which the grantor, jointly with Matthew Smyth, chaplain, now deceased, lately had by the gift and feoffment of Richard Westhall of Snayth, son of Thomas Westhall, formerly of Barnyslay. To have and to hold to the said prior and convent and their successors freely, quietly, etc., from the chief lord of that fee, by the services thence due and accustomed, for ever. Warranty (abbreviated). Witnesses, Thomas Hairon, Richard Wilde, and others. At Monkbretton, 6th February, 1444.

(35) Grant by Robert Diconson, son of John Diconson of Monkbretton, and Alice his wife to Richard, (*fo.* 22) prior of the monastery of blessed Mary Magdelene of Monkbretton and the convent thereof of all those lands, tenements, rents, etc., with the appurtenances, which the grantors lately had by the gift or feoffment of Thomas Heyron of Monkbretton and Hugh Kylen of Havercroft, in the vill and within the bounds of Monkbretton, and which the same Thomas and Hugh lately had by the gift and feoffment of the grantor Robert. To have and to hold to the prior and convent and their successors for ever, from the chief lords of that fee by the services due and accustomed. Warranty. Witnesses, John (*blank*), John Patrur, Thomas Halle, and others. Dated 12 March, 16 Hen. VI (1438).

(36)   Grant by John Frere, son of Richard Frere of Monkbretton, to William Hepworth, Richard Kydall, Thomas Cartwright of Barnyslay and John Autie, their heirs and assigns, of all those lands and tenements with their appurtenances, which he (the grantor) has in the vill and territory of Monkbretton.   To have and to hold to the grantees,[1] their heirs and assigns, (*fo. 22d*) for ever, from the chief lords of the fee by the services thence due and accustomed. Warranty.   Witnesses, Richard Oxspryng, John de Bretton, William Wylde, and others.   At Monkbretton, 29 April, 1422.

(37)   Release and quitclaim by William Hepworth and Richard Kydall to the prior and convent of blessed Mary Magdelene of Monkbretton and their successors for ever of all right, title and claims of and in all those lands and tenements with all the appurtenances, in Monkbretton which they (William and Richard) lately had, together with Thomas Cartwright and John Autye, by the grant of John Frere.   Dated 20 November, 1422.

(*Fo. 23*)   (38)   Grant by John son of Thomas del Wro of Carleton to Thomas de Cotyngam, his heirs and assigns, of 16*d*. of yearly rent, receivable from all the lands and tenements which he (the grantor) held by the gift of Thomas his father in the vill and territory of Monkbretton, and from a messuage with two buildings in Lambelane, and from the meadow called Lambesyke, and from all the tenements which he had by the gift of Alice his mother, in her widowhood, in the vill and bounds of Monkbretton.   To have and to hold the said rent, with all its appurtenances, freely, wholly, etc.   Warranty.   Power of distraint in case of nonpayment of the rent.   (*Fo. 23d*) Witnesses, Richard de Bretton, Robert Heiron, William de Selar, and others.   At Monkbretton, the day of St. John Baptist (24 June), 1349.

(39)   Grant by Henry Stayneton to William de Notton, William de Staynton son of Agnes de Staynton, and Thomas de Cotyngam, of all his lands and tenements in the vill and territory of Carleton near (*iuxta*) Rusetun, with all manner of pastures, meadows and other easements to the said lands belonging.   To have and to hold to the grantees and their heirs for ever, freely, quietly, etc., doing to the chief lords of that fee the services due and accustomed, and rendering yearly from the said lands to William, vicar of Bolton, 4 marks of silver for all other services and demands.   At Monkbretton the feast of the Assumption B.M. (Aug. 15), 1049.[2]   Witnesses, William Skargill, Roger de Novo Mercato, and others.

(40)   Quitclaim by Thomas le Renderer[3] (*fo. 24*) of Monkbretton to William Notton and John Barneburgh and their heirs, of all right and claim in all those lands and tenements, rents and services, which William de Notton, John de Barnburgh and he (Thomas)

---

[1] The second Richard Kydall is described in this clause as " chaplain."

[2] *Sic*—an obvious mistake for 1349.

[3] Called in the heading Thomas Cotyngam.

had by the grant of William de Notton in the vill of Monkbretton. Dated at Monkbretton, Monday after the feast of the Purification B.V.M. (2 Feb.), 25 Edw. III (1351).

(*Fo.* 24) (41) Grant (or confirmation) by William de Notton and John de Barnburgh to Sirs Walter Powre, parson of the church of Lek, and William de Wath, parson of the church of Wath, of all their messuages, lands, meadows, tofts, rents, and services, with the appurtenances in Bretton Monachorum, which they (the grantors) had by the gift of William de Staynton.   To have and to hold to the grantees, their heirs and assigns, well and in peace, from the chief lords of that fee, by the service due and accustomed, for ever. Witnesses, William de Staynton, John son of Godfrey de Staynton, William the cook (*coco*) of Erdisley.   Dated at Monkbretton, Monday, the morrow of the Circumcision (2 Jan.), 25 Edw. III (1352).

(*Fo.*24*d*)[1] (42) Grant by Thomas de Cotyngham, called Le Rendereur, of Monkbretton, to Sirs Walter Power, parson of the church of Leek, and William de Wath, parson of the church of Wath, of a messuage, sixty-two acres of land, four acres of meadow, six acres of pasture, and 4s. 4d. rent, with the appurtenances, which he had in Cudworth by the grant of Richard Dierd of Codworth; and also seven acres of land and meadow and the fifth part of 3s. 1d. rent, with the appurtenances, in the vill of Monkbretton, which he had by the grant of John son of Robert del Apelyerd of Carleton; and also a messuage and one bovate of land, with the appurtenances, in Monkbretton, which he had by the grant of Thomas Boswell of Erdislay; and also 1½d. of rent, with the appurtenances, in Carleton, which he had by the grant of Adam Kyng of Carleton; and also he has granted to the same Sirs Walter and William a messuage with curtilage, one bovate of land, three roods of pasture, and that pasture which is called Littelrode, with the appurtenances, in the vill and territory of Carleton, which he had by the grant of Richard son of John Watteman, junior.   He has also granted to them all his messuage, all his land and meadow, all the wood, and all his tenements, with the appurtenances, in the vill and territory of Carleton, which he had by the grant of (*fo.* 25) John son of Richard del Woode of Carleton, and all the lands and tenements in the same vill and territory, with the appurtenances, by the grant of Henry de Staynton, and a messuage and two tofts, seven and a half acres of land, and 3s. rent receivable from a certain plot of land called Lemmanrode, together with the homage and service of the tenant of the said plot, and also 16d. rent, with the appurtenances, in Monkbretton, receivable from all the lands and tenements of John Wro of Carleton in Monkbretton; to have and to hold to the said Sirs Walter and William, their heirs and assigns, all the aforesaid lands, tenements, rents, and services, with the homages and all other services of the tenants of the tenements whence those rents arise, with the wardships, reliefs, liberties, escheats, and easements, with their appurtenances, well

[1] Headed " Monkbretton, Carleton, Cudworth."

and in peace, from the chief lords of that fee by the services due and accustomed, for ever. Warranty (abbreviated). Witnesses, William de Notton, John de Barneburgh, Thomas[1] de Boswell of Erdislay, and others. Dated at Monkbretton, Monday next after the Epiphany, 25 Edw. III (1352).

(43) Licence, in the usual form, by King Edward [III] (*fo. 25d*) for five marks which the prior and convent of Bretton Monachorum have paid for the alienation to them by Thomas Rendour of the same vill, of 14s. of rent, with the appurtenances, in Penyston, Thurston, Oxspring, and Cudworth, for celebrating divine service in the church of the priory for the good estate of Thomas whilst he lives, and for his anniversary there yearly after his death. (*Fo. 26*) At Westminster, 4 Feb., in the 44th year (1371).[2]

(*Fo. 26d*)[3] (44) Grant[4] by Richard son of Robert Heyron, mason, chaplain, to William Wilde of Monkbretton, and Joan his wife and their heirs or assigns, of all those messuages with the buildings, and all those lands, tenements, and meadows, with all their appurtenances, which were Robert Heyron's, mason, his father, within the vill and fields of Monkbretton. To have and to hold to William and Joan and their heirs and assigns freely, wholly, etc., from the chief lord of that fee, by the services due and accustomed. Warranty. Witnesses, Richard de Bretton, John Diconson, Richard Auburne, and others. Dated at Monkbretton, 7 February, 1378.

(*Fo. 27*) (45) Release and quitclaim by John son of Robert Heyron of Monkbretton to William Wilde of Monkbretton and Joan his wife and their heirs or assigns, of all right and claim in all those messuages, with the buildings, lands, tenements, and meadows, with all their appurtenances, which were Robert Heyron's, his father, within the vill and bounds of Monkbretton. Warranty (abbreviated). Witnesses, Richard de Bretton, John Diconson, Richard Heyron, and others. Dated at Monkbretton, 9 February, 1378.

(46) Deed of exchange. Richard son of John Keresforth of Barnyslay, Thomas Halle of Pontefract, Richard Symmes of Barnyslay, senior, have granted to Richard Wilde of Monkbretton and his heirs and assigns all the lands and tenements, meadows, woods, and pastures, with all appurtenances, (*fo. 27d*) which they lately had by the grant of Nicholas Halle, prior of the house of St. John Apostle and Evangelist of Pontefract and the convent thereof, in Barnyslay and Dodeworth, in exchange for a messuage with the buildings and with the croft adjacent and with all lands, etc., which the said Richard Wilde had by hereditary right on the death of William Wylde, his father, in Monkbretton aforesaid. To have

---

[1] *Thome.*

[2] See Cal. of Letters Patent, 1367–70, page 357.

[3] Headed " Monkbretton," which continues to *fo. 30d.*

[4] In the margin is written " lande " with the letter " e " preceding it— the final letter of a word cut away in binding.

and to hold all the aforesaid lands, etc., to the said Richard Wilde, his heirs and assigns, in exchange for all the lands and tenements, with their appurtenances, which the said Richard Wilde had in Monkbretton aforesaid from the said prior and convent of St. John, by the services due and accustomed. Warranty to Richard Wilde and his heirs and assigns. Grant by the said Richard Wilde of Monkbretton to Master Thomas Mannyng, a secretary of the King, Thomas Halle, Richard Keresforth, and Richard Symmes, senior, their heirs and assigns, of a messuage with buildings, with the croft adjoining, and with all lands, etc., with their appurtenances, which he (Wilde) had by hereditary right after the death of William Wilde, his father, in Monkbretton, in exchange for all the lands, etc., which the said Richard son of John, Thomas Halle, and Richard Symmes, senior, had by the grant and feoffment of Nicholas, (*fo.* 28) prior of the aforesaid house of St. John and the convent thereof, freely and in peace, from the capital lord of that fee, by the services, etc. (as before). Warranty by Wilde. Witnesses, William Skergill, William Oxspryng, John Keresford, John Tynker, and others. Given at Barnysley and Monkbretton, 12 May, 38 Hen. VI (1460).

(47) Award[1] by William Bradfford and Robert Chaloner, arbitrators in an arbitration respecting "diverse claims, rights, and titles off landes and tenements some tyme in the holdynge and possession of Richard Wilde in Monkbretton, and also clames, chalenges, and demandes of certen rentes," betwixe Richard Leds, prior of the monastery of St. Mary Magdelene of Monkbretton, of the one part, and Richard (*fo.* 28*d*) Browne, prior of the monastery of St. John Apostle and Evangelist of Pontefract, Richard Keresford, and Richard Symmes of Barnyslay of the other part. The arbitrators award the said lands, late of Richard Wilde, to the prior of Monkbretton and his successors for ever, and the prior of Pontefract and Keresford and Symmes are to deliver to him all evidences they hold touching those lands, and to suffer a recovery thereof and (*fo.* 29) execute releases to the prior of Monkbretton. The prior of Monkbretton is to pay the prior of Pontefract, Keresford, and Symmes, 45[2] marks, and to release to them all arrears of rent from the property. The prior and convent of Monk Bretton are to make a sufficient grant to the prior and convent of Pontefract and their successors of licence and liberty within certain closes called Lemmanroid and Page roide (*fo.*29*d*) on the south-east side of Barnyslay brigge (and next adjoining unto the said bridge, the which closes are parcel of the aforesaid lands) for "attachement, knyttyng, festynynge, and makeyng off newe of a werre and milndamme for ye corne milne of Barnyslay," with free entry and issue for materials for making or repairing the said werre and milnedamme, or replacing them if necessary, paying yearly to Monk Bretton a "rose floure on the feast of the Nativity of St. John the Baptist, if demanded." (*Fo.* 30)

---

[1] This document is in English.

[2] Burton (*Mon. Ebor*, 93) says 55, but the number "xlv" in the Chartulary is quite plain.

Clause for observance by the parties of any amendment of this award by the arbitrators: the two convents to give obligations under seal for performance of the award. Sealed by the arbitrators, 22 September, 14 Edw. IV (1474).

(48) Obligation by Richard Browne, prior, and the convent of St. John the Apostle and Evangelist, of Pontefract, to Richard Ledes, prior, and the convent of the house of the Blessed Mary Magdalene (*fo.* 30*d*) of Monkbretton, in the sum of £100 sterling, for due performance of the provisions in the above award. Dated 24 September, 14 Edw. IV (1474).

(49) Release by Richard Keresford and Richard Symmes of Barnyslay (*fo.* 31) to John Genne of Workesburghe and John Calthorne of the same of all those lands, meadows, tenements, etc., with the appurtenances, which they (the grantors) lately had by the gift and feoffment of Richard Wilde in Monkbretton. To hold to the grantees, their heirs and assigns, for ever, from the chief lords of those fees, by the services due and accustomed. Witnesses, Ademer Burdett, Thomas Oxspryng, William Gilberthorpe, and others. Dated at Mukbretton [*sic*], 20 October, 14 Edw. IV (1474).

(50) Release and quitclaim by John Genne and John Calthorne to Richard Ledes, prior, and the convent of Monkbretton, and their successors for ever, of all right, title, claim, and demand of and in all the lands, meadows, tenements, with the appurtenances, in Monkbretton, etc., which they, the said John and John, had by the grant of Richard Keresford and Richard Symmes. (*Fo.* 31*d*) Dated at Monkbretton, 10 January, 14 Edw. IV (1474–5).

(*Fo.* 32 *and fo.* 33 *are blank.*)

(*Fo.* 33*d*)   *Carleton.*[1]

(51) Grant[2] on sale by Matilda de Ricroft, daughter of Thomas the clerk of Karleton, to Margery her kinswoman, of six acres of land in the territory of Carleton,[3] those namely which she (the grantor) bought from Richard her brother; to wit, three acres with the houses which are called Ricroft, and other three acres beside the pool of the prior of Bretton called Midehopflat. To hold from the grantor and her heirs to the grantee, her heirs and assigns, freely and quietly within and without the vill of Carleton, rendering thence to the said Richard and his heirs a pair of white gloves at Christmas yearly, and to the prior of Bretton 12*d*. yearly, for all service and secular action. Warranty. For this sale, quitclaim, and confirmation, Margery has given her 20s. of silver as a fine (*gersuma*). Witnesses, Richard Brasard, Jordan de Rouston, John son of Felix, Hugh de Carleton, and others.

---

[1] This heading continues to the reverse of the unnumbered folio which should be 36*d*.

[2] " Rycroft lande " within the margin.

[3] In the headings of this and the four following deeds the property is described as " called Rycroft "·or " Rycroft lande."

(*Fo.* 34) (52) Grant by Alice daughter of Claricie daughter of Richard de Ricroft of Carleton to Walter le tourner of Notton and his heirs, of a moiety of that messuage and three acres of land which she (Alice) had by hereditary right after the death of Claricie, in the vill and within the bounds of Carleton. To have and to hold to the grantee, his heirs and assigns, freely, quietly, etc., with all appurtenances, liberties, and easements, from the chief lord of that fee, by the services due and accustomed. Warranty. Witnesses, John Hayrun, John son of Thomas, John Coke of Carleton, and others. Dated at Carleton, Saturday in the feast of St. Laurence, martyr, 38 Edw. III (1364).

(53) Grant by Walter de Berford, called Walter Tournor of Notton, and Alice his wife, to Thomas de Cotyngham, called Renderor, of one messuage and six acres of land, with the appurtenances, in Carleton, of which he (Walter) bought one moiety from Alice daughter of Claricie the daughter of Richard de Ricroft, and the other moiety they (the grantors) have of the portion of Alice aforesaid (*fo.* 34*d*) daughter of Richard del Ker, late a villein of the prior and convent of Monkbretton. To have and to hold to the grantee, his heirs and assigns, well and in peace, from the chief lords of the fee by the services due and accustomed. Witnesses, John son of Thomas del Wro of Carleton, Robert Heiron of Bretton, and others. Dated at Carleton on the feast of St. Nicholas, Bishop (6 Dec.), 47 Edw. III (1373).

(54) Grant by Thomas de Cotyngham, called Rendrour, to John de Helay, son of Alice del Apilyerd of Carleton, and his heirs or assigns, of that messuage and those six acres of land, with all the appurtenances, which he (the grantor) had in Carleton by the gift of Walter de Bereford, called Tourneor, of Notton, and Alice his wife. To hold and to have to the grantee, his heirs and assigns, freely, etc., from the chief lords of the fee, by the services due and accustomed, (*fo.* 35) for ever; rendering to the grantor or his assigns 5s. sterling yearly. Power for distraint in case the said rent in arrear. Seals of the parties to the alternate parts of this charter indentate. Witnesses, John son of Thomas del Wro, Robert Hayron, Richard son of Roger, and others. Dated at Carleton, Monday after the feast of Mathias, Apostle, 48 Edw. III (1374).

(55) Grant by Thomas Cotyngham, called Rendrour, to the prior of Monkbretton (*fo.* 35*d*) and the monks there serving God, of a rent of 5s. issuing from a messuage and six acres of land, with the appurtenances, in Carleton, formerly Richard Ricroft's, receivable from John Helay, son of Alice Apelyerd of Carleton, his heirs and assigns. To hold and to have the said rent to the grantees and their successors, freely, etc., from the chief lords of that fee, by the services due and accustomed, for ever. Witnesses, Robert Hairon of Bretton, Richard son of Roger of the same, John Pull, and others. Dated at Monkbretton, the day of St. Nicholas (6 Dec.), 49 Edw. III (1375).

(56)   Grant by Adam Kyng of Carleton to William de Notton, John de Barneburgh, and Thomas le Renderour, of a rent of three halfpence, with the appurtenances, in Carleton; to wit, a penny receivable from the heirs of Alan de Scolay for a certain piece (*dola*) of meadow which he holds from the grantor in the same, and a half-penny from the heirs of Thomas de Frytheby from a piece (*pacia*) of pasture and alder grove (*alneti*) which he holds from the grantor in the same.[1]   To hold and to have, with the homages and all other services of the tenants, to the grantees, their heirs and assigns, from the chief lords of that fee, by the services due and accustomed, for ever.   And Adam grants that the said tenants may hereafter render the same services to the grantees.   Witnesses, John de Staynton, Robert Heyron, Richard the clerk, and others.   Dated at Monk Bretton (*Bretton Monachorum*), Monday after the feast of the purification B.M., 25 Edw. III (1351–2).

(57)   Grant by Richard son of John Watteman of Cudworth, junior,[2] to Thomas de Cotyngham of Monkbretton, of a messuage with curtilages, one bovate of land, and three roods of pasture, and that pasture which is called Littelrod, with the appurtenances, in the vill and territory of Carleton, which Roger de Roreston sometime held.   To have and to hold, with the appurtenances, to the grantee, his heirs and assigns, freely, etc., with the commons and all ease-ments to the said holding belonging, within and without the said vill of Carleton, from the chief lords of that fee by the services thence due and accustomed, for ever.[3]   Witnesses, Thomas de Staynton, William de Staynton, Arthur de Bossevile, and others. Dated at Carleton, Monday before the feast of the Nativity of St. John Baptist, 1346.

(Fo. 36)   *Cudworth.*[4]

(58)   Grant[5] by Robert Bynchestre of Cudworth and Joan his wife to John Michell, chaplain, William Barker of Roderham, and John Sperk of Codworth, their heirs or assigns, of that messuage with the buildings thereon and all other appurtenances, which they (the grantors) previously had in the vill of Cothworth by the gift and feoffment of Robert Heyron, chaplain.   To hold and to have to the grantees, their heirs and assigns, freely, etc., from the chief lord of that fee, by the services due and accustomed.   Witnesses, Richard Bet' of Dodworth, Richard Adde, John Marshall, and others. Dated at Codworth, the eve of the Nativity of St. Mary Virgin, 1395.

(59)   Grant by John *(fo. 36d)* Sparke of Codworth to Richard Kydall, chaplain, Thomas Richarson, chaplain, of Bolton, and

---

[1] The following folio, which commences here, is unnumbered.

[2] Written *junior* without mark of contraction; possibly therefore meaning younger son of John Watteman.

[3] The reverse of the unnumbered folio commences here.

[4] This and the succeeding folios (*dorses*) headed " Cudworth " to folio 65.

[5] " Sparke lande " written in the margin.

Richard Normanvyle of Billyngley, of that messuage with the buildings thereon and all other appurtenances, which he had, jointly with John Michell, chaplain, and William Barker of Roderham, who are now dead, by the gift and feoffment of Robert Bynchester and Joan his wife, in the vill and within the bounds of Cotheworth. To have and to hold to the grantees, their heirs and assigns, freely, etc., from the chief lord of that fee, by the services due and accustomed. Witnesses, Richard Barton of Cothworth, Thomas Whetlay, William Jonson, and others. Dated at Cotheworth, 4 January, 11 Hen. IV (1409–10).

(60) Grant by Richard Kydall, chaplain, (*fo.* 37) to the prior and convent of Monkbretton and their successors, of the messuage, with the appurtenances, in the lower town (*inferiori villa*) of Codworth; which messuage he, together with Richard Normanvile, now deceased, and Thomas Richardson, chaplain, lately had. To hold to the grantees and their successors, from the chief lord of that fee, by the services due and accustomed. Witnesses, William Hepworth, vicar of Royston, Richard Poplay, John Frankysch, and others. Dated at Cudworth, in the feast of Holy Trinity, 12 Hen. IV (1411).

(*Fo.* 37*d*)[1] (61) Grant by Richard Byard of Coutworth to William de Notton, John Barneburght, and Thomas le Renderour of Monkbretton, of a messuage with the buildings, sixty-two acres of arable land, four acres of meadow, and six acres of pasture, with the hedges (*hayis*), woods and fosses, and all other appurtenances, as they lie in divers places; to wit, the said messuage, fifty acres of land, four acres of meadow, and six acres of pasture lie together in the place called Aylsithrop, and six acres of land in a certain place called Thornwellflat, between the land of Thomas Belle on the west and the land of William son of John del Hall on the east and abut at one head on the Schortclay and at the other on the Hanganclyff, and one acre of land lies in a certain place called Clay, between the land of Thomas Belle and the land of Adam son of the reeve and abuts on the Toftes and on Thornewell, and one acre lies at the Cloghes between the land of Thomas Belle and the land of Ralph del Hill and abuts on the north field and on the beck, and one acre of land lies in the north field between the land of Mabote daughter of Robert del Pull and the land of Richard Le Marshall and abuts on Northsyke and on the Longeclay, and half an acre lies at Brodhengdik (*fo.* 38) between the land of Thomas Belle and the land of Richard Daudson and abuts on Brodheng and on the Northfeld, and half an acre lies at Brombutts between the land of Thomas Belle and the land of Ralph del Hill and abuts on the field of Schafton and on the Northfeld, and one acre lies at the head of the vill between the land of Thomas Bell and the land of John son of William and abuts on Dandecrosse and on Sedecop, and one acre of land lies at the Hedewell between the land of Thomas Belle and the land of

[1] Headed " Cudworth ": in the margin was written probably " Byard Lande," this has been cut down in the rebinding, and only the second word and three final letters of the first word remain.

Richard son of Albreda and abuts on Hedewel and on the Furlange below the garden of Adam the reeve.   The grantor has given to the said grantees 4s. of rent, receivable from a messuage and eight acres of land in Cudworth which (que) William del Hall held from him, and another rent of 4d., receivable from the same William Hall with the homages and services of the said William; and also all other lands and tenements, rents, and services of all his tenants, which he had on the day when these presents were made, in the vill of Cudworth.   To have and to hold all the aforesaid, with all their appurtenances, wardships, reliefs, escheats, marriages, and whatsoever other appurtenances, to the grantees, their heirs and assigns, well and in peace, wholly, freely, and quietly, from the chief lords of that fee, by the services thence due and accustomed, for ever.   (Fo. 38d) Witnesses, Thomas Belle, John son of Geoffrey de Staynton, Thomas Byard, William Hall, and others.   Dated at Monkbretton, Tuesday in the feast of St. Andrew Apostle, 1350,[1] 24 Edw. III.

(62)   Grant by John son of Robert Pull to Richard Bayard and Avice his wife of all those tenements, with their appurtenances, which Robert his father gave him (John) by charter, in the vill and territory of Cudworth, except the houses, curtilages, garden, and six acres of arable land, with the appurtenances, which John le taillour, son of Adam son of Jordan, and Mabel his wife hold in fee at Pull.   To have and to hold to the grantees and their heirs and assigns, freely, etc., with all commons, liberties, and easements, for ever, from the chief lords of that fee, by the services due and accustomed.   Warranty.   He has likewise granted to the same grantees and their heirs and assigns 12d. of yearly (fo. 39) rent, receivable from Alice daughter of Benedict Tirell and her heirs, and 6d. of yearly rent receivable from Diota Bell and her heirs, and 4d. of yearly rent receivable from John del Hall and his heirs, and a penny of yearly rent receivable from one bovate of land which Adam his (the grantor's) brother lately held, and a penny of yearly rent receivable from Peter Scot and his heirs; with the homages, services, wardships, reliefs, etc., belonging to the said tenements which the said Alice, Diota, John, and Peter held from him in the vill of Cudworth, together with all the aforesaid things belonging to the said bovate which Adam held.   Witnesses, Godfrey de Staynton, Thomas his brother, Henry[2] de Byrthwat, Arthur de Bossewell, and others.   Dated at Cudworth, the day of St. Peter in Cathedra, 1324.

(63)   Release and quitclaim by Thomas Cotyngham, called le Renderour, of Monkbretton, to the prior and convent of Monkbretton and their successors, of all right and claim in all those lands and tenements, with the appurtenances, in Cudworth, which were formerly Richard Bayerd's, whether[3] in any (fo. 39d) rent or service

---

[1] This is written " Millesimo quinquagesimo," obviously a mistake.

[2] Written " Herico."

[3] *Seve.*

issuing from the same tenements. Witnesses, John de Barneburgh of Doncaster, Thomas Belle of Cudworth, John Birtwaith, and others. Dated at Monkbretton, 20 April, 35 Edw. III (1361).

(64) Confirmation by Thomas Biard of Cudworth to Dom. John de Birthwait, prior, and the convent of Monkbretton and their successors, of all those lands and tenements, rents, and services, with their appurtenances, which he had in the vill of Cudworth, and which were formerly Richard Bayard's, his brother. To hold and to have to the prior and convent, and their successors for ever. Witnesses, Thomas Bossewell, John de Staynton, John de Barneburgh, and others. (*Fo.* 40) Dated at Cudworth, 8 September, 1363.

(65) Grant by Mabel daughter of Robert de Pul, lately wife of John le Taillor of Cudworth, in her pure widowhood and lawful power, to Thomas Cotyngham of Monkbretton, his heirs and assigns, of a certain annual rent of 4s. 5d., together with the reversion of 2s. 2½d. after the death of Richard Biard of Cudworth, from the tenements which were Robert de Pull's, which tenements Richard Bayard formerly held in the vill and territory of Cudworth. To have and receive the said rent and reversion, with the appurtenances, to the grantee, his heirs and assigns.[1] Power for distraint if payment be in arrear. (*Fo.* 40d) Witnesses, Thomas de Erdisley, William the cook (*coco*), Thomas[2] Bell, etc. Dated at Monkbretton, 12 January, 26 Edw. III (1352-3).

(66) Grant by John de Pull, dwelling (*manens*) in Roreston, to Thomas de Cotyngham of Monkbretton, his heirs and assigns, of a certain annual rent of 4s. 5d., together with the reversion of 2s. 2½d. after the death of Richard Baiard, from the tenements formerly Robert de Pul's, which tenements Richard Baiard sometime held in the vill and territory of Cudworth. To have and receive the aforesaid rents, with the appurtenances, to the grantee, his heirs and assigns, for ever. (*Fo.* 41) Witnesses, Thomas de Bossewell, Thomas[3] de Bell, John de Balne, and others. Dated at Cudworth, 14 February, 32 Edw. III (1358-9).

(67) Grant by Ralph son of Peter de Hill of Notton to Thomas de Cotyngham, his heirs and assigns, of a yearly rent of 3s. 4d. sterling receivable from one bovate and two acres of land with the meadow adjoining, which Richard son of Henry[4] the shepherd (*barcarii*) of Cudworth holds to himself and his heirs from the said Ralph within the fields and bounds of Cudworth. To have and to receive, with all the appurtenances, freely, etc., to the grantee, his heirs and assigns, from the said tenements. Warranty. Power for distraint if payment in arrear. (*Fo.* 41d) Witnesses, Richard Baiard,

---

[1] The copying is rather confused here, some words from a warranty being mixed up with this sentence.

[2] Thome.

[3] Thome.

[4] Herrici.

Thomas his brother, Richard son of Richard de le Cher, and others. Dated at Cudworth, Monday in the feast of St. Thomas of Canterbury, 1342.

(*Fo.* 42)[1] (68)   Grant by Thomas son of Adam de Cudworth to Dom. Thomas Bate, chaplain, his heirs and assigns, of that half bovate of land and meadow which the grantor bought (*perquesivi*) from John Belle of Cudworth, in Cudworth, and that half bovate of land and meadow which he bought from John de Pull in Cudworth, and an acre of land lying on Le Heghrode in the field of Cudworth which he bought from John Taillour, his brother, and three and a half roods of land lying on Le Fernileghs which he bought from Thomas Byard of Cudworth, in Cudworth, and an acre of land and meadow which he had by the gift of Adam son of Jordan (*Jurdani*) de Cudworth, in Cudworth.   To hold and to have all the aforesaid, with all appurtenances, to the grantee, his heirs and assigns, freely, etc., from the chief lords of that fee, by the services due and accustomed.   Witnesses, Thomas Bell of Cudworth, Thomas son of Jordan, John de Baldiker, and others.   Dated at Cudworth, Tuesday after Michaelmas, 1361.

(*Fo.* 42*d*)   (69)   Grant by charter indentate, by Thomas Bate of Roston, chaplain, to Thomas son of Adam de Cudworth and Agnes his wife, for life and for the life of the survivor, of those two half-bovates of land and meadow, with the appurtenances, which he (the grantor) had within the bounds of the vill of Cudworth, by the grant of the said Thomas son of Adam.   To hold and to have aforesaid, wholly and in peace, from the chief lords of that fee, by the services due and accustomed.   And after the death of the grantees remainder to John Haiwarde, servant of Roger de Pecten, fellow-monk[2] (*commonachi*), and his heirs or assigns; to hold from the chief lords as before.   Witnesses, Thomas,[3] Thomas Baiard, Thomas son of Jordan, and others.   Dated at Cudworth, Wednesday after the feast of St. Luke Evangelist, 1361.

(*Fo.* 43)   (70)   Grant by John son of Robert Haywarde, sometime servant (*s'vus*) of Roger de Pecton, fellow-monk, to Thomas de Cotyngham, "rendrour" of Monkbretton, and his heirs or assigns, of all those lands and tenements, with all and singular their appurtenances, which formerly belonged to Thomas son of Adam de Cudworth, in the vill and territory of Codworth.   To hold and to have to the grantee, his heirs or assigns, freely, quietly, etc., from the chief lords of that fee, by the services due and accustomed. Witnesses, Thomas Bell, Thomas Judson, Richard M'shall.   Dated at Cudworth, Wednesday after the Nativity of St. John Baptist, 1368.

   (71)   Release and quitclaim by Thomas Belle of Cudworth (*fo.* 43*d*) to Thomas Cotyngham, his heirs and assigns, of all right

---

[1] " Hayward Lande " written in the margin.

[2] It is not stated of whom Roger was fellow-monk.

[3] Surname omitted.

and claim in a certain yearly rent of 11*d*., which the said Thomas de Cotyngham was accustomed to pay him yearly for half a bovate of land called Barleland, which he (Cotyngham) had by the grant of John Haywarde, within the fields of Cudworth. Witnesses, John Geste, John M'shall, Robert Bakester, and others. Dated at Cudworth, 6 March, 1370.

(72) Grant by Thomas de Cotyngham, clerk, to Robert son of Peter de Cudworth, baker (*pistori*), and Dionisia his wife and the heirs between them lawfully begotten, of all those lands and tenements, with all the appurtenances, which the grantor had within the vill of Cudworth by the grant of John Haywarde. To hold (*fo.* 44) and to have to the grantees and their heirs, as before, wholly and in peace, from the grantor and his heirs, rendering to them yearly, or to his assigns, 7*s*. 9*d*. sterling, and doing to the chief lords of that fee the services due and accustomed. Power for distraint if rent in arrear, and to re-enter and retain if distraint insufficient. Warranty. Seals to the alternate parts of this charter in witness. Witnesses, Thomas Belle, (*fo.* 44*d*) Thomas Judson, Richard Marshall, and others. Dated at Cudworth, Saturday after the feast of St. Mark Evangelist, 1369.

(The following is annexed.)

" Memorandum; that the within written Robert and Dionisia died without heir of their bodies lawfully begotten and all the within written lands and tenements descended to the prior and convent of Monkbretton, as heirs and assigns of the within written Thomas de Cotyngham."

(73) Grant[1] by Adam Chapman of Cudworth to Thomas the clerk, son of William Bell of the same, of a messuage built upon (*superedificat'*), with all appurtenances and easements, and with all his (the grantor's) movables and immovables (*mobilibus et immobilibus*) lying in the vill of Cudworth, namely, between the messuage of Robert Chapman on the south side and the messuage of Ralph de Hyll on the north side and abutting on the highway on the west and on the garden of Robert Chapman on the east. To have and to hold the said messuage in length (*fo.* 45) and breadth, and all his movables and immovables, to the grantee, for a yearly rent of 6*d*. after the death of Adam, for the service of the blessed Mary of Roston. Witnesses, Arthur Boswel, John son of Godfrey de Staynton, Richard Biard, and others. Dated at Cudworth, Thursday after the Purification of St. Mary, 1342.

(74) Grant by Thomas the clerk, son of William Bell of Cudworth, to Matilda wife of Adam Chapman, and Avice her daughter, of the property named in the preceding deed.[2] To have and to hold

---

[1] There has been a note in the margin, "... mlande," but the first word has nearly all been cut away in the rebinding.

[2] A few words omitted but the meaning seems clear, the reading is " et Avice filie sue, sicut jacet in longitudine et in latitudine videlicet, etc. ut habetur in carta suprascripta."

C

the said messuage, with all its appurtenances, to Matilda and Avice and their heirs, freely, etc.,[1] by the services thence due and accustomed, namely, by rendering thence yearly 6*d.* to the service of the blessed Mary of Roston after the death of the aforesaid[2] Adam, and to the service of the blessed Mary before his death one penny. If it shall happen that Avice die without lawful heir of her body, remainder to the other heirs begotten between Matilda and Adam, and on failure of such (*fo.* 45*d*) heirs remainder to Robert son of Adam Chapman, and if Robert die without lawful heir of his body the property to remain to the said Adam Chapman, his heirs and assigns, for ever. Witnesses, as in the preceding deed. Dated at Cudworth, Sunday after the Purification B.M.V., 1342.

(75) Grant by John Jenkynson of Schafton and·Joan his wife to John Pharom[3] and Isabella his wife, their heirs and assigns, of three acres of land, with the appurtenances, in the vill and fields of Cudworth; whereof one acre lies at Ower Cudworth between the land of Thomas Wombwell on the south and the land of the prior of Bretton on the north and abuts at one head on the King's road leading to Barnyslay as far as the west called Crosacre, and three roods lie on Schortsetcop between the land of John Qwetley on the south and the land of the prior of Bretton on the north, one head abutting on Owertongren continuously to the east and the other on Hyngandbank continuously to the west, and one acre (*fo.* 46) lies in Southfede[4] in Selildroyde between the land of William Scargyll on the south and the land of John Quetley on the north, one head abutting on the land of William Oxspryng on the east and on Mabstegyll towards the west, and one rood lies in Southfeld in Le Qwetlay between the land of Richard Oxspryng on either side and abuts on the land of William Oxspryng on the east. To have and to hold the said three acres of land, with the appurtenances, to the said John Phayrun and Isabel his wife, their heirs and assigns, freely, quietly, etc., from the chief lords of that fee, by the services due and accustomed. Witnesses, John Ruston, Thomas Oxspryng, and others. Dated at Phayrun, 19 February, 28 Hen. VI (1450–1).

(76) Grant by John Farom[5] of Cudworth and Isabella his wife to Thomas Farom their son and Isabella his wife, of a messuage in Cudworth in which they (the grantors) now dwell. To have and to hold, with the appurtenances, to the grantees and the heirs and assigns of Thomas for ever, (*fo.* 46*d*) from the chief lords of that fee, by the services due and accustomed. Release and quitclaim by the said grantors to the said grantees and the heirs of Thomas, of all right

---

[1] Before the words "pro serviciis," "de capit' dominis" has been written, and then crossed out.

[2] Written *predicte.*

[3] In the heading, Pharon. The name was doubtless really meant for Fairholme: in 2 Rich. II there was a John Fayrhome residing in the adjoining village of Carlton. See also the name in 76, 77 and 79.

[4] Probably a mistake for *Southfelde.*

[5] In the heading written John Pharom, Thomas Pharon.

and claim of and in three acres of land in Cudworth whereof one acre lies in the south field there between the land late of William Scargyll, esquire, on the north and the land lately William Qwetley's on the south, and another acre lies there in Le Oldefeld, called Le Crosacre, half an acre lies in Le Smallbrygfeld between the land of the said William Qwetley on one side and the land lately John Humlok's on the other, half an acre lies in the north field there beside the land of Thomas Oxspryng beside Le Bellcrosse in the said field. Witnesses, Robert Rokley, Richard Hyll, and others. Dated 22 February, 19 Edw. IV (1480–1).

(*Fo.* 47) (77) Grant by Thomas Fayrom[1] of Cudworth and Isabella his wife to William Wadeloufe and John Ellys, of a messuage with garden adjoining in Cudworth, and three acres of land lying separately in the fields, with all their appurtenances, namely, one acre in Oldefeld, another acre in Southfelde, half an acre in Smalbrygfeld, and half an acre in Northfeld. To hold and to have to the grantees, their heirs and assigns, for ever, from the chief lords of that fee, by the services due and accustomed. Appointment of John Ward of Cudworth and Richard Bolton of Carleton as attorneys to deliver seisin. Witnesses, Thomas Oxspryng, Thomas (*fo.* 47*d*) Wodward, and others. Dated at Cudworth, 14 May, 20 Edw. IV (1480).

(78) Grant by William Wadelouffe and John Ellys to Richard Ledes, prior of Monkbretton, and the convent and their successors, of the properties named in the preceding deed. To have and to hold to the grantees and their successors for ever, from the chief lords of those fees, by the services due and accustomed. Witnesses, Nicholas Ruston, Robert Rokley, John Warde, and others. Dated at Cudworth, 5 August, 20 Edw. IV (1480).

(79) Grant by John Jenkynson of Schafton and Joan his wife (*fo.* 48) to John Fayrhome of Fayrhome in Brereley and their heirs and assigns, of two acres and a rood of land, with the appurtenances, lying in divers places in the fields of Cudworth, whereof one rood lies in a place called Le Qwethelaybeghe between the land of William Skargyll on the north and the land of William Carlyll on the south, and half an acre lies on Waltyrstones between the land of John Ruston[2] on the east and the land of Richard Oxspryng on the west, and another half acre abuts on Smalbryghyll towards the west and on Le Overtownegrene towards the east between the land of John Qwetley on the north and the land of John Humblok on the south, and another half acre lies in Le Oldefeld at Gateshadyls between the land of John Whetley on the south and the land of Edmund (*Ed'i*) Rokley on the north, and another half acre lies in Le Northfeld between the land of Richard Oxspryng on the east and the land of William Skargyl on the west. To have and to hold, with all the appurtenances, to the said John Fayrhome, his heirs and assigns, from the chief lords of that fee, by the services due and accustomed,

[1] Pharom in the heading.
[2] This is written, " in terrā Joħi Ruston," no doubt a mistake.

for ever.   Witnesses, Richard Oxspryng, John Pytt, and others.
Dated at Cudworth, Monday after the feast of St. Lucy the virgin,
17 Hen. VI (1438).

(*Fo.* 48*d*)   (80)   Grant by John Farom to Thomas Methlay of
Newstede, esquire, William Wadelowfe, and John Ellys, of two and
a half acres of land lying separately in the fields of Cudworth; whereof
one acre lies in Smalbrygfeld between the land of the prior of Monkbretton on the south and the land of William Wetley on the north
and abuts on Cudworth grene, half an acre lies in Le Oldefeld between
the land of William Whetley on the south and the land of William
Skargyll on the north and abuts on Schaftonstye to the west, half
an acre lies in Le Southfelde at Wolderstonnes between the land of
William Oxspryng on the west and the land of Nicholas Ruston on
the east and abuts upon Siliroide, one rood lies in Leghwhetlay between the land of William Carelyll on the south and the land of
William Mylner on the north and abuts on Sililsyke, and one rood
lies in Rawlande on either side and abuts on the land of William
Oxspryng to the east, with the appurtenances, in Cudworth.   To
have and to hold to the grantees, their heirs and assigns, for ever,
from the chief lords of those fees, by the services thence due and
accustomed.   Witnesses, (*fo.* 49) John Newile, Thomas Oxspryng,
and others.   Dated at Cudworth, 6 April, 9 Edw. IV (1469).

(81)   Grant by William Wadeluffe and John Ellys to the prior and
convent of Monkbretton and their successors for ever, of two and a
half acres of land lying separately in the fields of Cudworth, whereof
one acre lies in Smalbrygfeld, half an acre lies in Le Oldefeld, half an
acre lies in Le Southfeld, a rood lies in Leghwheley, and a rood lies
in Rawlande, with all the appurtenances, which the grantors lately
had, jointly with Thomas Methlay, by the grant of John Farom.
To have and to hold to the grantees and their successors for ever, from
the chief lords of those fees, by the services thence due and accustomed.   Witnesses, John Newile, Thomas Oxspryng, and others.
Dated at Monkbretton, 4 October, 21 Edw. IV (1481).

(*Fo.* 49*d*)   (82)   Grant[1] by Thomas Aubrey of Hegholme in Bargh
to William Carlehyll of Cudworth and Emmota his wife, their heirs
and assigns, of all his lands and tenements, rents, services, and reversions, with all their appurtenances,[2] to the said William and Emmota,
their heirs and assigns, freely, etc., from the chief lords of those fees,
by the services due and accustomed.   Warranty.   Appointment of
William Fell of Cudworth as attorney to deliver seisin.   Witnesses,
John Nevill, Thomas Dodworth, and others.   Dated at Cudworth,
the feast of the Apostles Simon and Jude, 1427; 6 Hen. VI.

(*Fo.* 50)   (83)   Release and quitclaim by Thomas Aubrey of Hegholm
in Bargh to William Carlehill of Cudworth and Emmota his wife,

[1] Written in the margin, " . . . . . yll lande," the first word (cut in the
rebinding) was probably " Carlyll."
[2] No vill is named, apparently some words are omitted here.

their heirs and assigns, of all right and claim in all those lands, tenements, rents, services, and reversions, with all the appurtenances, which they lately had by his grant in the vill and within the bounds of Cudworth. Witnesses, John Newell of Brerelay, Thomas Dodworth of Barnyslay, and others. Dated at Cudworth, the feast of St. Andrew Apostle, 1427.

(*Fo.* 50*d*) (84) Grant by William Hynderwell of Pomtfret and Emmota his wife, lately the wife of William Carlehyll, late of Cudworth, decd., to Thomas Chaloner, clerk, William Wynke, chaplain, and John Halle of Manston, of all the grantor's lands and tenements, rents, and services, with all their appurtenances, in Cudworth aforesaid, which were lately the said William Carlehyll's and Emmota's. To hold and to have to the grantees, their heirs and assigns, for ever, from the chief lords of those fees, by the services thence due and accustomed. Appointment of Henry Carlehill (son of Emmota) as attorney to deliver seisin. (*Fo.* 51) Witnesses, William Scargill, esquire, Thomas Barneby, vicar of Darfield, and others. Dated at Cudworth, 23 April, 4 Edw. IV (1464).

(85) Release and quitclaim by John Carlehyll, kinsman and heir of William Carlehyll, and Emme his wife, to wit, the son of Thomas son of the aforesaid William and Emma, to James Haryngton, knt., Thomas Metheley, esquire, and William Wadelowe, of all right and claim of and in a messuage, with the appurtenances, in Cudworth, and in all other lands and tenements, with their appurtenances, in the same vill, which were lately the said William's and Emme's, to the grantees, their heirs and assigns. Witnesses, (*fo.* 51*d*) Thomas Oxspryng, Henry Bryge, John Cusworth, and others. Dated at Cudworth, 6 May, 21 Edw. IV (1481).

(86) Grant by Thomas Chaloner, vicar of the parish church of Pountfret, and William Wynke, chaplain, to James Haryngton, knt., Thomas Metheley, esquire, and William Wadelowe, of a messuage and all other their (the grantor's) lands and tenements, with the appurtenances, in Cudworth, which jointly with John Halle of Manston, now decd., they lately had by the gift and feoffment of Emma Carlehyll, late the wife of William Carlehyll, senior. To hold and to have to the grantees, their heirs and assigns, for ever, from the chief lords of that fee, by the services thence due and accustomed. Appointment of Thomas Croft and Robert Rokley as attorneys to deliver seisin. (*Fo.* 52) Witnesses, Thomas Oxspryng, Henry Bryge, John Cusworth, and others. Dated at Cudworth, 1 May, 21 Edw. IV (1481).

(87) Grant by James Haryngton, knt., Thomas Metheley, and William Wadelowe, to Richard Ledes, prior of the monastery or house and church of blessed Mary Magdalene of Monkbretton and his successors,[1] of a messuage and all other their lands and tenements,

---

[1] " Et successoribus suis." The usual words, " et Conventui," were no doubt accidentally omitted; they occur in the *habendum* clause.

with the appurtenances, in Cudworth, which they (the grantors) lately had by the gift and feoffment of Thomas Chaloner, vicar of Pountfret, and William Wynke, chaplain. To have and to hold to the aforesaid prior and convent and their successors for ever, from the chief lords of that fee, by the services thence due and accustomed. Appointment of Thomas Oxspryng and Thomas Smyth (*fo.* 52*d*) as attorneys to deliver seisin. Witnesses, John Bradforth, Brian Bradforth, Thomas Lyster, and others. Dated 21 November, 1 Ric. III (1483).

(88) Quitclaim by William Awbray of Hegham to James Haryngton, knt., Thomas Methelay, esquire, and William Wadelowe, their heirs and assigns, of all right and claim in all those lands and tenements in the vill and territory of Cudworth and within the bounds thereof, which William Carlehyll formerly bought (*perquisivit*) from Thomas Awbray. (*Fo.* 53) Witnesses, Richard Hopkynson, vicar of the church of Bolton, Thomas Oxspryng, and others. Dated 15 January, 22 Edw. IV (1483).

(89) Release and quitclaim by William Awbray of Hegham to Richard Ledys, prior of Monkbretton, and the convent thereof and their successors, of all right and claim of and in all those lands and tenements in the vill or territory of Cudworth, which William Carle-hyll formerly bought from Thomas Awbray. Warranty. (*Fo.* 53*d*) Witnesses, as in the preceding deed, and same date.

(90)[1] Grant by William Scargill and Elisabeth his wife to William Wadyloue and Thomas Oxspryng, their heirs and assigns, of a parcel of arable land in Cudworth called Wyteleghes, parcel of the grantor's demesne land lying together in length and breadth between the common pasture of the same vill on the south and the land formerly William Carlehyll's on the north and abutting on the common pasture at each end. To have and to hold, with the appurtenances, to the grantees, their heirs and assigns, from the chief lords of that fee, by the services due and accustomed, rendering thence yearly to the grantors and the heirs of William 3*s*. 4*d*. (*Fo.* 54) Power for distraint if rent in arrear and for re-entry if in arrear for a year. Witnesses, John Lake, Robert Bradford, William Pytt, and others. Dated at Cudworth, 4 June, 1 Edw. IV, V[2] (1483).

(91) Demise by Thomas Oxspryng and William Wadelowe (*fo.* 54*d*) to Richard Ledes, prior of Monkbretton and the convent thereof and their successors, of a parcel of arable land in Cudworth, called Whyteleghes, lying together in length and breadth between the common pasture of the same vill on the south and the land formerly William Carlehyll's on the north and abutting on the common pasture at each end, which they (Thomas and William) lately had

---

[1] In the margin opposite is written, " . . . . . . eleghes "; the earlier portion of the word has been cut off in binding.

[2] *Sic*—" anno regni Regis Edwardi quarti quinti post conquestum anglie primo."

by the grant of William Scargyll and Elizabeth his wife. To have and to hold to the said prior and convent and their successors, for ever, from the chief lords of that fee, by the services due and accustomed. Witnesses, Richard Wentworth, Thomas Metheley, and others. Dated at Cudworth, 5 November, 1 Ric. III (1483).

(92) Release[1] and quitclaim by Richard Amyas, gentleman, to Thomas, prior of Monkbretton and his successors, of all right, title, etc., in an acre of land, with the appurtenances, in Cudworth, as it lies there in eight selions in a certain close called Willam rode. (*Fo.* 55) Dated 20 September, 10 Hen. VIII (1518).

(93) To all faithful of Christ, etc., Nicholas Ruston of Cudworth, son and heir of John Ruston, late of the same, greeting. Whereas the said John, on the 5th day of May, 7 Edw. IV (1467), sold and granted to Richard Ledes, prior of Monkbretton and the convent thereof and their successors, three roods of land, with the appurtenances, as they lie in Cudworth aforesaid between the land of William Carlehyll, on either side abutting on " Cudworth broke " at one head and on Cudworth common at the other; know that I the said Nicholas, for me and my heirs, have by these presents ratified and confirmed the said sale and grant. (*Fo.* 55*d*) Witnesses, John Sparke, Thomas Jenkynson, Robert Rokley, and many others. Dated 1 December, 22 Edw. IV (1482).

(94) Grant[2] by Roger Loterell of York to Nichola his daughter and her heirs, of all his lands and tenements in Cudworth, which he had of her inheritance after the death of Agnes, late his wife, by the law of England. To have and to hold to the grantee and her heirs for ever. Witnesses, Thomas de Staynton, Robert de Staynton, William de Notton, and others. (*No date.*)

(95) Grant by Nichola (*fo.* 56) Loterell, daughter of Roger Loterell of York, to John son of Adam son of Mell de Wolvelay and Clarice his wife, and the heirs of John, of all her (the grantor's) lands and tenements in Cudworth, which she had by the gift of her father, who held them by the law of England after the decease of her mother, of her (Nichola's) inheritance, and which fell or might fall to her by hereditary right or otherwise, with the reversion of all lands which ought to fall to her after the death of William de Kent of York. To hold and to have all the aforesaid to John and Clarice and the heirs of John, from the chief lords of that fee, by the services due and accustomed. Witnesses, William de Notton, Robert de Hyrland, Robert Monk, and others. Dated at Cudworth, Tuesday after the feast of the Annunciation B.M.V., 14 Edw. III (1340).

(96) Grant by Adam son of John de Wolvelay of Cudworth to William Hode of Hyndeley, Achilles Bossewyll, (*fo.* 56*d*) esquire, and John de Skyres, vicar of the church of Felkyrk, and Edmund de Byrkyn of Campsall, their heirs and assigns, of all his lands and

---

[1] " Una acra in Willyam Royde " written in the margin.
[2] " [Te]rra Johis Boyne " written in the margin.

tenements, rents and services, with the appurtenances in Cudworth. To have and to hold to the grantees, their heirs and assigns, freely, from the chief lords of that fee, by the services due and accustomed. Witnesses, William Jonson, William Taillor, Thomas Wheteley, and others. Dated at Cudworth, Tuesday after the feast of St. Mark Evangelist, 6 Hen. IV (1405).

(97) Grant by William Hode of Coldhendeley, Achilles Bosse-wyll, John Skyres, vicar of the church of Felkyrk, and Edmund Byrkyn of Campsall, to Adam son of John de Wolveley of Cudworth and Helen his wife, for their lives or the life of the survivor, with all the appurtenances, which the grantors had by the gift and feoffment of Adam and Helen in the vill and within the bounds of Cudworth. To have and to hold (*fo.* 57) to the grantees (as before) without impeachment of waste, freely, quietly, etc., from the chief lords of that fee, by the services due and accustomed; after the deaths of the grantees, reversion to the aforesaid William Hode, his heirs and assigns, for ever, to be held from the chief lords as before stated. Witnesses, Richard Becar of Cudworth, William Jonson, and others. Dated at Cudworth, the feast of St. Martin in the winter (11 Nov.), 1405, 7 Hen. IV.

(98) Grant by Edmund Byrkyn of Clipston to John Bowyn of Cregylston and Joan daughter of William de Walton of Cold (*fo.* 57*d*) Hendley, of all lands and tenements, with the appurtenances, which he had by the grant and feoffment of Adam de Wolley, in the vill and fields of Cudworth. To have and to hold to John and Joan and the heirs of their bodies lawfully begotten, freely, quietly, etc., from the chief lords of that fee, by the services due and accustomed, for ever. And if it shall happen that John and Joan die without lawful heirs between them begotten, remainder to the right heirs of William Hode of Coldhendley, for ever. Warranty to John and Joan and their heirs. Witnesses, John de Rueston, Edmund (*Ed'o*) de Rokley, and others. Dated at Cudworth, the feast of Corpus Christi, 18 Hen. VI (1440).

(99) Release and quitclaim by William Walton of Coldehendley, Margery his wife, and John their son and heir, to John Boyne of Chapelthorpe, and Joan his wife and the heirs of their bodies lawfully begotten, of all right and claim of and in a messuage with all other the appurtenances, in[1] Cudworth, formerly Adam Wolley's. Witnesses, John Gayle, then vicar of the parish church of Felkyrk, Henry Benks, Robert Goy, and others. Dated at Cudworth, 8 November, 36 Hen. VI. (1457).

(100) Grant by John Boyne to Thomas Blacker and John Hayghe of a messuage built and thirty acres of land and meadow in Crigleston, with the appurtenances, and a messuage and sixteen acres of land and meadow in Cudworth, with the appurtenances. To have

---

[1] The next folio commences here; it is unnumbered. Some number has been inserted at the heading and then smeared out.

and to hold to the grantees, their heirs and assigns, for ever, from the chief [lords][1] of those fees, by the services due and accustomed. Warranty. Witnesses,[2] John Wayde, William Hayghe, Thomas Porter, and others. Dated at Crigleston, 12 June, 6 Edw. IV (1466).

(101) Demise, delivery, and feoffment by Thomas Blacker and John Hayghe to John son of John Boyne, and Agnes his wife, daughter of John Sprygonell, of a messuage built, and thirty acres of land and meadow in Crigelston, with the appurtenances, and a messuage and sixteen acres of land and meadow in Cudworth, with the appurtenances, which properties the grantors lately had by the gift and feoffment of John Boene, senior. To have and to hold all the aforesaid to the grantees and the heirs and assigns of the grantee John for ever, from the chief lords of those fees, by the services due and accustomed. Witnesses, Oliver Hayghe, Robert Pell, and others. Dated at Crigelston, 13 June, 6 Edw. IV (1466).

(102) Grant by John[3] Boene[4] to Richard Ledes, prior of Monkbretton, of a messuage and sixteen acres of land and meadow in Cudworth, with the appurtenances. To have and to hold to the grantee and his successors for ever, from the chief lords of those fees, by the services due and accustomed. Witnesses, William Oxspryng, esquire (*armigero*), Thomas Oxspryng, and others. Dated at Cudworth, 5 February, 7 Edw. IV (1468).

(103) Grant[5] by William Matley of Rytforth in the County of Notyngham and Eustacia his wife, (*fo.* 57d) one of the daughters and heirs of William Depyng, to Thomas Mountney of Monkbretton, gentleman (*generoso*), and Richard Nicolls of Barnyslay, of a moiety of a messuage and croft adjoining and a moiety of an acre and a half of land, with the appurtenances, in the vill and fields of Cudworth. To have and to hold to the grantees, their heirs and assigns, for ever, from the chief lords of those fees, by the services due and accustomed. Witnesses, Richard Amyas, gentleman (*generoso*), Robert Marche, John Farnley, and others. Dated at Monkbretton, 24 April, 13 Hen. VIII (1521).

(104) Release and quitclaim by William Matley of Rytforth in the County of Notyngham and Eustacia his wife, one of the daughters and heirs of William Depyng, (*fo.* 58) to the abovenamed Thomas Mountney and Richard Nicolls, of all right and claim in the property named in the preceding deed. Witnesses, Thomas Gren, Robert Darley, John Frans, and others. Dated at Monkbretton, 27 April, 13 Hen. VIII (1521).

[1] Word omitted.

[2] The dorse of the unnumbered folio commences here.

[3] The folio commencing here is numbered 57; it should be 59, but the foliation continues from the former number.

[4] "John Boyne" in the heading.

[5] In the margin is written "terra Willelmi Depyng, postea Willelmi Matley."

(105)   There are next copied four or five lines from the commencement of a release and quitclaim by Henry Matley, son and heir of the abovenamed William and Eustacia, to the prior of the monastery of the Blessed Mary Magdalen, the copy ending with those words, and " vacat " written in the margin.

(*Fo.* 58*d*)   (106)   Grant by Alice Kar, late the wife of Nicholas Kar of Westretforth in the County of Notyngam, in her pure widowhood, to Thomas Mountney, gentleman (*generoso*), and Richard Nicolls of Barnysley, of a moiety of a messuage and croft adjoining, and a moiety of an acre and a half of land, with the appurtenances, in the vill and fields of Cudworth, which descended to her by hereditary right after the death of William Depyng, her father.   To have and to hold to the grantees, their heirs and assigns, for ever, from the chief lords of those fees, by the services due and accustomed. Warranty.   Appointment of Thomas Ellis and Richard Beste of Cudworth as attorneys to deliver seisin.   (*Fo.* 59)   Witnesses, Richard Amyas, gentleman, Robert Marche, John Farnley, and others.   Dated at Monkbretton, 24 April, 13 Hen. VIII (1521).

(107)   Release and quitclaim by Alice Kar, late the wife of Nicholas Kar of Westrytforth in the County of Notingham, one of the daughters and heirs of William Depyng, to the grantees named in the preceding deed, of all right and claim in the moiety of a messuage, and of the moiety of an acre and a half of land, with the appurtenances, in the vill and fields of Cudworth, which she had by hereditary right after the death of the said William Depyng.   (*Fo.* 59*d*)   Witnesses, Thomas Grene, Robert Darley, John Fransse, and others.   Dated at Monkbretton, 27 April, 13 Hen. VIII (1521).

(108)   Release and quitclaim by Thomas Muntney of Monkbretton and Richard Nycolls to the prior of Monkbretton and the convent thereof and their successors, of all right and claim, etc., in a messuage, a croft adjoining, and an acre and a half of land, with all the appurtenances, in the vill and territory of Cudworth, which they (Thomas and Richard) lately had by the grant of William Matley of Rytforth, Eustacia his wife, and Alice Kar, widow. (*Fo.* 60)   Witnesses, Richard Amyas, gentleman (*generoso*), Thomas Grene, Robert Darley, and others.   Dated at Monkbretton, 20 May, 13 Hen. VIII (1521).

(*Fo.* 60*d is blank.*)

(*Fo.* 61)   (109)   Grant[1] by Thomas Sayvell of Southwell and Nicola his wife, daughter and heir of William Hyll and Agnes his wife, to William Johnson of Cudworth, of a tenement with croft and toft and half an acre of land adjoining, with all the appurtenances, as it lies between the toft of the prior and convent of Bretton in the vill of Cudworth on one side and the land called Hartland on the other. To have and to hold (*fo.* 61*d*) to the grantee, his heirs and assigns, freely, quietly, etc., from the chief lords of that fee, by the services

---

[1] " Terra ·Thome Humbelok " written in the margin.

due and accustomed, for ever. Witnesses, Thomas de Whetley, Richard Beter, John Sparke, and others. Dated at Cudworth, 4 July, 2 Hen. IV, 1401.

(110) Grant by William Johnson of Cudworth to Thomas Humbloke of Cudworth of the property named in the preceding deed. To have, etc., to the grantee, his heirs and assigns, as before. (*Fo.* 62) Witnesses, as in the previous deed. Dated at Cudworth, 20 May, 1402.

(111) Grant by William Homloke, son and heir of John Homloke, to Edward Holdome, of all lands, tenements, meadows, woods, and pastures, with all the appurtenances, which he (William) has in the vill and within the bounds of Cudworth in the County of York. To hold and to have to the grantee, his heirs and assigns, for ever, from the chief lords of that fee, by the services due and accustomed. Witnesses, Thomas Wortley of Wortley, knt., Henry Everyngham, esquire (*armigero*), Richard Whetley, gentleman (*generoso*), and others. Dated at Cudworth, 27 April, 9 Hen. VII (1494).

(*Fo.* 62*d*) (112) Release and quitclaim by William Homlok[1] of Doncaster, cutler, to Edward Holdam of Barnysley, merchant (*merc'*), of all actions, real and personal, suits, debts, accounts, transgressions, and demands whatsoever against the said Edward, which he (William) ever had or has, or may have in future from the beginning of the world to the day of the making of these presents. Dated 6 July, 9 Hen. VII (1494).

(113) Grant by William Holdam, chaplain, to John Roke of Barnysley, mercer, and Joan his wife, of all those his lands and tenements, rents, and services, with the appurtenances, which lately were Edward Holdam's, his father, situated and lying in the parish of Ruston in the County of York. To have and to hold to the grantees and the heirs lawfully begotten between them, from the chief lords of that fee, by the services due and accustomed. (*Fo.* 63) In default of such issue remainder to John Genne, jun., and Margaret his wife and their heirs as above, for ever; to be held as before. Dated at Ruston, 26 August, 22 Hen. VII (1506).

(114) Appointment by William Oldom, chaplain, of Richard Nicolls and William Wolfe, as his attorneys to deliver seisin of the property named in the preceding deed, to John Roke and Joan his wife, the grantees therein mentioned. Dated as in last deed.

(*Fo.* 63*d*) (115) Grant by John Genne and Margaret his wife, one of the daughters and heirs of Edward Holdom, and Alexander Nicolls and Joan his wife, the other daughter and heir of the said Edward, to Thomas Oxspryng and John Hopkynson, of all messuages, lands, tenements, meadows, woods, pastures, with the appurtenances, in Cudworth. To have and to hold to the grantees, their

[1] "Hunblok" in the heading.

heirs and assigns, from the chief lord of that fee, by the services due and accustomed.   Warranty (abbreviated).   Appointment (abbreviated) of Richard Beste and Thomas Ellis as attorneys [to deliver seisin ?].   Dated 3 March, 22 Hen. VII (1507).

(116)   Release and quitclaim by the grantors named in the previous deed[1] (fo. 64) to the same grantees, their heirs and assigns, of all right, title, etc., to and in the same properties.[2]   Dated 5 March, 22 Hen. VII (1507).

(117)   Release and quitclaim by Thomas Oxspryng and John Hopkynson to Thomas Tykhyll, prior of Monkbretton, and the convent thereof, of all right and claim of and in all the messuages, lands, etc. (as before), in Cudworth, which they (Thomas and John) lately had by the gift and feoffment of John Gen and Margaret his wife and Alexander Nicolls and Joan his wife.   (Fo. 64d) Dated 3 February, 3 Hen. VIII (1512).

(118)   Release and quitclaim by Gerard Gen, son and heir of John Gen late of Barnysley, and Margaret his wife, one of the daughters and coheirs of Edward Holdome, to John Hopkynson, his heirs and assigns, of all right and claim of and in all those his messuages, lands, and tenements in Cudworth in the parish of Ruston, which he (Gerard) has by the grant of John Gen, his father and Margaret his mother.   Warranty.   (Fo. 65) Dated 4 November, 16 Hen. VII (1500).

(119)   Release and quitclaim (in consideration of a certain sum of money paid by the transferee) by Richard Roke, son and heir of John Roke and Joan his wife, one of the daughters and heirs of Edward Holdome, to John Hopkynson, his heirs and assigns, now in full and peaceable possession and seisin, of all right, estate, title, and claim of and in a messuage and ten acres of land, meadow, and pasture, with the appurtenances, in Over Cudworth in the County of York.   Warranty.   Dated 6 April, 20 Hen. VIII (1528).

(Fo. 65d) (120) Acknowledgment by Richard Roke of the receipt from William, prior of Monkbretton, of 4 marks sterling, in full satisfaction for all his (Richard's) possession, right, title, etc., of or in a messuage, with the appurtenances, in Cudworth in the County of York, lately Edward Oldom's.   Sealed with his seal and dated 6 July, 21 Hen. VIII (1529).

(Fo. 66)   Erdysley.[3]

(121)   Deed of sale by Thomas de Lifewardene to Jordan de Insula dwelling in Halton in consideration of 90 marks of silver which Jordan gave him on the day of the Purification B.M.V., 1245,

---

[1] The first is called " John Gen " in this deed.

[2] In the present document they are stated to have lately been Edward Holdome's, and to have descended to Margaret and Joan by hereditary right.

[3] Written here in the margin, continued as a heading until fo. 120d. The vill is Ardsley, near Barnsley.

of all his right and claim in the vill and territory of Erdesley. To hold and to have to him (Jordan), his heirs or assigns, freely, etc., with all appurtenances, liberties, and easements within the vill of Erdisley and without, in woods, in plains, in pastures, etc., doing forinsec service as belongs to so much land for all secular service, as is contained in the charter which he (Thomas) had from Sir Thomas de Melton. Warranty. (*Fo.* 66*d*) Witnesses, Sir Thomas Fitz William, Sir Henry Vernoil, Sir Adam de Normaneil, Sir Robert de Wikerley, Sir John Bosevile, Sir Ralph de Euermeles, knights, Raoul (*Rayulo*) Wamenell, Ralph Hagett, Roger de Schessefeld,[1] William de Wath, Jordan de Mar, Adam Penell, and many others.

(122)   Grant by Thomas de Lifewarderye[2] to Jordan de Insula in Haleton, in consideration of 90 marks of silver to him paid by Jordan in hand, of all the land he (Thomas) had in the vill and territory of Erdisley, with all the appurtenances, in wood, in plain, in meadows, etc., and in homages and services of free men [and] villeins. To hold and to have to the grantee and his heirs, freely, quietly, etc., with all liberties and easements (*fo.* 67) belonging to the said land, within and without the vill of Erdisley, doing homage and foreign service as belongs to the said land, to the said Thomas and his heirs for all secular service, as is contained in the charter which he (Thomas) had by the gift of the said Thomas de Melton.[3] Warranty, with sigillum. Witnesses, Sir Thomas son of William, Sir Henry de Vernol, Sir Ralph de Normavill, Sir Robert de Wikslay, Sir John Bosvile, knights, Rainer de Wambwell, Ralph Haget, William de Wath, Jordan de Mar, Adam Paynell, and others.

(123)   Confirmation by Thomas son of Lambert de Multon to Jordan de Insula and his heirs, for his homage and service, of all the land in the vill and territory of Erdislay, with all the appurtenances, which Sir (*fo.* 67*d*) Thomas de Muleton, his grandfather, gave to Sir Thomas de Lyfewarderye. To hold to Jordan and his heirs from the confirmor and his heirs in fee and inheritance, freely and quietly, with all liberties and easements belonging to the said land, as the deed of gift of Sir Thomas, his grandfather, [and] confirmation of Sir Lambert, his father, more fully and better witness; doing therefor to the confirmor and his heirs yearly the service which belongs to the said land. Warranty. Witnesses, Sir Thomas de Muleton, the confirmor's uncle, James de Bussell, rector of the Church of Serebek, Stephen, rector of the Church of Holbek March, Reginald de Rising, William de Freskeney, Thomas Bek, Randolf le Bretton, Adam Druery, William Elis, and others.

(124)   Grant by Jordan de Insula of Halghton (*fo.* 68) to Jordan his first-born son and Isabel his wife and the heirs between them procreated, of all his manor of Erdisley without retention, with the

---

[1] *Sic*, but no doubt intended for Scheffefeld.

[2] *Sic*, probably miscopied for " Lifewardene."

[3] *Sic*, but Thomas de Melton has not been previously mentioned in this deed. The name is altered in the MS., but is apparently Melton. This item and the preceding one are rather confusedly written.

homages, wardships, reliefs, escheats, rents, services, and all other
things to the said manor belonging.   To hold and to have all the
said manor, with the appurtenances, to the grantees and their heirs
(as before) from the chief lord of the fee, by the services due and
accustomed, freely, quietly, etc., for ever.   Warranty.   If the
grantees shall die without heirs as above, the manor, with the appurtenances, to revert wholly, after their deaths, to the grantor and
his heirs.   Alternate seals of the grantor and grantees in witness.
Witnesses, Adam de Wanerkyle,[1] John[2] de Burton, Henry de
Rysscheworth, Adam Achard, (*fo.* 68*d*) John de Flintyll, Peter de
Bosevile, Roger de Waton, and others.   Dated at Erdisley, Monday
after the feast of Peter *ad vincula*, 27 Edw. [I] (1299).

(125)   Grant by Jordan son of Jordan de Insula and Isabel
his wife to William Scot and Alice the grantor's daughter, and the
heirs of their bodies lawfully begotten, of the reversion of their manor
of Erdisley, with the homages and services of the free tenants,
wardships, reliefs, escheats, etc., and all other liberties and appurtenances whatsoever, within and without the vill of Erdisley,
in any way belonging or appertaining; which manor Sir (*dominus*)
Robert de Leuisham, parson of a mediety of the church of Darfield,
holds for his life by the demise of Jordan the present grantor, by
service of £6 of silver payable yearly.   To hold and to have
the said manor to William and Alice and the heirs of their bodies,
with all the appurtenances as aforesaid, from the chief lords of the
fee, by the services hitherto due and accustomed, and receiving the
said (*fo.* 69) £6 yearly from the said manor by the hands of the
said Sir Robert, tenant thereof, or his executors after his death,
as long as the term of years continues.   If the grantees should die
without heir of their bodies as above the said manor, with the
appurtenances, as aforesaid, shall after their death wholly revert.[3]
Witnesses, John de Wodehalle, Robert de Bosevill, Henry de Rokele,
Robert de Barneby, Roger de Etherthorp, William Croke, Adam
Bosevile, Walter Mody, and others.   Dated at Darffeld, Monday
in the eve of the beheading of John Baptist, in the twelfth year of
the reign of the Lord Edward son of King Edward, formerly the
illustrious King of England (28 Aug., 1318).

(126)   Grant by John (*fo.* 69*d*) Scot, knt., to John de Dronsfeld,
John Woderove, Hugh de Wombewell, and Thomas de Wollay,
chaplain, of all his lands and tenements, meadows, woods, pastures,
rents, and services of all his tenants, with all appurtenances, in the
vills of Darffeld, Erdisley, and Wombewell.   To have and to hold to
the grantees, their heirs and assigns, freely, quietly, etc., for ever,
from the chief lords of that fee, by the services thence due and accustomed.   Witnesses, Thomas Bosvill of Ardislay, Thomas de Her-
lynton, Thomas Belle of Cotheworthe, and others.   Dated at

[1] *Sic*; perhaps a mistake for " Wanervyle."
[2] " John " repeated.
[3] It does not say to whom—presumably to the grantor, Jordan.   William
and Alice did not, however, die without heirs of their bodies.

Erdisley, 7 July, 1380, in the ninth year of the reign of King Richard II¹ (1385).

(*Fo.* 70) (127) Release and quitclaim by John Scot, knt., to the grantees named in the previous deed, their heirs and assigns, of all right and claim in the manor of Erdisley and in all lands and tenements, etc. (as above), which the said John de Woderove, Hugh de Wombewell and Thomas de Wolley² had by his gift and feoffment in the vills of Erdislay, Derffeld, and Wombewell. Witnesses, Thomas de Bosvill of Erdislay, Thomas de Harlinton, Thomas de Belle of Cotheworthe, Richard del Hyll, Richard Withe of Erdyslay, and others. Dated at Erdislay, 10 July, 1385, 9 Ric. II.

(*Fo.* 70*d*) (128) To all sons of Holy Mother Church to whose notice these letters indentate shall come, Brother William, prior of the monastery or priory of Saint Mary Magdelene of Monkbretton of the order of Saint Benedict, diocese of York and the convent of the same place, health in Him who is the true health and the one refuge of those hoping in Him, etc., Reciting that the noble man, John Scot, knt., has granted and given certain yearly rents, possessions, and many and large other temporal goods (*fo.* 71) to the monastery to be possessed for their perpetual uses, whereby they and the monastery have been not a little relieved in their necessity and indigence; they therefore, the said prior and convent, desiring to make a spiritual return for the said noble man's liberality, have by these presents granted for themselves and their successors to the said John Scot that immediately after his death they will provide a fellow-monk of the said monastery, in orders, at their own charges, to celebrate daily for ever at the altar of St. Mary Magdelene for the soul of the said John, and for the souls of William Scot, knt., and Alice his wife, the father and mother of John, of Elizabeth, John's wife, Bartholomew Briansons, Robert de Bardelby, clerk, Henry de Hemyngburgh, clerk, and for the souls of his brothers, sisters, the heirs, and ancestors of John, and of all the faithful dead; under this condition, that if the manor of Erdisley, the lands and tenements be recovered against John de Dronsfeld, John Woderove, Hugh Wombewell or Thomas de Wollay, chaplain, (*fo.* 71*d*) enfeoffed by the said John Scot of the said manor, lands, and tenements, or against their assigns, by a title good and anterior to the said feoffment, or if the said John Scot shall hereafter have issue of his body lawfully begotten, the prior and convent and their successors shall be quit and exonerated from providing the said chantry, or if a portion of the said property be so recovered (as above) against the said feoffees, their heirs or assigns, then the prior and convent and their successors shall be exonerated from a proportionate quantity of the chantry according to their clear conscience. Dated at the said monastery, 7 July, 1385.

¹ The date is undoubtedly 1385 (9 Ric. II), but the last numeral " V " is omitted in the deed. Hunter, *South Yorks.*, ii, 279, is incorrect in these dates.

² John Dronsfeld's name is omitted here. It appears in the warranty immediately following.

(*Fo. 72*)   (129)   Deed by William de Notton and John de Brampton, parson of a mediety of the church of Hogholand,[1] executors of William Scot, knt., acknowledging that they have received from the prior and convent of Monkbretton all the moneys and grain, which the said prior and convent and their predecessors, before the making of this deed, by loan or otherwise received from William or his bailiffs. And because the said William was liable to the prior and convent in £49 for the manor of Erdysley, in which manor brother Richard de Halughton, formerly prior of Monkbretton, and the then convent, had a·term of seven years, and at the time when William married Alice his wife, the prior and convent delivered and rendered the said manor to William for his obligation to them made of the said £49, and William paid nothing thereof in his lifetime: And similarly William was liable to the prior and convent, in 10 marks in part payment of 100 marks due to them for a perpetual chantry in their house of Monkbretton, for the soul of Bartholomew de Brianson, (*fo. 72d*) and was likewise liable to them in 80 marks of the legacy of the said Bartholomew to William de Went, formerly prior, and the convent, of the same place, and paid nothing thereof in his lifetime: And also the priors and convents of the same place made to William divers obligations respecting great money services for security to be made to the said chantry, by their sealed letters, and for the treasure and divers goods of William deposited in the priory for safe custody: Having seen those letters, and had sufficient information by the examination of divers worthy persons sworn on the Gospels in the presence of many noble[men] to the truth of the premises, and of our certain knowledge, who have known the truth, and moreover, all things being reckoned, the said William was liable to the prior and convent, beyond the money and grain delivered to them, in £39 12s. 4d.   And the prior and convent have voluntarily (*fo. 73*) remitted the same sum: We (the executors), in full satisfaction of all debts for which William was liable to the prior and convent, have paid and delivered to them all the moneys and grain aforesaid which we have received from them as above, and all actions and demands which we as executors of the said William Scot have against them, by reason of the premises we have remitted and released for ever by these presents, sealed with our seals.   Dated at Monkbretton, 9 April, 20 Edw. III (1346).

(130)   Licence, in the usual form, by King Richard [II] (*fo. 73d*) to Thomas de Wolley,[2] chaplain, to grant to the prior and convent of Monkbretton five messuages, three hundred and sixty-six acres of land, twenty-one acres of meadow, thirty acres of wood, and 21s. 8d. rent, with the appurtenances, in Erdysley, Darffeld, Wombewell, Wranbroke, Skelbroke, and Wath (not held in chief), worth yearly, in all issues, 9 marks 9s. 10d., according to the true value, as found by inquisition held by Hugh Ardern, Escheator in Yorkshire.   To hold to the prior and convent, and their successors,

[1] High Hoyland.
[2] Printed " Wellay " in the Calendar of Patent Rolls.

as of the value of £10 in part satisfaction of a licence granted to them to acquire lands, etc., to the value of £20 (*fo.* 74) yearly.[1]   At Leycester, 17 September, 16 Ric. [II] (1392).[2]

(131)   Release and quitclaim by John Woderove and Hugh de Wombewell (*fo.* 74*d*) to Thomas de Wolley, chaplain, his heirs and assigns, of all right and claim in the manor of Erdisley and in all lands, tenements, rents, and services, with their appurtenances, in Erdislay, Darffeld, and Wombewell, which they lately had, jointly with the said Thomas and John. Dronsfeld (now dead); saving to Hugh, his heirs and assigns, common of pasture in all the said lands which are in Wombewell after corn and hay are cut and carried, as he was accustomed to have before the said feoffment.   Dated 8 April, 14 Ric. II (1391).

(132)   Licence by William Fitz William, knt., lord of Emley, to Thomas Wolley, chaplain, (*fo.* 75) to grant to the prior and convent of Monkebretton and their successors for ever, thirty acres of land and nine acres of meadow, with the appurtenances, in Wombewell, which are held of Thomas de Berley, who holds from the licensor. Dated 6 September, 16 Ric. II (1392).

(133)   Licence by Robert Nevill[3] of Horneby, knt., to Thomas de Wolley, chaplain, to grant to the prior and convent of Monk-bretton (*fo.* 75*d*) and their successors, for ever (which priory is of the foundation of Robert's ancestors), a messuage, two hundred and twenty-six acres of land, twelve acres of meadow, thirty acres of wood, 18s. 6½d. rent, with the appurtenances, in Erdislay and Darffeld, which are held immediately from him (Robert); saving to him, his heirs and assigns, the services thence due and accustomed. Dated 6 September, 16 Ric. II (1392).

(134)   Licence by John son of the King of England, Duke of Aquitaine and Lancaster, Earl of Derbeie, Lyncolne, and Leycester, Steward (*senescallus*) of England, for 10 marks paid to him by Thomas de Wolveley, (*fo.* 76) chaplain, to grant to the prior and convent of Monkbretton, the following two hundred acres of land, ten acres of meadow, thirty acres of wood, 16s. rent, with the appurtenances, in Derffeld and Erdyslay, held by knight service from Robert Nevill of Horneby, knt., as of his manor of Brereley, holding from the said Duke; twenty-four acres of land and six acres of meadow, with the appurtenances, in Wombewell, held by service of 5s. and one broad arrow (*catapulte*) or 2d. yearly, held from Thomas de Barley, holding from William Fitz William, knt., holding from the Duke:

A messuage, with the appurtenances, in Wrangbroke, held of the Duke in socage and by service of 8d. yearly, as of his manor of Auston.

D

A messuage and five acres of land, with the appurtenances, in Wrangbrok, held in socage and by service of 2s. 4d. yearly from John Depeden, knt., and Elizabeth his wife, in right of Elizabeth, holding the messuage from the Duke.

Another messuage and seven acres of land in Wrangbrok, held by service of 2s. 3d. yearly from the prior and convent of Monke-bretton and William Lorde, the holders from the Duke.

Three acres of land in Wrangbrok, held in socage by service of 19d. yearly from John Winteworth, holding the said acres from the Duke.

Fourteen acres of land, 3s. (fo. 76d) 1½d. rent in Skelbrok and Wrangbroke, held from the Duke in chief, by knight service and doing suit at his Court of Pontfrett, three weeks to three weeks, as was found by inquisition taken by William Gascoigne, Steward of the Honour of Pontefract.

To hold to the prior and convent and their successors for ever; and licence to them to receive and hold the same; saving to the Duke and his heirs all customs and services due to them. Dated at his Castle of Pontefret, 10 August, 16 Ric. II (1392).

(135) Grant by Thomas de Wolvelay, chaplain, by licence (fo. 77) of the illustrious King Richard and of all mediate [lords] to the prior and convent of Monkbretton, of his manor of Erdisley and all lands, tenements, rents, and services, with their appurtenances, which were formerly John Scot's, knt., in Erdisley, Darffeld, and Wombewell. To have and to hold to the grantees and their suc-cessors for ever, freely, quietly, etc., from the chief lords of the fee, by the services due and accustomed. Witnesses, William Fizt [sic] William, knt., Robert de Rokelay, knt., Thomas Barley, John Bossevill, Thomas Bossevill, Richard de Kenisforth, Robert Monk, Richard Whitt of Calthorn, Robert Qwayntrell, Robert Goddefray, and others. Dated at Erdisley, 22[1] September, 1392, 16 Ric. II.

(Fo. 77d) (136) Grant by John de Lisurs, with assent of Elienor his wife, to Roger son of Richard, for his homage and service, of a toft in the vill of Erdisley, with a croft, which Alda held, beside (iuxta) Stoc Welle, and a rood of land in the territory of the same vill, upon the high ground in the north field, lying between the land of William Bramewd and the land of Adam son of Simon. To hold and to have to him and his heirs from the grantor and his heirs, with all appurtenances, liberties, and easements, freely, quietly, and wholly, rendering to the grantor and his heirs 12d. for all secular service, demand and custom. Witnesses, John de Rokeleie, Thomas de Bosevill, Helias de Otleham,[2] William of the same, Adam son of Simon, William Bramewd, and others.

(Fo. 78) (137) Grant by Thomas the chamberlain (camerarius) of Erdisleia and Elianor his wife to God and the church of Saint

---

[1] Hunter (South Yorks., ii, 280) says 2 September, but the date is plain in the MS.

[2] Sic; perhaps meant for " Bileham," as in the next deed.

Mary Magdelene of Bretton and the monks there, in pure and perpetual alms, of a toft in the vill of Erdisley, and the croft which Alda de Erdisley held, beside Stokwelle, and a rood of land in the territory of the same vill, on the high ground towards Le Nord, lying between the land of William Bamwod and the land of Adam son of Simon. To hold and to have freely, quietly, etc., with all liberties and easements and commons to the said vill of Erdisley belonging. Witnesses, John de Rokeley, Thomas de Bosvyll, Elias de Bileham, Gilbert the serjeant (*seruiente*), Thomas de Muleton, Adam son of Simon, Ralph de Akitorp, John son of Hugh de Bretton, and others.

(*Fo. 78d*) (138) Quitclaim by Robert son of William Bramwod of Erdisley to Jordan de Insula of Halcton, his heirs or assigns, of all right in all the land, with the appurtenances, without retention, which belonged to him (Robert) after the death of his said father, in the vill of Erdisley. To hold and to have, freely, quietly, etc., with all liberties, etc.; for this concession and quitclaim Jordan has given him 4 marks of silver in recognition. Witnesses, Sir[1] Robert de Wikercesley, Sir John de Bosevile, knts., Roger de Eclesfeld, William de Liseurs, Henry de Bileh', John de Pelton, Henry Durell, William Crok, Richard his son, Simon White (*Albo*), Adam the cook (*coco*) of Erdisley, John Cointerell, William de Ederetorp, clerk, and others.

(139) Quitclaim and confirmation by Thomas Braynewode (*fo. 79*) to Jordan de Insula, junr., and his heirs, of the charter and quitclaim which Robert Braynewode, his father, made to Jordan de Insula, purchaser, of Daderodis, with the appurtenances. Witnesses, Robert Bosevile, Adam de Brerethysill of Wath, Adam Mody of Billinglay, Robert de Humsingdon, William de Normanton, and many others.

(140) Grant by William de Lisurs to Jordan de Insula and his heirs or assigns, for his homage and service, of that essart which is called Weterode, with the meadow, and all the appurtenances, without retention, in the territory of Erdislay. To hold and to have from the grantor and his heirs, in fee and inheritance, freely, quietly, etc., with all liberties and easements appertaining to the said land, rendering yearly to the grantor and his heirs 1*d.* at Christmas, at Erdisley, for all services, etc. (*Fo. 79d*) For this grant Jordan has given him 100s. in recognition. Seal. Witnesses, Sir[2] John de Bosevil, Sir Robert de Wikereysley, knts., Adam Panell, Rainer de Wombwell, John de Chelton, Hugh de Crigleston, Simon White (*Albo*) of Erdisley, John Qinterel, John son of Margaret of the same, Rainer de Bosco, William son of Rois, William de Ederethorp, clerk, and others.

(141) Grant by William de Lisurs, made on the day of St. Leonard, 1251, to Jordan de Insula and his heirs, or to whom he shall desire to give, sell, assign, or bequeath, for his homage and service,

[1] In each case " domino."
[2] In each case " domino."

of that essart which is called (*fo.* 80) Wetherode,[1] with the meadow and wood, and all other appurtenances, without retention, in the territory of Herdislay.   To hold and to have to him and his heirs or assigns, from the grantor and his heirs or assigns, in fee and inheritance, freely, quietly, etc., with all appurtenances, liberties, commons, and easements, belonging to the land; rendering to the grantor and his heirs or assigns 1*d.* yearly, at the gate of the said Jordan at Erdisley, at Christmas, for all services, etc.   For this grant Jordan has given him 100*s.* in recognition.   Witnesses, Sirs[2] John de Bosevill and Robert de Wekerlay, knts., Adam Paynell, Rainer de Wambuell, John de Schelton, Hugh de Crigelestun, Simon White (*Albo*), and others.

(*Fo.* 80*d*)   (142)   Quitclaim by Jordan[3] son of Robert Braynwode to Jordan son of Jordan de Lile, and his heirs or assigns, of all right and claim in any land or tenement within the bounds of Erdisley which his (the quitclaimor's) ancestors formerly held.   Dated at York, at Christmas, 1300.

(143)   Release and quitclaim by John Clogge of Erdislay to Sir William Scot, knt., and his heirs and assigns, of all right and claim in a plot of land in the eastern part of Dadderodes, upon which Sir William's foss is extended (*stratum est*), and the said plot is parcel of a certain essart called Ibbotterode.   (*Fo.* 81) Dated at Erdislay, Thursday in the feast of the Exaltation of Holy Cross, 20 Edw. III (1346).

(144)   Demise by Sir Richard de Roderham, parson of the church of Peniston, William de Fyncheden, junr., and Thomas de Methelay of Thornhyll, to Sir William Scot, knt., and Alice his wife, of their (the grantors') manors of Halghton, to wit, the manor which was Jordan de Insula's and the manor which was John de la Roche's, with all rights, reversions, services, rents, and all other appurtenances; and likewise their (the grantors') manor of Erdyslay and a plot of land and meadow called Normanrode, and also all the land and meadow of Bromfeld, with common pasture in Wombwell and in the common wood of Wombwell, with road to the same wood, and also a messuage and all the land which was Katherine de Bosvell's, with the appurtenances, in Erdyslay, and also all their (the grantors') tenements in Byllinglay which were formerly Walter Mody's, or Adam's (*fo.* 81*d*) his son and heir, together with the reversion of one tenement, which Emma who was wife of Walter Mody holds from the grantors, in the same vill, by the grant of the said Adam son of Walter, and all rents and services, homages, reversions, wastes, woods, essarts, and all other rights and appurtenances, to the said Sir William and Alice for their full lives; after their death remainder to William their son and the heirs of his body; if he shall die without such heir, remainder to Thomas his brother and the heirs of his

---

[1] Not Westroyd, as Hunter has it (*South Yorks.*, ii, 280).

[2] " Domino " in each case.

[3] Hunter (*South Yorks.*, ii, 280) says this release was by Robert Braynwood.

body; if he shall die without such heir, remainder to Nicholas his brother and the heirs of his body; if he shall die without such heir, remainder to John his brother and the heirs of his body; if he shall die without such heir, (*fo.* 82) remainder to Frances his sister and her heirs for ever, from the chief lords of the fee, by the services due and accustomed. Witnesses, Sirs John de Eland and Nicholas de Worteley, knts., John de Wodhall, Robert de Bosevill, Thomas de Staynton, and others.

(145)[1] Grant by Gilbert de Broddebryg to Henry del Brom and his heirs or assigns, of all the land which he (Gilbert) had in the essart called Ranke rode, in the territory of Wambwell between the land of the same Henry and the water called Dowhe, with all appurtenances, as far as the middle of the water. To hold and to have to Henry, his heirs or assigns, from the grantor and his heirs, in fee and inheritance, freely, quietly, etc., with all liberties and easements, in plains, in woods, etc., with commons within and without the vill of Wambwell as belong to so much land; rendering to the grantor and his heirs an arrow yearly for all services and demands. (*Fo.* 82*d*) For this grant Henry has given him 5*s.* of silver and half[2] a bushel of beans in recognition. Seal. Witnesses, Reiner de Wombwell, Jordan de Insula, Roger de Halet, John de Schelton, Hugh de Bacun, Roger de Skires, John Douell, and others.

(146) Grant by William de Lisurs to Henry de Brom and his heirs or assigns, except religious or jews, for his homage and service, of all the land which he (William) had in Farhthingforht in the territory of Erdyslay, to wit, six roods with the length and breadth, as they lie in parcels. To hold and to have from the grantor and his heirs in fee and inheritance, freely, quietly, etc., with all liberties, easements, and commons to so much land in Erdislia belonging; rendering thence yearly to the grantor and his heirs a pair of white gloves, or ½*d.* for all services, customs, and (*fo.* 83) demands. For this grant Henry has given him 4*s.* of silver in recognition. Seal. Witnesses, Jordan de Insula, Rainer de Bosco, Adam son of Claricia, John son of Simon, Simon White (*Albo*), Adam the cook, John Conteres, William son of Roys, and others.

(147) Quitclaim by Thomas son of . . . . . .[3] to Henry de Brom and his heirs of the servile service which he does or ought to do to the quit-claimor at W'dehall. For this quitclaim Henry has given Thomas 20*s.* sterling in hand and his yearly ferm is increased from 2*s.* to 5*s.* 2*d.* for all his land and the said service. (*Fo.* 83*d*) Seal. Witnesses, Henry de Novo Mercato, Thomas de Horbury, Richard de Tange, knts., Rainer de Wallwell, William de Billam, John de Bosevile, Robert de Crigileston, Thomas de Ecclesffeld, and others.

---

[1] " Brome lande " written in the margin.

[2] Hunter (*South Yorks.*, ii, 280) reads this " two," but the word in the MS. is " dm̃."

[3] Omitted in the MS.

(148)   Quitclaim by Thomas son of Randolph Bulloc to William Scott and Alice his wife and the heirs of William, of all his tenements in the vills of Wombwell and Erdislay, as well those tenements which are called Le Brom Lande as all his other tenements whatsoever in the said vills, with all appurtenances, commons, and roads to the common[1] of Wombwell, and other easements to the said tenements in any way belonging.   To have and to hold to William and Alice and the heirs of William from the chief lords of the fee, by the services due and accustomed for all other services.   (Fo. 84) Witnesses, Sirs[2] John Darcy, John de Eland, Nicholas de Worttley, Adam de Everingam, knts., Thomas de Walghum, clerk, Robert Parunch, John de Habinttheby, William de Miggelay, and others.   Dated at Calthorn, Wednesday after the feast of St. Dunstan, Archbishop, 6 Edw. III (1332).

(149)   Grant by Dionisia formerly wife of Randolph Bullocc of Barnysley, in her widowhood, to Thomas her son, of all her tenement, in woods and in meadows, with the appurtenances, as it lies in the vill and bounds of Wombwell, in a certain place called Le Brom.   To have and to hold to the grantee, his heirs and assigns, from the chief lords of that fee, freely, quietly, etc., with commons and easements, by the services due and accustomed to be done, for ever.   Witnesses, Godfrey de Stanton, Edmunde de Bosewill, Roger son of Hugh de Wombwell, John Clayton, and others.

(Fo. 84d)   (150)   Demise at term by Thomas son of Randulph Bullocc of Barnisley to William Scott of Birthwayt, of all those lands and tenements, meadows and pastures, with the appurtenances, called Le Brome, as they lie in length and breadth within the bounds of Wombewell, saving to Thomas the growing wood in the said tenement, which he retains for felling, burning, and carrying, as he pleases.   To have and to hold to William, his heirs and assigns, from Martinmas, 1331, for the full term of ten years next following, from Thomas and his heirs, freely, quietly, etc., rendering to them yearly 28s.   Alternate seals to the two parts of this indenture. Dated at Calthorn, Monday after the feast of Exaltation of Holy Cross, in the year abovesaid.

(Fo. 85)   (151)   Grant and quitclaim by Alice, formerly wife of Richard le Wondeward of Erdislay, in her free widowhood and lawful power, to Robert de Bosevill and his heirs or assigns, of two roods of land in the territory of Erdysley, whereof one rood lies on Adeerdeslay between the land of the same Robert and the land formerly Richard the cook's, the south head abutting upon Normanrode and the other rood on the same Adcerdislay between the land of the same Robert and the land of John son of Rayner and abuts on the same Normanroide, and moreover 1d. yearly rent from Randulph Bullocc and Dionisia his wife and their heirs, receivable at Christmas, issuing from one rood of land on which a chamber is

---

[1] Written " ad cŏie."
[2] In each case " domino."

situated, at Le Brom. To hold and to have to the said Robert and his heirs and assigns as chief lord of the fee, with all wardship, reliefs, escheats, treasure-trove (*fortunis*), falling to the said rent. Warranty, for a certain sum of money paid to her in hand. Dated at Erdisley in the . . . . .¹ year of the reign of King Edward III. Witnesses, Peter Bosevill, Thomas de Swathe, and others.

(*Fo.* 85*d*) (152) To all, etc., John son of Roger son of Thomas de la Wodehalle, greeting. Whereas Thomas le hunter of Calthorne did suit at the court of Roger son of Thomas, John's father, for a tenement which he held from him within the bounds of Wambewele, in a place called Brom, and he now holds from John. John, for the health of the souls of his ancestors, has released and quitclaimed, for ever, to the said Thomas and Dionisia his wife and the heirs or assigns of Dionisia, all that suit. Witnesses, Robert de Bosevile, Geoffrey de Staynton, Henry de Rokley, John de Cad, Robert son of John Wambwell, and others.

(153) Indenture witnessing that William (*fo.* 86) Scott has granted to John his son and his heirs and assigns all his (William's) land called Le Bromland. To have and to hold to John, his heirs and assigns, with all commons and appurtenances, from the chief lords of that fee, by the services due and accustomed, rendering to William, his heirs and assigns, 100s. yearly; power of re-entry or distraint at will in case rent in arrear. Mutual seals in witness. Witnesses, William de Multon, Roger Curson, William de Notton, Thomas de Cresacre, and Philip de Bosevil. Dated at Halghton, Sunday after the feast of Exaltation of Holy Cross, 10 Edw. III (1336).

(154) Grant by Elinor formerly wife of John de Lysurs (*fo.* 86*d*) to God and the blessed Mary Magdalene of Bretton and the monks there serving God, in pure and perpetual alms, of three acres of land in the territory of Erdislay, with all the appurtenances, namely, half an acre in the place called Hundigleie between the land of William Bramwod and the land of Adam son of Simon, and half an acre in Old (*Uet*) Erdisley which she had next to the land of Helias de Bilham towards the east, besides half an acre and a rood in the place called Crumlandes between [the land of] William Bramwod and the land of Ralph son of Bacun, and half an acre in the same place between the land of the said Helias and the land of Robert son of Cecilie, and half an acre in the place called Crinocclyf between the land of Adam son of Simon and the land of Roger son of Edwin, and a rood of land below Crinocclyf beside the land of Adam son of Simon, and half an acre in the north field between the land of the said Helias and the land of Robert son of Cecilie, beside the place called Litelleie Clyf. Witnesses, John de Rokeleye, Helias de Byllam, Adam son of Simon, William Croc, Ralph son of Jordan, Thomas Tyrell, and others.

¹ Omitted in MS.

(*Fo.* 87) (155) Confirmation by Thomas son of John de Leisurs of Erdyslay to God and St. Mary Magdalene of Bretton and the monks serving God there, of the gift of Elienor his mother, namely, three acres of land in the territory of Herdisleye, with all the appurtenances belonging to so much land.[1] Witnesses, John de Rokeleie, Helias de Bilham, Adam son of Simon, William Croke, Ralph son of Jordan, Thomas Tyrell, Arnold de Kinesleye, Hugh de Bosco, and others.

(156) Grant by Roger de Edrictorp to God and the blessed Mary Magdelen of Bretton and the monks serving God there, in pure and perpetual alms, of a toft, with the appurtenances, in the vill of Erdisley, which John de Selton held from him for 6*d.* yearly, which toft the said John de Selton afterwards gave to the said monks by his charter, similarly for 6*d.* yearly to be paid to him (John) and his heirs. (*Fo.* 87*d*) Roger now quitclaims to the monks the said toft with the aforesaid 6*d.*, and with all easements and liberties belonging to so much land. Witnesses, William son of William, John de Rokeleia, Reiner parson of Derefeud, Walter de Louais, Richard Croco, Ralph Borbot, John Lesuris, and many others.

(157) Grant by John de Scelton to God and St. Mary Magdelene of Bretton and the monks there, of a toft in the vill of Erdisleia, with the appurtenances, that toft, namely, which was Richard Prat's, in length and breadth as it lies beside the road from Erdislaie to Wirkesburc, towards the south. To hold and possess from the grantor and his heirs, freely, quietly, etc., in wood, in plain, etc., with all liberties and free customs of the said vill, belonging to so much land, rendering to the grantor or his heirs for all service, etc., 6*d.* yearly. (*Fo.* 88) Witnesses, William son of William, Richard de Wambwelle, John de Rockleia, Hugh parson of Darffeld, Thomas his brother, and many others.

(158) Grant by Simon son of Richard the miller of Erdisleia to God and St. Mary Magdelen of Birtton and the almoner of the same place, of a toft in the vill of Erdisley, with the buildings and other appurtenances, namely, that toft which lies [? between][2] the toft of Hugh de Ednketorp and the toft of Thomas son of Hayun de Hacwrh and the King's road on the south side. To hold and to have, freely, quietly, etc., with all appurtenances, rendering yearly a silver halfpenny to Thomas son of Hyun de Haicwrh or his assigns, for all services and demands. Witnesses, Sir (*dom*) John Bolouk, Ralph de Haya, Adam Cook, Gregory de Batelay, William the clerk of Bretton, and many others.

---

[1] Hunter (*South Yorks.*, ii, 280) reads this as a grant of the " house ' of Eleanor, and, in fact, the word is written " domu," but the reference to the land shows that this is only a copyist's error for " donum," and that the deed is merely a confirmation of the preceding one.

[2] There has been an alteration in the MS. here.

(*Fo.* 88*d*) (159) Deed by Agnes de Darley, daughter of Adam and Alice de Erdislay, who held from the prior and convent of Bretton a bovate of land, with the appurtenances, in Erdislay, for 4s. 6d. yearly, and because that rent has been in arrear for twenty years, by this deed she has granted, demised, and resigned to the said prior and convent, her chief lords, six acres of land, with the appurtenances, in Rohagh in Erdisley, which are of the said bovate. To have and to hold to the prior and convent and their successors, quietly, peaceably, and wholly, with all appurtenances and easements, until she, Agnes, or her heirs, in one day shall have paid 6 marks and 10s. for the said arrears. Warranty of the land until such payment shall have been made. Witnesses, Godfrey de Stanton, Thomas his brother, William de Notton, Robert de Celar, Robert son of Alexander, and others. Dated at Monkbretton, Sunday before the feast of St. Nicholas, bishop, 1317, the 11th year of the reign of King Edward, son of King Edward.

(*Fo.* 89) (160) Release by Richard de Halgton, prior of Monkbretton and the convent, to Thomas son of Robert de Bosevile, of 2s. of the 4s. 6d. which he was accustomed to render to the prior and convent, for a bovate of land in Erdisley, for so long as six acres of land in Rohagh remain to them in possession which they had by the demise of Agnes de Darlay. Seal of the prior in witness. Witnesses, Godfrey de Staynton, Adam de Bosevill, Philip his brother, William de Notton, Robert de Celar, and others.

(161) Grant by William son of John de Lisurs to God and the church of St. Mary Magdelene of Bretton and the monks there, of the homage and service of Adam son of Claricia, of a bovate of land in the territory of Erdislay, which he (Adam) held from the grantor by hereditary right of his wife Alice and their heirs, (*fo.* 89*d*) to wit, the service of that bovate which Peter, William's grandfather, the son of Geoffrey, formerly sold to Simon the serjeant (*seruienti*) and his heirs. To hold and to have in pure and perpetual alms, freely, quietly, etc., as well in homages and services as in wardships, reliefs, escheats, and other appurtenances belonging to the said bovate. Witnesses, Thomas son of William, Reiner de Wombwell, Peter de Rokkelay, Jordan del Hile,[1] Simon White, Adam[2] Cook, Reiner de Bosco, and many others.

(162) Quitclaim[3] by James de Bosevile, knt., to Katherine de Bosevile, of all right and claim in the lands and tenements which Robert de Bosevile gave her, namely, in Wykyrisley (*fo.* 90) a messuage and a bovate of land, with the appurtenances, in Derffeld, a toft and croft in the place called Ouurwodhall, and all that land which is called Foxwelland, and a plot of meadow containing one acre on the west side of Le Milnemore, and a bovate called Normanrode, and

---

[1] Hunter (*South Yorks.*, ii, 280) reads this " Hill," but the word is plain in the MS. No doubt it represents " Ile, de Insula."

[2] " Ade."

[3] Here " Normanroide " is written in the margin.

an acre of land abutting on Normanrodelidgate, and a toft and six acres of land which Robert de Bosevile had of the gift of Amabel his wife in the vill and territory of Erdysley.   Witnesses, Edmund de Percy, Godfrey de Stanton, Philip de Bosevile, William de Notton, Edmund de Bosevile, and others.   Dated at Le Neuhalle, Monday after the feast of St. Matthias Apostle, 1321.

(163)   Indenture witnessing that Katherine daughter of Robert de Bosevile, has granted (*fo.* 90*d*) to William Scot and Alice his wife all that plot of land and meadow called Normanrode with the ditches and fences enclosing that plot, and that acre of land lying at Normanrodelidgate, with the appurtenances.   To have and to hold, from the chief lords of that fee, to the said William and Alice and the heirs and assigns of William, with all appurtenances, commons, and easements, freely, quietly, etc., rendering yearly to Katherine during her life 16*s.* of silver from the said tenements, to whosesoever lands they shall come.   William recognises Katherine's right to distrain for the said rent.   Alternate seals to the present indenture.   Witnesses, Adam de Everingham of Rockelay, knt., Richard de Roderham, parson of the church of Peniston, Thomas de Barneby, parson of the church of Heton, John son of John de Wodhall, and others.   Dated at Erdislay, Tuesday in the Nativity of the Lord, 5 Edw. III (1331).

(*Fo.* 100)[1]   (164)   Grant by John de Bosevile and Alice his wife to Robert Bosevile their son, of 16*d.* of yearly rent receivable from Mabel daughter of Robert Anelacby, in Erdislay, 6*d.* yearly, from William son of Adam the cook of the same 7*d.* yearly, from Richard the cook of Erdyslay 3*d.* yearly, together with the homage of the said tenements, wardships, reliefs, and escheats, which may in any way fall by reason of the said rent.   To have and to hold to the grantee, his heirs or assigns, from the grantors and their heirs for ever, freely, quietly, etc., with all appurtenances. Witnesses, Sir Roger son of Thomas, Roger de Wambwell, Roger de Edirthorp, Thomas de Bosevile, Peter de Bosevile, and others.

(165)   Grant by Alice, formerly wife of Sir John Bosevile, knt., in her free widowhood (*fo.* 100*d*) and lawful power to Robert de Bosevile, her son, and his heirs or assigns, of that bovate of land, with all appurtenances, which Norman formerly held, in the territory of Erdislay, and is called Normanroyde, as it lies together in length and breadth.   Moreover she has given Robert six acres of land, lying in one parcel, at the eastern head of the vill of Erdislay, as they lie in length and breadth between the land formerly of William Coyntres on the west side, and the land formerly of William de Bosco on the east side, and the northern head abuts on the land of Elizabeth de Erdislay which is called Estewelflat, and the southern head abuts on the land of the same Elizabeth which is called Hancweleflat.

---

[1] *Sic*; doubtless a mistake of the person responsible for the pagination; there is no "lacuna" in the MS., as the heading for the following deed appears at the bottom of *fo.* 90*d.*

To hold and to have to the grantee, his heirs or assigns, from the grantor and her heirs, in fee and inheritance, freely, quietly, etc., with all liberties, easements, commons, in woods, in meadows, in pastures, etc., in all places common, belonging to the said land within and without the vill of Erdislay: rendering yearly to the grantor and her heirs 1d. at Christmas for all services, etc. Seal. Witnesses, Sir Roger son of Thomas, (fo. 101) Nicholas de Wortelay, John de Sothehil, knts., John de Bosevile, junior, Henry de Byry, William de Bosevile, John de Stanton, William de Mar, and many others.

(166) Release and quitclaim by William de Notton to William Scot and Alice his wife and the heirs of William, of all right and claim in a plot of land as enclosed and enfossed, called Normanroide, and in a messuage and seven and a half acres of land, with the appurtenances in the vill of Erdislay, which plot of land with the said messuage and seven and a half acres William and Alice had by the gift and feoffment of a certain Katherine de Bosevile in Erdislay. Witnesses, Robert Parnynge, William Basset, William son of William de Migelay, William de Wakefeld, Philip de Bosevile, and others.

(Fo. 101d) (167) Pleas at Westminster before John Prysot and his fellows, Justices de Banco, Hilary term, 27 Henry VI (1449). Ebor; As appears in Michaelmas term last past, roll 441 thus contained: Ebor; Richard, prior of Monkbretton, by Thomas Beaumont his attorney, seeks against William Bosevile 13s. rent with the appurtenances, in Monkbretton, Ardysley, Darffeld, Huland by Calthorn, and Calthorn, in right of his monastery, of which William unjustly and without judgment disseised him, etc. The case adjourned to Hilary term, when William failed to appear, (fo. 102) and judgment was given that the prior recover. But because collusion between the parties was suspected, against the form of the statute of mortmain, the Sheriff was directed to summon a jury of the neighbourhood within a month of Easter, to ascertain the prior's right, etc., and whether there was any fraud or collusion between the parties and to warn the superior lords, etc., and in the meantime to take the said rent into the King's hands, etc. (fo. 102d) (Case further adjourned to Michaelmas term, 28 Hen. VI.) The jury say (fo. 103) upon their oath, that the prior and all his predecessors, priors of the said monastery, were seised of the said rent with the appurtenances as a rent of service, in right of their monastery, from time beyond memory, and that William Riall formerly prior, was seised thereof in the time of the lord Henry late King of England, son of King John, to wit of 2s. rent from a certain plot of land four feet in length in Monkbretton, and a messuage with the appurtenances, in Derffeld, by the hand of John Broddesworth then tenant, and of 2s. 6d. from the capital messuage of the withinnamed William Boswell in Ardisley, by the hand of a certain Adam Forster then tenant of that messuage, and of 4s. rent from a certain close called Gilbertroyde otherwise Diconstubbyng in Huland, and of 2s. rent from a messuage called Canonhall and a certain essart called Dunstall in Calthorn, by the hand of John Orme of Calthorn tenant, and of 2s. 6d. rent from one (*fo.* 103d) bovate called Darley Oxgang in Ardesley, by the hand of a certain Agnes Darley then tenant. And the said William, formerly prior, and all his successors, priors of the said monastery, were successively seised of the said 13s. rent until the said William Boswell, on the 22 August, 22 Hen. VI (1444), disseised the present prior, unjustly and without judgment, from the time of which disseisin five years have elapsed, and that the rent is in arrear for those five years and is still unpaid, and that the prior has sustained damages, beyond the arrears to the value of ten shillings: and that there is no fraud or collusion between the parties against the statute of mortmain. The prior says that he has sustained greater damages than these assessed by the jury as above, and asks the Justices to increase them. Therefore it is adjudged that the prior have execution of the said judgment, and further that he recover against William his arrears and damages, assessed by the jury at 75s. and also 30s.(*fo.* 104) allowed by the Justices as increase at his request, in all 105s. And the aforesaid William is in mercy.

Names of the jury: Richard Wodhall,[1] Robert Rokley, Thomas Mokson, John Metheley, Robert del Legh, Thomas Watson, John Pilley, John Jenkynson, Richard Turton, John Galbar, William Stede, William Turton.

(168) Know all by these presents that I, Edward Hastynges, Sheriff of York, have received the mandate of the King in (these words), Henry by the grace of God, King of England and France, and Lord of Ireland, to the Sheriff of York, greeting. Know that it has been granted in our Court (*fo.* 104d) at Westminster that Richard, prior of Monkbretton, have seisin against Thomas Boswell, son and heir of William Boswell, of 13s. rent with the appurtenances, in Monkbretton, Ardyslay, Darfeld, Huland by Calthorn and Calthorn which the said prior recovered in our Court at Westminster, as the right of his monastery, against the said William, father of Thomas: We command you that forthwith you cause the prior to have full seisin of the said rent. Witnesses, R. Danby, at Westminster, 30 January, the 49th year from the commencement of our reign, and the first of the recovery of our royal power, by virtue of which writ, I have appointed and put in my place Thomas Sandbych, bailiff of Stayncrosse, John Wordesworthe, John Couper, and John Ravenfeld, my attorneys, jointly and severally to the due execution in my name of this writ. Dated at York Castle, under the seal of my office, 31 March in the aforesaid year (1471).

Henry (VI), King of England, etc., to the Sheriff of York, Mandate that of the lands and (*fo.* 105) chattels of William Bosvile in his bailiwick he levy 105s. which Richard, prior of Monkbretton, recovered for damages, which he had because the said William disseised him of 13s. rent in Monkbretton, etc. (as in the preceding document). Witnesses, J. Prisot, at Westminster, 22 November, the 28th year of our reign. Hillary xxvii, Ro. cxxxii.

---

[1] After each name "jur" is written.

(169) Edward (IV), King of England, etc., to the Sheriff of York. Whereas Richard, prior of Monkbretton, in the Court of Henry VI, lately in fact but not of right, King of England, at Westminster, to wit in Michaelmas term in the 28th year, before John Prisott and his fellows, Justices, recovered seisin against William Boswell of 13s. rents with the appurtenances, in Monkbretton, etc. (as before), (fo. 105d) but execution of the said judgment still remains to be done, as we have received by the information of the said prior: we command you that you cause Thomas Bosevill, son and heir of William Bosevell, who now receives the said rents, that he be before our Justices at Westminster in fifteen days of Michaelmas to show cause why the prior should not have execution. Witnesses, R. Danby, at Westminster, 4 July, in the 10th year of our reign (1470). Ro. cxxvii.

(170, in English) This writtyng indented witnes yat dyvers varius clames and demandez for the right title and possession (fo. 106) off certains Londes tenements, rents and arreragies of rentts late had and moved bitwyx Richard Ledes prior of ye monastre of Sent Mare Magdalen of Monkbretton on yat on partye and Henri Langton esquier and Isabell his wife late wife of John Boseville Esquier and ye feoffes to ye use of ye said Isabell on ye other partie were by yassent and agrement of ye said prior and Isabell put to yawarde dome and ordinance of hus Margarete late wife off Thomas Everingam squire, John Woderoffe squier, Thomas Dodworthe, William Bradfforth and Thomas Beamont as Arbitrators indifferentlie chosen by ye said prior and Isabell. And we takyng on hus ye said awarde dome and ordinance ye tuysday in ye firste weke off Lentyn in ye yere of ye reigne of King Henry ye sext after ye conquest xxxv att Ardisley by thagrementt of ye said prior and Isabell awarde ordeygnes and demes in yes premisses in ye forme ensuyng yt is to say yat ye said prior shall have and peassablie enioye to hym and to his successors without impedimente off ye sayd Isabell her heres and feoffes to her use a meas or a toft iiij acres and halff a rode of lande somtyme John Milner in Ardysley and iij rode of londe with medowe with yappurtenance in Ardysley lying in a place callyd Bradley with iij porcions of yng in ye More yng callyd Softende wych late were Jak Adam off Ardysley the (fo. 106d) wiche londs and tenements ye said prior late clemed as his eschete in ye right of his said monastery. And also ye said Isabell shall deliver to ye said prior before ye feste of Nativity of Sent John Babtiste next comyng al such charters and muniments as she has concernyng ye same. Also we award yat ye sayd Isabell and her ffeoffes to hir use shall paye to ye said prior and his successors yerelie at times usuall yes rentes underwrittyn yt is to say for lande and tenements in hill lying bisyde Cowclose yer callid ffrape thing ij shillings.

And also for a parcell of lond lying within ye same Cowclose whiche late was on Willym Cobbok, 2½d. Also for an acre of lande called Nodcaracre and Smythe Croft, 12d.; for lands and tenements somtyme Robert Godffray in Ardisley, 12d. Also for londes and tenements sumtyme Robert Quintrell's in Ardisley, 10½d.

Also for londes and tenements sumtyme Thomas Westall's and byfore Elisot Westall's in Erdysley, 5½d. Also for londes and tenements in Monkbretton somtyme John Wroo, 3s. And for teynd hay of ye same of olde tyme acustomyd to be payd 4d.

Also for ye same to yoffice of ye secreston of ye same place 16d. And also do to ye said prior and his successors all other service due to yam for all ye seid londes and tenements holdyn of yam. Also ye said Isabell her heiris and feoffes to (fo. 107) her use shall paye to ye said prior or his successors.

Also do to ye said prior and his successors all other services due to yam for all ye said landes and tenements holden of yam. Also ye said Isabell her heirs and said feoffes to her use shall paie to ye said prior or his successors att the seid fest off Nativity off Sent John for ye arreragies of ye rents of long tyme beyng be hynde to hym before yis award now paid 6l. 9s. 6d. Also ye said Isabell shall paie to ye said prior att ye said ffest 5s. in satisfaction of certeyns cornes late takyn by hir in Ardisley, and led away off parcells of ye said ground late Jac. Adam. Also we award ordeyn and deme yat ye said prior his successors shall paye [to crossed out] yerelie to ye said Isabell hir hers or feoffes to hir use att times usuell thes rentts underwriten yat ys to say for certeyn londes and tenements in Ardislay callyd Mabott londes and late John Scot knyght, 12d. And for iij londes lyng in Molcroft ageynst ye yate of ye olde hall a pair of withglowis or a peny. Also for certeyn londes and tenements in Ardislay callid Dand londes late John Herison and sometyme Robert Pirrie, 2s. Also wer ye said Isabell clames of ye same londes 3d. rent yerelye over ye said 2s., the wiche ye said prior sais and affermes not to be due we will and ordeigne yat upon resonable warnyng by hus made to ye said prior and Isabell (fo. 107d) yay shall mete before hus at Ardisley with sich evydences and proves as yai severallie mey have or gete in provyng or denying of ye payment of ye 3d. rent. And ther to take oure awarde.

Also ye said prior and his successors shall do to ye said Isabell hir heirs or feoffes at other service dew to yam for ye same londes and tenements holden of yam. Also ye said prior or his successors shall paye to ye said Isabell hir heirs or feoffes to hir use at ye said fest of Nativite of Sent John for a yarrerege of ye same rentes of long tyme beyng beynd to yam befor yis award not paied 29s. 6½d.

Also ye said prior shal paie to ye said Isabell att ye same fest 5s. in satysfaction of a waynful of corne in cheves callid otes of ye same Isabell and hir feoffes late takin and lede away by hym at Monkbretton. In Witness werof we ye said arbitrators to yis oure award dome and ordinancs have set our seals the day yere and place above said.

(171)   Bond of John Boswell esquire and John Monk to Richard, prior of Monkbretton, and his successors, in the sum of £100 (fo. 108) to be paid at Christmas next following. Sealed with their seals, and dated Friday after the feast of St. Wilfrid bishop. 20 Hen. VI (1441).

The condition is that if the said John Boswell and Isabell his wife shall abide by the award of William Scargill and William Mirfield esquires, arbitrators chosen by the said John and the prior respecting the right, title, and possession of a certain wood in Ardislay called Ardesleywod, alias the westwod of Ardislay, and respecting all other actions, real and personal, between the said John and the prior from the beginning of the world to the date of these presents, and shall faithfully observe and fulfil such award, then this obligation shall be null, otherwise remain in full force and effect.

(172) This writyng endentted witnes that (*fo.* 108*d*) where as certeyns clames debates variances and controversies were late had and movyd bytwix Richard, prior of Monkbretton, on that one partie and John Bosevyll of Newhall Squier on that other partie touching a wod callyd the westwod of Ardislay by a nothir name callyd Ardislay wod. And also the warde and maryage of Robert son and here of Edmunde Normanvile and off certeynes landes rentes and services in Ardislay and Monkbretton of the which clames, debates, variances and controversies and all other things the parties before said have putts and submyt thame to the award, dome and ordynances off William Skargill Esquier and William Mirfeld Esquier arbitrators indeferenlie [*sic*] chosen be the parties beforesaid: these the said arbitrators takyng uppon theme the said awarde, dome and ordenances the Saturday next after the fest of Sent Wilfride the yere of the regne of Kyng Henry sext after the conquest of yngland twenty, at Ardysley be agrement of the said parties awarde demes and ordeynes in the some that felowes that ys to saie that the said wod callid Westwod be another name called Ardisleywod shalbe departid bitwyx the said parties. And the said prior peseblie to have and recover to hym and to his successors forevermore the north partie of ye said wod fro the corner of a cloyss of William Boswell callid Dawerode foloyng the way callid Anstikergrene wich ledes fro a cloys callid Bromeroid through (*fo.*109) the said wod to Bernysley more in severaltie fro the said John his heirs and assignes or feoffes to his byhove. And the said John peseblie to have that other partie of the said wod to hym hys heris or assignes in severalite, that is to witt the sowthe partie of the said wod as it is departyd set assigned and lymyted be marks and boundes the day of makyng of this award and ordenance by the said arbitrators by the circuite off the same wod. And at all the tenants of Ardisley shall hafe and recover thare comon in the said wod as they ogthe do to do haffe and has used be long tyme. And also that William Bosvell shall be maide fully content be the said John of all parcelles conteyned in a chartre made by the said John to the said William of certan londs, tenements and wodds in Ardisley so that the said wod assigned to the said prior then no parcells ther off be conteyned in the same charter. And also that either partie before said at hys awne propre costs shall be maid as sure of the partie assignyd to hym his counsell shall dewise at the oversight of the said arbitrators, and the said John Boswell shall make

the said prior have a due knowlegge of such persones ageynes whome he may hafe a sufficant recovere in laghe and right that the said prior and his successors of the said wod assigned to hym and of bestes of athir partie escape in to ye partie assigned to other then the same bestes to be turnyd out with out inparkyn or other grevance had by the (*fo.* 109*d*) said parties. And also be cause of divers evydence shewyd to the said arbitrators touchyng the said award and mareage of the said Robert be the wyche the said arbitrators fyndes in laghe and right that the said prior and hys successors has better tytle and right to ye same warde then ye said John Boswell has, the said arbitrators awardes and demes that the said John Bosewell shall paye to ye said prior or his successors for the same warde and mariage and for takyng of tymber of the said prior in ye said wod 10 marcs at ye feste of Sent Martyne next comyyng. And also the said prior shall grauntt to the said John the said warde and mariegie of ye bodie of the said Robert at this tyme be hys seall be wrytyng endented wher off that one partie remanyng anents the said prior shall be sealled under the seale of armes of ye said John sawyng alway to the said prior and his successors the warde and kepyng of all the londes and tenements the whichver holden of the said prior be knyght service. And also savyng to the same prior and his successors theire right wen such warde a nother tyme happes to falle. And also that all suttes betwyx the said parties dependyng to be nonusued or dyscontynewed byfore the fest of Pasce nexte comyng. And th^t all clames of rents and londes beyng in debate or other variances had betwyx ye (*fo.* 110) said parties to be endid by the said arbitrators betwix this and Cristenmesse next sueyng. Into witnes of wiche thynges wele and truly to be holden and performed to this writyng endented as well we the said arbitrators have sette our sealls as the parties before said enterchaungeable have sette thar sealles the yere daie and place before sayd.

(173)   Grant[1] by Alexander Drax, son and heir of Robert Drax, to Thomas Wortley, son and heir of Nicholas Wortley, esquire, John Woderove, Henry Sothill, Thomas Everyngam, Nicholas Mounteney, Robert Barneby, esquires, Sir William de Barneby, vicar of a mediety of the church of Darfeld, and John Lake,[2] their heirs and assigns, of his manor of Wodehalle with all the appurtenances except the advowson of a mediety of a church of Darfeld. He has also granted to the same parties all other his lands, tenements, rents and services with all the appurtenances, which he has in the vills of Wodehall, Darffeld, Wombwell, Worsburgth and Ardyslay, together with the reversion of his manor of Collone, with their appurtenances, and of all other his lands and tenements in Crome, Wodehall and Darffeld, which Katherine

---

[1] " Drax lande " written in the margin.

[2] Apparently the name of one feoffee is omitted here, as in reciting their Christian names in the deed subsequently—which happens several times— an additional John is introduced.

Drax, late wife of the said Robert Drax, father (*fo.*110*d*) of the grant-
or, holds for term of her life, and which after her death revert
to him; to remain to the grantees, their heirs and assigns for ever,
to hold from the chief lords of that fee by the services due and
accustomed; under this condition, that they (the grantees) fulfil
his last will as more fully shown in certain indentures between
them made, and pay him or his heirs yearly 100 marks if demanded;
power of re-entry if such rent be in arrear.   Witnesses, John Wombwell, William Flemmyng, Thomas (*fo.* 111) Boseville, esquires,
William Wodehall, Thomas Flecher, and many others.   Dated at
Wodehall, 26 September, 1469, 9 Edw. IV.

(174, in English)   This indenture of covenant made betwene Elys
Byrtton Esquier and Thomas Oxspryng on ye one partie and Alexander
Drax on ye other partie Witnessith yt were Richard prior of the
monasterie of Sent Mare Magdalene of Monkbretton hath to hym
and his successors for ever certeyn londs and tenements in Darfeld
and Wombewelle of the same Alexander and his hers for ever by
certeyn service and rent of 6*s*. 2*d*.   And also the rent of a brode
arowe yerely goyng out of ye same yt is to wit 5*s*. 2*d*. yereof goyng out
of ij closis callid Brome lond in Wombewell, and 12*d*. of rent yerely
goyng out of certeyn londs in Darffeld called manger land.   And
also a brode arowe yerely goyng out of a close in Wombwell
callid Rawe Roid otherwise callid Rauff Roid, the same Alexander
by thes presentts will and grauntith for hym and his heirs yt the
same Alexander or his feoffes in ye same, if any, bee afore ye
fest of Cristenmes next comyng shall make or cause to be maid
unto ye same Elis and Thomas and ther heirs and assignes for ever
a sufficient sure and lawfull graunt in law of ye same (*fo.* 111*d*)[1]
service and rent as ye lernyd Councell of ye same Elis and Thomas
shall advice by fyne recover or otherwise at costs of ye same Elis
and Thomas.   And on this same Alexander by thes presents grantith
and agreith to make or cause to be maid unto ye same Elis and
Thomas and ther heirs for ever a sure and lawful estate in and of
iiij acres of lond and half an acre with the appurtenances in Wombwell aforsaid wiche lye severally in a feld yt callid ys on bromefeld on
ye west syde of ye Millnecarhawe in xviij selyons wereof xv lie to
gether in ye said overbromfeld, betwene ye londe of ye same prior
on every syde and iij selions residue lie in ye said feld betwene ye
lond of ye said prior on every side.   And moreover ye same Alexander grauntith y^t within xl days after ye seide graunt and suertie
so maide in and of the premisses y^t ye same Alexander and John
son and heire apparent of ye same Alexander by ther dede suffycient
in lawe shall relese al ther right and title in ye same service rent
and londs as thai have in ye same to the same Elis and Thomas
and thar heirs for ever with a warante.   In Witnes were of the
parties affore said hereunto severally have sette thar seills yeryn the
xviij day of August the xxij yere of the reigne of Kyng Edward
the iiij (1482).

---

[1] This page is headed " Wombwell."

E

(*Fo.* 112) (175) Fine at Westminster, the morrow of the Purification of the blessed Mary, in the first year of Richard the Third from the conquest (1484) in the presence of Thomas Bryan, Richard Neell, John Catesby and Humphrey Starky, justices of the King, between Thomas Matheley esquire and Thomas Lister, querents, and Alexander Drax esquire and Margaret his wife and John Drax his son and heir apparent, deforciants, respecting four and a half acres of land and 6*s.* 2*d.* rents, and also a rent of one arrow with the appurtenances in Darffeld and Wombwell. The said Alexander and Margaret and John recognise the right of the said Thomas Lyster to the tenements and rents as those which the querents have by the gift of the said Alexander and Margaret and John. And they remit and quitclaim from themselves and the heirs of Margaret to the aforesaid Thomas and Thomas and the heirs of Thomas Lyster for ever. And the aforesaid Alexander and Margaret and John concede for themselves and the heirs of Margaret by this warranty to the aforesaid Thomas and the heirs of Thomas Lister aforesaid the tenements and rents for ever. And for this recognition the said Thomas and Thomas give to the aforesaid Alexander and Margaret and John 20 marks of silver.

(*Fo.* 112*d*)[1] (176) Grant[2] by Robert son of Peter de Bosevile to the prior and convent of Monkbretton that they may make a fulling mill on the water of Derne, and construct, make, and attach a dam for the same mill on his soil (*solum*) in Erdislay, without hindrance by him or his heirs. Witnesses, Sir William Scot, knt., Hugh de Totehill, Robert de Stanton, and others. At Le Newhale, Friday after the feast of St. Wilfrid, Archbishop, 14 Edw. III (1340).

(*Fo.* 113) (177) A similar grant by Thomas son of John de Dodeworth to the prior and convent of Monkbretton, of liberty to make a fulling mill on the Derne, and a dam on his soil which is called Slogrode in the territory of Erdisley. Witnesses, as in the preceding deed with the addition of William de Notton and Adam de Birtwait. At Monkbretton, the feast of the Invention of Holy Cross, 1042.[3]

(178) Whereas[4] there has been dispute between the prior of Bretton on the one part and John Boswell of Ardyslay on (*fo.* 113*d*) the other respecting the lordship of the wastes and the woods growing thereon, which dispute, by the mediation of friends, John Gairgrawe and John Frankysse chosen on the part of the prior, and Avere Maston[5] and John Milner on the part of John Boswell, has been settled thus:—the said arbitrators have ordained that the prior and his successors, and John and his heirs henceforth shall have and hold all the waste within the lordship (*dominium*) of

---

[1] The heading " Erdisley " is resumed.

[2] In the margin is written " Attachiament' molendini fullonici."

[3] *Sic,* doubtless a mistake for 1342.

[4] Written in the margin—" de vastis & boscis."

[5] *Sic,* probably meant for Avery Manston.

Erdisley as undivided, as joint tenants and in common: but so that the Prior and his successors may not take or make any pits[1] for profit in the same, in the said wastes without the consent of John and his heirs, nor similarly John or his heirs or assigns without the consent of the prior and convent or their successors. Provided always that the said prior, Thomas, and his successors and John Boswell and his heirs may have and enjoy all the wood growing in and upon the said waste called Erdislaywode in common according to (*fo.* 114) the quantity of their acres within the vill of Erdislay, namely, taking thence yearly for every six acres of their land in Erdislay in the hands of either of them one waggon-load of wood.

(179) Grant[2] by Roger son of Thomas de la Wodehalle to Robert Parre of Erdislay of half a bovate of land with the appurtenances, in the vill of Erdislay, whereof a messuage with croft lies between the messuage of John del Hagh on the west and the messuage of William Smith on the east, and an acre of land lies on Borythrodeheved, and half an acre on Le Northrodes, and a rood on Northclyff, and half an acre lies on Olde Erdislay, and half an acre on Krinesklclyff, and a rood and a half on Ankkewellheved, and a rood of meadow lies on Le Eyngplas, and a rood of meadow lies on the west side of the moor, and a rood of meadow lies in Le Wetemore abutting on Thormlayeyng, and a selion of land lies on Hundurglay[3] (*fo.* 114*d*) and .....[4] of Hundinglay,[5] and a rood of land lies on the road of Hundinglay, and one butt lies on Hundinglay abutting on the moor. To hold and to have to the said Robert Perre, his heirs or assigns, from the grantor and his heirs, freely, quietly, etc., with all liberties, commons and easements to the said half bovate belonging within the bounds of Erdislay and without: rendering to the grantor and his heirs 2*s.* yearly for all services and demands. Witnesses, Peter de Boseville, Robert of the same, Rayner de Bosco, and others.

(180) Grant by Agnes, late wife of John Daude, daughter and heir of John Henryson of Erdislay, in her widowhood, to Richard Henryson, chaplain, and (*fo.* 115) William Haleday, of a messuage built, and all lands, meadows, pastures and woods, with all their appurtenances in Erdisley, which came to her by hereditary right after the death of her father. To have and to hold to the grantees, their heirs and assigns, from the chief lords of that fee, by the services thence due and accustomed, freely, quietly, etc. Witnesses, William Dodworth, William White, Robert Godfrey, John Wodhal, William Gudehale, and others. Dated at Erdisley, 5 August, 1404.

---

[1] *Puteos,* perhaps coal pit.

[2] "Daude land," written in the margin.

[3] See note 5.

[4] An erasure here, making a blank of about ¾ inch in the MS.

[5] The name is probably meant for Hundinglay in each case, but the writing of the first word is as above.

(181) Release and quitclaim by William Haliday of Pontfrect, formerly dwelling in Barnisley, to Richard (*fo.* 115*d*) Heyron of Barnisley, chaplain, his heirs and assigns, of all right and claim of and in all those lands, tenements, meadows, pastures and woods, in Erdisley, which, together with the same Richard, he formerly had by the grant and feoffment of Agnes Daude, daughter and heir of John Henrison of Erdisley, with the appurtenances. Witnesses, John Frankys junior, Edmund Normanvile, William Withe, and others. Dated at Erdisley, 19 January, 1416, 4 Hen. V.

(182) Grant by Richard Hayron, chaplain, to William de Haryngton, knt., William Hepworth, Richard Kydall, chaplains, and Richard de Popelay, esquire, of all the lands and tenements, meadows, woods and pastures, with their appurtenances, in Erdisley, which he, together with William Halyday, lately had by the grant and feoffment of Agnes Daude, daughter and heir of John Henryson, of Erdysley. To have and to hold to the grantees, their heirs and assigns, from the chief lords of that fee, by the services thence due and accustomed, for ever. Warranty. Witnesses, Thomas de Wombwell, James Cresaker, John Nevyll, Richard Oxspryng, and others. Dated at Erdyslay, 10 May, 1417.

(*Fo.* 116*d*) (183) Indenture witnessing that William Haryngton, knt., William Hepworth, Richard Kydall, and Richard Popley, have demised at ferm to Agnes late wife of John Daude of Erdisley, all those lands and tenements, meadows, woods and pastures, with the appurtenances, in Erdisley, which they (the grantors) have by the grant of Richard Hayron, chaplain. To have and to hold to Agnes from the day when these presents were made to the end of the term of eighty years next following, rendering thence yearly to the grantors, their heirs and assigns, 3s. 6d. for all services. If Agnes should die within the said term, all the said properties, with the appurtenances, to remain wholly to the prior and convent of Monkbretton and their successors, to have and to hold (*fo.* 117) from the present grantors and their heirs for the remainder of the term, rendering yearly to the grantors, their heirs and assigns, 10s. for all service. Seals of the parties to the two parts of this indenture.[1]

(184) Power of attorney by Richard Hayron, chaplain, to Adam Bate of Normanton and Robert Marshall, clerk, to deliver seisin of all those lands and tenements, meadows, woods and pastures, with the appurtenances, in Erdisley, which he sometime had together with William Haliday, by the grant and feoffment of Agnes, late wife of John Daud of Erdisley, to William de Haryngton, knt., William Hepworth, chaplain, (*fo.* 117*d*) Richard Kydall, chaplain, and Richard Poplay, or their attorney. Seal. Dated 10 May, 1417.

(185) Power of attorney by William Haryngton, knt., William Hepworth and Richard Kydal, chaplains, to Richard Popley, to

---

[1] The words " hiis testibus " are then written, but no names are given. The date is also omitted.

fo. 116 d.

fo. 161 d.

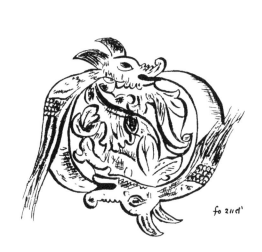

fo. 211 d.

fo. 246

H
O
SPECIMENS OF INITIAL LETTERS.
U
H

[p. 68]

receive seisin from Richard Hayron, chaplain, of all lands, tenements, etc., with the appurtenances, in Erdyslay, which, together with the said Richard Poplay, they have by the grant of the said Richard Hayron. Seals. Date as in preceding instrument.

(*Fo.* 118) (186) Power of attorney by William Haryngton, knt., to Richard Poplay to receive seisin from Richard Heyron, chaplain, of all the lands, etc., which, together with William Hepworth, Richard Kydall, and the said Richard Popley, he has in Erdyslay, and all those lands, etc., to be demised at ferm, by indenture thereon made. Seal. Dated 11 May, 1417.

(187) To all, etc., Richard Popley, greeting. Whereas the prior and convent of Monkbretton by writing indentate lately had and held to themselves and their successors for the term of eighty years by the (*fo.* 118*d*) grant and demise of me and William Haryngton, knt., William Hepworth and Richard Kydall, now deceased, all those lands, tenements, meadows, woods and pastures, with the appurtenances, in Erdislay, which I, together with the aforesaid parties, sometime had by the grant of Richard Heyron, chaplain, and which were formerly Agnes Daud's, daughter and heir of John Heryson: Know that I, the said Richard Poplay, have released and for myself and my heirs for ever quitclaimed to Richard[1] now prior of Monkbretton aforesaid, and the convent thereof and their successors, all right and claim in the said lands, etc., with the appurtenances, and in every parcel of the same. Dated 5 May, 1442.

(*Fo.* 119) (188) Grant[2] by Thomas Wode, son and heir of John Wode, late of Wath, to Thomas Oxspryng and Robert Wodhall, of half an acre of land with the appurtenances in the territory of Erdysley as it lies there in a place called Le Hakkings, between the land of the prior of Monkbretton on either side, one head abutting on Le Longflat, lately John Boswell's, on the north, and the other upon the side of Le Nodcaracre to the south. And he (the grantor) has further granted to the grantees all and singular his lands, tenements and meadows, with the appurtenances, in Hardesley aforesaid, in a close there of the said prior, called Thomasroyde, namely, two parts of the meadow lying and being in the said close. To have and to hold to the grantees and their heirs and assigns for ever, from the chief lords of that fee, by the services due and accustomed. (*fo.* 119*d*) Warranty. Appointment of Robert Rokley and John Hopkynson as attorneys to deliver seisin. Dated 2 October, 23 Hen. VII (1507).

(189) Release and quitclaim by Thomas Wode, son and heir of John Wod, late of Wath, (*fo.*120) to Thomas Oxspryng and Robert Wodehall, their heirs and assigns, of all right and claim in the properties named in the preceding deed. Dated 4 October, 23 Hen. VII (1507).

---

[1] Richard de Ledes.
[2] " Thomas Royde " written in the margin.

(*Fo.* 120*d*) (190)   Grant by Thomas Oxspryng and Robert Wod-hall to the prior and convent of Monkbretton of the properties named in the preceding two deeds, which they (the grantors) lately had by the grant of Thomas Wod, son and heir of John Wode, late of Wath.   To have and to hold to the grantees and their successors for ever, from the chief lords of that fee, by the services thence due and accustomed.   Appointment of Richard Best (*fo.* 121) and John Silverwod as attorneys to deliver seisin.   Dated 20 October, 23 Hen. VII (1507).

(*Fo.* 121*d*)   *Derfeld.*[1]

(191)   Grant by Sir Thomas de Horbiry to God and the blessed Mary Magdalene of Bretton, and the monks there, of Richard de Darfeld, son of Mauger, and all his issue and chattels, and all the land with the buildings and appurtenances which he (Richard) held from the grantor in the vill of Derfeld, namely, fourteen and a half acres of arable land and three roods of meadow, as they lie in strips (*per partes*) in the fields of Derfeld.   Moreover he (Thomas) has granted to the monks all the land which Hugh Roset formerly held from him in the vill of Darfeld, namely, two messuages (*fo.* 122) and seven acres of land and the meadow which belongs to the said land, with all the appurtenances and all right in the said land and the said Richard, his issue and chattels.   To hold and to have freely, etc., in as pure and perpetual alms as any alms may be granted.   Seal.   Witnesses, Sir (*Dom*) Thomas Fitz William, John de Boswell, Rayner de Wambwelle, Jordan de Insula, Roger de Berh, William de Wentworth, and others.[2]

(Monkbretton Chart, Lansdowne MS. 405, fo. 39)

(192)   Demise by Robert Mauger of Darfeld to Elizabeth daughter of the late Peter del Grene of (*fo.* 122*d*) Staynburgh and Agnes her daughter for life, of all that messuage with the croft, as it lies in the vill of Darfeld between the messuage of Roger Warde on the south side and the messuage which the same Roger holds at term from Agnes Coke on the north side.   He has also granted to the same Elizabeth and Agnes for term of their lives three roods of land lying together in the field of Darfeld in a place called Lang-elothell, between the land of Henry Hauard on the east side and the land of Edward de Bosevill on the west side, abutting at one head on the land of Richard Walentyn, and at the other on the King's highway.   To hold and to have with all commodities and easements belonging to Elizabeth and Agnes for life and the life of the survivor, freely, quietly, etc., rendering thence to the grantor, during his life, 5s. yearly; and after his death, if Elizabeth and Agnes shall survive him, to his heirs or assigns 6d. yearly.   Warranty to Elizabeth and Agnes for their lives or the life of the survivor of them.   Witnesses, (*fo.* 123) John de Wodhall, Richard Walentyn, chaplain,

---

[1] Darfield.   The heading continues as Darffeld or Derffelde to *fo.* 132*d*.

[2] Opposite the end of the charter is a side note in a later hand—" Sir Thomas Fitzwilliams lived in the reign of Henry the 3ᵈ [*sic*], in the beginning of his reign."

Roger Ward, Hugh le tayllour, and others. Dated at Derffeld, Thursday after the feast of the Nativity of St. John the Baptist, 1349, 23 Edw. III.

(193) Grant by Robert Mauger of Darfeld to Sir Robert de Hendeley, chaplain, his heirs and assigns, of all tenements, lands, meadows, pastures, rents and services, which he (the grantor) had by hereditary right after the death of Robert Mauger his father and after the death of Agnes his mother, as they lie separately in the vill and fields of Darfeld. To hold and to have, with all the appurtenances, to the grantee, his heirs and assigns, freely, quietly, etc., from the chief lords of that fee, by the services due and accustomed, for ever. (*fo.* 123*d*) Witnesses, Henry Lauvel of Wombwell, Hugh Mody of Darfeld, Adam de Overwodhall, William de Flecher senior, John son of Edward, and others. Dated at Darfeld, Friday before the feast of the Nativity of B.V.M., 1355, 29 Edw. III.

(194) Grant by Robert de Hyndelay, chaplain, to Robert Mauger of Derfeld and Elizabeth his wife, and the lawful heirs of their bodies, of all lands and tenements, rents and services, with all (*fo.* 124) the appurtenances, which he (the grantor) has by the gift and feoffment of the said Robert Mauger in Derfeld. To have and to hold to the grantees and their heirs, as before, freely, quietly, etc., from the chief lords of that fee, by the services thence due and accustomed. And if it happen that the said grantees die without such heir, remainder to Hugh Lauvel of Wombwell, his heirs and assigns, for ever, to hold from the chief lords as before. (*fo.* 124*d*) Witnesses, John de Wodehalle, Henry Lauvell, William de Haltgton, Adam de Wodehalle, and others. Dated at Darfeld, Thursday after the feast of St. Michael Archangel, 1055[1] (*Anno Dni. Millo quinquagesimo vto*).

(195) Grant by John Toppyng of Byllynglay to Robert Mauger of Darfeld and Elizabeth his wife, and the heirs and assigns of Robert, of all that half acre of land lying in one plot on the south side of the dumy[2] called Adam thorn in the field of Milnehouses, abutting at the west head on Le Syk,[3] and at the east head on Le Holgate leading from Milnehouses to Doncaster, namely, that half acre of land which he (John) had from Thomas de Bosvell of Midilwod as in exchange for half an acre of land lying in the fields of Darfeld separately in a place called Betwenyegates, between (*fo.* 125) Darfeld and Ouwerwodhall. To have and to hold to the grantees and the heirs and assigns of Robert, freely, quietly, etc., from the chief lords of that fee, by the services due and accustomed. Witnesses, Hugh Mody, John son of Edward, John Hanard, William le Fiechar, and others. Dated at Darffeld, Sunday in the feast of St. Luke Evangelist, 1355, 29 Edw. III.

---

[1] A mistake for 1355.

[2] I am unable to identify this word: the name " Adam thorn " suggests that it may have some connection with *dumentum*.

[3] *Sic*—Le Dyke in the next deed but one.

(196) Grant by Thomas Bosvell of Middelwod to Robert
Mauger of Darfeld, his heirs and assigns, of half an acre of land, as
it lies in length (*fo.* 125*d*) and in width on the south side of the vill
of Derffeld between the messuage and croft of William le flecher
and Margaret his wife on the north, and the land of the aforesaid
Robert on the south, abutting at the east head on the common
pasture of Derfeld called Le Lane, and at the west head on land of
Adam son of William de Ouerwodhall.   To hold and to have, with
all the appurtenances, to Robert, his heirs and assigns, freely,
quietly, etc., from the chief lord of that fee by the services due and
accustomed.   Witnesses, Sir (*domino*) William de Quenton, rector
of a mediety of the church of Darfeld, John de Wodhall, William de
[*sic*] flecher, Hugh le Thailler, and others.   Dated at Darfeld, Sunday
after the feast of the Invention of Holy Cross, 1351, 25 Edw. III.

(*Fo.* 126)   (197)   Grant by Robert Mauger of Darfeld to Hugh de
Wombwell, his heirs and assigns, of an acre and a half a rood of
land, with the appurtenances, in Darfeld, whereof half an acre,
with the appurtenances, purchased from Thomas Bosvell of Midel-
wod, lies on the south side of the vill of Darfeld between the croft
of William le Flecher and Margaret his wife on the north and his
(Robert's) land on the south, and the other half acre purchased
(*cu*)[1] from John Toppyng, and it lies in Millnehous feld on the south
[of] Adam thorn, and the east head abuts on Le Hollegate leading
from Millnehous towards Doncaster, and the west head abuts on
Le Dyke; and half a rood of land purchased from Roger Warde,
and it lies beside the said half acre of land bought from Thomas
Bosvell on the south side.   To have and to hold to Hugh, his heirs
and assigns, freely, quietly, etc., from the chief lords of that fee, by
the services due and accustomed.   Witnesses, (*fo.* 126*d*) Adam
de Ou'wodehall, Robert de Hindelay, chaplain, Richard Shepeshank,
and others.   Dated at Darfeld, Wednesday after the feast of the
Conception B.M., 1365 (39 Edw. III).[2]

(198)   Release and quitclaim by Hugh son of Henry Lannell of
Wombewell to John de Birthwat, prior of Bretton, and the monks
and convent thereof and their successors, of all right and claim in
two messuages, twenty-one and a half acres of land, and three roods
of meadow, in the vill of Darfeld, in which tenements the said prior
entered as in right of his church of St. Magdelen of Monk Bretton,
in the possession of Robert Mauger, son of Robert Mauger of Darfeld,
a villein (*nativi*) of the same prior and convent, who held them from the
prior and convent in villenage, and in that meadow which Hugh
Roset sometime held in Darfeld and was in possession (*fo.* 127) of
the said Robert son of Robert at the time of entry of the said prior.
Seal.   Witnesses, Sir (*domino*) William de Notton, Sir (*domino*)
Richard, parson of a mediety of the church of Derfeld, John de
Stanton, John de Barnburgh, Thomas Welle, and many others.
Dated at Darfeld, 3 April, 33 Edw. III (1359).

---

[1] Possibly " cu " is a mistake for " emi," or perhaps " pertinenciis " is
omitted here and below.

[2] In a later hand.

(199)   Grant by Roger son of Hugh Schepschank of Lambewell to Agnes, late the wife of Robert Mauger of Darfeld, clerk, her heirs and assigns, of a plot of arable land, and two acres and a rood of arable land lying in the fields of Derfeld; whereof the plot lies beside the common pasture of Derfeld, which is called Midelwodstrogs, between the land of Robert the clerk, son of Robert the clerk of Derfeld on one side, and Midilwodstrogs on the other, and abuts at one head upon le Clyntr'grene, and at the other head upon (*fo.* 127*d*) the land of the said Robert, and two acres lie at the head of the said plot, between the land of the said Robert the clerk on either side, one head abutting on the road leading from Derfeld to little Halghton and at the other head upon the road leading from Derfeld to Éderthorp and upon the land of the said Robert; the rood lies in a certain place called Longrodes between the land of the said Robert on one side and the land of the rector of the church of Derfeld on the other, and abuts at one head on Lathesgate and at the other on the croft of the said rector, beside the croft of Richard son of Valentine.   To have and to hold to Agnes, her heirs and assigns, with all commodities and easements, freely, quietly, etc., from the chief lord of that fee, by the services due and accustomed.   Witnesses, William Crok of Okythorp, Roger de Ederthorp, Thomas de Bosevill, and others.

(200)   Indenture between (*fo.* 128) Thomas de Scheffeld of Braythewell of the one part and Hugh de Wombewell of the other, witnessing that Thomas has granted to Hugh, his heirs and assigns, a certain yearly rent of 8*s.*, with the services appertaining to the same rent, issuing from a toft and a bovate of land in Derfeld, in exchange for a messuage and eighteen acres of land, with the appurtenances, in Mikkilbryng in Breithwell, which toft and bovate of land Elizabeth, who was the wife of Robert Mauger, now holds for term of her life.   To have and to hold the said rent and services, with the appurtenances, to Hugh, his heirs and assigns, from the chief lords of the fees, by the services due and accustomed, in exchange for the messuage of land aforesaid in Mikkilbryng.   Warranty by Thomas.   And the said Hugh has given and granted to Thomas, his heirs and assigns, from the chief lords of the fee, by the services due and accustomed in (*fo.* 128*d*) exchange for the said rent with the appurtenances, and Hugh and his heirs will warrant.   Seals of the parties in witness.   Dated 4 January, 1394.

(201)   Release and quitclaim by Thomas de Wombewell, son and heir of Hugh Wombwell, to the prior and convent of the monastery of the blessed Mary Magdalene of Monkbretton and their successors, of all right and claim in all those lands and tenements, with the appurtenances, in Derfeld on Dyrn', which Elizabeth, who was the wife of Robert Mauger of Derfeld, lately held for term of her life by grant of the late prior and (*fo.* 129) convent of Monkbretton.   He has also released to the present prior and convent and their successors all right and claim in the dam of the mill of Milnehous in Derfeld and in the attachment of the same, which attachment he lately had and claimed

by the grant of John son of Adam de Wodehall.   Witnesses, Richard
Normavile, John Frankysch, John Autye.   Dated in the feast of
the Purification B.M., 1407.

(202)   Release and quitclaim by Roger Wombwell, esquire to
Thomas prior of the monastery of the blessed Mary Magdalene (*fo.*129*d*)
of Monkbretton and the convent thereot and their successors for ever,
of all his right and claim, etc., in all those lands and tenements, meadows
and pastures, with the appurtenances, in Derfeld on Dern', which
Elizabeth, late wife of Robert Mauger, late of Derfeld, formerly
had and held for term of life by the grant of the late prior and convent of that monastery, predecessor of the present prior.   He
(Roger) has likewise released to the prior and convent and their
successors for ever all right and claim, etc., of and in the dam of
their mill of Milnhows by Derfeld and in the attachment thereof
and in all things appertaining.   Dated 24 November, 1514,
6 Hen. VIII.

(*Fo.* 130)   (203)   Assize at York before Ralph[1] Pole and Richard
Knygth to the same Ralph and John Nedeham, justices to take
assizes in the County of York, associated for this turn, the presence
of the said John not being expected, Monday in the third week of
Lent,[2] 36 Hen. VI (1458).
    The assize comes to recognise if John Wombwell, esquire and
William Pye, chaplain, unjustly, etc., disseised Richard prior of
Monkbretton, of his free tenement in Derfeld, after, etc.   The
prior, in his own person, complains that they disseised him of two
messuages, twenty-one and a half acres of land, and three acres of
meadow, with the appurtenances, etc.   The said John and William
come not, but a certain Henry Wheteley answers for them as bailiff,
and says nothing why the assize ought to stand over; therefore
let it be taken.
(*Fo.* 130*d*)   The jury, to wit, Elias Birton, William Cudworthe,
John Jenkinson, Richard Turton, John Nettylton, John Wright of
Fisshlake, Richard Rokis, John Cusworth of Roston, John
Burgeis of Bentley, William Hill of Worsburgh, Thomas Calthorn,[3]
and John Claiton, say upon oath that a certain John Birthwayt,
late prior, was seised of the tenement placed in view, in his demesne
as of fee, and in right of his said monastery, and the present prior,
being so seised, a certain Hugh Wombwell by the name of Hugh
son of Henry Lannell of Wombwell, grandfather of the said John
Wombwell, whose heir he is, to wit, son of Thomas son of the said
Hugh, by a certain writing of release, which the said present prior
produced here in Court the tenor of which writing is as follows:—
Noverint universi per presentes me Hugonem filium Henrici Lannell
de Wombwell remisisse, relaxasse, et omnino de [*me*] *et heredibus*

---

[1] Written here " Ried," but in the following line " Rad."   The name
was Ralph.
    [2] *Quagragessıme.*
    [3] Or Calthorp, there has been an alteration in the last letter.

meis imperpetuum quietum clamasse Johanni Birthwait priori de Bretton Monachorum, etc., sicut superius in quinto folio plenius apparet, released and quitclaimed to the said late prior, by the name of John Birthwait (*fo.* 131) prior of Bretton Monachorum and the convent thereof and their successors, all right and claim which he (Hugh) had in the tenements placed in view, by the name of two messuages, twenty-one and a half acres of land and three roods of meadow; and that Hugh afterwards died, and after his death a certain Thomas Wombwell, father of the said John Wombwell, whose heir he is, by the name of Thomas de Wombwell, son and heir of Hugh de Wombwell, by a certain writing which the prior similarly produced here in Court, the tenor of which follows in these words:—*Noverint universi per presentes me Thomam de Wombwell, filium et heredem Hugonis de Wombwell remisisse, relaxasse et omnino de me et heredibus meis imperpetuum quietum clamasse priori monasterii Beate Marie Magdelene de Monkbretton, etc., sicut supra in tercio folio perfeccius intitulat,* released and quitclaimed to the said John Birthwait, then prior, (*fo.* 131*d*) and the convent and their successors then seised all right and claim in the said tenements, by the name of all those lands and tenements, with the appurtenances, in Derfeld on Dyrn', which Elizabeth, who was wife of Robert Mauger of Derfeld, lately held for term of her life by grant of the late prior and convent of Monkbretton. And the jury further say on their oath that the present prior was seised of the said tenements, with the appurtenances, in demesne as of the fee and right of his monastery, until the aforesaid John Wombwell and William Pye disseised him unjustly and without judgment, not by force and arms. And they assess (*fo.* 132) the damages of the prior by reason of the disseisin beyond his expenses and costs touching the suit at 7 marks, and for the expenses and costs at 4 marks.

The jury asked what right the present prior has in the said tenements and which of his predecessors was seised and in the time of which King, and whether there be any fraud or collusion between the parties, concerning the recovery of the property, against the statute of mortmain, say on their oath that the present prior and all his predecessors, priors of the said monastery, were successively from time beyond memory, until the said John and William disseised the present prior in form aforesaid. And that a certain Roger, formerly prior, predecessor of the present prior, was seised in demesne as of the fee and right of his monastery in the time of the Lord H., formerly King of England, son of King John, and before the said statute; and that there is no fraud or collusion between (*fo.* 132*d*) the said parties respecting the recovery of the property, against the said statute. Therefore it is adjudged that the prior recover seisin and his damages, assessed by the jury at £7 6s. 8d. in form aforesaid. And John and William in mercy, etc.

(204) Precept by the King [Henry VI] to the Sheriff of York to cause the tenement in dispute between Richard, prior of Monkbretton and John Wombwell, esquire and William Pye, chaplain,

to be reseised of the chattels taken therein, and the tenement and chattels to be in the peace until a certain day which Ralph Pole and John Nedeham shall signify to him, and in the meantime to provide a jury of the neighbourhood (*fo.* 133) to view the property and to summon them to be before the said Ralph and John and their fellows at a certain place to be appointed, to make recognition thereof; and to put the said John Wombwell and William Pye, in pledge to attend. Witness myself at Westminster, 31 July, in the 33rd year (1455).

(*Fo.* 133*d*)   *Mylnhous.*[1]

(205)   Grant by John son of Richard de Bateley to God and the church of St. Mary Magdalene of Brettona and the monks there serving God, in pure and perpetual alms, of all his part of the mill of Milne-house, with the appurtenances, which he had by the gift of Ingram son of Adam de Kirkby, namely, the eighth part of all the said mill, with all the suit of his men, and with the work of five men yearly for one day; on the day when they work there they shall have from the said monks an allowance (*coredium*) at noon only. More-over he has quitclaimed to the monks all the liberty which he had in the said mill in the name of multure, so that if it happen there-after that he or his heirs grind their corn at the said (*fo.* 134) mill, they will give multure, as others do. All the above the monks shall possess freely, quietly, etc., without damage or hindrance by him or his heirs, in pure and perpetual alms. Witnesses, Sir (*domino*) Thomas Fitz-William, Roger his brother, John de Hoderode, John de Bosevil, Raner de Wombwell, and others.

(Monkbretton Chart., Lansdowne MS 405, fo. 38*d.*)

(206)   Grant by William Fitz-William to the monks of Bretton of a moiety of the mill of Millnehoses, namely, his share with all the suit belonging to the same mill, without the work of his men, in exchange for the mill of Wodehalle which[2] his grandfather gave them in pure and perpetual alms, and which they have quitclaimed to the grantor for the moiety of the said mill of Millehuses. The monks shall grind without multure all the corn (*fo.* 134*d*) of his demesne which grows in the field of Derfeld. This agreement he grants to the monks for the health of his soul and the souls of his ancestors, in pure and perpetual alms. Witnesses, William de Novomarcato, Thomas de Oregrane, then bailiff of the Earl John, Adam de Adlwych, William de Insula, Robert de Benerans, and many others.   (Monkbretton Chart., Lansdowne MS. 405, fo. 38*d.*)

(207)   Grant by Thomas son of Isabel to God and the blessed Mary of Bretton and the monks there, of all his share of the mill of Milnehouse, with all the appurtenances, without retention, namely, the fourth part of three parts of the moiety of the said mill. To hold and to have freely, quietly, in pure and perpetual alms. Witnesses, Roger de Monte Begon, William son of Adam, Gilbert de Notton, William, Matthew his son, and others.

(Monkbretton Chart., Lansdowne MS. 405, fo. 38*d.*)

[1] This heading, with slight variations of spelling, continues to *fo.* 142*d*, with the exception of *fo.* 140*d*, which is headed " Hyll."
[2] *Quem.*

(*Fo.* 135) (208) Confirmation by Robert son of Thomas son of Isabel de Horbiri to God and St. Mary Magdalene of Bretton and the monks there, in pure and perpetual alms, of the fourth part of three parts of a moiety of the mill of Milnehouse, with all the appurtenances, without retention, which his father formerly gave them. To hold and to have freely, quietly, etc. Warranty of this confirmation. Witnesses, Roger de Montebegon, John de Birikin, William de Stapilton, Gilbert de Notton, and others.

(Monkbretton Chart., Lansdowne MS. 405, fo. 39.)

(209) Fine[1] between the prior and convent of Bretton and Adam de Sicligtona (*fo.* 135*d*) and William de Horbere and Jordan de Sancta Maria and their heirs; that the said Jordan quitclaimed all his claim in the mill of Milnehuse, namely, the damage of his meadow, whereof he had gone to the King's Court: so that the said Jordan and his heirs shall grind without multure all their demesne corn from their house, next after that which shall be milling (*super molendinum*); and for half a mark of silver which they gave Jordan. The said mill shall remain in the same state in which it was on the day when Jordan took proceedings. Witnesses, Thomas de Ranavell, Adam de Sancta Maria, Nicholas his brother, Hugh de Novo Mercato, Robert de Rokelaie, Hugh de Bretton, and many others.

(210) Grant by Thomas son of William de Horbery to the monks of Roche (*Rupe*) of all his share in the mill of Milnehuse below Derfeld, with the dam and watercourse (*cum stagno et corsu aque*) and all his suit and every right, liberty, and easement, to him or his heirs belonging or which may belong in the said mill, without retention. To hold and to have in pure (*fo.* 136) and perpetual alms, free and quit of all secular service, exaction ·and demand. Witnesses, Sir Hugh the butler (*pincerna*), then steward of the Earl of Lincoln, Sir Hugh de Langthwait, Sir Richard de Wikyrsley, and others. (Monkbretton Chart., Lansdowne MS. 405, fo. 39.)

(211) Agreement made at Milnehuse, the eve of St. Barnabas Apostle, 1237, between the Abbot and convent of Roche (*Rupe*) of the one part and the prior and convent of Brettona of the other. The abbot and convent have granted to the prior and convent all their share in the mill of Milnehuse which they had by the gift of Thomas Horbiri with every right, liberty, and easement which belonged or might belong to them in the said mill, without retention: to hold and to have for ever, for 9*s.* to be paid to the said abbot and convent yearly, at Thirnesco. (*Fo.* 136*d*) And the prior and convent have remitted and quitclaimed to the abbot and convent the yearly rent of 3*d.* which they were accustomed to pay them. Seals of the parties to the alternate parts of this deed. The prior and convent to pay the first ferm for the said mill at Whitsuntide,

---

[1] This fine, although it begins in the usual way, " Hec est finalis concordia," etc., does not follow the customary form, and was not levied in the King's Court. There is nothing to show definitely who were plaintiffs and deforciants respectively. There is no date.

1238. Witnesses, Sir Robert de Wykersley, Sir John de Hoderode, Rainer de Wambwell, Ralph de Roche, Thomas de Eclesfeld, and many others.

(*Fo.* 137) (212) Grant by Robert Gode of Billyngley to John Dowdale, chaplain, and his heirs or assigns, of a garden called Pyke-nonyerd lying in Milnehuse within the bounds of Derffeld, namely, between the garden of John de Wodhall on the west, and the water of Derne on the east, and the garden formerly Robert Mauger's on the south, and the road leading to the mill on the north.   To have and to hold the said garden with all easements, to John, his heirs or assigns, freely, wholly, etc., from the chief lords of that fee, by the services due and accustomed; rendering thence yearly to the grantor and his heirs one grain of corn at Michaelmas, during the term of a hundred years next following, and after the completion of the said term 10*d.* yearly.   If the said rent of 10*d.* shall be in arrear for one month, power of re-entry.   (*Fo.* 137*d*)   Witnesses, Thomas Boswell of Erdisley, Roger his son, Thomas de Wodhal, Adam de Wodhall, William Frankes, Hugh Mody, Thomas Welle of Cudworthe, and others.   Dated at Derffeld, Wednesday in the feast of the Nativity B.M., 1378.

(213)   Grant by William Atkynson of Milnehouse to the prior and convent of Monkbretton, of a certain piece of land containing twelve ells in length and six ells in breadth, with the appurtenances, in Milnehouse, which piece of land is a parcel of a certain toft or croft of his, lying between the mill dam of the said prior and convent in Milnehouse on one side, and the tenement of John Byngley on the other, and the piece of land so granted by him lies between the road leading to the said mill in Milnehouse on one side, and abuts on the remainder of the said toft or croft towards the east, and it lies similarly to the dam of the said mill.   To have (*fo.* 138) and to hold to the prior and convent and their successors for ever from the chief lords of that fee, by the services due and accustomed. Witnesses, John Woddall of Darfeld, Robert Rokley of Billyngley, William Wakefeld of the same, and others.   Dated at Millnehouse, 20 June, 1423.

(214)   Grant by Richard Northcroft of Billyngley and Margaret his wife to the prior and convent of Monkbretton and their successors, of a certain piece of land with the appurtenances, in Milnehuse, which was formerly William Atkynson's, and which contains (*fo.* 138*d*) in length twelve ells and in breadth six ells, as it lies beside the dam of the mill of the said prior and convent in Millnehouse.   Moreover they (Richard and Margaret) have released and quitclaimed to the said prior and convent and their successors all right and claim in the said piece of land and appurtenances.   Witnesses, John Strafford of Derffeld, John Pye of Wombwell, John Sperk of Wadworth, Thomas Colet of Halghton, and others.   Dated 20 April, 1466.

(215) Grant by Thomas son of Adam de Horbiri, with the concurrence of his heirs to Richard (*fo.* 139) de Wodehall and his heirs, for homage and service and for 3 marks of silver and a horse which he has given Thomas in recognition, of fifteen acres of land of the demesne, with the appurtenances, in Derfeld, except his (Thomas's) mill, which he retains. Moreover he has given to Richard and his heirs all his share in Neu Enges at Middelwode, to hold from him and his heirs in fee and inheritance, freely, quietly, etc., in wood, in plain, etc., with all appurtenances, rendering thence yearly to him (Thomas) and his heirs 2s. for all service to that land belonging. Witnesses, Jordan de Sancta Maria, Hugh, parson of Derfeld, Hugh de Halgton, Hugh de Edrethorp, and Roger his son, Richard Coce, and Hugh Croc, and many others.

(216) Grant by Robert Wodhall of Derfeld to Thomas Ox-spryng senior and William (*fo.* 139*d*) Wadelouff, of an acre of meadow in Derfeld, with the appurtenances, as it lies between the meadow of Alexander Drax on either side, and abuts on the lane from Middel-wod towards the west and upon Dern' towards the east. To have and to hold to the grantees, their heirs and assigns, for ever, from the chief lords of that fee, by the services due and accustomed. Witnesses, Thomas Bosvile esquire, Alexander Drax esquire, John Hopkynson, and others. Dated at Derfeld, 3 October, 3 Hen. VII (1487).

(217) Grant by Robert Midilwode and Marjorie his wife to William Wodehall of Ouerwodehal, his heirs and assigns, of two roods of meadow lying in the meadow called Le Newyng, with the appurtenances, whereof one rood lies between the meadow of the said William on the south, and the meadow of Robert Drax on the north, and abuts at one (*fo.* 140) head upon the water of Derne on the east, and the other head abuts on the common lane (*communem lane*) of Midilwode on the west, and the other rood lies between the meadow of the said William on the south and the meadow of Robert Drax on the north, and abuts at one head on Le Oldhed on the east, and the other head abuts on the common lane of Midil-wode on the west. To have and to hold to the grantee, his heirs and assigns, freely, quietly, etc., from the chief lords of that fee, by the services due and accustomed. Witnesses, Robert Rokeley of Byllynglay, Hugh Blome of Midelwode, John Anotson of Barnysley. Dated at Midelwode in the feast of St. Martin in winter, 1439.

(218) Quitclaim[1] by Dionisia de Eyvill to God and blessed Mary Magdalene of Bretton and the prior and monks there, (*fo.* 140*d*)[2] of Alan de Le Hille called the miller, formerly her villein, with all his issue (*sequela*) for ever. Witnesses, John de Bretton, Thomas Wacelyn, Wastard, Roger de Berlyng', and others.

[1] " Hyll " written opposite, in the margin.
[2] Headed " Hyll."

(219) Grant by brother Roger, the humble minister of Bretton and the convent of the same place, to Ralph son of Richard Wace and his heirs, of all that land in Le Hill which his father sometime held from the grantors, with all the appurtenances, within the vill and without. To hold and to have to the grantee and his heirs, from the grantors, in fee and inheritance, freely, quietly, etc., with all easements, liberties and commons appertaining; rendering to the grantors yearly 2s. for all service and demand. (Fo. 141) Warranty, as far as the charter of the donor can warrant to them. Witnesses, Jordan de Insula, Hugh de Edriethorp, William Croc, Ralph de Okinthorpe, and others.

(220) Grant[1] by William de Westbretton, knt., to God and the church of St. Mary Magdalene of Bretton and the monks there, of a rent of 4s. for his anniversary yearly, to be done on the day of his death, from a certain essart called Gilberode in the territory of Holand, which essart Gilbert son of Cornelius formerly held as his free tenement from the grantor. Moreover he has given the grantees the homage and service of the same Gilbert, with reliefs and other appurtenances which can arise from a free holding. To hold and to have to the grantees in pure and perpetual (fo. 141d)[2] alms as freely, quietly and honourably as any alms may be given, whether he (the grantor) be living or dead, and when he dies they are to receive his body. Witnesses, Sir Adam de Hirefend, knt., Thomas de Kirkeston, Walter de Duesend, Robert de Barkett, and many others.

(221) Grant[3] on sale by Thomas Oxspryng to Richard Nicolls and John Hopkynson, for a certain sum of money to him in hand paid by them, of two acres of land, with the appurtenances, in the territory of Mylnehous. To have and to hold to the grantees, their heirs and assigns, for ever, from the chief lords of that fee, by the services due and accustomed. (Fo. 142) Dated 20 December, 22 Hen. VII (1506).

(222) Release and quitclaim by Thomas Oxspryng to Richard Nicolls and John Hopkynson, their heirs and assigns for ever, of all right, claim, etc., of and in two acres of land with the appurtenances, in Mylnehous. (Fo. 142d) Dated 21 December, 22 Hen. VII (1506).

(223) Demise by Richard Nicolls and John Hopkynson to Thomas Tykkell, prior of Monkbretton, of two acres of land, with the appurtenances, in the territory of Milnehous, in the County of York, which they (Richard and John) lately had by the gift and feoffment of Thomas Oxspryng, gent. To have and to hold to the said prior and his successors for ever, from the chief lords of that fee, by the services due and accustomed. Appointment of

---

[1] " Holand " written opposite, in the margin.
[2] This folio and fo. 142d are headed " Mylnehous."
[3] " Oxsprynglande " written in the margin.

William Warton and Richard Beste as attorneys to deliver seisin. (*Fo.* 143) Witnesses, Robert Wodall, Thomas Ellis, William Wormley, and others. Dated at Monkbretton, 4 November, 23 Hen. VII (1507).

Parva Halgton.[1]

(224) Grant by William son of Alice Valantyn, " arousmyt,"[2] John son of Edward Boswill, and Beatrice daughter of Richard the carter (*certer*) of Milnehouse, to William Broun and Diota his wife and their heirs and assigns, of all that messuage with the croft which they (the grantors) had by hereditary right after the death of Isabel daughter of William the smith of Great Houghton, called " *tali mali*," as it lies in length and breadth in the vill of Little Houghton on the west side of Le Peryerd. To have and to hold, with all appurtenances, to the grantees, their heirs and assigns, freely, quietly, etc., from the chief lord of that fee (*fo.* 143*d*) by the services due and accustomed. Warranty.[3] Witnesses, William de Halgton, Hugh Mody, Richard Yne, William Normanton, and many others. Dated at Parva Halgton, Thursday before the feast of Ascension, 1352.

(225) Grant by William Brone of Parva Halghton to Adam his son, of a messuage with the buildings, and all other appurtenances, as it lies in the territory of Halghton, and abuts on the King's highway and on Croswelle. To have and to hold to the grantee, his heirs and assigns, wholly, well, and in peace, from the chief lords of that fee, by the services due and accustomed. (*Fo.* 144) Witnesses, John de Dudelay, John Cowper, William Marschalle, William de Hunsyngdone, and others. Dated at Halghton, Tuesday before the feast of St. Wilfrid, Archbishop, 1385.

(226) Grant by Adam Broune son of William Broune to Robert Pache, son of Richard Horcefent of Billyngley, of a messuage, with the buildings and all other appurtenances, as it lies in the territory of Halgthon, whereof one head abuts on the King's highway and the other on Crossewell. To have and to hold to the grantee, his heirs and assigns, freely, quietly, etc., from the chief lords of that fee, by the services due and accustomed. (*Fo.* 144*d*) Witnesses, Ralph Normanvill, William Franks of Byllynley, John son of Adam de Wodehall, John Marshall of the same, John Bossevill of Midelwode, and others. Dated at Halghton, Sunday after the feast of the Apostles Philip and James, 12 Rich. II (1389).

(227) Grant by Robert Pache of Parva Halghton to Richard son of Henry Schepherd of the same and Alice, Robert's daughter, wife of the said Richard, of a messuage built up with the croft and all appurtenances, as it lies in the vill and territory of Parva Halgton, one head abutting on the King's highway and the other on Crossewell,

---

[1] Written in the margin, but the heading " Parva Haltona " continues to *fo.* 146*d*. The vill is Little Houghton in the parish of Darfield.

[2] *i.e.*, arrowsmith.

[3] In the warranty the grantee's wife's name is given as Dionysia.

F

as in certain charters thence made is more fully contained.   To
have and to hold to Richard, Alice, his wife, and the heirs of their
bodies lawfully begotten between them, to wit, after the death of
the same Robert Pache; freely, wholly, quietly, etc., from the chief
lord of that fee, by the services due and accustomed, for ever: if
Richard and Alice shall die without (*fo.* 145) such heir, and particularly without heir of the body of Alice, the property to remain to
John Woddehall of Derffelld, John Teylor of Wombewell, William
Dudley of Magna Halgthon, Adam Hyne of the same, Richard
Woddehall of Parva Halgton, William Scheperd of Hymlyngfeld,
their heirs and assigns, wardens (*custodibus*) of the services of the
Holy High Cross and St. Mary Virgin in the parish church of Darf-
feld, and so remain for ever.   Warranty.   Seals of the grantor to
the two parts of these indentures, one remaining with Richard
and Alice, the other with the remainder men.   Witnesses, John
Boswell of Ardisley, Thomas de Wombewell, esquires, Thomas del
Hyll, Thomas de Wodhall, and others.   Dated at Littell Halgthon,
Monday in the feast of St. Peter in Cathedra, 1416.

(*Fo.* 145*d*)   (228)   Grant by John Teilior of Wombewell to Richard
Heryson, son of Robert Heryson, of a messuage built upon, with
croft and all appurtenances, as it lies in the vill and territory of
Parva Halghton, whereof one head abuts on the King's highway,
and the other on Croswell: which he (John) had by the gift and
feoffment of the late Robert Pache.   To have and to hold to the
grantee and the lawful heirs of his body, freely, wholly, etc., from
the chief lords of that fee, by the services due and accustomed,
for ever.   If the grantee shall die without such heir, the said property
to remain to John Woddeall of Darffeld, William Dudley, Adam
Hine, Richard Woddhall, William Scheperd, their heirs and assigns,
wardens of the services of the Holy High Cross and St. Mary Virgin,
in the parish church of Darffeld, and so remain for ever.   (*Fo.* 146)
Witnesses, Robert Hogley, John Ellyott, Thomas Collet.   Dated
at Litylhaghton in the feast of St. Luke, 15 Edw. IV (1475).

(229)   Release and quitclaim by John Withe of Parva Halghton
to John Herison and Richard Heryson, sons of Robert Heryson,
late of Parva Halghton, of all actions real and personal, which he
has had, or could in any way have in future against them by reason
of a contract of agreement made by Robert Heryson, father of John
and Richard, respecting lands and tenements in the said Halghton,
or any matter or cause, from the beginning of the world to the day
of the making of these presents.   Dated at Darfeld in the feast of
the Nativity of the blessed Mary, 1486.

(*Fo.* 146*d*)   (230)   Grant by John Heryson and Richard Heryson
to William Wadylove and John Ellys, their heirs and assigns, of
two tofts and an acre of land, with the appurtenances, in Parva
Halghton; to have and to hold for ever, from the chief lords of
that fee, by the services due and accustomed.   Warranty.   Appointment of Robert Wodhall and Richard Elyot as attorneys to deliver

seisin.   Witnesses, Henry Brige, Robert Wodward, James Tellour, and many others.   Dated 1 January, 1 Ric. III (1484).

(*Fo.* 147)   (231)   Release and quitclaim by William Wadylove and Robert Drax, prior of Monkbretton, and the convent and their successors, of all right, title, and claim in two tofts and an acre of land, with the appurtenances, in Parva Halghton, which he (William) lately had, jointly with John Elys deceased.   Dated 6 December, 15 Hen. VII (1499).

(*Fo.* 147*d*)   *Magna Haltona.*[1]

(232)   Grant by Jordan[2] de Halton to God and St. Mary Magdalene of Bretton and the monks there for the health of his soul and the soul of Adam his brother, and his wife and ancestors and successors, of a toft in the vill of Halton, that toft, namely, which lies between the toft of Gilian, who was wife of Aissolf, and the toft of Gilian, who was wife of William son of Ralph, and a rood of land in the territory of the same vill upon Holdffeld, in pure and perpetual alms.   To hold and to have freely and quietly, in wood and plain, and with all other easements, liberties and commons of the said vill of Halton to so much land belonging.   Witnesses, William son of William, Henry le Walays, John de Rokeley, Morice de Askarne, Adam Painnell, Robert de Ekelisfeud, Roger de Edrictorp, Ralph Barbott, and many others.   (Monkbretton Chart., Lansdowne MS. 405, fo. 18.)

(233)   Grant by Hugh de Shafton, son and heir of Robert Shafton, to Anote and Alice his (Hugh's) sisters, and their heirs or assigns, of a messuage and nine acres of land in the vill and territory of Magna Haltona, which fell to him by hereditary right after the death of his father. (*Fo.* 148) To have and to hold from the lord of the fee, to the grantees, their heirs and assigns, freely, quietly, etc., with all liberties, easements, etc.; rendering thence yearly 32*d.*, saving forinsec service, and doing to the lord of the fee the service due and accustomed.   Dated at Magna Haltona, Wednesday after the feast of the Apostles Peter and Paul, 1310.   Witnesses, John de Rupe, William Croke, Roger de Hedrik, Walter Mody, William Frankysshe, and many others.

(234)   Grant by Alice daughter of Robert de Shafton to Thomas Belle and Avice his wife, of a plot of land of her messuage lying in Magna Haltona, to build a house; which plot contains forty feet in length, abutting at the eastern head on the messuage of Thomas Belle and at the western head towards the messuage of Henry de Belam, and contains thirty feet in breadth, lying between the public road and the remainder of her messuage.   To hold and to have to the grantees and the heirs between them lawfully begotten, (*fo.* 148*d*) with all appurtenances and easements to so much land within and without the vill of Magna Halton and appertaining, from the chief lord

---

[1] Great Houghton in the parish of Darfield.   The subsequent headings, to *fo.* 153*d* inclusive, are " Maior Haltona."

[2] Burton erroneously calls him *John* (*Mon. Ebor.*, 95), and in the Lansdowne Chartulary he is called *Jordan de Insula.*

of the fee, by the services thence due and accustomed, freely, quietly, etc.   Warranty.   If the grantees should die without heir as above, the property after their death to revert to the grantor and her heirs.   Witnesses, John de Woddehall, Jordan de Insula, John Harynghel, William Croke, Walter Mody, and many others.

(235)   Grant by Adam Rogerson of Littilhalton, to Joan daughter of Robert Bakester of Wath, in her pure virginity, and to the heirs between the grantor and her lawfully begotten, of all his messuages, edifices, lands, tenements, meadows and pastures, with the appurtenances, which he had in Mykilhalton in the parish of Derffeld. To hold and to have to the said [Joan][1] and the heirs as above, freely, quietly, etc., from the chief lord of that fee, by the services due and accustomed.   (*Fo.* 149)[2] Witnesses, Thomas Dode, William Roger, Adam Godlyng, Roger de Hendelay, and many others. Dated at Halton the feast of All Saints, 1389.

(236)   Grant by Matilda Parsonman of Wath, daughter and heir of Adam Rogerson, formerly of Lyttilhalton, and Joan his wife, in her pure widowhood, to John Curson of Magna Halgton, gent., of a messuage with garden and four acres of land and meadow, with all the appurtenances, in the vill and within the bounds of Magna Halgton, which descended to her by hereditary right after the death of Adam and Joan.   To have and to hold to the grantee, his heirs and assigns, from the chief lords of that fee, by the services due and accustomed.   Warranty.   For this grant, John has given her £4 of money.   (*Fo.* 149*d*) Witnesses, Richard Hyn of Magna Halgton, Thomas Scolay of the same, William Wilbor of the same, and many others.   Dated at Halgton aforesaid, 16 April, 1472.

(237)   Appointment by Matilda Parsonman of Wath (described as above), of John Wyghtman of Magna Halgton, as her attorney to deliver seisin to John Curson of the same, of the property named in the preceding deed.   Same date as in previous deed.

(238)   Grant by Robert (*fo.* 150) Brerlay of Mangna Halgton [*sic*] to John Curson of Holwell, gent., of an acre and a half [of arable land][3] in Odsstorth in the fields of the vill of Halgton, which descended to the grantor by hereditary right after the death of Robert Brerlay his father; which lie in plots in Odsstorth aforesaid, between the land (of the lord ?)[4] of the said vill on the east side, and the land of Robert Weg on the west, and abuts at one end on the land of the lord towards the north, and on Odsstorth towards the south. To have and to hold to the grantee, his heirs and assigns, from the chief lord of the fee, by the services due and accustomed, for ever.

[1] Omitted.

[2] This folio is not numbered in the MS.

[3] Omitted here; it occurs later in the habendum and warranty clauses.

[4] The word possibly a contraction of " domini," but there has been an alteration.

Witnesses, John Wyghtman, William Hyte, Richard Sysson, and many others.   Dated at Halghton aforesaid, 3 April, 13 Edw. IV (1473).

(239) Appointment by Robert Brerlay, grantor of the previous deed, of John Wythman of Halgton as his attorney to deliver seisin to John Curson, the grantee named in the previous deed, of the property mentioned.   (*Fo.* 150*d*) Date as in last deed.

(240) Grant by Robert de Brerlay of Magna Halgton to John Curson of Holwell, gent., of a close containing five acres of land lying in the field called Odsstorth beside Ladycrose, in the fields of Magna Halgton, which descended to him (Robert) by hereditary right after the death of Robert Brerlay his father; which close lies between the land of the lord of the vill on either side, and abuts on the land of the said lord at either end.   To have and to hold to the grantee, his heirs and assigns, rendering to the chief lord of the fee the services due and accustomed.   Warranty.   Witnesses, Robert Card, Richard Hyn, John Wightman, and others.   Dated at Halgton aforesaid, 15 May, 16 Edw. IV (1476).

(*Fo.* 151) (241) Appointment by Robert Brelay[1] of Magna Halgton of John Wightman of Halgton to deliver seisin to John Curson of the close named in the preceding deed.   Date as in previous deed.

(242) Grant by Nicholas Curson, brother and heir of Thomas Curson, son and heir of John Curson, to William Wadeluffe and Richard Eliott of Halghton, of a close containing five acres of land with the (*fo.* 151*d*) appurtenances, lying in the field called Odstorth beside Ladycrose in the fields of Mykylhaghton, an acre and a half of land, with the appurtenances, in Mykilhaghton aforesaid, and a messuage with garden and five and a half acres of land and meadow, lying in plots in the fields of Mikylhaghton, with the appurtenances. To hold and to have to the grantees, their heirs and assigns, for ever, from the chief lords of those fees, by the services due and accustomed.   Warranty.   Appointment of John Berwyke as attorney to deliver seisin.   Witnesses, Thomas Oxspryng,[2] John Lake, Christopher Watson, Robert Wodhall, John Carlill.   Dated at Monkbrett', 5 January, 20 Edw. IV (1481-2).

(*Fo.* 152) (243) Release and quitclaim by William Wadylove to the prior and convent of Monkbretton and their successors, of all right, title, claim, etc., of and in a close containing five acres of land, with the appurtenances, lying in the field called Odstorth beside Ladycrose, and in an acre and a half of land, with the appurtenances, a messuage with garden, and five and a half acres of land and meadow lying in plots in the fields of Mikilhaghton, with the appurtenances, which he (William) lately had, jointly with Richard Elliott.   Dated 10 March, 21 Edw. IV (1481-2).

[1] *Sic.*   Brerlay afterwards in the deed.
[2] Written Oxpsryng.

(244)   Grant by John Sayvile of Spolding, in the County of Lincoln, gentylman, and Agnes his wife, to Thomas de Dodworth of Galber, in the County of York, Jordan Marschall of Bretton in the same County and Richard son of John de Byrtton of Derton in the same County, their heirs and (*fo.* 152*d*) assigns, of a messuage of land and five acres of arable land, with the appurtenances, more or less, as they lie in the vill and fields of Haughton in the County of York. To have and to hold to the grantees, their heirs and assigns, from the chief lords of that fee, by the services due and accustomed, for ever.   Witnesses, Oliver Woderofe of Wollay, John Barnby of Barnby, William de la Hawe of Kesborowh, and others. 6 July, 8 Hen. VI (1430).

(245)   Grant by Elizabeth late wife of William Shaghe of Sandall, in her widowhood, to Richard Ledes, prior of Monkbretton, of a messuage and five acres of arable land, with the appurtenances, in the vill and fields of Haughton.   (*Fo.* 153) To have and to hold to the grantee and his successors for ever, from the chief lords of those fees, by the services due and accustomed. Warranty. Appointment of John Sparke as attorney to deliver seisin.   Witnesses, William Bradford, George Frannkysh, Thomas Oxspryng, and others.   Dated at Haugheton, 20 August, 10 Edw. IV (1470).

(246)   Grant by Elizabeth, late the wife of William Shaw, daughter and heir of Richard Birtton, late of Swalwell, in her pure widowhood, to William Bradford, George Frannkysch, and John (*fo.* 153*d*) Bradford, of five acres of land and meadow in Halghton, which were formerly John Seywille's.   To have and to hold, with the appurtenances, to the grantees, their heirs and assigns, from the chief lords of that fee, by the services due and accustomed. Warranty.   Appointment of Richard Shellito and John Ellis to deliver seisin.   Witnesses, William Oxspryng, Thomas Oxspryng, Robert Baxter, Christopher Watson, Richard West, and others. Dated 5 November, 11 Edw. IV (1471).

(*Folio* 154 *is blank*.)

(*Fo.* 154*d*)   *Byllyngley*.[1]

(247)   Grant by Adam son of Swane for the health of his soul to the church of St. Mary of Lunda, and the monks serving God there, of the tithe of the wild colts throughout his lordship every year, where- ever the herds of mares shall be: he also grants to them all the ferm which Ravan de Halcton was wont to render to Swane son of Eilric and Robert son of Ravan rendered to him (Adam) after the death of his (Robert's) father.   This donation he makes in free and per- petual alms, for the care of his soul and (the souls) of his heirs.[2]

(248)   Grant by Helias Sorel to God and St. Mary Magdelene of Bretton and the monks there, of a toft which was Robert's beside

---

[1] Similar heading to *fo.*156*d* inclusive.

[2] This deed is printed in full by Hunter (*South Yorks.*, ii, 126), who calls it ' a very remarkable charter."

the cold spring, and an acre and a half of land on the east side nearest to the said toft, in pure and perpetual alms, for the health of the souls of himself and of Qenylde his wife, and for the souls of all their ancestors, with all the appurtenances. Witnesses, William son of Adam, Hugh son of Alan, William de Alretun, Reyner the scribe, William the mason, Alan the cook, William the baker.

(*Fo.* 155) (249) Confirmation by John de Shelton to Hugh son of William de Byllyngley and his heirs and whomsoever he shall at any time desire to give, bequeath, sell or assign to, for his homage and service, of two bovates of land, with the tofts and crofts adjacent, and moreover the croft of Emlot, with all the appurtenances, in the vill and territory of Billynlay, those namely which Hugh West formerly held from him (John); except one acre and a half of land which Hugh son of Helias holds of the same bovates, for a penny payable to the said Hugh son of William and his heirs yearly; and except a certain plot of the toft which Richard de Barneburghe holds for a penny payable yearly to the same Hugh and his heirs, of which two bovates of land, with the appurtenances, the said Hugh West (released ?)[1] all his right which he had or could have to the said Hugh son of William and his heirs or assigns, in fee and inheritance, freely, quietly, and peaceably, with all liberties and easements, in plain, in wood, in meadows, etc., with commons to the said land of William belonging, with the services and escheats of the said tenants, namely, Hugh son of Helias and Richard de Barneburghe, to the said holding belonging; rendering thence yearly to him (John de Shelton) and his heirs 6s. of silver and 8d. (*fo.* 155d) for all secular services, etc. Warranty and acquittance; doing suit to the mill of, as other free tenants of the same vill do. For this grant, warrant, and confirmation the said Hugh son of William has given the grantor 6s. of silver in recognition. Witnesses, Sir John de Wekyrslay, John son of William de Bolton, Richard Crok, Roger de Ediricthorp, and others.

(250) Grant by Hugh son of Robert Malet of Mekelbring to Thomas son of Reginald de Ketelberg, of 3s. yearly rent in Byllynglay, namely, from Hugh Bayard 12d., and from the heirs of John son of Elias 2s., with all right which in any way could fall to him (the grantor) from lands and tenements by reason of the said rent. To have (*fo.* 156) and to hold from the grantor and his heirs to the grantee and his heirs or whomsoever he should wish to give, bequeath, or assign to, freely, quietly, etc., with all appurtenances, wardships, reliefs, etc., belonging to the tenements, for which the said rent is paid, rendering yearly to the grantor and his heirs one close at Christmas, for all secular service, etc. Seal. Witnesses, Sir William de Thornill, knt., Sir William, rector of Maltby, John de Hyll, then steward, and others.

---

[1] There appears to be something omitted here: the wording is " quarum duarum bovatarum terre cum pertinenciis dictus Hugo West totum ius suum quod in illis habuit vel habere potuit." Probably " habendum et tenendum " ought to follow.

(251)   Grant by Hugh son of Robert de Mekelbring to Thomas de Ketelberg, clerk, and his heirs or assigns, of a rent of four quarters of oats and half a quarter of wheat yearly at Michaelmas from the land which John son of Elias and Hugh Byard held from him (the grantor) in the vill of Byllyngley.   To hold and to have to the grantee and his heirs or assigns in fee and inheritance well, in peace, freely and quietly, rendering to the grantor and his heirs yearly (*fo.* 156*d*) one clove at Christmas for all service and demand. Warranty, in consideration of a certain sum of money which Thomas has [paid] him in hand.   Witnesses, Roger the reeve, Richard Pluket, Richard Frink, Adam de Skauceby, and others.

(252)   Grant by Richard de Hawile, son of Robert Maleth, to Thomas son of Reginald de Ketelberg, clerk, or his assigns, or whomsoever at whatever time he shall desire to give, sell, assign, or at his last moment (*in extremis*) to bequeath to, for a certain sum of money, which he has given the grantor in hand, of a yearly rent of 11s. 8*d.* in the vill of Billyngley, to be received yearly, namely, from Hugh Bayard of Billyngley for a bovate of land 2s., from Hugh son of Elias for four bovates of land, with the appurtenances, 6s., and from Robert de Wambwell for a certain mill 3s. 8*d.*   To hold and to have to the grantee and his assigns from the grantor and his heirs in fee and inheritance, freely, quietly, etc., without any (*fo.* 156)[1] retention, with all escheats, wardships, reliefs, and other appurtenances: rendering yearly to the grantor and his heirs one clove at Easter, and to the prior of Blythe (Blida) 4s. 2*d.* for all service secular, exaction and demand.   And if it happen that Thomas, in possession of the same rent, die, the rent shall remain to Denis (*Dionisio*) son of William de Doncaster, brother of the said Thomas, and his heirs or assigns.   Seal.   Witnesses, Sirs Thomas de Bella Aqua, Ivo de Heriste, knts., William son of Thomas, Peter de Botherfeud,[2] Thomas de Scauceby, and others.

(253)   Grant by John son of William de Doncaster to Sir Alexander Ledes and Margaret his wife, of all his (John's) right (*fo.* 156*d*) in the vill and territory of Byllyngley, namely, in a certain tenement and a yearly rent of 4s. receivable from the land and tenement which Hugh Gode formerly held from him (the grantor), with all appurtenances, in homages, services, wardships, etc.   To have and to hold and receive to the grantees and the heirs and assigns of Alexander for ever, doing to the chief lord the service due and accustomed. Witnesses, Sirs Roger son of Thomas, Henry de Tynneslowe, Peter de Rotherfeld, knts., Stephen de Bella Aqua, William de Wyntworth, and others.

(254)   Grant by Thomas Doncaster to Sir Alexander Ledes and Margaret his wife and their heirs, of all his rent in the vill of Byllyngley (*fo.* 156)[3] from Hugh Biard, from Elias son of John, from Hugh

[1] *Sic.*   Three leaves are so numbered.
[2] Probably a mistake for Rotherfeud, see 253.
[3] *Sic.*

son of Hugh, and from John de Womvelle for the tenement which they held from him (the grantor) with homages, wardships, reliefs, escheats, and all other rights from the same rent in the same vill to him belonging.   To hold and to have from the lord of the fee, freely, quietly, etc., in fee and inheritance, rendering yearly to the said lord the rent due and accustomed, and to the grantor and his heirs for warranty a clove at Easter for all services, etc.   For this grant, concession and confirmation of charter, the said Sir Alexander has found Bartholomew, the grantor's nephew, with the habit and all other things necessary to enter religion in the house of Drax.   Witnesses, Sir William son of Thomas, Sir Roger son of Thomas, Sir John le Buk, Sir Ralph Salweyn, and others.

(*Fo.* 156*d*)   (255)   Licence by Robert, prior of Blyth (*Blida*) and the convent of the same place, to Master Henry Eynesham, mason,[1] to grant to the prior and convent of Monkbretton 18*s.* 8½*d.* of yearly rent with the appurtenances in Byllyngley, issuing from six bovates of land which are held from thèm (Robert and his convent) in that vill.   To hold and to have the said rent with the appurtenances, to the said prior and convent[2] and their successors for ever.   And for this permission to Henry, the prior and convent of Monkbretton have agreed, for themselves and their successors, to do to the prior and convent of Blyth and their successors all services from the same tenements due to them and accustomed, the statute of mortmain notwithstanding.   Seals of the two priories alternately to the two parts of this writing indentate.   Witnesses, Sir John Flemyng, knt., John de Bella Aqua, Geoffrey de Staynton, William de Notton, Philip de Bosevile, and others.   Dated at Blida before the feast of St. Boniface, 1322.

(*Fo.* 157)   (256)   Licence by Robert, prior and convent of Blyth (*Blida*) to the prior and convent of Bretton and the monks there, to obtain and enter upon all the tenements formerly of Master Henry Le Mason in their vill of Byllyngley, which formerly the said Master Henry held from them (the prior and convent of Blida) in chief: so that the prior and convent of Bretton may hold the said tenements from them according to the form of an agreement between the priories.   Dated at Blida, the day of St. Dionysius, 1324.

(257)   Let it appear to all by these presents that I, Henry Eynesham, from profound affection, beholding the good will of the convent of the monastery of Monkbretton, give and concede to the same convent 10*s.* of silver for a certain yearly pittance, which 10*s.* the collector or collectors (*fo.* 157*d*) of pittances for the time being shall receive from the ferm and rent of Billyngley for ever: so that the said convent may be in full seisin of the said pittance during my life, and seisin, God willing, shall continue in perpetuity,

---

[1] The description "magister" and "cementarius" seems rather incongruous, and Hunter suggests that he may have been "one of the architects to whom we owe the magnificent edifices which arose in that age." (*South Yorkshire*, i, 382.)

[2] *i.e.*, of Monk Bretton.

notwithstanding that the said prior and convent have granted to me the said ferms to the end of my life. I desire and grant that the collector of ferms of the vill of Bolton pay yearly during my life 3s. 4d. to the cellarer of Monkbretton for the time being, so that on St. Leonard's day he may distribute such money amongst the poor of the parish of Bolton, for the souls of myself and others, as is contained in the ordinances. Dated at Monkbretton, 4 June, 1328.

(*Fo.* 158)   *Thyrnescho.*[1]

(258)   Grant by John Wadylowff of Thyrnescho to John Grym bald and Margaret his wife, of the same, of two tofts and six acres of land, with the appurtenances, which the grantee John held from the grantor.   To have and to hold to the grantees and the heirs of their bodies lawfully begotten, freely, quietly, etc., from the chief lords of that fee, by the services due and accustomed.   If the grantees should die without heirs as above, the property to revert to the right heirs of the grantor.   Witnesses, Richard Swalw [*sic*][2] of Thirnescho, John son of Randolf, Alan Grymbald of the same, and others.   Dated at Thirnescho, Monday before the feast of Corpus Christi, 1402.

(*Fo.* 158d)   (259)   Appointment by John Wadelowe of Thirnescho of Richard Swalowe of the same as attorney, to deliver seisin to John Grymbald and Margaret his wife, of two tofts with crofts adjoining, and six acres of land, with the appurtenances, as more fully appears in his charter of feoffment.   Dated at Thirnescho, as above.

(260)   Release and quitclaim by John Swalow " del Mose " in the parish of Campsall to John Grymbald of Thirnescho, of all actions, real and personal, which the said John Swalow had, has, or could have against him by reason of any matter from the beginning of the world to the day of the making of these presents.   Dated at Thirnescho, 2 February, 7 Hen. V (1416).

(*Fo.* 159)   (261)   Grant by Thomas Hardyng, son and heir of John Hardyng of Thirnescho, to John Calthorn and Robert Alott, of two tofts and six acres of land, with the appurtenances, as they lie in the vill and territory of Thirnescho.   To have and to hold to the grantees and their assigns, freely, quietly, etc., from the chief lords of that fee, by the services due and accustomed.   Witnesses, John Elys, rector of the church of Thirnescho, Thomas Wytte of the same, Stephen Helum, and others.   Dated 3 April, 7 Edw. IV (1467).

(262)   Release and quitclaim by Thomas Hardyng, son and heir of John Hardyng of Thirnescho, to John Calthorn and Robert Alott, their heirs and assigns, of all right and claim in two tofts

---

[1] The heading continues to *fo.*160d. The vill is Thurnscoe, near Doncaster.
[2] Perhaps the Richard Swalowe of the next deed.

and six acres of land, with the appurtenances, in Thirnescho. (*Fo.* 159*d*) Witnesses, John Ellis, rector of the church of Thirnescho, Thomas Witte, Stephen Helum of the same, and others. Dated 6 April, 8·Edw. IV (1468).

(263) Grant by John Calthorn and Robert Alott to William Belle of Hikylton and Thomas Halle of the same, of two tofts and six acres of land, with the appurtenances, as they lie in the vill and territory of Thirnescho. To have and to hold to the grantees, their heirs and assigns, freely, quietly, etc., from the chief lords of that fee, by the services due and accustomed. Warranty. (*Fo.* 160) Witnesses, John Elys, rector of the church of Thirnescho, Thomas Witte and John Palmer of the same, and others. Dated 3 April, 1468.

(264) Appointment by Robert Alott of John Calthorn as his attorney to deliver seisin to William Belle of Hykylton and Thomas Halle of the same, of two tofts and six acres of land, with the appurtenances, in Thirneschow, according to the form and effect of a certain charter to them made thereof. Dated as in the last deed.

(265) Grant by Thomas Halle of Hikylton, to Richard, prior of Monkbretton and the convent thereof and their successors, of two tofts and six acres of land, with the appurtenances (*fo.* 160*d*) in Thirnescho, which he (the grantor) jointly with William Bell of Hikylton, now deceased, lately had by the grant and feoffment of John Calthorn and Robert Alott. To have and to hold to the said prior and convent and their successors for ever, from the chief lords of that fee, by the services due and accustomed. Witnesses, John Elys, rector of the church of Thirnescho, John Palmer, Thomas Witte, and others. Dated at Thirnescho, 4 October, 1.Ric. III (1483).

(266) Release and quitclaim by John Calthorn to William, prior of Monkbretton and the convent thereof and their successors, of all right and claim of and in two tofts and six acres of land, with the appurtenances, in Thirnescho, which Richard, late prior, predecessor of the present prior, had by the grant and feoffment of Thomas Halle of Hikylton. (*Fo.* 161) Witnesses, Richard Syms, Thomas Oxspryng, John Mettcalffe, chaplain, and others. Dated 23 February, 3 Hen. VII (1488–9).

(*Fo.* 161*d*)   *Hykylton.*[1]

(267) Grant by Randulf (*Randulphus*) de Novo Mercato to God and St. Mary Magdelene of Bretton and the monks there serving God, in pure and perpetual alms, of six bovates of land, with the appurtenances, in the territory of Hikilton; namely, that bovate, with the toft which Walter the reeve held, and that bovate, with the toft which Elias de Thirliskon held, and that bovate, with the toft which Swane held, and that bovate, with the toft which Simon

[1] This heading continues to *fo.* 172*d*. The vill is Hickleton, near Doncaster.

held, and that bovate, with the toft which Hugh Horn held, and that bovate which Fulk Hare and Fulk son of Ranneld held, with the toft of the latter. To hold and to have as freely and quietly as any pure and perpetual alms may be given. Witnesses, Master Roger de Hampol, Sir Adam de Novo (*fo.* 162) Mercato, Sir Henry his brother, Sir Robert, parson of Gamelestun, Sir Rainer Malet, Sir Richard de Wambwell, and others.

(Monkbretton Chart., Lansdowne MS. 405, fo. 36.)

(268) Confirmation by Ralph son of Ranulf (*Rainulfi*) de Novo Mercato to God, etc. (as in the previous charter), of all the land which his father gave the monks, in pure and perpetual alms, as in the charter of his father, which they have, witnesses; namely, in the territory of Hikylton. Witnesses, Sir Adam de Novo Mercato, Sir Henry his brother, Richard de Wambwelle, Reiner Malet, Robert, parson of Hotun, and others.

(269) Grant by Adam, prior of Bretton, and the convent thereof, (*fo.* 162*d*) to Nichola daughter of Sir Randulf de Novo Mercato and her heirs and assigns, of six bovates of land, with the tofts and crofts and all appurtenances, in the territory of Hikilton, with all the liberties, easements and free commons of the said vill, as pertains to it ; namely, the bovate of Swane with the croft, and the bovate of Hugh Horn with the toft, and the bovate of Simon with the toft, and the bovate of Fulk Hare and Fulk son of Reginald, with the toft which was the said Fulk's son of Reginald, and the bovate of Walter the reeve with the croft, and the bovate of Elias de Thyrnescho with the toft; for her homage and service, to her, her heirs or assigns. To hold and to have from the grantors, freely and quietly, in fee and inheritance; rendering to them yearly 4*s.*, for all services, etc., to them belonging. Witnesses, Adam de Novo Mercato, Henry de Novo Mercato, John de Rokeleia, William de Bylby, and others.

(270) Surrender and quitclaim by the lady Nichola de Hikilton (*fo.* 163) to God and the church of St. Mary Magdalene of Bretton and the monks there serving God, of all the land which she held from the prior and monks of Bretton, within and without the vill of Hykilton, with all the appurtenances, as in lordships, homages, and all other services and escheats belonging to the said land, as the charters of her father Sir Randulf de Novo Mercato and her brother Ralph, which they (the prior and convent) have, witness. For this surrender they have given her 100 marks of silver in hand. Seal. Witnesses, Sir Adam de Novo Mercato, Sir Thomas Fitz William, Sir John de Novo Mercato, Sir Robert de Stapelton, and others.

(Monkbretton Chart., Lansdowne MS. 405, fo. 36.)

(271) Quitclaim by Randulf son of Randulf de Novo Mercato to Nichola his sister and her heirs or assigns, of all the land without retention, namely, two bovates of land, with (*fo.* 163*d*) the appurtenances, which Jordan his brother held from the prior and monks of Bretton, in the vill of Hikilton. So nevertheless, that Nichola and her heirs or assigns may have and hold this aforesaid land,

with the appurtenances, from the said prior and convent, as their charter, which she has, witnesses. Seal. Witnesses, John de Rokeley, Henry de Tancresley, Master William de Mustain, and others.

(272) Grant by Nichola daughter of Randulf de Novo Mercato to God and St. Mary Magdalene of Bretton and the convent there, for the souls of herself and her ancestors, and particularly for the soul of Jordan her brother, of three acres of land in the territory of Hikilton, namely, the toft and croft which Walter the reeve held, which contain an acre and a rood which lies in the field of Waterfall between the land of Roger son of Walter and the land of William son of William, and another [rood] which lies in Dalefurlang, (*fo.* 164) and a third which lies in Mikelhaghe Furlang, between the land of John Carter and of Reginald Spyve, and a fourth which lies between the land of Ralph the reeve and of Walter the reeve, and a fifth which lies in the field of Enstwelles between the land of Randolf the reeve and Walter the reeve at the stone bridge, and three roods which extend from the field of Barneburg to Langedickare, in pure and perpetual alms. These three acres she has given to the said church and monks specially for an obit which they shall do yearly for ever for the soul of Jordan her brother, namely, on the 3rd January. Witnesses, John de Rokeley, Reginald, parson of Hikilton, Robert Testard, parson of Hotun, Randolf son of Randolf de Novo Mercato, and others.

(Monkbretton Chart., Lansdowne MS. 405, fo. 36d.)

(273) Quitclaim by Robert Curzon to the prior and convent of Monkbretton, of all right and claim in the tenement called Le Monkhouwe in Hikilton. Witnesses, William Scott, knt., William de Notton, Robert Haryngel, John son of Nicholas de Tours, John son of Godfrey de Stenton, and others. Dated at Hikilton, 17 September, 13 Edw. III (1339).

(*Fo.* 164*d*) (274) Consent by Robert Haringel that the prior and convent of Monkbretton shall not be hindered by him or his heirs from digging marl in a certain place called Le Monkhouwe in Hikilton, nor from carrying it, or causing it to be carried wheresoever they will on their own land. Witnesses, William Scott, knt., William de Notton, Robert Curzon, and others. Dated at Hikilton, 3 September, 13 Edw. III (1339).

(275) Edward, by the grace of God, etc., to the Sheriff of York: we command you that in your full county [court] (*Com'*) you cause to be recorded the suit which is in the same county [court] without our writ between Richard de Halghton, prior of Bretton, and the monks there, and John de Morby of Hikilton respecting a cow of the said John, taken and unjustly detained, as is alleged; and have the record before our justices at Westminster within fifteen days of St. Hilary, under your seal and the seals of four (*fo.* 165) lawful men of the same county, and fix the same day for the parties, that then, etc.

(The cow was taken on the toft of the said John which is of the prior's fee, for arrears of 9*d.* yearly, not paid for twenty years before the day of seizure: and William de Ebor, prior of Monkbretton, predecessor of the present prior, was seised by such tenant.)

(*Fo.* 165*d*)   (276)   Grant[1] by Elena daughter of Beatrice de Hikilton, in her widowhood and free power, to John de Wilde of the same, for a certain sum of money which he has given her in hand, of a certain part of her messuage built in the same [vill] containing in length fifteen feet.   She has also given him a plot of land lying at the head of the said house towards the west, containing in length ten feet, which lies between the land of the prior and convent of Bretton on one side and the land of William son of Beatrice on the other, whereof the heads abut on her house and on her land to the west.   To have and to hold the said part of the said house and the said plot of land to the said John le Wilde, his heirs and assigns, well and in peace, freely, quietly, etc., from the chief lords of that fee, by the services due and accustomed.   Dated Sunday after the feast of the Apostles Peter and Paul, 1312.   Witnesses, Thomas de Asseberi, Giles de Hykilton, John Couper, Adam the smith, and others.

(*Fo.* 166)   (277)   Grant by Robert Daudeson of Hikylton to Richard Wilde of the same, his heirs and assigns, of one half of a messuage in the vill of Hikylton, lying between the toft of Roger de Preston on one side and the messuage of the said Richard on the other; whereof one head abuts on Le Westecrofte and the other on the road leading through the middle of the vill of Hikilton.   To have and to hold, with all the appurtenances, to the grantee, his heirs and assigns, freely, quietly, etc., from the chief lords of that fee, by the services due and accustomed.   Witnesses, William Spynk, Thomas Heley, Thomas Rille, and others.   Dated at Hikilton, Monday before the feast of Gregory the Pope, 22 Ric. II (1399).

(278)   Grant by Roger (*fo.* 166*d*) Preston, lord of Hikylton, to Richard Wilde of Hikilton, his heirs and assigns, of an acre and a rood of arable land, with the appurtenances, in the fields and territory of Hikilton; whereof one rood lies in Waterfalffeld between his (Roger's) own land on either side and abuts at one head upon Tranelandhades and at the other on Dalehades, and half an acre lies in Oustewelfeld, and abuts at one head on Labegate (or Lambegate) and at the other on Stanegranes; and another rood lies in Waterfalfelde between his (Roger's) land on either side and abuts on Tranelandehades and Dalehades; and another rood lies in the west field of the same vill in a place called Dyrtelandes, between the land formerly Treton [*sic*] on the east and the land of the prior of Monkbretton on the west, and abuts at one head on the highway

---

[1] In the margin is written " lande," apparently part of a word, the beginning of which has been cut away.

towards Bernysley and Doncaster and at the other head on Stremi-haxsewelsyk. To have and to hold to the grantee, his heirs and assigns from the chief lords of the fee, by the services due and accustomed, for ever. Witnesses, Robert Daudeson, Richard Campion, William Spynk, and others. Dated at Hikilton, Monday in the feast of St. John of Beverlay, Archbishop, 20 Ric. II (1396).

(*Fo.* 167) (279) Grant by William Littilwod of Hikilton and Joan his wife to Henry Strafford,[1] rector of the church of Tretton,[2] and William Bell of Hikilton, of a messuage built in Hikilton with garden adjoining, as it lies between the land of the prior and convent of Monkbretton on the north and the tenement of Thomas Preston on the south, and abuts on the highway towards the east, and five roods of land lying separately in the fields of Hickilton, with the appurtenances. To have and to hold to the grantees, their heirs and assigns, for ever, from the chief lords of that fee, by the services due and accustomed. Warranty. Witnesses, Thomas Preston of Hikilton, William Wilson, chaplain, Thomas Hall, and others. Dated at Hikilton, 6 May, 1471.

(*Fo.* 167*d*) (280) Release and quitclaim by Robert Palden of Doncastere to Henry Strafford, rector of the church of Treton, and William Bell of Hikilton, their heirs and assigns, of all right, title, and claim, of and in a messuage built with garden adjoining, and five roods of land lying separately within the bounds of Hikilton, with the appurtenances, which they lately had by the gift and feoffment of William Littilwood and Joan his wife. Witnesses, Thomas Preston of Hikilton, Thomas Hall, Christofer Watson of Bolton, and others. Dated at Hikilton, 4 July, 1471.

(281) Release by Henry (*fo.* 168) Strafford, rector of the church of Treton, and William Bell of Hikilton, to Richard de Ledes, prior of the monastery of the blessed Mary Magdalene of Monkbretton, of a messuage built in Hikilton, with the garden adjoining, as it lies between the tenement of the prior and convent of the said monastery on the north and the tenement of Thomas Preston on the south, and abuts on the highway towards the west, and five roods of land lying separately in the fields of Hikilton, with the appurtenances. To hold and to have to the said prior and his successors for ever, from the chief lords of those fees, by the services due and accustomed. Witnesses, Thomas Preston, William Oxspryng, Thomas Oxspryng, Christofer Watson, and others. Dated at Hikilton, 20 June, 1471.

(*Fo.* 168*d*)[3] (282) Grant by John de Doddesworth, chaplain, to Thomas Baty of Hikilton and Diota his wife, their heirs and assigns, of a messuage, four and a half acres of land, a rood and a half of

---

[1] Called Stafford in Hunter's Hallamshire.

[2] *i.e.*, Treeton.

[3] A name has been written in the margin, now partly cut away; the letters remaining are ". . . . . e lande."

arable land, as they lie within the vill and territory of Hikilton. To have and to hold to the grantees, their heirs and assigns, freely, quietly, etc., from the grantor and his heirs, doing to the chief lords of that fee the services due and accustomed, namely, to the prior of Bretton three silver pennies yearly. Witnesses, Robert Daudson, Richard Smyth, Walter Campeon. Dated at Hikilton, 6 February, 51 Edw. III (1376–7).

(*Fo.* 169) (283)   Grant by Dionisia, who was the wife of Thomas Bate, to John Smyth of Hikilton and Margaret his wife, her daughter, of a tenement built and six acres of land with the appurtenances in Hikilton, which were Thomas Bate's, her late husband.   To have and to hold to the grantees, their heirs and assigns, from the chief lords of that fee, by the services due and accustomed.   Witnesses, Roger de Preston, John Cresacre, Robert del Marshe, and others. Dated at Hikilton, Christmas, 1398.

(284)   Release and quitclaim by William, son of Richard Bate, to John Smyth of Hykilton and Margaret his wife, their heirs and assigns, of all right and claim in a tenement built and six acres of land with all the appurtenances in Hikilton, which the said John and Margaret had (*fo.* 169*d*) by the gift and feoffment of Dionisia, who was wife of Thomas Bate, and which belonged to the said Thomas in Hikylton.   Witnesses, Roger Preston, Alexander Anne, Hugh Suward, and others.   Dated at Hikylton, 3 January, 1398.

(285)   Grant by John Axe of Hikilton to John Bradford, Brian Bradford, and Robert Chaloner, of a moiety of a messuage in Hikilton and six acres of land lying separately in the fields of Hikilton. To have and to hold with the appurtenances to the grantees, their heirs and assigns, for ever, from the chief lords of that fee, by the services due and accustomed.   (*Fo.* 170) Witnesses, Christofer Watson of Bolton on Derne, Thomas Baxter, Thomas Sisson, and others.   Dated at Hikilton, 31 December, 1485.

(286)   Appointment by John Bradford, Brian Bradford, and Robert Chaloner of Thomas Wodward as attorney to receive seisin of the property named in the preceding deed, according to the form and effect of a certain charter thereof made to them by John Axe. Dated as in previous deed.

(287)   Surrender by John Bradford, Brian Bradford, and Robert Chaloner (*fo.* 170*d*) to Richard Ledes, prior of the monastery of the blessed Mary Magdalene of Monkbretton, of a moiety of a messuage, with the appurtenances, in Hikilton, and six acres of land lying separately in Hikilton aforesaid, which they had lately by the gift and feoffment of John Axe of Hikilton.   To have and to hold the said moiety of the said messuage and six acres of land with the appurtenances, to the said prior and his successors for ever, from the chief lords of that fee, by the services due and accustomed.   Appointment of Thomas Oxspring as attorney to

deliver seisin.   Witnesses, Thomas Wodward, Richard Grubber, John Ellis, and others.   Dated at Monkbretton, 20 May, 1485.[1]

(288) Grant by William Walker (*fo.* 171) of Bolton to John Hikilton, of a moiety of a toft and three roods of land with the appurtenances, as they lie in length and width in the vill and fields of Hikilton, whereof the said moiety lies between the land of Roger Preston on one side and the tenement of Thomas Bate on the other, one head abutting on the King's highway and the other head on Westecroft, and the three roods lie between the land of the prior of Bretton on one side and the land of Roger Smyth of Barnebur on the other, the heads abutting on the King's street (*stratum*) and the other heads on the land of Thomas de Metham, knt.   To have and to hold to the grantee, his heirs and assigns, freely, quietly, etc., from the chief lords of that fee, by the services due and accustomed.   Witnesses, Roger de Preston, Adam Kyrham, and others. Dated at Hikilton, 20 February, 9 Rich. II (1385–6).

(289) Release and quitclaim by John Hikilton to John Syke of Bulklyffe of a moiety of a toft and three roods of land, with the appurtenances, as they lie in length and width in the vill and fields of Hikilton, whereof the said moiety lies between the tenement of Thomas Preston on one side and the tenement of Robert son of (*fo.* 171*d*) Richard on the other, the head abutting on the King's street and the other head on Wescroftes, and the three roods lie between the land of the prior of Bretton on one side and the land formerly Roger Smythe's on the other, the heads abutting on the King's street and the land formerly Thomas Metham's, knt.   To have and to hold to the grantee, his heirs and assigns, freely, quietly, etc., from the chief lords of that fee, by the services due and accustomed.   Witnesses, Richard Wentworth, Thomas Preston, esquires, Robert Wetteley, and others.   Dated 30 May, 38 Hen. VI (1460).

(290) Appointment by John Hikilton of Robert Wetelay as his attorney to deliver seisin of the above property to John Syke of Bulklyffe.   Date as in previous deed.

(*Fo.* 172) (291) Grant by John Sike of Bulklyfe to Thomas Oxspryng and William Bell of Hikilton, of a moiety of a toft and three roods of land, with the appurtenances, as they lie in length and width in the vill and fields of Hikilton (described as in the last deed but one).   To have and to hold to the grantees, their heirs and assigns for ever, from the chief lords of that fee, by the services due and accustomed.   Witnesses, Thomas Preston, Thomas Stodfold, chaplain, and others.   Dated 12 August, 11 Edw. IV (1471).

(292) Demise and delivery by Thomas Oxspryng (*fo.* 172*d*) and William Bell of Hikilton to Richard Ledes, prior of the monastery of the blessed Mary of Magdalene of Monkbretton and the convent

---

[1] The dates of the three deeds relating to this property are all plainly written, but obviously there is some inaccuracy, probably the latter deed should read " 1486."

G

there and their successors for ever, of a moiety of a toft and three roods of land in Hikilton, with the appurtenances, whereof, etc. (property described as before), which [property] they lately had of the gift and feoffment of John Sike of Bulclyffe.   To have and to hold to the grantees for ever, from the chief lords of that fee, by the services due and accustomed. Witnesses, Thomas Preston, Richard West, and others. Dated at Hikilton, 5 May, 15 Edw. IV (1475).

(293)   Grant by Randulf son and heir of Randulf to Thomas son of Henry de Goldthorp, his heirs and assigns, of a toft in the vill of Hikilton (*fo.* 173) with all manner of liberties and easements, lying between the toft of William Spinc and the toft of Walter Child, and two acres and a rood of arable land, whereof an acre and a half lie in the field of Barnburg on Synyngland, between the King's highway and the land of William called Batet of Hikilton, and abuts upon the King's highway, and one head abuts on the land of Alan son of Helwise de Mar, and one rood lies on Haverhil in the field of Hikilton between the land of Roger Spinc and the land of Thomas Boye, and abuts on the King's highway, and the other [head] on Haverhildie, and half a rood lies on Piletcroft between the land of the parson and the land of Roger Spync, and a rood lies beside the bridge[1] between the land of Walter Child and the land formerly Randulf de Buklay's, and abuts on the land of Thomas Boye and the other [head] on the beck of Barnburg; with all liberties and appurtenances. To hold and to have to the grantee and his heirs and to whomsoever he shall desire to give, leave, sell, or assign from the grantor and his heirs, freely, quietly, etc., rendering to the prior of Bretton yearly for the said toft 6*d.* for all services and demands, and 2*d.* to the light of the blessed Virgin Mary in the church of Hikilton in the feast of St. Peter ad vincula for all demands. Warranty. For this grant Thomas has given the grantor a toft and a croft with the land belonging, in Goldthorpe. Witnesses, Sir Peter de Roderfeld, William son of Beatrice de Hikilton, Richard Wilde, and others.

(*Fo.* 173*d*)   [*Cad*]*by.*[2]

(294)   Grant by William de Nosmarche to God and St. Mary Magdalene of Bretton and the monks there serving God, of a bovate of land in Cadby, which was Luke's, with all the appurtenances and all the liberties of the same vill, free and quit of all secular services, in pure and perpetual alms. Witnesses, Reginald, parson of Hikilton, Jordan de Sancta Maria, William de Ligla, and others.
(Monkbretton Chart., Lansdowne MS. 405, fo. 38.)

(295)   Confirmation by Ranulf de Hikilton to the same house and monks of a bovate of land in Cadby, which his father gave them, namely that bovate which was Luke's, with all appurtenances

---

[1] A blank of about one inch in the MS.

[2] " Cadby " has evidently been written as a heading in the margin, but the binder has cut away all but the last two letters.

and all liberties of that vill, in wood, in plain, etc., free and quit of all secular services, in pure and perpetual alms. Witnesses, Reginald, parson of Hikilton, Jordan de Sancta Maria, William de Ligla of Broddisworda and Randolf his brother, Richard de Wath, Richard Gornun, Robert Mastrel, and many others.

(Monkbretton Chart., Lansdowne MS. 405, fo. 37.)

(*Fo.* 174) (296) Grant by William, prior of Bretton, by the general council of all the chapter, to Ralph de Unad and his heirs in fee and inheritance, of a bovate of land in Cadby, that namely which was Luke's, with all the appurtenances, free and quit of all secular service: rendering yearly to the grantors 5s. Witnesses, William de Nosmarche, Ranulf de Nosmarche, Reginald his brother, and others.

Memorandum, that Sir Robert Langtwayt, chaplain, heir and tenant of the above-written lands and tenements, on the 20th April, 6 Edw. IV (1466), at Cadby, in the presence of John Philipson, Thomas Wolsy, chaplain, Thomas Wodward, and others, surrendered all his estate and title of and in the above written lands and tenements, and every parcel thereof to Richard Ledes, then prior of Monkbretton, his lord, and his successors for ever.

Addewyk super Statum.[1]

(297) Grant by Thomas son of William to God and the blessed Mary Magdalene (*fo.* 174d) of Bretton and the monks there serving God, of all the service which William the clerk and Walter Payt of Adwik owed him, namely each year 9s. of rent and half a windle of white peas;[2] and with all other services which could fall to him or his heirs, namely in homages, services, wardships, reliefs, etc., from the land, in perpetual alms, saving the service due at Tikhill and the King's forinsec service as belongs to land of that fee. Witnesses, Sir John de Lungvilers, Sir Philip de Cortilingston, etc.

(Monkbretton Chart., Lansdowne MS. 405, fo. 16.)

(298) Grant by Ralph Haket to God and the church of St. Mary Magdalene of Bretton and the monks there serving God, with his body, of two bovates of land with tofts and crofts and all the appurtenances, in the vill and territory of Addewic; whereof Ralph the miller holds one, together with the said Ralph and his issue and chattels, and Henry brother of Thomas holds the other, together with the said Henry and his issue and chattels; and a moiety of all the mill of Addewic, with all the suit and the appurtenances, to the said mill belonging ; (*fo.* 175) namely for a pittance to the convent on the day of the death of the same Ralph for ever. To have and to hold from Ralph and his heirs in free, pure, and perpetual alms for ever, with all liberties, etc., in wood, in plain, etc.,

[1] Adwick-le-street. " Addewik super St " . . . . . . written in the margin— some letters being cut off. The succeeding page is headed as above.

[2] *Dimid' windell' albarum pisarum.* The windle was a measure for corn, straw, etc., usually a bushel, but varying in different localities (*Eng. Dialect Dict.*).

to the said land and mill belonging.   Seal.   Witnesses, Sir
Geoffrey de Nova Villa, Sir Alexander de Nevil, William Torte-
mains, and others.   (Monkbretton Chart., Lansdowne MS. 405, fo. 18.)

(299)   The court of the lord, the prior of Monkbretton, held at
Athewike on Thursday, the 19 February, 1 Hen. IV (1399–1400).

Inquisition taken there by the oath of John Payte, John Donnyng,
John Dewy, who say on their oath that the heirs of Robert Euyre
owe suit of court for one rood of meadow lying in a place called
Brodyngs.   Also they say that Roger Elis, chaplain, holds one rood
of land abutting on Le Est strete beside Hyngand, late in the tenure
of Robert Mennd, and renders yearly three farthings.   Also that
John Beyne comes not, therefore he is in penalty.   John Payte
holds a messuage and ten acres of land with the appurtenances,
and renders yearly 3s., and for forinsec service 5d., and homage and
fealty, and whoever collects the rent shall have, by order of the
prior, a bushel of peas.   John Beyne holds a rood of land abutting
upon Le Est strete and renders yearly three farthings.   John Dounyng
holds a messuage and twenty acres of land and renders yearly 6s.,
and forinsec service.   (Fo. 175d) John Dewe holds three roods of
land, and two roods are of the right of his wife, and renders yearly
for two roods 1½d., and the other roods lie at Leycrosse, and for one
rood he renders yearly three farthings.

Doncaster.[1]

(300)   Grant by John de Newton, chaplain, to John de Scauceby
of Doncaster, lyster, and Joan his wife and their heirs and assigns, of
a messuage with the buildings thereon, and with the appurtenances,
in Doncaster, as it lies in Le Marsshegate, between the lane which
leads towards the water of Done on one side, and the messuage of
John Pynder of Barnyslay on the other; whereof one head abuts
on the messuage of Henry le milner, and the other upon the waste
(*fo.* 176) of the lord of Doncastre.   He has also given the said John
and Joan and their heirs 16d. of yearly rent with the appurtenances,
in the said vill of Doncastre, receivable from the messuages of
John Pynder, Henry le milner, John de Balne, lytster, and from
the messuage formerly Henry Gramore's, knt., namely from each
messuage 4d. yearly, at the four terms of the year appointed in
Doncastre.   To have and to hold the said messuage and rent, with
all the appurtenances, to the grantees, their heirs and assigns, well
and in peace, freely, quietly, from the chief lords of the fee, by the
services due and accustomed.   Witnesses, John Frer, Richard
Lewer, Robert de Eland, and others.   Dated at Doncaster, the
feast of All Saints, 1369.

(301)   Grant by John de Scauceby, litster, of Doncaster, to
William Pynder of Barneslay, his heirs and assigns, of a messuage
with the buildings thereon, with the appurtenances, in Doncaster,
as it lies in Le Mersshegate between the lane which leads towards

[1] The Doncaster heading continues to *fo.* 178d.

the water of Done (*fo.* 176*d*) on one side and the messuage of the said William Pynder on the other, whereof one head abuts on the messuage of the heirs of Richard Lewer, and the other on the waste of the lord of Doncaster. He has also granted to the said William and his heirs 16*d.* of yearly rent, with the appurtenances, in the said vill of Doncaster, receivable from the messuages of the heirs of John Pynder, the heirs of Richard Lewer, and of Emma, late wife of John de Balne, lytster, and from the messuage of William Waytte, namely from each messuage 4*d.* yearly, at the four terms of the year appointed in Doncaster. To have and to hold to the grantee, his heirs and assigns, freely, quietly, etc., from the chief lords of that fee, by the services due and accustomed. Witnesses. William Barbour, Robert de Eland, John Herman, and others. Dated at Doncaster, Saturday after the feast of the Apostles Peter and Paul, 15 Ric. II (1391).

(302) Grant by William Pynder of Barnisley to Thomas Luttryngton of the same, and his heirs or assigns, of all his (William's) lands and tenements, rents and services, with all the appurtenances, which (*fo.* 177) he had [or] has in the vill and within the bounds of Doncaster. To hold and to have to the grantee, his heirs and assigns, freely, wholly, etc., from the chief lords of that fee, by the services due and accustomed. Witnesses, William Barbur, Richard Herman, James Cutteler, and others. Dated at Doncaster, Sunday after the feast of St. Martin in winter, 1410.

(303) Appointment by William Pynder of Barnyslay of William Clerk of Barnisley, to deliver seisin to Thomas Luttryngton of Barnysley and his heirs or assigns, of all the lands and tenements, rents and services, with the appurtenances, lying in the vill and within the bounds of Doncaster, according to the tenor of a certain charter to the said Thomas by him (William Pynder) made. Dated at Barnysley, Sunday after the feast of St. Martin, 1410.

(*Fo.* 177*d*) (304) Grant by John son of Richard Kerysforth of Barnyslay, Thomas Chawmberlayn and Thomas Chaworth, chaplain, to Thomas Lotryngton and Isabel his wife, of a messuage with the buildings thereon, with the appurtenances, in Doncaster, as it lies in Le Marsshgate, between the lane which leads towards the water of Don on one side and the messuage late William Pynder's of Barnyslay on the other, one head abutting on the messuage late Henry Milner's and the other on the waste of the lord of Doncaster. They have likewise granted to Thomas and Isabel a certain yearly rent of 16*d.*, with the appurtenances, in Doncaster, receivable from the messuages, lands, and tenements which William Pynder of Barnislay, Henry Milner, John de Balne, lytster, Henry Gramery, knt., and their heirs, and their tenants, previously held from us and our feoffors freely in the same vill of Doncaster, namely 4*d.* from each,[1] which messuage aforesaid, together with the said rent

---

[1] Payable at " the usual terms appointed in the vill of Doncaster "—namely Easter, the Nativity of St. John, Michaelmas, and Christmas, by equal portions.

(*fo.* 178) they (the grantors) lately had, jointly with Richard Keres-forth, now deceased, by the grant of the said Thomas Lotryngton. To have and to hold the said messuage and rent, together with all the services of the said Henry Milner and the other three, and their heirs or assigns, to Thomas and Isabel and their assigns, for the life of either of them, from the chief lords of that fee, by the services due and accustomed; but so that after the death of the said Thomas Lotryngton and Isabel, the said messuage and rents, with the appurtenances, remain to William son of the said Thomas Lotryng-ton, to have and to hold to him and his assigns for his life; after his death, remainder to John son of the aforesaid Thomas for his life; after his death, remainder to Robert son of the said Thomas for his life; after his death, to Richard brother of the said Robert son of Robert[1] for his life; after his death, remainder to the prior and convent of Monkbretton, their successors and assigns; to have and to hold for a term (*fo.* 178*d*) of forty years thence next following, from the chief lords of those fees, by the services due and accustomed. And after the end of such term of forty years remainder to Edmund de Normanville of Billyngley, Adam Bate, John Normanvile, and Robert Marschall, clerk, their heirs and assigns for ever;[2]   to have and to hold from the chief lords of those fees, as before.   Witnesses, Richard Lytster, then mayor of Doncaster, William Barbor, Thomas Mysyn, and others.   Dated at Doncaster, 5 April, 1416.

Memorandum that the abovewritten John, Thomas and Thomas desire and grant that all the abovewritten tenements, rents, and services, after the death of all the above written, namely Thomas Lutryngton, Isabel his wife, William, John, Robert, Richard, his sons, remain to the prior and convent of Monkbretton and their successors for ever; doing for the soul of the said Thomas Lutryngton yearly one solemn placebo and dirige choral, and one mass choral at the high altar of the same priory, because the said John, Thomas, and Thomas were enfeoffed on that condition.

(*Fo.* 179)   *Wrangbrok.*[3]

(305)   Grant by Roger de Montbegun to God and St. Mary Magdalene of Bretton and the monks there serving God, for his soul and the soul of Adam son of Swane, and the souls of his father and mother and all his ancestors, of all his land in Wrangebroke, namely four bovates, with all the appurtenances, in wood, in plain, etc., free and quit of all secular service and exaction in pure and perpetual alms.   Witnesses, William the priest, William de Peningeston, Simon his brother, John Tyrel, Henry de Byry, and others.

(Monkbretton Chart., Lansdowne MS. 405, fo. 4.)[4]

(306)   Confirmation by Thomas de Burgo, son of Thomas de Burgo, to God and the church of St. Mary Magdalene of Bretton and

---

[1] There is some confusion here; the wording is " remaneant Ricardi fratri predicti Roberti filii *Roberti* ": the last word should presumably be " Thome."

[2] There is no limitation to the heirs of these remainder men.

[3] The Wrangbrok headings continue to *fo.* 187*d*.

[4] See *fo.* 13, No. 15 (p. 16).

the monks serving God there, freely and quietly, of whatsoever Adam son of Swane gave them, and by his charters confirmed,in pure (*fo.* 179*d*) and perpetual alms, in wood, in plain, etc., and in all things which belong to him (Thomas); saving to him and his heirs the mill of Langedene dale. He also confirms to them Carltona, with all its appurtenances, as much as to him belongs, and the church of Roreston, with all the appurtenances, as much as to him belongs, and four bovates of land in Wrangebrok, with the appurtenances, in pure and perpetual alms, which Sir William de Nevilla, his grandfather, and Amabel his wife gave the monks by their charter. This grant and confirmation he has made free from secular service. Witnesses, Richard de Alatun, Robert de Birkethwat, Garin de Thornell, and others.

(307)   Grant by Adam son of Robert de Wrangbrok to God and the blessed Mary Magdalene of Bretton and the monks there serving God, of all his land of Ravenescroft[1] as it lies in length and breadth without retention; to hold from him and his heirs for ever, freely and quietly, in fee of alms, rendering to them yearly 3*s*. sterling for all secular service and exaction. This grant (*fo.* 180) he has made to them for the health of his soul and for 4 marks and 8*d*. sterling which the monks have given him in recognition, and for 4 marks which they have given him in hand for the relief of the said land of Ravenescroft, that they may be quit of relief of that land against his heirs for ever, and that no heir of his may be able to demand anything from them for the said land except the yearly farm of 3*s*. Witnesses, Gilbert de Notton, William his son,[2] Adam de Notton, John Tyrel,˙ and others.   (Monkbretton Chart., Lansdowne MS. 405, fo. 7.)

(308)   Grant by Maurice de Askarne to God and St. Mary Magdalene of Bretton and the monks there serving God, of the rent of 3*s*. yearly which they were accustomed to render to him for a certain piece of land called Rasvenscrofte which Adam son of Robert de Wrangbrok gave them, as his charter, which they have, witnesses; wherefore he (the grantor) desires that they may have and hold the said rent as freely, quietly, and honourably as any alms may be given and held. Witnesses, Hugh le butteiller, then steward of Doncaster, John de Hec, Thomas de Hoebir, Henry de Sellesc, and many others.   (Monkbretton Chart., Lansdowne MS. 405, fo. 7*d*.)

(*Fo.* 180*d*)   (309)   Grant by Adam son of Robert de Wrangbrok to God, etc. (as above), in pure and perpetual alms, without retention, of six acres and a rood of land in the field of Wrangbruk, namely an acre and a half on Hulin beside Le Rig, and also on Hulin an acre and a half at Flaskedoles, and an acre in Midelfurland at Pype doles, in length and breadth as it is between Clifurelang and Brokfurlang; and all his land in Cheverilriding which makes two acres and a rood, which lies between Munkeflat and the land of Ralph son of Gemel, in length and breadth, as it is from the water

---

[1] " Ravenescroft " written in the margin opposite this charter.
[2] " Fil " interlined in a later hand.

as far as Midelfurlang.   Wherefore he wills that the monks may hold
and possess the said land freely, quietly, etc., as pure and perpetual
alms should be.   Witnesses, John de Schelton, Walter de Deulener,
Adam Burnel, Richard Burnell, and others.

(Monkbretton Chart., Lansdowne MS. 405, fo. 6.)

(310)   Grant by William son of (*fo.* 181) Gemel de Wrangbrok
to God, etc. (as before), of six acres of land in the fields of Wrangbrok
and of Skelbrok, in pure and perpetual alms; namely in the field of
Wrangbrok the land which lies between that of the monks and Ralph
the grantor's brother at Meneland, and the land at Swalh which lies
between Ralph and Reiner, and one rood of land on the hill which
lies between William de Horncastell and Adam Jubbe and his (the
grantor's) land which lies on the hill beside the monks towards the
west at Long Acre, and one rood between Adam Jubbe and Adam
son of Godfrey and his (the grantor's) land which he held beside
the monks near Ravenescroft towards the north.   And in the field
of Schalebrok three roods which he (the grantor) had at his part
beside Waterfall, and half an acre to the south[1] at Waterfall, and an
acre which he had next beside the street, and a rood which lies
between [the land of] his brothers, Adam and Ralph, as he held it
in length and breadth.   Witnesses, John Wacelin, Gilbert de
Notton, William son of Adam, Walter Deuener, and others.

(Monkbretton Chart., Lansdowne MS. 405, fo. 10.)

(311)   Grant by William son of Gamel de Wrangbrok to the
monks of Bretton of an acre of land in Wrangbrok, namely half an
acre which is next to the house of the said monks towards the west,
and another half acre next to their culture which is called Rydinges
towards the north; rendering to him and his heirs 2*d.* yearly for all
service.   Witnesses, William son of Adam, Adam de Rainevilla,
and others.

(Monkbretton Chart., Lansdowne MS. 405, fo. 10.)

(*Fo.* 181*d*) (312) Confirmation by Adam son of Roger de Wrangbrok
to God and blessed Mary Magdalene of Bretton and the monks there
serving God, of all lands, possessions, and rents, with all the appurtenances, in pure and perpetual alms, which they have by the gift of
William son of Gamel de Wrangbrok, his grandfather, or by any of
his ancestors to the said monks given or conveyed.   Moreover he
(Adam) has given to them in pure and perpetual alms the yearly rent
of 2*d.* which they were accustomed to render him for an acre of land,
which his said grandfather gave them as by his charter, which they
have, witnesses.   Witnesses, John de Flynthill, John Bysette, and
others.

(Monkbretton Chart., Lansdowne MS. 405, fo. 12.)

(313)   Quitclaim by Peter de Hornecastell to the prior and convent (*fo.* 182) of Bretton, of half a bovate of land in Wrangbrok, that
namely which he held in demesne from Garvase Pulam; free and
quit of all service and all action [and] claim by him and his heirs.

[1] The wording is "propinginorem poli," the latter word being, I think,
a mistake for " soli."

For this quitclaim the prior and convent have given him 24s. Witnesses, Garvase Pulan, William de Sumerevile, William son of Gamell, and others.   (Monkbretton Chart., Lansdowne MS. 405, fo. 8d.)

(314) Confirmation by Garvase Pulann of Wrangbrok to the prior and convent of Bretton, of the sale to them by Peter de Hornecastell of half a bovate of land in Wrangbrok which he held in demesne from Garvase. Witnesses, Peter Hornecastell, Ralph his son, Richard Pulain, and others.

(Monkbretton Chart., Lansdowne MS. 405, fo. 8d.)

(315) Grant[1] by John Jubbe of Wrangbrok and Richard Jubbe of Upton to John Pullene of Wrangbrok of a tenement in Wrangbrok built on as it lies between the cottage of the nuns of Hampole on the west and the land of Peter de la Hay on the east, and extends to the beck of the said vill towards the south, together with twelve acres of arable land lying in (fo. 182d) the fields and territory of Wrangbrok, Slepill, and Skelbrok; whereof one acre lies in Haverlands between the land of John Bargan on the north and the land of the monks of Bretton on the south, and a rood of land lies in the same field between the land of John Jubbe on the west and the land of John Wodward on the east, another half acre lies in Mykilffurland between the land of William Lord on the west and the land of the said monks on the east, one rood lies in the same culture between the land of the said monks on the west and the land of William Shepherd on the east, another half acre lies in Le Estfeld between the land of William Bargan on either side, and one rood lies in the same culture between the land of John Jubbe on the west and the land of the said monks on the east, half a rood lies in the same field between the land of the said monks on either side, one acre [lies] in the same culture between the land of John Haitfeld on the west and the land of John Wodward on the east, half an acre lies in the same culture between the land of William Lord on the west and the land of William Bargan on the east, one acre lies between the land of the said monks on the north and the land of John Adamson on the south, half an acre lies in the same field between the land of William Bargan on the north and the land of the said monks on the south, one acre lies in the same culture between the land of the prioress of Hampall on the north and the land of William Lord on the south, half an acre lies in the same field between the land of the said monks on either side, half an acre lies in Slephill between the land of the said prioress on the west and the land of Richard Slephill on the east and abuts on Lynges of Skelbrok, half an acre lies in the same field between the land of John Adamson on the west and the land of the prioress on the east and abuts on Le Lynges aforesaid, half an acre lies in the same culture between the land of William Lord on the west and the land of Reginald Pullayne on the east and abuts on the aforesaid Lynges and upon the stone of Robert Hode[2] towards

---

[1] " Terra Johannis Pulleyne " written in the margin.

[2] A well, about six miles north of Doncaster, and half a mile east of Skelbrook, on the old north road. In the reign of Henry VII it was known, as it still is, by the name of Robin Hood's Well.

the north, an acre (*fo.*183) lies in the same field between the land of the said prioress on the west and the common land on the east and abuts upon their (the grantors') land towards the north, half an acre lies in the same field between the land of William Calthorn on the south and the land of the lord of Skelbrok on the north and abuts on their (the grantors') land towards the west, half an acre lies in the same field between the land of William Calthorn on the north and the land of the said lord on the north [*sic*] and abuts on the King's highway towards the east, half an acre lies between the land of William Calthorn on the north and the land of John Janyn on the south and abuts on the same highway to the east.[1] To hold and to have to the said John Pulayne for his life, freely, quietly, etc., from the chief lords of that fee, by the services due and accustomed, rendering thence yearly to the lord of Burghwaleis 5*d.* and to the prior of Bretton 3*s.* 7*d.* And after the death of the said John, remainder to John his son and the heirs of his body; and if he shall die without such heir, remainder to the right heirs of John Polayne for ever. Witnesses, John Wentworth of Elmesall, William Lorde of Wrangbrok, Richard de Wrangbrok, and others. Dated at Wrangbrok, Sunday in the feast of Holy Trinity, 1322.[2]

(*Fo.* 183*d*) (316) Grant by John Jubbe of Wrangbrok to John Pullayne of Wrangbrok of a tenement built in Wrangbrok, as it lies between the cottage of the nuns of Hampolle on the west and the land of Peter Dalahay on the east, and extends to the beck of the same vill towards the south, and sixteen acres of arable land as they lie in the various fields and territories of Wrangbrok, Sclephill, and Skelbrok. To have and to hold with all the appurtenances, to the grantee, his heirs and assigns, freely, quietly, etc., from the chief lords of that fee, by the services due and accustomed. Witnesses, John Wentworth of North Elmsal, esquire, William Lord of Wrangbrok, Richard Bargen of the same, and others. Dated at Wrangbrok, the feast of the Assumption of the blessed Virgin Mary, 8 Hen. V (15 August, 1420).

(317) Grant by John Pulan of Wrangbrok to William Wadelufe and John Ellis of a messuage lying in Wrangbrok between the tenement of the prioress of (*fo.* 184) Hampole on the west and the land late Peter de la Hay's on the east, and sixteen acres and three roods of land lying separately in the fields of Wrangbrok, with the appurtenances. To have and to hold to the grantees, their heirs and assigns, for ever, from the chief lords of that fee, by the services due and accustomed. Witnesses, Thomas Oxspryng, Thomas Lord, Thomas Clayton, and others. Dated at Wrangbrok, 24 April, 2 Hen. VII (1487).

(318) Release and quitclaim by William Wadelouffe to the prior and convent of Monkbretton of all right, title, etc., of and in all those messuages, lands and tenements, meadows and pastures,

---

[1] The quantities specified do not exactly amount to twelve acres.
[2] " Miřo III^{mo} vicesimo secundo," but undoubtedly a mistake for 1422.

with the appurtenances, in the vills and territories of Wrangebrok, Slephill, and Skelbrok; which he (William) lately had, together with John Ellis now deceased, by the grant of John Pullan. (*Fo.* 184*d*) Dated at Monkbretton, 20 January, 12 Hen. VII (1496-7).

(319)   Release and quitclaim by William Pullayne, son and heir of a certain John Pollayne of Wrangbrok, deceased, to Thomas, prior of Monkbretton, and the convent thereof, of all right, claim, etc., of and in a tenement and twelve acres of arable land, with the appurtenances, in Wrangbrok, Slephill, and Skelbrok in the County of York, which are more fully set forth in a certain ancient charter of feoffment made thereof by John Jubbe and Richard Jubbe of Upton, to a certain John Polayne, ancestor of the said William Polayne. To have and to hold to the grantees and their successors for ever. Dated 13 January, 10 Hen. VIII (1518-9).

(*Fo.* 185) (320[1]) All men beying present her and for to cum shall knawe that I John Pullan of Wrangbrok have gyffyn and grantyd and have maid faste by my present writyng to John Pullan, my son, his heres and assignes, vj acres and a rode of arebill land os it lyes in divers places of the felds of Wrangbrok. In Primis the croke acre lyes next ye meis (messuage) of Joh. Grason of ye west party and next ye meis of Oliver Byard of ye est part and butts of ye hy gait of ye sowth part of ye rynyng broke of ye north part. And a rode lyes next ye mes of prior of bretton abba of the west part and est part bothe. An a halff acre butt of ye hare hill of ye nort part and of ye sayd prior of ye sowthe and of Thomas lord of ye west part and est part bothe. And a rode at ye blake rawe and butts off Arthur Wentworthe of ye west part and of John Grason of ye north part and of the sayd prior of ye est part and sowthe part bothe. And a nacer [*sic*] in the est feylde callyd Gowers butts of barnysdale ryg of ye est part and of thomas Lorde of the sowthe part and of ye said prior of ye north part and west bothe. And a nacer butts of ye sayd prior of ye north and of ye heris [*sic*] of Xpofer Wilkok of ye sowth part and of William Gascone of ye est part. And three rodes butts of Thomas Lorde of ye north and of ye sayd prior of ye sothe [*sic*] and west part bothe. And a nacer in ye mor croft bounded of ye lyngs of birton abba of ye est part and of ye heres of ye roklesses and William gascone of ye west part and of ye said prior of ye north part and of ye heres and rokeless of ye sowth part. And a halffe acre lyes in ye Haverlands and bonds of the by stret of ye est part and of ye sayd prior bothe north and west and of said William gascone of ye sowth. The forsaid six acre and a rode wt all ye appurtenace yto (*fo.* 185*d*) belongyng to be had and to be holden to John Pullan the yunger to his heirs and assignes. Warranty, seal. Witnesses, William Wode, Oliver Heryson, Thomas Lorde, and other mo. Gyffyn at Wrangbrok. In ye fest of Sent Michall ye archangell, in the yere of reyng of King Edward IV after ye conquest of yngland the eighth yere (1468).

---

[1] This document is in English.

(321)   Grant by William Pullan of Barmbe on Don, son and heir of a certain John Pullan of Wrangbrok, lately deceased, to Thomas Montney and Thomas Oxspring, gentleman, of six acres and a rood of arable land, with the appurtenances, lying separately in the territories of Wrangbrok and Skelbrok.   To have and to hold to the grantees, their heirs and assigns, from the chief lords of those fees, by the services due and accustomed.   Appointment of Robert Darlay of Ardyslay and Robert Hawme of Wrangbrok as attorneys (*fo.* 186) to deliver seisin.   Witnesses, Richard Amyas, Richard Nicolls, John Darley, and many others.   Dated at Wrangbrok, 5 January, 5 Hen. VIII (1513–4).

(322)   Release and quitclaim by William Pullan of Barnby upon Don in the County of York, milner, son and heir of a certain John Pullan of Wrangbrok, deceased, to Thomas Montney and Thomas Oxspryng, of all right, title, claim, etc., of and in all those six acres and a rood of land, with the appurtenances, in the territories of Wrangbrok, Slephill, and Skelbrok, which he (William) lately had by hereditary right after the death of his said father.   (*Fo.* 186*d*) Witnesses, Sir (*domino*) John Adde, chaplain, Robert Vicars, Robert Marsche, and others.   Dated at Wrangbrok, 6 January, 5 Hen. VIII (1513–4).

(323)   Release and quitclaim by Thomas Montney and Thomas Oxspryng in the County of York, gentlemen, to Thomas, prior of Monkbretton, and the convent thereof and their successors, of all right, claim, etc., of and in all those six acres and a rood of land, with the appurtenances, in the territories of Wrangbrok, Slephill, and Skelbrok, which they lately had by the grant of William Pullan of Barmby upon Dune.   (*Fo.* 187) Dated at Monkbretton, 20 March, 5 Hen. VIII (1513–4).

(324)   Grant by John Adamson of Wrangbrok and Joan his wife to   John Woderofe, Hugh de Wombwell, Sirs (*dominis*) Thomas de Wollveley, John Mason, and John Doudale, chaplains, of all their (the grantor's) messuages, built on and not built on, together with all their lands and tenements, rents, services, and all other appurtenances, which they lately had in Wrangbrok and Slephyll and the fields thereof.   To hold and to have to the grantees, their heirs and assigns, freely, quietly, etc., from the chief lords of that fee, by the services due and accustomed.   Witnesses, John de Wentworth, John Ouston, Thomas Sampule, and others.   Dated at Wrangbrok, 10 May, 14 Ric. II (1391).

(*Fo.* 187*d*) (325)   Licence by John de Depedene, knight, and the lady Elizabeth his wife, to Thomas de Wollay, chaplain, to grant to the prior and convent of Monkbretton and their successors, for ever, a messuage and five acres of land, with the appurtenances, in Wrangbrok, which are held from them in right of the said Elizabeth, and to the prior and convent to receive the same, the statute of Mortmain notwithstanding, saving to them, their heirs and assigns, the services due and accustomed.   Dated 6 September, 16 Ric. II (1392).

(326)   A similar licence by John de Wentworth to Thomas Wollay, chaplain, to grant three acres of land, with the appurtenances, in Wrangbrok, held from him, to the same grantees.   Same date.

(*Fo.* 188) (327) Grant by Thomas de Wollvelay, chaplain, by licence of King Richard and of all mediate interests, to the prior and convent of Monkbretton, of all his messuages, built on and not built on, with all his lands and tenements, rents and services, and all other appurtenances, formerly belonging to John Adamson and Joan his wife, in Wrangbrok and Slephill and the fields thereof.   To have and to hold to the grantees and their successors for ever, freely, quietly, etc., from the chief lords of the fee, by the services, due and accustomed.   Witnesses, John de Winteworth, John de Auston, Thomas Sampaule, and others.   Dated at Wrangbrok, Friday before Michaelmas, Anno dom. mill. nonagesimo secundo [1092 *sic*] et anno regni dom. Regis Ricardi secundi post conquestum Anglie sexto decimo (1392).[1]

(*Fo.* 188*d*)   *Newhall.*[2]

(328)   Grant by Robert de Wath, clerk, and Juliana his wife, to Philip de Bosevile of six and a half acres of arable land in the fields of Newhale in the place called Terre Rodes; they have also given him all their meadow in the said vill of Newhale as it lies in length and breadth in divers places, namely in Le Schepenker, Calverode, and Longyngs.   To have and to hold, with the appurtenances, to the grantee, his heirs and assigns, from the chief lords of that fee, by the services due and accustomed yearly, freely, quietly, etc. Witnesses, Stephen de Bella Aqua, Godfrey de Staynton, and others.

(329)   Grant by Robert de Wath, clerk, and Juliana his wife, to Philip de Boswel, of an acre of land, with the appurtenances, in Newhal, which used to be a toft and a croft lying between the land of the prior of Bretton on either (*fo.* 189) [side] and abutting on Newhale Green towards the west.   To have and to hold from the chief lords of that fee to the grantee, his heirs and assigns, freely, quietly, etc., with all appurtenances, commons, and easements belonging to the said land within and without the said vill, doing to the said chief lords the services due and accustomed.   Witnesses, Godfrey de Staynton, William de Notton, and others.

(330)   Quitclaim by Adam son of Robert Broun of Wath, clerk, to the prior and convent of Monkbretton of all right and claim in the properties described in the two foregoing deeds, " all which they (the prior and convent) had by the gift of the said Robert my father and Juliana my mother."   (*Fo.* 189*d*) Witnesses, Sir Philip de Bosewell, chaplain, William his brother, and others.   Dated at Monkbretton, the feast of St. Augustine, Bishop of the English, 1343.

---

[1] There is a discrepancy in these two dates.   The latter one is correct.

[2] The heading "Newhall" continues to *fo.* 195*d*.   *Fo.* 189*d* is headed " Newhall Brampton ":   Newhall, in Brampton Bierlaw.

(331)   Grant by Robert son of Peter de Wath to Philip de Bosewill of a yearly rent of 5*d*., with the appurtenances, in Melton in
Brampton, receivable as to 4*d*. from Juliana daughter of William
Tebaud for a messuage and three roods of land which she held from
him in the same vill, and as to a penny from Thomas Haliday for the
land which he held from Peter the grantor's father and from the
grantor in the same vill; together with all the services of the said
Juliana and Thomas and their heirs, which they were accustomed to
do to him and his ancestors.   To hold and to have to the grantee,
his heirs and assigns, from the chief lords of that fee, freely, quietly,
etc., with all the appurtenances, as in homages, reliefs, etc., doing
to the said chief lords the services thence due and accustomed.
Witnesses, Godfrey de Staynton, Edmund de Percy, and others.

(*Fo.* 190)   (332)   Grant by William de Melton beside Wath to John
de Birthwait, junior, and Thomas Cotyngham, of an annual rent of
2*s.* 9*d.*, receivable from those tenements in Newhal in Brampton
beside Wath which were John Schephird's there, namely from a
messuage and six acres and a rood of land, which tenements William
Stele and Alice his wife, Adam Nelder and Agnes his wife, John
Trugge and Elisota his wife, Robert Gene, John Bobker, William
del Abdy, and Robert Pety, held from the grantor on the day when
these presents were made.   To have and to hold to the grantees,
their heirs and assigns, well and in peace, from the chief lords of that
fee by the services due and accustomed, together with homages,
fealties, and all other services of the said William, Alice, etc. (the
holders above named), and their heirs, which they were bound to
do to him (the grantor) for the said tenements with wardships,
marriages, etc., when they fall.   Witnesses, John del Wodhall, and
others.   Dated at Bretton, the eve of All Saints, 34 Edw. III (1360).

(333)   Grant by John son of Katerine de Brampton beside Wath
to Thomas de Cotyngham, his heirs and assigns, of the reversion of
all the lands and meadows which Henry son of Walter de Melton and
Alice his wife hold from him (the grantor) for term of their lives
(*fo.* 100*d*) as they lie in length and breadth in the fields of Brampton
beside Wath, in a certain place called Terreroyds, within the fee and
lordship of the prior and convent of Monkbretton.   To have and to
hold the said reversion, with all the appurtenances, to the grantee,
his heirs and assigns, freely, quietly, etc., from the chief lords of that
fee by the services due and accustomed.   Witnesses, William de
Wyntworth and others.   Dated at Brampton beside Wath, Wednesday after the feast of the Assumption of the blessed Virgin Mary,
35 Edw. III (1361).

(334)   Grant by John son of Robert de Wath to Thomas de
Cotyngham of four acres of land in Smeythecroft in the fields of
Newall, abutting on Grewalebroke and lying between the demesne
land of the prior and convent of Monkbretton on either side.   To
have and to hold, with all the appurtenances, to the grantee, his
heirs and assigns, from the chief lords of that fee, by the services

due and accustomed. Witnesses, (*fo.* 191) Roger Bacon of Wath, John Sayvill of the same, and others. Dated at Wath, Friday in the feast of St. Petronilla virgin, 1364.

(335) Grant by Richard Whitte of Erdyslay to Thomas de Wolveley, chaplain, his heirs and assigns, of five acres of land, with all the appurtenances, as they lie together within the bounds of Newhall between the land of the prior and convent of Monkbretton on the south and Newallane on the north, which five acres he (Richard) had by the grant of Thomas de Wodhall of Wath. To have and to hold to the grantee, his heirs and assigns, freely, quietly, etc., from the chief lord of that fee, by the services due and accustomed. Witnesses, Robert de Hesilheved, and others. Dated at Newhall, Tuesday after the feast of St. Matthew Apostle and Evangelist, 1092.[1]

(*Fo.* 191*d*) (336) Licence by Thomas Flemmyng, knt., lord of Wath, to Thomas de Wollay, chaplain, to grant to the prior and convent of Monkbretton and their successors, for ever, five acres of land, with the appurtenances, as they lie together within the bounds of Newall, which are held from him, and to the prior and convent to receive them. To hold to them and their successors for ever, the statute of Mortmain notwithstanding, saving to him and his heirs the services due and accustomed. Dated 24 September, 16 Ric. II (1392).

(337) Grant by Thómas de Wolvelay, chaplain, by licence of the King and of all mediate interests, to the prior and convent of Monkbretton, of five acres of land, with all the appurtenances, as they lie together within the bounds of Newhall between the land of the said prior and convent on the south and Newallane on the north, and which he (Thomas) had by the gift and feoffment of Richard Whitte of Erdyslay. To have and to hold to the grantees and their successors for ever, freely, quietly, etc., from the chief (*fo.* 192) lord of that fee, by the services due and accustomed. Witnesses, Robert Hesilhed, William de Melton, and others. Dated at Newhall, Thursday before Michaelmas, anno dm̃ millo nonagesimo secundo [1092 *sic*] et anno regni dom. regis Richardi secundi post conquest. sexto decimo (1392).

(338) Release[2] and quitclaim by John Crecy, son and heir of William Crecy, to Thomas Tikihill [*sic*], prior of the monastery of the blessed Mary Magdalene of Monkbretton, and the convent and their successors for ever, of all right, claim, etc., of or in all those messuages, lands, tenements, rents, and services, with all the appurtenances, in Newhall, Wath, and Brampton, now in possession of the said prior. (*Fo.* 192*d*) Witnesses, John Wombwell, gentleman, Thomas Lyster, counsellor at law, and others. Dated 10 June, 21 Hen. VII (1506).

---

[1] *Sic;* a mistake for 1392: a caret mark is inserted after the word " millesimo," but the correction was not made.

[2] " Cresy land " written in the margin.

(339)   Grant by John Cressy of Wath in the County of York to Brian Bradforthe, senior, and Thomas Oxspryng, of three acres of land, with the appurtenances, in Newhall by Wath aforesaid, as they lie in a place called Terrerods, otherwise called Qwitleys, whereof one acre lies within the land of the prior of Monkbretton on either side, one head abutting on the land of the same prior called Tastardyng towards the south, and the other head on the land of the same prior towards the north, and another acre lies between the land of the same prior on either side, one head abutting on the land formerly John Pope's called Tasterdyng towards the south, and the other head abutting on the land of the same prior called Brodhyng towards the north, and the third acre lies between the land of the same prior on either side called Brodhyng and Monkker, one head abutting on the aforesaid land called Terrerods towards the south, and the other on Brodyng aforesaid towards the north.   To have and to hold to the grantees, their heirs and assigns, for ever, from the chief lords of those fees, by the services due and accustomed. (*Fo.*193) Dated 24 December, 2 Hen. VIII (1510).

(340)   Grant by John Cressy of Wath to Thomas Oxspryng and Richard Nicholls of an acre of land, with the appurtenances, in Newhall by Wath, as it lies in a certain place called Mylneflatts between the lands of the prior of Monkbretton on every side.   To have and to hold to the grantees, their heirs and assigns, for ever, from the chief lords of those fees, by the services due and accustomed.   Dated 27 January, 2 Hen. VIII (1510–11).

(341)   Release and quitclaim by John Cressy of Wath to Thomas Oxspryng and Richard Nicholls, their heirs and assigns, for ever, of all right, title, claim, etc., of and (*fo.* 193*d*) in the acre of land named in the preceding deed.   Dated 28 January, 2 Hen. VIII (1510–11).

(342)   Release and quitclaim by Thomas Oxspryng to the prior and convent of Monkbretton and their successors for ever, of all right, title, claim, etc., of and in three acres of land, with the appurtenances, in Newhall, as they lie in a place called Terrerods otherwise called Qwitleis, which acres, with the appurtenances, he lately had jointly with Brian Bradford; and in another acre of land, with the appurtenances, in Newhall, as it lies in a certain place called Milneflats, which he lately had jointly with Richard Nicholls deceased, by the grant of John Cressy.   Dated 10 August, 5 Hen. VIII (1513).

(343)   Grant by John Cressy, (*fo.* 194) gentleman, to Thomas Oxspryng and Richard Nicholls of an acre of land lying in a place called Qwitleis belonging to the manor of Newhall, between the land of the prior and convent of Monkbretton, now in the tenure of Thomas Mountney, on either side, abutting on the meadow called Popeyng towards the south and on the land late John Abdy's and late John Tynlay's towards the north, with the appurtenances, in Newhall. To have and to hold to the grantees, their heirs and assigns, for ever, from the chief lords of that fee, by the services due and accustomed. Dated at Newhall, 14 August, 3 Hen. VIII (1511).

(344) Release and quitclaim by John Cressy, gentleman, to Thomas Oxspryng and Richard Nicholls, their heirs and assigns, for ever, of all right, title, claim, etc., of and in the acre of land and appurtenances named in the preceding deed[1] (described as before). (*Fo.* 194*d*) Dated 16 August, 3 Hen. VIII (1511).

(345) Release and quitclaim by Thomas Oxspryng and Richard Nicholls to Thomas, prior of Monkbretton, and the convent thereof and their successors, for ever, of all right, title, claim, etc., in the acre, with the appurtenances (described as before), which they had by the grant of John Cressy, gentleman. Dated 10 March, 4 Hen. VIII (1512–13).

(*Fo.* 195) (346) Release and quitclaim by William Cressy, brother and next heir apparent of John Cressy, to Thomas Thykhill, prior of Monkbretton, and the convent thereof and their successors, for ever, of all right, title, etc., of and in all those messuages, lands, tenements, rents, and services, with the appurtenances, in Newhall, Melton, Wath, Brampton, and Raynber, now in possession of the said prior. Witnesses, Thomas Roklay, esquire, John Baxster, gentleman, Robert Roklay, with others. Dated at Monkbretton, 5 August, 4 Hen. VIII (1512).

(347) To all the faithful, etc., John Brome of Brampton, greeting. Whereas William Faueborne lately held to himself and his heirs freely, by charter, certain lands and tenements in Brampton aforesaid, and also held and occupied for a term of years a moiety of one bovate of land in the same, containing nine acres of land called Hareoxgange, by the demise of the prior of Monkbretton, which aforesaid lands and tenements held freely William Fauceborne alienated to me the said John Brome, among which lands there remained three acres and one rood of land not separated, parcel of the aforesaid (*fo.* 195*d*) moiety of a bovate of land, of which three acres and one rood a rood lies in a certain field called Cliffeld in one selion between the land of John Wombwell called Hurelthyng on the west and the land of the aforesaid prior on the east and abuts upon Powreyngwelle towards the south and on the land of Robert West to the north, two roods lie separately in a certain field called Wyntwelfeld in two selions upon Maresdalebuttes, of which one rood lies between the land of the said prior on the east and the land of John Darley on the west and abuts on the land of John Wombwell to the north and south, the other rood lies in the same space between the land of the said prior on the west and the land of William Spencer on the east and abuts on the land of John Wombwell at the south end and north end, two acres and a rood lie separately in a certain field called Westefelde, namely three roods together lie in three selions between the land of the said prior on the east and the land of William Spencer on the west and abut on Hurelecroft towards the north and on Foredolegate to the south, half an acre lies in the same

---

[1] " Whiteleys " instead of " Qwitleis " in this deed. In the following deed it is " Wyitleys."

field in a certain space called Agane the Cryste between the land late Richard Petty's on the east and the land of John Wombwell on the west and abuts on Crosseslake to the south, half an acre lies in the same space in one selion between the land of John Wombwell on the east and the land of the said prior on the west and abuts on Crosseslake on the south, half an acre lies in the same space in one selion between the land of the said prior on either side and abuts on Crosseslake on the south,—Know that I the said John Brome have released and quitclaimed to Richard Ledes, the prior, and the convent of the house (*fo.* 196) of the blessed Mary Magdalene of Monkbretton and their successors for ever, all right, title, etc., of and in the said three acres and one rood[1] as parcel of the said moiety of a bovate of land, with the appurtenances, in Brampton.   Seals of John Brome and the prior to the alternate parts of this writing indentate. Witnesses, Thomas Oxspring, Richard West, John Darlay, and others.   Dated 12 August, 14 Edw. IV (1474).

West Melton.[2]

(348)   Grant[3] by Alice Spenser of Adwik, daughter and heir of Hugh Spenser late of the same, deceased, to John, earl of Salop, of all her lands and tenements, meadows, pastures, rents, and services, with all the appurtenances, lying in the vill and fields of West Melton, which descended to her by hereditary right after the death of her said father.   (*Fo.* 196*d*)[4] To have and to hold to the said John, his heirs and assigns, for ever, to the behoof and use of Thomas Chamber, son of Richard Chambyr, from the chief lords of that fee, by the services due and accustomed.   Witnesses, John Wytton of Adwyk, chaplain, Richard Wade of the same, John Lownde of the same, and others.   Dated at Adwyk aforesaid, 7 January, 11 Edw. IV (1471-2).

(349)   Delivery and demise by Gorge, earl of Salop, to Thomas Chawmber of Rotherham, of all those lands and tenements, meadows, pastures, rents, reversions, and services, with the appurtenances, which John late earl of Salop, his father, had by the grant and feoffment of Alice Spenser late of Adwyk, daughter and heir of Hugh Spenser late of the same, deceased, in the vills and fields of the same aforesaid and West Melton.   To have and to hold to the grantee, his heirs and assigns, freely, quietly, etc., from the chief lords of those fees, by the services due and accustomed.   Appointment of Thomas Ellerton and William Gurre, senior, as attorneys (*fo.* 197) to deliver seisin.   Witnesses, Thomas Okes of Adwyke, and others.   Dated at Adwyke aforesaid, 26 October, 9 Hen. VII (1493).

(350)   Release and quitclaim by George, earl of Salop, to Thomas Chambyr of Rotherham of all right, title, etc., in tenements, lands,

---

[1] The specifications do not seem quite to amount to that quantity.
[2] Near Wath-on-Dearne.
[3] In the margin is written "terra Thome Chamber in Melton."
[4] The heading is "West Melton," which continues to *fo.* 200*d*.

etc. (as in the last deed), in the vill and fields of West Melton, which lately John earl of Salop, his father, had by the grant of Alice Spenser (as before). (*Fo.* 197*d*) Dated 2c November, 9 Hen. VII (1493).

(351) Grant by Thomas Chambir of Rotherham to Thomas Oxspryng and Richard Nicholls of a messuage built in West Melton, with the toft and croft adjacent, containing two acres of land, as it lies between the messuage of Robert West on the east and the land of the lord prior and convent of Monkbretton on the west, and five acres of land and meadow to the same messuage belonging, as they lie separately within the fields of West Melton aforesaid, whereof two and a half acres of land lie in the Westfield, an acre lies in Le Rawes, half an acre of land lies in Wynterwelfeld, half an acre of land lies in Wolthawyte, a rood lies in Colysmore, and a rood of meadow lies in town ende close, with the appurtenances in West Melton. To have and to hold to the grantees, their heirs and assigns, for ever, from the chief lord of that fee, by the services due and accustomed. Witnesses, John Wombwell, esquire, Thomas Montnay, and others. Dated at West Melton aforesaid, 16 October, 3 Hen. VIII (1511).

(*Fo.* 198) (352) Release and quitclaim by Thomas Chambir of Rotheram to Thomas Oxspryng and Richard Nicols, their heirs and assigns, for ever, of all right, title, and claim of and in the property described in the previous deed.[1] Dated 18 October, 3 Hen. VIII (1511).

(353) Release and quitclaim by John Chambyr, son and heir of Thomas Chambyr of Rotheram, (*fo.* 198*d*) to Thomas Oxspryng and Richard Nicols, their heirs and assigns, for ever, of all right, title, and claim in one messuage built in West Melton, with toft and croft adjacent, etc. (as in the previous deed). Date as in previous deed.

(354) Release and quitclaim by Thomas Oxspryng and Richard Nicols of Barnysley to Thomas, prior of Monkbretton, and the convent thereof and their successors for ever, of all right, title, and claim of and in a messuage built in West Melton, with toft and croft, etc. (described as in the last deed but two).[2] (*Fo.* 199) Dated 10 May, 4 Hen. VIII (1512).

(355) Grant by Thomas Chambur of Rotheram to Thomas, prior of Monkbretton, and the convent thereof and their successors for ever, of a messuage, five acres and three roods of land, and a rood (*fo.* 199*d*) of meadow, with the appurtenances, in West Melton in the parish of Wath on Derne, which were lately William Spenser's, son of Hugh Spenser. To have and to hold to the grantees for ever, from the chief lord of that fee, by the services due and accustomed. Dated 3 June, 5 Hen. VIII (1513).

[1] In this deed the locations of the five acres are not given at length as in the former deed, " etc." being substituted.

[2] In this deed " Wolthwaite " instead of " Wolthawyte," and " Coylys more " instead of " Colysmore." The property is stated to be that which the grantors had by the gift of Thomas Chambur, of Rotheram.

(356)   Release and quitclaim by John Baxter of Bolton, esquire, to Thomas, prior of Monkbretton, and the convent thereof and their successors for ever, of all right, title, etc., of and in a messuage, five acres and three roods of land, and a rood of meadow, with the appurtenances, in West Melton by Wath on Derne, which the said prior and convent lately had by the gift and feoffment of Thomas Chamber of Rotheram, and which were late the property of William Spenser, son of Hugh Spenser.   Dated 5 June, 1513, 5 Hen. VIII.

(*Fo.* 200) (357) Grant[1] by William Lounde to Thomas Oxspryng and Richard Nicols of two acres of land lying together in the fields of West Melton between the land late John Abdy's on the west and the land called Blannchelande on the east, and abutting on the toft of the said William Launde towards the south and on the land of John Wombwell towards the north, with the appurtenances, in West Melton.   To have and to hold to the grantees, their heirs and assigns, for ever, from the chief lords of that fee, by the services due and accustomed.   Witnesses, John Wombwell, esquire, Thomas Mountnay, and others.   Dated at West Melton, 21 November, 3 Hen. VIII (1511).

(358)   Release and quitclaim by William Launde (*fo. 200d*) to Thomas Oxspryng and Richard Nicols, their heirs and assigns, for ever, of all right, title, etc., of and in two acres of land described in the preceding deed.   Dated at West Melton, 24 November, 3 Hen. VIII (1511).

(359)   Release and quitclaim by John Launde, son and heir of the late William Launde, to Thomas Oxspryng and Richard Nicols, their heirs and assigns, for ever, of all right, title, etc., of and in the same two acres of land.   (*Fo.* 201) Dated at Monkbretton, 4 September, 8 Hen. VIII (1516).

(360)   Release and quitclaim by Thomas Oxspryng and Richard Nicols to Thomas, prior of Monkbretton, and the convent thereof and their successors for ever, of all right, title, claim, etc., of and in two acres of land which they (the grantors) had by the grant of William Launde, as they lie in the fields of West Melton (described as in the previous deeds).   (*Fo.* 201d)[2] Dated at West Melton, 24 November, 4 Hen. VIII (1512).

Wyntworth.

(361)   Grant by John son of Aisolf, with the consent and counsel of his wife and his heirs, to God and Saint Mary Magdelene of Bretton and the monks there serving God, of all his tenement below the road[3] in Wyntworth, with the appurtenances, which Hugh son of Henry held from him, and the service of that tenement which he

---

[1] " Lounde lande " written in the margin.

[2] Headed " Wyntworth " here and on *fo.* 202d.

[3] Hunter (*South Yorkshire*, ii, 79) refers to this tenement as " Underway," and mentions an old manor house at Wentworth, nearly opposite the chapel, which he believed to have been the original Underway.

(John) did to Adam son of Swane, lord of Newhall, namely homage, suit of Court from three weeks to three weeks, with a plough in Lent and a reaper in autumn, without retention, in pure and perpetual alms. Witnesses, Jordan son of Aisolf, Thomas his brother, Richard son of Jordan son of Aisolf, William son of Thomas son of Aisolf, Michael and John his brother,[1] William de Nosmarche and others.   (Monkbretton Chart., Lansdowne MS. 405, fo. 28*d*.)

(*Fo.* 202) (362) Grant by the prior and convent of Bretton to William son of William de Winteworth and his heirs, of all their (the convent's) tenement below the road in Winteworth, with the lands, meadows, pastures, and all other appurtenances, within and without the vill which John son of Aisolf gave them (the grantors), with all common and other easements to the said vill belonging, in wood, in plain, etc., rendering to the grantors yearly, and to their successors, 6s. of silver, with homage, suit of Court at Neualla from three weeks to three weeks, with two boonworks, together with a plough in Lent and a reaper in autumn, and with divers riding-horses and lodgings for guests to be taken with them (the grantors) to Synods and Convocations.   To have and to hold to the grantee and his heirs for ever.   Witnesses, Henry de Nosmerche, Robert de Wodhouse, Richard de Kelwik, Roger de Bretton, and others.

(363)   Agreement (*fo.* 202*d*) between Roger, prior, and the monks of Bretton, and William son of William de Wentworth, namely that the prior and monks have demised and quitclaimed to the said William and his heirs for ever one yearly entertainment (*hospicium annuum*) and the riding-horses which they were demanding from him according to custom; respecting which a dispute was raised between the said parties, in the Court of Neuhale.   For this demise and quitclaim William and his heirs will pay to the house of Bretton for ever 2s. 6d. yearly, saving all other services and rents which William and his heirs are bound to render to the prior and monks.   Witnesses, Sir Henry de Novomarcato, Reiner de Wambwell, Robert de Wodehuse, William son of William de Wath, and others.
(Monkbretton Chart., Lansdowne MS. 405, fo. 31.)

(364)   Indenture witnessing that the prior and convent of Monkbretton have granted and demised to John son of Robert de Wodhall and Alice his wife all that tenement in the vill of Wyntworth as it lies and is contained within the bounds and other limits at a certain love-day (*ad quandam diem amoris*) assigned and viewed, and as it lies on the north side of the chapel of Wyntworth.   To have and to hold to John and (*fo.* 203) Alice and the lawful heirs of their bodies, from the prior and convent and their successors, rendering to them 6d. yearly for all services.   If John and Alice shall die without such heir, the property, with all its appurtenances, shall revert to and re-

---

[1] Hunter (*South Yorkshire*, ii, 79) says, "Michael and John his (*i.e.* William's) brother." The wording in the MS., however, is very plainly "fratre suo," and there is nothing to show a connection between these two men and the Aisolf family.

main with the prior and convent and their successors.   If the rent
be in arrear for six weeks, power for the grantors to retake and retain
the property.   Seals of the parties to the two parts of this indenture,
alternately.   Witnesses, John de Wodall, Thomas his brother,
Robert de Roklay, and others.   Dated at Monkbretton, 10 October,
1367.

(365)   Confirmation by Hugh son of Henry de Wyntworth, by
the counsel and permission of his heirs, (*fo.* 203*d*)[1] to God and Saint
Mary Magdelene of Bretton and the monks serving God there, of
eleven acres of land from his demesne in Wintworth, namely an
acre and a half at the head of the vill, at the east, an acre in Lange-
furlands, half an acre opposite the mill, and half an acre opposite the
road of Waht (*sic*), and the other acres in the field as they lie, with
all commons and all easements of the said vill, namely in wood, in
plain, etc., quit and free of all service, in pure and perpetual alms.
Witnesses, Robert son of Henry, Richard son of Barnard, and Walter
his brother, William son of Richard, Rainer de Wodehus, and others.
(Monkbretton Chart., Lansdowne MS. 405, fo. 29.)

(*Fo.* 204)   *Mekisburgh.*

(366)   Grant[2] by Alexander Atkyn of Kynwoldmarche in the
County of Derby to Thomas Wyntworth of Doncaster, esquire, and
Ivo York of Connesburgh, of all those lands and tenements, rents
and services, with all appurtenances, which he (Alexander) lately
had by the gift and feoffment of John Webster of Mekesburgh, in
the vill, fields, and territories of Mekesburgh in the County of York.
To have and to hold to the grantees, their heirs and assigns, for ever,
from the chief lords of that fee, by the services due and accustomed.
Witnesses, William Wavaso of Demby,[3] Henry Wavysor of the same,
Henry Wightman, and others.   Dated at Mekysburgh, 10 May,
17 Hen. VI (1439).

(367)   Grant by Thomas Wentworth of Doncaster, esquire, and
Ivo York of Connesburgh (*fo.* 204*d*)[4] to Thomas Ploghwright of
Hoton Robert of a messuage with the toft and croft adjoining, in
the vill of Mekesburgh, which they lately had by the gift and feoffment of Alexander Atkyn of Kynwolmersh in the county of Derby,
and which lie between the messuage formerly William Bacon's on
the west and the messuage of the prior of Bretton on the east.   To
have and to hold to the grantee, his heirs and assigns, for ever,
freely, quietly, etc., from the chief lords of that fee, by the services
due and accustomed.   Witnesses, William Wavasor of Denyby,
Henry his brother, Henry Wightman, and others.   Dated at Mekisburgh, 29 February,[5] 20 Hen. VI (1441–2).

[1] Headed " Mekysburgh," but the Mexborough deeds do not begin until
the next page.

[2] Opposite is written in the margin " Plowrygthe lande."

[3] For Denaby.

[4] Headed " Mekysburgh."

[5] *Sic;* but the year indicated, 1442, was not leap year.

(368)   Grant by William Plugwrygh late of Stokun to Thomas Medeley of Newsted, esquire, John Whitehed of Mekeysburgh and John Wodson of the same, of a messuage with (*fo*. 205) toft and croft adjoining, in the vill of Mekisburgh, which messuage lies between the land late Percival Cresacre's on the west and the tenement of the prior of Monkbretton on the east, with two acres of land and meadow lying in the fields and meadows of the said vill, whereof half a rood of land lies on Rekenyll between the land of the said prior on the south and the land of Thomas Wavasor on the north, abutting on Cop at one head and on the land of George Frankisch at the other, and half a rood lies in the same space between the land of the prior on either side, abutting at one head on Copp and at the other on the land of John Bussell, one rood lies between the land of the said prior on either side, abutting on Standgate and Adwikgate, a rood lies on Gorland between the land of the same prior on the east and the land of John Whitehed on the west, abutting on Almuntfurlong, half an acre lies on Slatebanke between the land of the prior on the south and the land of Hugh Abney on the north, abutting on Le Moredike at the west head and on Slatebankesyke on the east head, a rood of meadow lies on Ridcroft Stones between the land of the said prior on the south and Ricroftesyke on the north, abutting upon the meadow of the same prior to the west and on Ricroftesyke to the east, half a rood of meadow lies in Le Northyng between the meadow of Thomas Wavasor on the east and the meadow of John Hunt on the west, abutting on Derne at the north head and on Midelholmsyke at the south head, a rood lies there between the meadow of the said prior on the west and the meadow of the same prior and of John White-hed on the east, abutting upon Derne at the north head and on Midel-holmesyke at the south head, half a rood of land lies in Le Whit-offurrs between (*fo*. 205*d*)[1] the land of George Frankysch on the north and the land of the said prior on the south, abutting on Rekynhyll at the west head and on longe Clay at the east head.   To have and to hold with the appurtenances, and all lands, tenements, and mead-ows formerly Thomas Plogwryght's in the vill, fields, and meadows of Mekesburgh, to the grantees, their heirs and assigns, for ever, from the chief lords of that fee, by the services due and accustomed. Witnesses, Thomas Wavasor of Denyby, esquire, Thomas Wynter of the same, Thomas Whitehede, and others.   Dated 15 July, 19 Edw. IV (1479).

(369)   Demise and grant by Thomas Medelay of Newstede, esquire, John Whithede of Mekesburgh, and John Wodson of the same, to Richard Ledes, prior (*fo*. 206) of Monkbretton, and the con-vent thereof and their successors for ever, of a messuage with the toft and croft adjoining in the vill of Mekesburgh, as it lies between the land late Percival Cresacre's on the west and the tenement of the said Richard the prior on the east, and two acres of land and meadow lying separately in the fields and meadows of the said vill, with the appurtenances, which the grantors lately had by the grant of William

---

[1] Headed " Mekysburgh."

Ploghwright, late of Stokum. To have and to hold to the grantees for ever, from the chief lords of that fee, by the services due and accustomed. Witnesses, Thomas Vavasor, esquire, Thomas Whithede, John Philipson, and others. Dated at Mekesburght, 3 May, 21 Edw. IV (1481).

(*Fo. 206d is blank.*)

(*Fo. 207*)   *Swath.*[1]

(370) Grant[2] by Henry de Brom to Henry his son, and his heirs, legatees, or assigns, except Religious or Jews, for his homage and service, of all the land, with the appurtenances, without retention, which he (the grantor) formerly bought from Adam Blaber, in the territory of Swathe, within the bounds of Wirkesburg. To hold and to have from the grantor and his heirs in fee and inheritance, freely, quietly, etc., with all liberties and easements belonging to the land, rendering to them yearly 3s. of silver for all services, etc., grinding their corn growing on the land at the mill of the lord of Rockeley, at the twentieth measure,[3] if within one day or one night after they come there they are able to grind [it], if not they shall go away where they will without hindrance. (*Fo. 207d*) Witnesses, Robert de Slethley, Robert de Berch, Matthew de Shepeley, Walter de Seyvile, Robert de Wambwell, and others.

(371) Grant by Henry son of Henry de Brom to Robert son of Sir John de Bosovile [*sic*], his heirs and assigns, of that bovate of land with the messuage and appurtenances, without retention, which he (the grantor) had by the gift of Henry his father in the territory of Wirkysburg, that bovate namely which is called Blabirmegand. To hold and to have to the grantee, his heirs and assigns, from the grantor and his heirs, in fee and inheritance, freely, quietly, etc., with all liberties, easements, and commons thereto (*fo. 208*) belonging, rendering thence yearly to the grantor and his heirs 3s. for all suits, services, etc. Warranty, in consideration of a certain sum of money paid by the grantee in hand. Witnesses, Sirs Roger son of Thomas de la Wodehall, Nicholas de Wrtelay [*sic*], Sir Nicholas de Turribus, Peter de Bosevile, Richard de Birg, Adam son of Ralph de Derlay, Henry del Blacker, Robert Perre of Erdisley, and others.

(372) Grant by Henry son of Henry del Brom to the prior and convent of Monkbretton and their successors of all the rent and all (*fo. 208d*) the services which Robert de Boswevile was accustomed to do for a messuage and a bovate of land, with the appurtenances, in Wyrkisburg called Blabirtofte and Blabiroxgangs, with mandate of

[1] Swaith, near Worsborough. The handwriting (except the headings of the deeds) appears to change here. The heading, " Swath," continues to *fo.* 210d: but in the table of contents at the beginning all the following deeds are included under " Worsborough Dale " from this point until " Smythlay " is reached, *fo.* 261.

[2] " Blaberoxgang " written in the margin opposite.

[3] *i.e.* giving one part in twenty as payment for grinding.

intendance and payment to Robert accordingly. Witnesses, Godfrey de Staynton, William de Notton, Philip de Bosevile, Edmund de Bosevil, John de Kynnesley, and others.   Dated at Monkbretton, Friday in the feast of the Circumcision, 1301.

(373) Surrender and confirmation by Henry son of Henry del Brom to the prior and convent of Monkbretton, his chief lords, of the yearly rent of 3s. with the appurtenances, in Wirkysburg, receivable from Robert de Bosevile and his heirs for a messuage (*fo.* 209) and a bovate of land which he held from the grantor in the same vill, called Blabiroxgangs, together with all the services of the said Robert and his heirs therefrom.   To have and to hold to the prior and convent and their successors, in pure and perpetual alms, freely, quietly, etc., with all appurtenances, etc. Witnesses as in the preceding deed.

(374) Grant by Robert de Bosevile to Philip de Bosevile of a toft and bovate of land, with the woods and meadows adjoining, and the appurtenances, in Sunathe in Wirkisburg, (*fo.* 209*d*) that toft namely and that bovate of land which he (Robert) had by the gift of Henry del Brom, and are called Blabirtofte and Blabiroxgangs. To have and to hold, from the chief lords of the fee, to the said Philip and his heirs or assigns, freely, quietly, etc., with all appurtenances, etc., within and without the said vill of Wyrkysburg, doing to the said chief lords the yearly services due and accustomed, namely to the prior and convent of Monkbretton and their successors 13s. 4d. yearly. Witnesses, Sir James de Bosvile, knt., Godfrey de Staynton, Henry de Rocley, William de Notton, Edmund de Bosvile, William de Derley, and others.

(*Fo.* 210) (375) Appointment by Robert de Bosevil of John de Wombwelle, his son, as his attorney to deliver seisin to Philip de Bosevile of a messuage and bovate of land with the meadows and woods adjoining, and the appurtenances, in Sunath in Wirkisburg, which he has given to the said Philip by his charter.   Dated at Le Neuhalle, Thursday after the feast of St. Valentine, 15 Edw. II (1321–2).

(376) Grant by Philip de Bosevile to Henry de Eynesham of that tenement (*fo.* 210*d*) with the appurtenances, which is called Blabirland in Wyrkysburg, as wholly as he (Philip) had it by the gift of Robert Bosevile, his uncle.   To have and to hold to Henry, his heirs and assigns, from the chief lords of that fee, by the services due and accustomed.   Witnesses, William Scot, Thomas de Staynton, William de Notton, Richard de Wayard of Cothewych, Richard son of Roger, and others.

(377) Release and quitclaim by William son of Peter de Bosevile and Isabel and Elizabeth, sisters of the said William, to the prior and convent of Monkbretton and their successors, of all right and claim in all those lands and tenements in Wyrkysburg which are called Blabyrland and [in] all those lands and tenements which they

(the releasors) had in Monkbretton, except 3s. of yearly (*fo.* 211) rent to them from Lemmeley Rode. Seals. Witnesses, Sir William Scot, Sir John de Eland, Sir Nicholas de Wortelay, Sir Adam de Evirringham, knights, Thomas de Staynton, William de Notton, Adam de Byrthwayt, Richard son of Roger, William de Staynton, and others. Dated at Ardysley, in the feast of the blessed Bartholomew Apostle, 1341.

(378) Grant by Peter de Rokelay to God and Saint Mary Magdalene of Bretton and the monks there, with his body, in pure and perpetual alms, of the homage and service (*fo.* 211d)[1] of Henry del Brom and his heirs from one bovate of land, with the appurtenances, in the territory of Wyrkysburg in the place called Swathe, which he (Henry) held from the grantor for 3s. yearly. To hold and to have, freely, quietly, etc., in homages, rents, wardships, reliefs, escheats, and other services thereto belonging, to make a service each year for his (the grantor's) soul on the day of his burial. Warranty, as pure and perpetual alms. Witnesses, Richard the chaplain of Wyrkysburg, Robert de Rokeley, Nicholas Legat, Robert de Turs, Henry de Rokelay, Richard his brother, Simon the clerk of Wirkysburg, and others.

(*Fo.* 212) (379) Grant[2] by Roger de Montebegon to God and the church of Saint Mary Magdalene of Bretton and the monks there, with his body, in pure and perpetual alms, of thirty acres of land, with the appurtenances, in the territory of Wircesburht, in the place called Thirnethueit. To hold and to have freely and quietly, with all easements belonging to so much land of the said vill. Witnesses, Sir Richard de Vescy, John de Lamara, Richard Blanchard, Henry de Munedene, John de Peningestun, Ralph Hagat, and others.

(380) Grant by Roger de Montebegon to Simon de Wirkeburc, clerk, for his homage and service, of nineteen acres of land in the vill of Wyrkisburc, whereof fifteen acres lie between Wigefal and Oslekneith, and four acres within the vill of Wirkeburc in four parts, (*fo.* 212d) to wit, Kolne croft, and the toft which lies beside the land of the church of Wirkesburc towards the south, and the ings which were sometime Syward's, and three perches of land in length and twelve in width beside the house of the same Simon towards the west. To hold from the grantor and his heirs to the grantee and his heirs or to that one of his children he chooses, freely, quietly, etc., by service of 4s. 6d. to the grantor and his heirs yearly, for all service, etc., to them. Witnesses, William son of Adam, William Lungvilers, Eudo de Lungvilers, Peter de Bircekneith, Hugh de Pilleia, John de Rocceleia, Henry de Tancerleia, and others.

(381) Grant by brother Roger, (*fo.* 213) prior (*humilis minister*) of Bretton, and the convent there, to Hugh son of Geoffrey son of

---

[1] Headed " Wyrkysburgth," which heading (with some slight variations in spelling) continues to *fo.* 226d.

[2] " Wardefeld " written opposite in the margin.

Clyluhic de Wirkesburc and his heirs, of all the land, with the buildings and all other appurtenances, without retention, that namely which Geoffrey his father formerly[1] held from the grantors, within the bounds of Wirkesbur'. To have and to hold to him and his heirs in fee and inheritance, from the grantors, freely, quietly, etc., in wood, in plain, etc., and in all other easements, liberties, and commons belonging to so much land of the vill of Wirkesburg; rendering yearly to the grantors 3s. of silver, for all service and demand. Hugh and his heirs may not give, pledge, or sell any of the land without the grantor's licence. Warranty, so far as the charter of the donor of the land to the grantors shall be able to warrant. Witnesses, William de Koryltun, Adam Cossard, then (fo. 213d) steward of the prior of Bretton, Stephen de Harlay, and many others.

(382) Grant by Adam, prior of Bretton, and the convent thereof to William the sergeant (servienti) of Wirkesburg and his heirs, for his homage and service of a messuage in the vill of Wirkesburg lying between the house of Simon the clerk and the house of Ailsi, and three acres of land in the territory of the same vill, namely in Ketell croft six and a half roods of land, and an acre which is over against Turneshac, and a rood and a half in the place called Crokrode, with all appurtenances. To hold and to have to the grantee and his heirs, freely and quietly, rendering yearly to the grantors 3s. for all service and secular exaction. Witnesses, William son of Adam, John Rocklei, Henry de Tankresley, Simon parson of Tankreslei, and others. (Monkbretton Chart., Lansdowne MS. 405, fo. 49d.)

(Fo. 214) (383) Grant by Adam son of Peter de Birkine to God and Saint Mary Magdelene and the monks of Bretton, of the service of Roger de Montebegon from the land of Wirkesburg which he holds from the grantor, namely 4s. payable yearly at Martinmas, and five acres of meadow in Smethehale beside the meadow of the monks of Pontefract at the west side, for the health of his soul and the souls of his ancestors and heirs, and for all living or dead who have sinned by him or on account of him, in pure and perpetual alms. Witnesses, John Tyrel, German de Cornhil, Reginald son of Elias, John his brother, Peter son of Adam de Birkyne, Robert de Struet', and many others.

(384) Confirmation of the preceding grant, by John son of Adam son of Peter de Birkine, (fo. 214d) in pure and perpetual alms, for his soul and his wife's and the souls of his father and mother and ancestors and heirs. Witnesses, William de Nevilla, Rainer Flameng, Hugh, dean of Silkeston, John Tirel, Gilbert de Notton, Adam son of Orm, Hugh de Stapelton, and many others.

(385) Grant by John de Rokeleia to God and Saint Mary Magdelene of Bretton, and the monks there, of a toft in the vill of Wirkesboro', and two acres of land in the territory of the same vill, in pure and perpetual alms, that (fo. 215) toft namely which was Ketel's, as

---

[1] " Quod," doubtless a mistake for " quondam."

it lies in length and width, and one acre of land which abuts on le Turneshac, and one acre which abuts on Smaleby, as far as the mill of Sir Roger de Monte Begon, as they lie in length and width.   To hold and to have from the grantor and his heirs, freely, quietly, etc., in wood, in plain, etc., with all liberties and easements and free common of the said vill as belongs to so much land.   So nevertheless that the prior and convent of Bretton shall do a service yearly for the souls of the grantor's father and mother for ever, and the convent shall provide, from the rent of the aforesaid land, a good recreation on the day on which the anniversary ought to be done.   Witnesses, William Fitz-William, William Fitz-Adam, Richard[1] de Wambwel, Henry de Tancrislae, Elias, parson of Edlington, Simon, parson of Tanceslaia, Hugh de Bilaham, William de Rokeleia, Simon his brother, and many others.

(Fo. 215d)[2] (386) Grant by Juliana formerly wife of John de Rokelay, in her widowhood, to God and the church of Saint Mary Magdalene of Bretton and the monks there, of 4s. yearly from the rent of her land, which Ralph Fisher of Wirkesboro holds from her, namely from the bovate of land which was Ralph de Stutevill's.   If the tenant Ralph or his heirs should fail to pay the rent at the term appointed, the prior and monks may take the land into their hands until full payment.   This donation she has made to the monks to do yearly service for the soul of her said husband on the day of his anniversary, namely service in convent (fo. 216) and a mass by a priest, and by the others the proper psalms for his soul and the souls of all the faithful dead.   The subprior of Bretton may receive the said 4s. for a corrody for the convent on the day of the anniversary. Witnesses, Sir Peter de Byrktuait, Sir Robert son of Adam, Roger de Notton, parson of Felekyrke, Hugh de Berc,[3] Robert de Rockeley, Simon his brother, Roger Solin, Roger de Bergh, and others.

(387)   Surrender and quitclaim by Raener son of Adam Hert of Erdislay to God and the church of Saint Mary Magdalene of Bretton and the monks there, of all the moiety of the land, with the appurtenances, which he held from the same prior and monks in the territory of Wirkesburg, namely a moiety of that bovate of land which Thomas son of Orm sometime held, and a moiety of that bovate which Hugh (fo. 216d) son of Lewyn sometime held, and a moiety of four acres of land which lie between the wood of Erdisley and the field of Wirkesboro.   Witnesses, Sir Richard de Tankerley, Sir John de Boswell, knights, Reyner de Wambewell, Hugh de Crygleston, Nicholas Legat, William Fischer, and others.

(388)   Grant by Brother R., prior (humilis minister) of Bretton, and the convent thereof, to Richard Grusci, goldsmith, of York, and

[1] The name very plainly is " Ric' " in the Chartulary; Hunter (South Yorkshire, ii, 283) gives it as " Nicholas," but adds " qu. Richard ? "
[2] The heading of this page is " Workesburg Daylle."
[3] Hunter (South Yorkshire, ii, 283) calls this " Bere," but the word seems plain in the Chartulary. No doubt it is a variation of " Bargh."

his heirs or assigns, for his homage and service, of a bovate and a half and four acres of land, with the appurtenances, in the territory of Wirkesboro', (*fo.* 217) namely that bovate with the appurtenances, at Derley, which Hugh son of Lewin held from Sir Robert de Rokkeley, and that half bovate, with the appurtenances, which Thomas son of Orm held, and four acres of land which lie between the wood of Herdesley and the field of Wirkesboro', with free common of the said vill of Wirkesboro' as much as belongs to so much land. To hold and to have to the grantee and his heirs or assigns from the grantors in fee and inheritance, freely, quietly, etc., in wood, in plain, etc., and in all other easements and liberties of the same vill of Wirkesboro', rendering yearly to the chapel of St. Mary the Virgin of their (the grantor's) house for the support of the lamp 6*d*. for all services, doing to them forinsec service as belongs to a bovate and a half of land, where twelve carucates make a knight's fee. (*Fo.* 217*d*) Witnesses, Sir Henry de Novo Mercato, Sir Roger de Notton, Sir Robert de Skeknesse, then steward of the abbot of York, Sir Robert de Stapelton, and many others.

(Monkbretton Chart., Lansdowne MS. 405, fo. 49d.)

(389) Surrender and quitclaim by Richard Grusci, goldsmith of York, to God and the church of Saint Mary Magdelene of Bretton and the monks there, of all the land, with the appurtenances, which he held from the said monks in the territory of Wirkesboro, namely that land which Simon de Rockeley gave them; but so that the monks shall pay him (Richard) for life 9*s*. yearly at York at Whitsuntide, and moreover they (the monks) shall pay yearly to the chapel of St. Mary of Bretton, to find a light, 12*d*. Be it known that if Juliana, (*fo.* 218) Richard's wife, shall survive him, the monks shall pay her yearly 9*s*. for her lifetime at the same term at York; and, after the decease of both, the monks shall pay the 9*s*. yearly with the 12*d*. to the chapel of St. Mary of Bretton to find a light. Witnesses, Sir Roger de Notton, Sir John de Hoderode, Sir John de Bosevile, Reiner de Wambwell, Ralph son of Ralph de Wirkesboro, and others.

(Monkbretton Chart., Lansdowne MS. 405, fo. 50)

(390) Grant by brother Roger, prior (*humilis minister*) of Bretton, and the convent thereof, to Reiner son of Adam Hert and his heirs (*fo.* 218*d*) or assigns, for his homage and service, of a moiety of all the land, with the appurtenances, which Simon de Rockelay gave them in the territory of Wirkesboro, namely the moiety of that bovate of land, with the appurtenances, which Hugh son of Lewyn sometime held at Derlay, and a moiety of the half bovate, with the appurtenances, which Thomas son of Horm held, and a moiety of the four acres, with the appurtenances, which lie between the wood of Erdeslay and the field of Wirkesboro. To hold and to have to the grantee and his heirs or assigns from the grantors and their successors, in fee and inheritance, freely, quietly, etc., with all liberties, easements, and commons belonging to the land, rendering yearly to them 5*s*. of silver, for all service and demand. The monks will warrant as far as the charter of their donor can warrant to

them.   Witnesses, Sir John de Bosevil, Reiner de Wambwell, Adam Collard, Henry de Brom, William de Derley, and others.

(*Fo.* 219) (391) Grant by brother Roger, prior (*humilis minister*) of Bretton, and the convent thereof, to Roger de Brom and his heirs or assigns, for his homage and service, of a moiety of the property which Simon de Rockelay gave them (description as in the previous deed).   To hold and to have to the grantee and his heirs from the grantors and their successors, etc. (as in the previous deed), (*fo.* 219*d*) rendering to them yearly 5*s.* of silver for all service and demand (as in the preceding deed).   Witnesses, Sir John de Bosevil, Reiner de Wamwell, Henry de Brom, Adam Cossard, Robert de Smythelay, Roger de Berch, William Darlay, and others.

(392) Confirmation by Peter son of John de Rockelay to God and the church of Saint Mary Magdelene of Bretton and the monks (*fo.* 220) there, in pure and perpetual alms, of all the lands which Simon de Rockeley gave them in the territory of Wirkisburg, with the appurtenances; to wit, on Derley a bovate of land which Hugh son of Leuwin sometime held, and half a bovate which Thomas son of Orm held, and four acres lying between the wood of Herdesley and the field of Derley.   Witnesses, Sir Henry de Tankerley, Sir Roger de Notton, Sir John de Hoderode, Richard de Orul, then bailiff of Steyncros, Reiner de Wambwell, Ralph de Rupe, and others.

(393) Grant[1] by Simon son of Robert de Rockeley (*fo.* 220*d*) to God and blessed Mary Magdelene of Bretton and the monks there, in perpetual alms, of a bovate and a half and four acres of land, with the appurtenances, in the territory of Wirkesboro, namely that bovate of land at Derley which Hugh son of Leuwin held from the grantor's father, and that half bovate which Thomas son of Oryn held, and four acres as increment lying between the wood of Herdesley and the field of Wirkesboro, with free common of the vill of Wirkesboro as belongs to so much land.   To hold and to have, freely, quietly, etc., in wood and plain, etc., and in all other easements and liberties of the same vill of Wirkesboro, saving forinsec service as belongs to a bovate and a half of land, where twelve carucates make a knight's fee. (*Fo.* 221) Warranty.   Witnesses, Robert Fitz-Adam, Henry de Tancreley, John de Hoderode, Roger de Notton, Reiner de Wambewell, Roger de Berch, Ralph de Rupe, and others.

(394) Grant[2] by Robert Fitz-Adam de Wirkesburg to Thomas son of Richard de Swathe and his heirs, or to whom he shall desire to give, bequeath, sell, or assign, a messuage and three acres of land in the territory of Wirkesburg, lying in a place called Le Wellehusses, which messuage and land Robert Fitz-Adam quitclaimed to him

---

[1] This deed is quoted by Hunter (*South Yorkshire*, ii, 283), but incorrectly. He states that the description of Simon is *son of Robert*, only; whereas the charter clearly describes him as *Simon son of Robert de Rockeley*. Hunter then unnecessarily goes on to prove that Simon was a Rockley.

[2] " Wellehousse " written in the margin opposite.

(the grantor). To have and to hold to the grantee and his heirs or assigns in fee and inheritance, with all appurtenances, free commons, and easements to the said messuage and land belonging within the bounds of Wirkesburg. Rendering thence yearly (*fo.* 221*d*) to the grantor 6*d.* of silver for all secular service and demand. Witnesses, William the smith of Erdesley, Richard the cook of the same, William Crok, John Quinterest, Richard le forester, and others.

(395) Grant by Thomas son of Richard de Swath to John son of Thomas de Kyemslay[1] and his heirs [or] to whom he may desire to give, bequeath, sell, or assign a messuage and three acres of land as they lie in length and breadth in the territory of Wirkesburg in a certain place called Le Wellehouses. To hold (*fo.* 222) and to have to the grantee, his heirs or assigns, with all appurtenances, liberties, commons, and easements belonging, doing yearly to the lords of the fee the service due and accustomed, for all secular services, exactions, and demands. Warranty, for a certain sum of money paid to him by John in hand. Witnesses, William de Crigilston, William Crock, William de Normanton, Robert de Huntyndon, Ralph de Wodehall, Adam de Derelay, and many others.

(*Fo.* 222*d*) (396) Grant by John son of Thomas de Kynneslay to Henry de Aynesham, the mason, and his heirs, or to whomsoever he shall desire to give or assign, of a messuage and three acres of land, with the appurtenances, in Wirkesburgh, which he (John) had by the gift and feoffment of Thomas son of Richard de Swath, as they lie in length and breadth within the bounds of Wirkesburg in a certain place called Wellehouses. To have and to hold, etc., as in the preceding deed, with similar provision as to service. (*Fo.* 223) Witnesses, Stephen de Bella Aqua, Godfrey de Staynton, William de Notton, Adam de Boseville, Philip his brother, Adam the clerk, and others. Dated at Monkbretton, Friday in the feast of St. Thomas Martyr, 1318.

(397) Grant by Richard son of Richard de Wumbowell (*fo.* 223*d*) to God and blessed Mary Magdelene of Bretton and the monks there, of an acre of land in Dinielees next to the land of William Steward towards the east as it lies in length and breadth, in pure and perpetual alms. Witnesses, John Rokesley, Simon and William his brothers, William the mason, John the cellarer, Peter Stute, Richard Pulam, Robert his son, Roger the baker, and others.

(398) Grant by Jordan Tagun to God and Saint Mary Magdelene of Bretton and the monks there (*fo.* 224) of two houses with fifteen acres of land and the fourth part of an acre from his essart in Swatha, which Osbert and Godwin held, and three acres of land which Robert Tagun held from him, namely these which are below his (the grantor's) house in Duneleis, in pure and perpetual alms, with all appurtenances, in wood, in plain, etc., free and quit of all secular exaction.

---

[1] " Kynsley " in the heading.

Witnesses, William de Novo Mercato, Osbert de Bretton, Robert his brother, Hamon de Bretton and Hugh his brother, Robert Pele, Ingelric brother of Richard Cardunal, Geoffrey Herdesly, William son of Roger, and others.

(399)   Quitclaim by Juliana, sometime wife of Simon Brenur of Wirkesbur, in her widowhood and lawful power, (*fo. 224d*) to God and the church of blessed Mary Magdelene of Bretton and the monks there, of all the part of her dower from the land which Simon her husband held from the same monks in the territory of Wirkes-boro, with all the appurtenances, etc.   Witnesses, Peter de Rokelay, Robert Pilay, Simon son of Henry the smith of Wirkesburg, Adam the cook of Erdislay, John **Fitz**-Simon of the same, Simon le Blund, Gregory de Batelay, and others.

(400)   Surrender by Richard son of Simon le Brenur of Wirkes-burg to God and the church of Blessed Mary Magdelene of Bretton and the monks there, of all the land which he held in the territory of Wirkesburg (*fo. 225*) from the said monks, with all liberties and easements appertaining.   Witnesses, Peter de Rokelay, Robert Pillay, Simon son of Henry the smith of Wirkesburg, Adam the cook of Erdislay, John Fitz-Simon of the same, Simon le Blund, Gregory de Batelay, and others.

(401)   Grant by brother R., prior (*humilis minister*) of Bretton, and the convent there, to Emma sometime wife of Simon Spitilman of Wirkesburg and her heirs or whichever of her sons (*fo. 225d*) she shall desire to give or sell to, for her homage and service, of all the land which Richard son of Simon le Brenur of Wirkesburg formerly held from them (the grantors) as it lies in length and width in the territory of Wirkesburg.   To hold and to have from the grantors, freely, quietly, etc., in wood, in plain, etc., within and without the vill of Wirkesboro, with all liberties to so much land belonging; but so that the said Emma or any of her successors may not give, sell, or pledge the land, except as aforesaid, either to Religious or into the hands of the Jews.   Rendering yearly to the grantors 5s. ster-ling, for all service and secular demand.   Warranty so far as the charter which they (the grantors) have of the land can warrant to them.   Witnesses, Sir Adam Eviringam, (*fo. 226*) knight, Sir John de Hoderede, knight, Sir Robert de Holande, knight, Peter de Rokkelay, Richard Tankreslay, Robert de Pillay, Adam Colard, and many others.

(402)   Demise and quitclaim by Richard the smith of Holand to Sir Henry de Novo Mercato and his heirs of all the service, with the homage and appurtenances, which he (Richard) had from Richard de Bosco, namely all the service which he was bound to render yearly to the quit-claimor.   To hold and to have to Henry and his heirs, freely, quietly, etc., doing the homage and service which belongs to Stephen Harlay and his heirs, namely 2s. 6d. yearly.   Witnesses, (*fo. 226d*) Rayner de Wambwelle, Jordan de Cretona, John de

Holande, William de Cretona, William Haleblast', Robert the clerk of Wath, and many others.

(403) Grant by Simon son of Simon de Darlay to Adam his son for his service in the pilgrimage which he made to the cross of Droholm[1] for the good of the grantor's soul, of a toft with a certain essart and all the appurtenances, in the territory of Wirkesburg as it lies between the land of Simon Sorell on the south and the common on the north and the spring of Agnes on the west and the common towards Milnethorpe on the east. To hold and to have to the grantee, his heirs or assigns, freely, etc., for ever, with all liberties and easements, doing yearly the service due to the prior of Bretton for the time being (fo. 227) 6d. for all service and demand. Warranty, according to the warrant which he (the grantor) has from Prior William and the convent of Bretton. Witnesses, Sir Henry de Tankersley, Ralph de Rupe, Robert de Pillay, Simon de Sorell, and others.

(404) Grant by Ralph son of Ralph de Wirkesburg to God and the church of Saint Mary Magdelene of Bretton and the monks there, of 12d. yearly on Palm Sunday from his capital toft and fee in Wirkesburg, for a maundy[2] (fo. 227d)[3] on the Thursday following, in pure and perpetual alms. Power of distraint on non-payment of the said rent. Witnesses, Peter de Rokkelay, Robert de Pillay, Thomas the clerk of Staynburg, Richard the smith of Holand, and others.

(405) Grant[4] by Jordan de Wiggefall of Wirkesburg to Richard his son and his heirs of all (fo. 228) that messuage with the buildings, and all those lands and tenements, meadows and woods, with the appurtenances, which fell to him (Jordan) by inheritance after the death of Simon de Wiggefal, his father, within the bounds of Wirkesburg, except a certain essart called Littelstubbings. To have and to hold to the grantee, his heirs and assigns, from the chief lords of the fees, by the services due to them and accustomed, freely, quietly, etc., with all appurtenances, etc. Witnesses, Henry de Rockelay, John del Hill of Wirkesboro, Henry del Wodehouses of the same, William son of Henry of the same, and others. Dated at Wirkesburg, Wednesday in the feast of St. Peter ad vincula, 1330.

(Fo. 228d) (406) Grant by John Pay, son of John Pay of Kayam and Elizabeth his (the grantor's) wife, daughter of William son of Richard Judson of Wigfal, to Robert del Loyne of Wirkesburg, of all lands and tenements, with all the appurtenances which they had in the fields and territories of Wirkesburg, all which

---

[1] " Ad crucem Drōholm," the last word probably a mistake for " Bōholm." The cross of the Cluniac priory of Bromholm, in Norfolk, a cell of Castleacre, was a well-known relic, reputed to be made of the wood of the true cross, and attracted large numbers of pilgrims with costly offerings.

[2] A benefaction of clothing, food or money. *New English Dictionary.*

[3] Headed " Wygffall "—as are the following folios to 233d.

[4] " Wiggefall " written in the margin opposite.

I

descended to Elizabeth by hereditary right after the death of the said William her father.   To have and to hold to the grantee, his heirs or assigns, freely, quietly, etc., from the chief lords of those fees, by the services due and accustomed.   (*Fo.* 229) Witnesses, Richard de Kersforth of Barneslay, William de Dodworth of Derton, William del Hill of Wirkesburg, Thomas de Swath, William de Burton of the same, and others.   Dated at Wygfall in Wirkesburgdale, Sunday after Michaelmas, 1384.

(407) Grant by Robert del Loyne of Wirkesburg to Richard de Keresforth of Barneslay, Thomas Emson of the same, Thomas and Richard his (the grantor's) sons, their heirs and assigns, (*fo.* 229*d*) of all those lands and tenements, with the appurtenances, which he (the grantor) had by the grant of John son of John Pay of Kayam and Elizabeth his wife, within the bounds of Wirkesburg, which Elizabeth had by hereditary right after the death of William son of Richard Judson of Wygfall, her father.   To have and to hold to the grantees, their heirs and assigns, freely, quietly, etc., from the chief lords of those fees, by the services due and accustomed.   Witnesses, Robert de Rokelay, knight, Robert his son, Robert Monke, Richard del Hill, John del Hyll of Wirkesburg, and others.   Dated at Wigfall in Wirkesburg, the morrow of St. James Apostle, 1407.

(*Fo.* 230) (408) Grant by William de Burton of Luccburgh[1] in the county of Leycestre and Elizabeth his wife to the lady Elizabeth, lady of Bellomonte, of the same county, Robert de Roklay, Richard de Wortelay, esquires, of the county of York, John de Wortelay, junior, esquire, and Henry Langus of Wirkesburg in the same county of York, of all those messuages, lands and tenements, woods, meadows and pastures, with all the appurtenances, which lately descended to the said Elizabeth, William's wife, by hereditary right after the death of William de Wigfalle, her father, in Wigfalle in Wirkesburg and within the bounds of the same.   To have and to hold to the grantees and the heirs (*fo.* 230*d*) and assigns of the said Henry Langus, freely, quietly, etc., from the chief lords of those fees, by the services due and accustomed, for ever.   Witnesses, Robert Monke of Wirkesburg, Richard del Hill of the same, William Joneson of the same, Henry Fischar and William Fischar of the same, and others.   Dated at Wygfall in Wirkesburg, 1 September, 1422.

(*Fo.* 231) (409) Release and quitclaim by Henry Elyson of Wirkesburg to William Gilberthorp in the same, his heirs and assigns, of all his estate and claim in a messuage with toft and croft, and the appurtenances, which he (Henry) had by hereditary right after the death of Joan his mother and by the gift of Elizabeth Burton his (? aunt) in Wirkesburg aforesaid.   Witnesses, Robert Pilley, William del Hill, William Elmehyrst, Robert Elyson, and others. Dated at Wygfall, (*fo.* 231*d*) 7 June, 6 Edw. IV (1466).

---

[1] Loughborough.

(410)   Grant by Henry Elison to William Gilberthorp of Wirkesburgh, his heirs and assigns, of a messuage with toft and croft as it lies between the messuage late Robert Roklay's on the south and the land of William del Hill called Brode Royde on the north and the land of William Elmehyrst on the west and the common pasture called Wigfall Gryne on the east, a moiety of which messuage, with the lands adjacent, he (Henry) had by hereditary right after the death of Joan Wigfal, his mother, and the other moiety by the gift of Elizabeth Burton, his aunt, in Wirkesburg aforesaid.   To have and to hold to the grantee, his heirs and assigns, from the chief lord of that fee, by the services due and accustomed.   (*Fo.* 232) Witnesses, Robert Pilley, William Hill, William Elmehyrst, Robert Fyschar, Robert Elyson, and others.   Dated at Wygfall, 6 June, 6 Edw. IV (1466).

(411)   Grant by Henry Elison of Wirkesburg to Robert Elison and Robert Cawodd of Wirkesburgh, of a messuage built on, with two gardens and a close, lying together, with their appurtenances, in Wirkesburg, namely in a certain place there called Wigfall between the common pasture on the east and the land of William Elmehirst on the west and abutting on the land of John Roklay to the south and on the land of William Hill called Broderoyde to the north.   To have and to hold (*fo.* 232*d*) to the grantees, their heirs and assigns, for ever, from the chief lords of that fee, by the services due and accustomed.   Witnesses, William Gilbertthorpe of Wirkesburg, Robert Fyschare, William Elmehirst, Richard Broddesworth and Thomas Kyllen of the same, and others.   Dated at Wirkesburg, the feast of the Nativity of the blessed Virgin Mary, 1467.

(412)   Release and quitclaim by William Gilberthorp of Wirkesburg to Robert (*fo.* 233) Elison and Robert Cawod of Wirkesburg, of all right and claim in that messuage built on, with two gardens and a close, with the appurtenances, in Wigefall within the bounds of Wirkesboro, which he lately had by the gift of Henry Elisson of Wirkesburg, lying in a certain place called Wygefall, between the land of William Hill called Broderode towards the north and the land of John Roklay towards the south.   Witnesses, John Scalehorne, chaplain, William Hill of Wirkysburg, (*fo.* 233*d*) John Gen, John Alott and John Holyn of Erdesley, and others.   Dated at Wirkesburg, in the feast of the Exaltation of Holy Cross, 1467.

(413)   Demise, feoffment, and delivery by Robert Elysson and Robert Cawode of Wikesburg [*sic*] to Richard, prior of the monastery, house, or church of blessed Mary Magdelene of Monkbretton, of the property in Wygfall as described in the last deed but one.[1]   To have and to hold (*fo.* 234) to the prior and his successors for ever, from the chief lords of the fee, by the services due and accustomed.   Appointment of John Spark, Thomas Cudworth, and John Elys as attorneys to deliver seisin.   Witnesses, John Webster, William Hill, William Pytte, and others.   Dated 12 January, 1467.

[1] Except that the bounding lands are now described respectively as " late " of William Elmeherst, John Rokley, and William Hill.

(*Fo.* 234*d*)[1] (414) Grant[2] by Robert de Roklay, knight, to Thomas
Gawde of a messuage built on, with two crofts adjoining, formerly
Henry de Fyschar's of Wirkesburg, as it is situated in the same
vill between the messuage of John Hankoc on the south, and on the
north between one of the said crofts, which croft abuts on Dawe
well towards the north; the other croft abuts on Crosse Cliff Bank
towards the west and on the meadow called Lyttell Enge towards the
east; with all lands, meadows, pastures, and appurtenances, which
he (the grantor) lately had by the gift and feoffment of John de
Wolthwayt, son of Elena Fischar, in the vill and territory of Wirkesburg.   To have and to hold (*fo.* 235) to the grantee, his heirs and
assigns, freely, from the chief lords of that fee, by the services due
and accustomed, for ever.   Witnesses, Richard del Hill of Wirkesburg, William Joneson, Robert son of John de Roklay, William del
Hagh, William Robynson, all of the same.   Dated at Wirkesburg,
at Martinmas, 1416, 4 Hen. V.

(*Fo.* 235*d*) (415) Release and quitclaim by Robert de Roklay,
esquire, son of Robert de Roklay, knight, to Thomas Gaude, his
heirs and assigns, of all right and claim in a messuage built on in
Wirkesburg, with two crofts adjoining, with all lands, meadows,
etc., with the appurtenances, which the said Thomas lately had by
the gift and feoffment of the said Robert de Roklay, knight, in the
same vill, and were formerly Henry Fischar's of Wirkesburgh, as in
a certain charter thereof to the said Thomas is more fully contained.
(*Fo.* 236) Witnesses, Robert Monke of Wikesburg, Thomas de
Calthorne, Richard del Hill, William Joneson, Robert son of John
de Roklay, and others.   Dated at Wirseburg, the feast of Saint
Andrew Apostle, 1416, and 4 Hen. IV.

(*Fo.* 236*d*) (416) Release and quitclaim by Robert de Roklay,
esquire, to Thomas Gaude of Wirkesburg and his executors, of all
manner of actions, real or personal, respecting any trespass, agreement, obligation, etc., or any matter or cause between them, from
the beginning of the world to the day of the making of these presents;
sealed with his seal the 20 April, 8 Hen. VI (1430).

(*Fo.* 237) (417) Release and quitclaim by John Webster, son and
heir of John Webster of Wirkesburg and Elizabeth his wife, to
John, earl of Salopp, James Haryngton, knight, and Henry Stafford,
rector of the church of Treton, and the heirs and assigns of the same
Henry, of all right, title, and claim of and in a messuage with two
gardens adjoining, in Wirkesburg, and in all other lands, meadows
and pastures in Wirkesburg, with their appurtenances, which the
said John, earl of Salopp, James, and Henry lately had by the gift
of the said John Webster and Elizabeth his wife in the same.   (*Fo.*
237*d*) Witnesses, Henry Helleson, Robert Elleson, William Elmehirste, and others.   Dated 5 August, 5 Edw. IV (1465).

[1] The heading " Wyrkysburgh " recommences here.
[2] " Terra Thome Gawde " written in the margin opposite.

(*Fo.* 238) (418) To all the faithful in Christ, etc., the prioress of Nonapilton and the convent thereof, greeting in the Lord. Know that whereas James Haryngton, knight, and Henry Stafford, rector of Treton, have and hold from us a messuage in Wirkesburg, with two crofts adjoining, and all other lands, tenements, etc., in Wirsburgh, which Robert Roklay, knight, sometime gave to Thomas Cawode and his heirs for ever, as in a certain charter thereof is more fully contained. Know that we have given licence to the said James and Henry to place in mortmain or alienate to a certain religious man and to the prior of the monastery of blessed Mary Magdelene of Monkbretton and his successors, or to any ecclesiastic, the said messuage, crofts, and all other lands, tenements, etc., (*fo.* 238*d*) with the appurtenances. Saving to us and our successors the services due and accustomed. Given in our Chapter House, 5 July, 6 Edw. IV (1466).

(419) Delivery and feoffment by John, earl of Salopp, James Haryngton, knight, and Henry Stafford, rector of the church of Treton, to Richard, prior of Monkbretton, of a messuage, with two crofts adjoining, (*fo.* 239) and all other lands, tenements, etc., with the appurtenances, in Wirkesburg, which Robert Roklay, knight, formerly gave to Thomas Gawde and his heirs for ever, and which they (the grantors) lately had by the gift and feoffment of John Webster of Wirkesburg and Elizabeth his wife. To have and to hold to the said Richard and his successors for ever, from the chief lords of those fees, by the services due and accustomed. Appointment of Thomas Oxspring as attorney to deliver seisin. (*Fo.* 239*d*) Witnesses, Robert Cawod, William Elmehirst, John Glewe, and others. Dated at Wirkesburg, 5 April, 7 Edw. IV (1467).

(420) Release and quitclaim by Elizabeth, late wife of John Webster late of Wirkesburg, in her widowhood, to James Harynton, knight, and Henry Stafford, rector of the church of Treton, their heirs and assigns, for ever, of all right, title, and claim of and in all those messuages, crofts, lands, meadows, etc., with the appurtenances, in Wirkesburg, which were lately Thomas Gawde's, and which the said Thomas had by the gift of Robert Roklay, knight. (*Fo.* 240) Dated 27 November, 18 Edw. IV (1478).

(421) Release and quitclaim by Henry Webster, son of John Webster, of Lincoln, (*fo.* 240*d*) to Thomas, prior of Monkbretton, and his successors for ever, of all right, title, etc., of and in a messuage, with the appurtenances, in Wirkesburgh and two crofts adjoining, and of and in all those lands and tenements, with the appurtenances, in Wirkesburg, which were lately Thomas Gawode's which he had by the gift and feoffment of Robert Roklay, knight. Witnesses, Thomas Oxpringe, gentleman, William Hysott, clerk, Robert Marshe, Richard Portar, Robert Tyndall, George Elys, (*fo.* 241) Thomas Buttery, and many others. Dated 29 October, 6 Hen. VIII (1514).

(422) Grant[1] by John Webster of Wirkesburg and Elizabeth his wife to John, earl of Salopp, James Harynton, knight, and Henry Stafford, rector of the church of Treton, of a messuage in Wirkesburg, with two crofts together adjoining, and all other lands, meadows, and pastures in Wirkesburg which Robert Roklay, knight, formerly gave to Thomas Gawde and his heirs for ever. To have and to hold, with the appurtenances, to the grantees and the heirs and assigns of Henry, for ever, (*fo.* 241*d*)[2] from the chief lords of that fee, by the services due and accustomed. Witnesses, Robert Cawode of Wirkesburg, William Elmehirste of the same, John Glewe, Henry Elleson, Robert Elleson, and others. Dated at Wirkesburg, 5 June, 4 Edw. IV (1464).

Wyrkysburghdale.

(423) At[3] the Court of the Prioress of Appillton[4], held at Wirkeburght, 18 April, " anno regni H. x° " (1432), Matilda wife of Roger Genne, daughter of John Elmehyrst, comes here in Court and claims by hereditary right a messuage and a bovate of land, with the appurtenances, after the death of William son of William son of John Elmehirst, whose heir of blood she is. Which messuage and bovate of land, with the appurtenances, were granted (*fo.* 242) to the said Matilda, to hold to her and her heirs, by the ancient services, according to the custom of the manor. And she gives-in the name of inheritance 13*s.* 4*d.*, by the pledge of Roger Genne, her husband; and the same gives for the marriage-fine[5] of Matilda 5*s.*

(424) At the Court of Wirkesburg, held there on Monday after the feast of Exaltation of Holy Cross, 34 Hen. VI (1455), Roger Genn by John Wygfall and Robert Fyssher, tenants of base tenure, sworn, surrendered a messuage, with the appurtenances, late in the tenure of the same Roger, into the hands of the lady the prioress of Appilton, to the use of Nicholas Worteley, esquire; which messuage, with the appurtenances, were granted to the said Nicholas, to have and to hold to him and his heirs for ever, according to the custom of the manor, by the ancient services and yearly rent, payable to the said prioress and her successors, of 15*s.* 7*d.*, and he gives the lady for fine and entry 6*s.* 7*d.*, and did fealty, and was admitted tenant, etc.

(*Fo.* 242*d*) (425) At the Court of Joan Ryther,[6] prioress of Appilton, held at Wirkesburg on Monday before the feast of Saints Simon

[1] In the margin is sketched, in pencil, with a finger pointing to " John Webster," a shield bearing a *lion rampant within a bordure* (Talbot, Earl of Shrewsbury—Salopp).

[2] The heading commences here " Wyrksburgh Dale," which continues (with slight variations in the spelling) to *fo.* 258*d.*

[3] In the margin is written " Derleyclyff," and below, in red ink, " Frankyschelande."

[4] Nun Appleton, a Cistercian priory founded *c.* 1150, near the river Wharfe, in Yorks. (See also No. 418.)

[5] *Mercheta.*

[6] Prioress 1459–1471.

Fo. 156.

Fo. 72.

Fo. 241

Arms of John,
3rd Earl of Shrewsbury.
(Salopp) No. 422.

MARGINAL DRAWINGS.

and Jude, 37 Hen. VI (1458), it is there contained, etc., Nicholas
Worteley, esquire, by Robert Fyssher, reeve and a tenant, sworn,
surrendered, in full Court, into the hands of the lady a messuage
and all other lands and tenements, with their appurtenances, which
lately he had in Wirkesburgh Dale, and surrendered to the said
Robert to the use of William Gen and his heirs for ever. And
touching this came the said William and took from the lady the said
messuage, lands, and tenements, with the appurtenances. To have
and to hold to him, his heirs and assigns, for ever, by the services
according to the custom of the manor and yearly rent of 15s. 7d.
And he gives the lady a fine[1] for entry, and did fealty and was admitted tenant.

(426) At the Court of Joan Ryther, prioress of Appilton, held
at Wirkesburg on Thursday after Martinmas, 38 Hen. VI (1459),
it is there contained, etc., William Genne, by John Gen, a tenant,
sworn, and the reeve (fo. 243) surrendered in full Court into the hands
of the lady a messuage and all other lands and tenements, with their
appurtenances, which he had in Wirkesburgdale, to the use of John
Cresacre, esquire, and his heirs, for ever. And touching this came
the said John Cresacre and took from the lady the said messuage,
lands, and tenements, with all the appurtenances. To have and
to hold to him and his heirs and assigns for ever, by the services
according to the custom of the manor and yearly rent of 15s. 7d.
And he gives the lady for fine for entry 5s., and did fealty, and was
admitted tenant.

(427) At the Court of the prioress and convent of Nunappilton,
held at Worsseburgh on Monday after the feast of St. Peter which
is called *ad vincula*, 1 Edw. IV (1461), it thus stands on record, etc.,
John Cresacre, esquire, by Richard Broddesworth, tenant, sworn,
and reeve, surrendered into the hands of the lady, the prioress, a
messuage and all other lands and tenements, with the appurtenances,
which he lately had and held from the same lady in Worsseburgh-
dale by service according to the custom of the manor, to the use
of John Frannkysshe, of Bilyngley, his heirs and assigns, for ever.
And touching (fo. 243d) this, came the same John Frannkysshe and
took from the said lady the said messuage, lands, and tenements,
with the appurtenances. To have and to hold to him and his heirs
and assigns for ever, by the services according to the custom of
the manor, and yearly rent of 15s. 7d., to be paid to the lady. And
he gives the lady a fine of 40d. for entry, and was admitted tenant.

(428) At the Court of the Lady Joan Ryther, prioress of Appilton, held there on Tuesday after the feast of the Exaltation of
Holy Cross, 11 Edw. IV (1471), John Frannkyssh, by Richard
Broddesworth, a tenant, sworn, surrendered into the hands of the
lady, the prioress, a messuage and a bovate of land, with the appurtenances, in Worsseburgdale, to the use of Robert Frannkyssh, son

---

[1] Amount of fine omitted.

of the said John.   And touching this came here in the same Court the same Robert, and took from the lady the said messuage and bovate of land, with all the appurtenances.   To have and to hold to him, his heirs and assigns, by the services according to the custom of the manor.   And he gives the lady as fine for entry 6s. 8d., and was admitted.

(Fo. 244) (429) At the Court of the lady, Matilda Tailbus,[1] prioress of Appilton, held there on Thursday after the feast of St. Luke Evangelist, 5 Hen. VII (1489), came Robert Herryson and Richard Keresforth, and took from the lady a messuage, with the lands, meadows, and pastures appertaining, in Worsseburgh, which Robert Frannkyssh surrendered.   To have to the same Robert and Richard and their heirs, according to the custom of the tenure of the manor there, by the rent and service due and accustomed; and he gives for fine 10s., whereof he paid in hand 6s. 8d., and for certain considerations is pardoned the remaining 3s. 4d.; and did fealty and was admitted tenant thereof, as appears in face of the said Court.

(430)   At the Court of the lady, Ann Langton,[2] prioress of Appilton, held at Worsburgh, 10 May, 4 Hen. VIII (1512), (fo. 244d) Robert Hareson, in absence at the Court, surrendered into the hands of the lady the prioress a messuage and all lands and tenements which he lately had and held in Worsburghdail, on Darlayclyff, late Robert Frankysh's, to the use of Thomas Roklay, esquire, Charles Barnby, Richard Nicols, Richard Cawodd, and John Halle, chaplain, at this court, and they took the said messuage, lands, and tenements, with the appurtenances; to hold and to have to themselves, their heirs and assigns, by the services according to the custom of the manor there, for ever; rendering yearly to the prioress and her successors 15s. 7d.   And they give the lady as fine for entry 10s., and were admitted tenants.

(431)   To all faithful of Christ, etc., Thomas Gen, brother and heir of William Gen, greeting.   Know that whereas the said William, by a certain charter granted to John Cresacre, senior, esquire, all the lands and tenements, meadows, pastures, and woods, with all the appurtenances, which (fo. 245) descended to him (William) by hereditary right after the death of Roger Gen lately deceased, in Darlayclyff, in Worsborghdale, or within the territory of Worsborgh, to have and to hold to him, his heirs and assigns, as in the said charter is more fully contained: and the same John by his deed granted to John Frankish, senior, or his heirs and assigns, all the said lands, etc. (as before), which he had by the gift of the said William in Derleyclyff and in Worsborghdale or within the territory of Worsborgh; to have and to hold to him, his heirs and assigns, for ever, as in the same deed is more fully contained.   Know that I the aforesaid Thomas have ratified and confirmed the estate, title,

---

[1] Confirmed 1489, died 1506.

[2] Called "Langley" in York. Archiep. Reg. Savage, fo. 486, but Langton in conventual leases and elsewhere.   She was appointed by lapse in 1506.

and possession of the same John Frankish, his heirs and assigns, of all the said property (described as before), and have released and quitclaimed for ever to him, his heirs and assigns, all my right, title, etc., against him. (*Fo.* 245*d*) Witnesses, John Shyres of Allertweytt, senior, Robert Baxter of Bolton on Dern, Robert Tynlay of Wath, John West of the same, Richard Bacon of the same, and many others.   Dated at Wath, 21 May, 1464, 4 Edw. IV.

(*Fo.* 246) (432) Exemplification of a suit at Westminster before Thomas Bryan, knight, and his fellows, Justices De Banco, Michaelmas term, 5 Hen. VII, Ro. 403 (1489).

EBOR.   Richard Keresford, senior, and Robert Henryson, by Thomas Rayner, their attorney, seek against Robert Frankeshe, clerk, twenty acres of land, eight acres of meadow, five acres (*fo.*246*d*) of pasture, two acres of wood, and 6*s.* 8*d.* of rent, with the appurtenances in Wirkesburgh, as their right and inheritance, and in which the same Robert Frankesse has no entry except after a disseisin by John Frankesse of the said Richard and Richard[1] Henrison. Robert Frankeshe in his proper person appeared, and defends, etc., and called to warrant thereof John Drakes, then present in Court in his proper person, and warrants, etc.   And touching this the said Robert [*sic*] and Robert seek against John the said tenements and rent in the form aforesaid.   (*Fo.* 247) And the said John as tenant by his warranty defends, etc., and says that John Frankesshe did not disseise the said Robert and Robert Henrison as the said Richard and Robert Henrison by their writ and statement suppose and thereupon places himself on the country, etc.   And Robert and Robert seek leave to interlocute and have it.   And afterwards the same Richard and Robert come again into Court in the same term by their attorney aforesaid.   And the said John Drakes, solemnly called, returned not, but withdrew in contempt of Court, and made default.   Therefore it is adjudged that the said Richard and Robert Henrison recover seisin against Robert Frankesshe, and that Robert Frankesshe have of the land of the said John Drakes the value, and the said John Drakes be in mercy, etc.

(The exemplification is sealed and dated at Westminster, 18 November, in the 5th year.)

(*Fo.* 247*d*) (433) Grant[2] by Hugh de Nevil, chief lord of Brelelay,[3] to Adam son of Robert de Swathe, and his heirs or assigns, except Religious, Jews, and the chief lords of the fee, of an essart as it lies within the bounds of Derley between the land of Adam son of Oryn, and an essart called Lauedi Rode, whereof at one head it abuts on the essart called Therprode and at the other head on the wall between that essart and the essart of Henry Ketilbarne.   To have and to hold to him, his heirs and assigns, from the grantor and his heirs,

---

[1] *Sic.* Throughout the deed the copyist seems to have been in a state of confusion as to the Christian names of the plaintiffs.

[2] " Spynk hous " written opposite in the margin.

[3] Brierley.

without retention by them, in fee and inheritance, freely, quietly, etc., (*fo.* 248) with all liberties, easements, and commons belonging to the said essart; rendering yearly to the grantor and his heirs 3*s.* 2*d.* for all services, etc., saving forinsec service, as belongs to such a holding. Warranty of the said essart, with the messuage and all other things belonging to the said essart. Witnesses, Henry de Rockelay, Richard of the same, Henry de Blacker, Adam de Derlay, Henry of the same, Reiner de Bosco, William the clerk, and others.

(434) Grant by Hugh de Nevile, (*fo.* 248*d*) lord of Berelay, to Henry son of Reyner de Swathe, his heirs and assigns, except Religious and Jews and the chief lord, of all that land, with the messuage and appurtenances, without retention, which Jordan Ketilbarn and Robert Ayre sometime held, in the territory of Derlay. To have and to hold to the grantee, his heirs and assigns (except as aforesaid), in fee and inheritance, freely, quietly, etc., with all liberties, etc., within and without the bounds of Derlay, thereto belonging. Rendering yearly to the grantor and his heirs or assigns 8*s.* for all services, etc., save forinsec service, as belongs to such a holding. (*Fo.* 249) Witnesses, Henry de Rockelay, Richard his brother, Henry de Blacker, Adam son of Ralph de Derlay, and many others.

(435) Grant by Thomas de Camera to Henry son of Henry de Rockelay of all that essart which Sir Hugh de Nevile sold to Adam son of Robert de Swath, and [which] lies within the bounds of Wirkesburgh between the land which Adam son of Oryn sometime held and Le Lauedi rode, one head abutting on Thorprode and the other on Murmor[1] between the said essart and the essart which Henry Ketilbarne formerly held. To have and to hold to the grantee, his heirs and assigns, with the wood and meadow, and all other appurtenances, from the lord of the fee, by the services thence due to him and accustomed, for all other services and demands. (*Fo.* 249*d*) Witnesses, Adam de Derlay, Richard of the same, Henry son of William de Wirkesburg, and others.

(436) Grant by Henry de Rocklay to Adam called Godeayre, son of Adam de Swathe of Wirkesburg, and his heirs, of an essart of land and meadow lying within the bounds of Wirkesburg which [is called] Le Seckerrode, as it lies in length and breadth between Le Lafnedirode on one side and Darthingtonrode on the other, and abuts at one head [upon] Yreperode and at the other on Ketelbernrode. To have and to hold, with all the appurtenances, to the grantee and his heirs and (*fo.* 250) assigns from the chief lord of that fee, by the services due to him and accustomed, freely, quietly, etc., with all liberties, etc., to the said essart belonging. Witnesses, John de Rockelay, Richard del Wodehouses of Wirkesburg, William son of Henry of the same, William de Derlay, John del Hill, John de Swathe, and others. Dated at Wirkesburg, Wednesday after Sunday in which is sung Quasi modo geniti, 1326.[2]

---

[1] The copyist apparently misread the word " murum," which is plain in the last deed but one.

[2] The first Sunday after Easter.

(437)   Grant by John son of John del Wode of Wirkesburgh to Thomas Spynk (*fo.* 250*d*) of Erdeslay and his heirs or assigns, of a moiety of an essart of land called Ayrode, as it lies in Wirkesburg on the west side of the tenement of Adam Godehair and abuts at the west head on a plot of meadow and wood called Jhonker, which fell to the grantor by hereditary right after the death of his said father, in the vill of Wirkesburg aforesaid.   To hold and to have the said moiety, with all appurtenances, to the grantee, his heirs or assigns, freely, quietly, etc., from the chief lords of that fee, by the services due and accustomed, for ever.   Witnesses, John de Swath of Wirkesburg, John del Hyll, William son of Henry of the same, Robert le ffissherr, Adam the clerk of the same, and others.   Dated at Wirkesburg, Wednesday before the feast of St. Thomas Apostle, 1343.

(*Fo.* 251)   (438)   Grant by Thomas Spynk of Erdeslay to Adam Godehayr of Wirkesburg, his heirs or assigns, of all that moiety of the essart of land in Wirkesburg called Ayrode, which the grantor had by the feoffment of John son of John del Wode of Wirkesburg. To hold and to have, with all the appurtenances, to the grantee, his heirs and assigns, freely, quietly, etc., from the chief lords of that fee, by the services due and accustomed, for ever.   (*Fo.* 251*d*) Witnesses, John de Swath of Wirkesburg, William son of Henry of the same, John del Hill, Richard del Stons, Adam the clerk of the same, and others.   Dated at Wirkesburg, Saturday in the feast of the Apostles Philip and James, 1344.

(439)   Grant by Richard de Oxpryng to John Glwe of Wirkesburghdale, his heirs and assigns, of a messuage called Spynkeshouse, with a croft adjacent, with all other appurtenances, in Wirkesburgdale, one head abutting on Sekkeroyde on the west side and the other on a certain lane on the east side, and lying between Grymewell on the south and Berntonroydes on the north.   To have and to hold (*fo.* 252) to the grantee, his heirs and assigns, from the chief lord of that fee, by the services due and accustomed.   Witnesses, Richard del Hill of Wirkesburgdale, Roger Genne, Thomas Clerkson, William Robynson, and William Jonson of the same, and others. Dated at Wirkesburgh, 8 May, 1413.

(440)   Grant by Thomas Bosevile of Erdesley (*fo.* 252*d*) to Henry Glu of Wirkesburgh of an essart of land called Le Laderoyde, as it is enclosed by fence and ditch lying in Derleyclyff within the bounds of Wirkesburgh; and also a meadow called Grymehing lying at the east end of the said essart and abutting upon Swathker. To have and to hold, with all the appurtenances, to the grantee, his heirs and assigns, freely, quietly, etc., from the chief lords of that fee, by the services due and accustomed.   Rendering thence to the grantor and his heirs and assigns yearly twelve silver pence, and rendering yearly to the prior and convent of the abbey of Monkbretton and their successors 5*s.* of silver, and also rendering to the prioress and convent of Nunapilton and their successors 4*s.* of silver

yearly, (*fo.* 253) for all secular service and demand. Witnesses, Adam the clerk of Wirkesburgh, William del Hill, Thomas de Swath, William de Burton, Roger de Thornhill of the same, and others. Dated at Derleyclyff in Wirkesburg, Sunday after the feast of Martinmas, 1386.

(441) Acknowledgment by William son and heir of Roger de Thornehhill, (*fo.* 253*d*) lately dwelling in Wirkesburgdale, of the receipt from John Glue of Wirkesburg, on the day of the making of these presents, of 6s. 8d. in full payment of a greater sum in which he was liable to William by his bond for a certain garden bought from him. At Doncaster, Saturday, 1 June, 4 Hen. VI (1426).

(442) Grant by William son and heir of Roger de Thornhill, lately dwelling in Wirkesburgh dale, to John Glue of Wirkesburg, his heirs and assigns, of a certain small garden lying within the bounds of Wirkesburgh beside the messuage of the said John called Lady-zerdes, abutting on Ladyrode at the (*fo.*254) eastern head, and at the western head on the common before the messuage of the said John. To have and to hold, with the appurtenances, to the grantee, his heirs and assigns, freely, quietly, etc., from the chief lord of that fee, by the services due to him and accustomed. Witnesses, Richard del Hill of Wirkesburg, William his son, William Jonson, Henry Fyshar, Richard Smyth of Barneslay, and others. Dated at Wirkesburg, Tuesday, 18 May, 1423.

(*Fo.* 254*d*) (443) Grant by John Glewe, son and heir of John Glewe, now deceased, for a certain sum of money paid to him in hand, to Brian Bradford, Thomas Oxspryng, and William Wadylove, of two messuages and all lands and tenements, meadows, woods, etc., with the appurtenances, in Wirkesburg, formerly his said father's. To have and to hold to the grantees, their heirs and assigns, for ever, from the chief lords of that fee, by the services due and accustomed. (*Fo.* 255) Appointment of John Bolton and Thomas Wodward as attorneys to deliver seisin. Witnesses, Thomas Wortley, knight, Robert Wodhall, John Calff, chaplain, and many others. Dated 4 August, 11 Hen. VII (1496).

(*Fo.* 255*d*) (444) Release and quitclaim by the same John Glewe to the same grantees and their heirs and assigns, of all right, title, etc., of or in all those messuages, lands, tenements, rents, reversions, and services, with the appurtenances, in Workesburgh, which were lately John Glewe's, his father. (*Fo.* 256) Witnesses, John Thopclyff, Thomas Lyster, Thomas Baxter, and others. Dated 26 August, 12 Hen. VII (1496).

(445) Release and quitclaim by Alice late wife of John Glewe and mother of John Glewe his son, in her pure widowhood, (*fo.* 256*d*) to the same three grantees, their heirs and assigns, as above, of all right, title, etc., of the messuages, etc., as in the previous deed. (*Fo.* 257) Witnesses, Thomas Lyster, Richard Hopkynson, vicar of Bolton, Richard Hunter, clerk, and others. Dated 20 August, 11 Hen. VII (1496).

(446)   Release and quitclaim by Thomas Oxpryng to Robert, prior of Monkbretton, and the convent thereof and their successors, of all the right, claim, estate, etc., which he (Thomas) had together with Brian Bradforthe and William Wadelowyffe, now deceased, of the gift of John Glew, son and heir of John Glew, of or in all the messuages, etc., as in the last two deeds. (*Fo.* 257*d*) Dated at Monkbretton, 10 April, 13 Hen. VII (1498).

(*Fo.* 258) (447) Acknowledgment by John Glewe, son and heir of John Glewe of Workesburg, that he has this day received from William, prior of Monkbretton, £4 in full satisfaction of £21 13s. 4d. for all his (John's) lands and tenements in Workesburg, sold to the same prior and his successors for the said sum, and he acquits the prior and his successors thereof by these presents, sealed. Dated 5 January, 6 Hen. VII (1490-1).

(448)   Release and quitclaim by Margaret (*fo.* 258*d*) Smyth, widow, late wife of Richard Smyth of Kirk Sandall, formerly wife of John Glewe, to William, prior of Monkbretton, and the convent thereof and their successors, of all her right, title, claim, etc., of and in the same property in Worsbore as in the last deed but one and previous deeds, formerly the said John Glewe's late her husband. (*Fo.* 259) Witnesses, John Pek, esquire, Ralph Barneby, esquire, Thomas Grene, gentleman, and others. Dated at Monkbretton, 24 November, 17 Hen. VIII (1525).

(449)   Grant by William, prior of Monkbretton, and the convent thereof, (*fo.* 259*d*) to Margaret Smyth, widow, formerly wife of John Glewe, of a yearly rent of 10s. issuing from a close called Bebbeall More, with the appurtenances, in Fysshelake, now in the tenure of Thomas Grene, gentleman. To have and receive the said rent to Margaret and her assigns, for the term of her life. Power of distraint in case the rent is in arrear for forty days. Alternate seals of the parties, to the two parts of this writing indentate. (*Fo.* 260) Given in the grantor's chapter house, 24 November, 17 Hen. VIII (1525).

Smythlay.[1]

(450)   Grant by Sir John Schepeschank, chaplain, and John Wystardrode, to Richard de Smythlay and Joan his wife and the heirs of their bodies, of all the lands and tenements which they (the grantors) had by the gift and feoffment of the said Richard in the vills and fields of Smythlay, Wombewell, and Hymlyngfeld. To have and to hold, with the appurtenances, to the grantees and the heirs of their bodies, from the chief (*fo.* 260*d*)[2] lords of that fee, by the services due and accustomed. Dated at Smythlay, the feast of the Apostles Simon and Jude, 13 Ric. II (1389). Witnesses, Thomas Barlay, Hugh Wombewell, Ralph Normanvill, and many others.

---

[1] Written here in the margin and as a heading on the next page, and *fo.* 261*d*, " Smithley and Hemingfield in Wombell."

[2] Headed " Smythlay," as also is *fo.* 261*d*.

(451)   Grant by Richard son of Richard de Wambewell to God and Saint Mary Magdelene of Bretton and the monks (*fo.* 261) there, of all the land, with all the appurtenances, without retention, which Richard Aldham held[1] from him (the grantor) in the territory of Smethley.   To hold and to have freely, quietly, and peaceably, in wood, in plain, etc., with all free common in the vill and without, and all other easements and liberties to the said vill of Smethley belonging.   Rendering thence yearly 4*d.* to the altar of St. Nicholas of the chapel of St. Mary of Wambewelle on the day of St. Nicholas, for all services and secular demands, save forinsec service of the King, as belongs to one bovate of land where twelve carucates and one and a half bovates make a knight's fee, and saving the service of Wath.   Witnesses, Sir (*fo.* 261*d*) William son of William, Sir Jordan de Sancta Maria, Reiner de Wombewell, John de Rockeley, and many others.

(452)   Let it appear to all by these presents, that whereas I Robert son of John de Wombewelle, have by usurpation occupied the custody and marriage of the land and heir of Adam de Bosco of Smythley, over the prior of Monkbretton, and the said prior impleaded me before the Justices, by writ of the King, respecting the said custody and marriage, I acknowledge that I have no right therein, and if I shall have had or can have any right in the said custody and maritage I release and quitclaim it to the said prior and convent and their successors, by these presents, so that neither I nor my heirs shall be able to claim any right in the said custody and marriage, or escheat if it shall occur, in the tenements formerly of the said Adam de (*fo.* 262) Bosco deceased, in Smythley in Wombewelle. Witnesses, Richard de la Wodehalle, Godfrey de Staynton, William de Notton, Hugh de Smythlay, John de Kynnesley, and others.

(453)   Grant by Adam, prior of Bretton, and the convent thereof to Master Thomas the physician of Scelton and his heirs or assigns, for his homage and service, of a bovate of land in Smythley, with the appurtenances, that namely which Richard de Wambewell gave them (the grantors).   To have and to hold from the grantors and their successors, in fee and inheritance, freely, quietly, etc., in wood and plain, etc., (*fo.* 262*d*)[2] and in all easements and liberties, within and without the vill, as belongs to so much land: rendering thence yearly to the grantors and their successors 4*s.* yearly for all service to them and 4*d.* yearly to the altar of St. Nicholas of the chapel of Wambewelle, and doing the forin ec [service] of the King and the service of Sir William de Wath and his heirs.   Witnesses, William son of William, Adam de Sancta Maria, Jordan his brother, John de Rockeley, Thomas de Crigeliston, and many others.

(*Fo.* 263) (454)   Grant by Roger son of Robert de Berch to God and blessed Mary Magdelene of Birtton and the monks there, of that

---

[1] A finger-point opposite this in the margin, in different ink.
[2] This page is not headed.

essart which was William de Mundesder's, which lies between the essart of Henry Palefrai and the essart of Edric as it lies in length and width, in pure and perpetual alms, to hold and have freely and quietly, and wholly, as pure and perpetual alms.   Witnesses, William Fleming, and others.[1]

Barneby.

(455)   Grant[2] by Alan de Bretton (fo. 263d)[3] to God and Saint Mary Magdelene of Bretton and the monks there of all the land of his demesne in Barneby, which Robert de Athelwald held freely [and] quietly from the grantor and his heirs, with all commons of the same vill; rendering yearly 8d. at Whitsuntide and 8d. at Martinmas.   This land he has granted to the monks for his soul and the souls of his ancestors and heirs, in pure and perpetual alms, free and quit of all secular exaction.   Witness, Robert.

Barghe.

(456)   Grant[4] by Ralph[5] de Rupe and Leticia his wife, for the health of their souls and the souls of John their son and Hugh de Suualuhil (sic), to God and the church of Saint Mary Magdelene of Bretton and the monks there, in pure and perpetual alms, of a culture of land, with the appurtenances, in the territory of Barghe, that namely which is called Roger Rode as it lies between the land of the prior of Pontefract and Derne; whereof one head (fo. 264) abuts on Ravenkell Rode and the other on the land formerly Hugh de Berg's. To hold and to have freely and quietly, with all easements, liberties, and commons of the said vill of Berg, to so much land belonging, without annoyance by the grantors or their heirs.   Witnesses, John de Hoderode, John de Bosuuel, Robert de Berg, John the grantor's son, Robert Turs, and many others.

Swalohyll.[6]

(457)   Confirmation by Jordan de Horbiri and Eugenia his wife (fo. 264d) to God and the church of Saint Mary Magdelene of Lunda and the monks there, of a moiety of the land of William the smith of Swaleuehil, and the service of the same, with all easements which ought to belong to a moiety of the said land, which Swane de Holande granted and gave them; freely and quietly, for the health of the souls of themselves and of the said Swane and all their ancestors, in pure and perpetual alms.   Witnesses, Master Peter de Doncaster, Henry his brother, Reginald the scribe, William de Horbiri, Thomas his brother, and others.

[1] No vill is named, either in the deed or the heading.

[2] " Barneby " written in the margin opposite.

[3] Headed " Barghe."

[4] " Barghe," " Rog' royde," are written in the margin; in the heading, " de una cultura terre vocata Roger Royde in territorio de Barghe."

[5] Erroneously called " Roger " by Burton (Mon. Ebor., 92).

[6] Swallow Hill, in Darton.

(458) Quitclaim by Reginald son of Helias de Sothil of twenty acres of land, those namely which William the smith held in Sualewehil and that which Swane de Hoiland gave the monks of Bretton, in pure and perpetual alms; whereof there was a suit between him (Reginald) and the said monks in the court of Roger de Cestria of Pontefract by precept of the King; he has ceded all his right to the aforesaid monks for three marks which they have given him. Witnesses, Robert de Walas, Adam de Rainavill, William de Staplton, and many others.

(Fo. 265)   *Dartton.*

(459) Grant by Ernald de Barnabi to God and Saint Mary Magdelene of Bretton and the monks there, of two acres of land of his demesne in Dertona, with the appurtenances, in pure and perpetual alms, free and quit of all secular exaction. Witnesses, Hugh de Berch, Adam de Berch, Hugh de Bretton, William son of Roger, etc.

(460) Grant by brother Adam de Norhampton,[1] prior (*humilis minister*) of Bretton, and the convent there, to Henry son of Henry Brid[2] of Ketelbarnethorp and his heirs for ever, of a croft within the bounds of Derton, called Robert croft, (*fo. 265d*)[3] one head whereof extends to the south to the road which leads to Derton and the other to the north as far as the land of William son of Adam de Derton, and one side is on the west beside the land which Roger Kenbodi holds and the other side on the east goes with the King's highway between the said land and Hoderode, as the said croft lies in length and breadth. To hold and to have from the grantors and their successors to the grantee and his heirs, in fee, freely and quietly, with all liberties, commons, and easements to so much land belonging within and without the bounds of Derton, rendering yearly to the grantors and their successors 12*d.*, for all secular services and demands. Warranty so far as the said croft shall be warranted to the grantors. Seal of the convent to this writing, and Henry has affixed his seal to the transcript remaining with the monks. Witnesses, Sir Ralph, then parson of Derton, Robert Bergh, Henry son of Matilda de Ketaburg, and many others.

(Fo. 266)[4]   *Cublay.*

(461) Grant by Nicholas Burdett, lord of Denby, to William son of Richard de Bilclyff, lately dwelling at Waturhall in Peniston, his heirs and assigns, of a messuage and all the land, with the meadow to the said messuage belonging, with all the appurtenances, called lez Rodes, which formerly John Cublay held, within the bounds of Peniston. To have and to hold to the grantee, his heirs and assigns,

[1] Adam de Nortampton occurs 1259 and 1266.

[2] In the heading " Byrd."

[3] No heading.

[4] Not headed, but " Cublay " is written in the margin. Afterwards the heading is " Cublay " or " Cubley " to *fo.* 270*d.* Cubley, in the parish of Peniston.

freely, quietly, etc., from the chief lord of that fee, by the services due to him and accustomed. Witnesses, Richard de Oxpringe, John de Hesilhede of Thurleston, Thomas del Rodes of the same, Nicholas de Wordulworth of Peniston, and others. Dated at Peniston, Tuesday, 5 June, 1408.

(*Fo.* 266*d*) (462) Obligation by Nicholas Burdett, lord of Denby, to William son of Richard de Bilclyff, lately dwelling at Waturhall in Peniston, and his heirs and executors, in forty marks sterling, payable at Peniston at Michaelmas next following; for which payment he (Nicholas) binds himself, his heirs and executors, and all his goods and chattels, wheresoever found, by these presents. Dated at Denby, 1 July, 1408.

(463) Release and quitclaim by John son of Roger At-church (*fo.* 267) to Amabel his sister, of all right and claim in a messuage and eight acres of arable land and meadow, as they lie within certain bounds of Peniston, at Le Rodes, in a place called Le Longehirst. Witnesses, William del Hill, John son of Peter, John Salforth, and others. Dated at Peniston, Saturday after Sunday in [which is sung] Quasi modo geniti,[1] 1328.

(464) Grant by Amabel daughter of Henry son of Roger At-church to William del Hill of Thurleston and his heirs, of a messuage and eight acres of land and meadow, with the appurtenances, lying within certain bounds in (*fo.* 267*d*) the vill and territory of Peniston at Le Rodes, in a place called Le Longehyrst. To have and to hold to the grantee, his heirs and assigns, from the chief lord of that fee, by the services due and accustomed, freely, quietly, etc., with all appurtenances, liberties, commons, and easements to the land belonging. Witnesses, John le procurator of Peniston, Thomas de Heselheved, and others.

(465) Release and quitclaim by Richard Waterhall to Richard Oxpring, son of Richard Oxpring of Cudworth, of all right, estate, title, and claim, etc., in a messuage or a plot of land called Coblay, in the vill (*fo.* 268) of Peniston, situate and being beside the chapel of St. John in Peniston, and in all other lands and tenements there called Coblay, and also of and in an acre of land lying in the fields of Peniston, and similarly of and in a certain plot of land containing by estimation eight acres in Peniston, with the appurtenances, called Longhirst. Dated at Coblay, 11th kal. January, 30 Hen. VI (1451–2).

(466) Release and quitclaim by William Waturhall, son and heir of Richard Waterhall, to Richard Ledes, prior of Monk (*fo.* 268*d*) Bretton, and his successors, of all right and claim in a messuage or plot of land called Coblay in the vill of Peniston, situate and being beside the chapel of St. John in Peniston, and also of and in all other lands and tenements there called Coblay, and of and in an acre of

---

[1] First Sunday after Easter.

J

land lying in the fields of Penyston, and a certain plot of land containing by estimation eight acres in Peniston, with the appurtenances, called Le Longhyrst; all which the said prior lately had by the gift and feoffment of William Oxpring, esquire, son and heir of Richard Oxpring, senior, esquire. (*Fo.* 269) Witnesses, Thomas Oxpring, Robert Wodhall, Thomas Sandbeck, and others. Dated 16 May, 15 Edw. IV (1475).

(467) Grant by William Oxspring, esquire, to Thomas Oxspring, his brother, William Barnaby, vicar of the church of Derfeld, William Bradfford, John Lake, Robert Chaloner, and William Wordesworth, vicar of the church of Peniston, of the properties mentioned in the preceding deed.[1] To have and to hold, with the appurtenances, to the grantees, (*fo.* 269*d*) their heirs and assigns, for ever, from the chief lords of that fee, by the services due and accustomed. Witnesses, Richard Barnaby, John Swyfte, Thomas Grene, and many others. Dated 8 August, 11 Edw. IV (1471).

(468) Release and quitclaim by the grantees of the previous deed,[2] to Richard, prior of Monkbretton, and the convent thereof and their successors, (*fo.* 270) of all right, title, estate, etc., of and in the properties, as in the preceding deed.[3] Dated 28 August, 11 Edw. IV (1471).

(469) Demise by Thomas Oxspring, William (*fo.* 270*d*) Barnby, vicar of the church of Derfeld, John Lake, and Robert Chaloner, to Richard, prior of Monkbretton, and the convent thereof and their successors, of the same properties which lately they (the grantors) had jointly with William Bradford and William Wordsworth, vicar of the church of Peniston, now deceased, by the gift and feoffment of William Oxspring. To have and to hold to the grantees and their successors for ever, from the chief lords of that fee, by the services due and accustomed. Witnesses, Aimer Burdet, esquire, John Swifte, and others. Dated at Penyston, 20 June, 21 Edw. IV (1481).

(*Fo.* 271)[5]   *Brokhouse.*

(470) Grant by William son of John Skott of Browkhous by Skoles to John de Kyrkby of a messuage called Browhous by Skoles, with the buildings and with all lands, woods, meadows, pastures, commons, easements, and liberties which he (the grantor) had by

---

[1] In this grant the acre in the fields of Peniston is described as between the land of Nicholas Stevenson, chaplain, on the north, and the land called " Seyntroneland " on the south; and the plot, stated in the previous deed to contain eight acres, is now estimated at four acres. The chapel is called the chapel of St. John the Baptist.

[2] Except the two vicars.

[3] Longhirst is here estimated at four acres.

[4] Longhirst is here estimated at four acres, and the land previously called " Seyntroneland " is called " Seint John land."

[5] " Browkhowes " written at the top in the margin. The heading is " Brokehowes " or " Brokehowse " to *fo.* 273*d*.

hereditary right after the death of his father, within the bounds of Thurulston. To have and to hold, with all appurtenances, to the grantee, his heirs and assigns, freely, quietly, etc., from the chief lord of that fee, by the services due and accustomed. (*Fo. 271d*)[1] Witnesses, Nicholas Burdett, John Skott of Turlyston, Thomas de Rodes, and others. Dated at Browkhous, the feast of St. John Baptist, 1392.

(471) Grant by John Kyrkby of Preston by Pontefract to Thomas son of Richard de Kyrkby, his heirs and assigns, of all those lands and tenements which he (John) had by the gift and feoffment of William Skott, within the bounds of Thurleston, to wit, that messuage, with all the appurtenances, called Browkhous by Skoles. To hold and to have to the grantee, his heirs and assigns, freely, quietly, etc., from the chief lords of that fee, by the services due and accustomed. (*Fo. 272*) Witnesses, John de Hesylhed, Thomas de Rodes, Thomas de Appylyerd, and many others. Dated at Brok-hous by Skoles, Sunday after the feast of St. John Baptist, 1393.

(472) Appointment by John de Kyrkby of William de Kirkby, his son, as attorney to receive seisin in his name, of that messuage, with the buildings, and all lands, with the appurtenances, which William son of John Skott had in Brokehous and within the bounds of Thurulston by hereditary right after the death of his father, according to the tenor of a charter by the said William to him (John) made. Dated at Penyston, Saturday before the feast of St. John Baptist, 1392.

(*Fo. 272d*)[2] (473) Grant by William Kirkby, son and heir of Richard Kirkeby of Brokhouse, to John Nevyll of Lyversegh, knight, Aimer Burdhed, esquire, and William Kay, chaplain, of a messuage in Turleston called Le Brokehousez, and also all other his lands and tenements, with the appurtenances, in Thurleston aforesaid. To have and to hold all the aforesaid, to the grantees, their heirs and assigns, from the chief lords of that fee, by the services due and accus-tomed. (*Fo. 273*) Witnesses, John Jenkynson of Denby, William Stede of Wynteworth, William Elys of Holand, and others. Dated 20 January, 10 Edw. IV (1470–1).

(474) Appointment by William Kirkebe, son and heir of Richard Kirkebe of Brokehouse by Scolis, of Nicholas son and heir of Aimer Burdhed and John Elys of Thurleston, as his attorney to enter upon and deliver seisin (*fo. 273d*) of and in a messuage, lands, and tene-ments, with the appurtenances, in Thurlleston, to John Nevill of Lyversegh, knight, Aimer Burdhed, esquire, and William Kay, chap-lain, their heirs and assigns, according to the form and effect of a certain charter to them made. Witnesses, John Jenkinson of Denby, William his son, John Elys, Thomas Grefe, John Cusworth, and others. Dated as preceding deed.

---

[1] Headed " Brokhowse."

[2] *Ibid.*

(475) Grant by John Nevile of Lyversegh, knight, Aimer Burd-hed, esquire, and William Kay, chaplain, to Richard Ledes, prior of Monkbretton, and the convent thereof and their successors, for ever, of a messuage in Thurleston called Brokhouses, and all other lands, (*fo.* 274) meadows, and pastures, with the appurtenances, in Thurleston aforesaid, which formerly were William Kirkby's, son and heir of Richard Kirkby of Brokhouse. To have and to hold to the grantees and their successors for ever, from the chief lords of those fees, by the services due and accustomed. Witnesses, Thomas Oxspring, John Jenkinson, William Stede, Richard West, William Elys, and others. Dated at Thurleston, 6 January, 22 Edw. IV (1482–3).

Oxspryng.

(476) Grant[1] by Henry son of John son of Agnes de Ospring (*fo.* 274*d*) to Baldwin del Hill, Thomas de Heselheved, his brother, and their heirs and assigns, of the land of Broderode and of Lonynges and of Stonicnoll, with the meadow and wood adjacent, as all the said land lies wholly and abuts on the east side to the stream running beside Le Storthes and on the west side to Brounescroft and lies from the side on the north to the land of Alan son of Thomas the shepherd and on the south to the land called Betoncrofte, which Matthew the smith holds. To have and to hold all the said land, with the wood, meadow, and other appurtenances, to the said Bald-win [and] Thomas, their heirs and assigns, from the lord of the fee, freely and peaceably, with all liberties, commons, and easements within the bounds of Oxspring and without belonging to the land, with free entry and exit through the middle of the grantor's land at all times of the year, without hindrance, doing to the said lords of the fee the services due and accustomed. Warranty for a certain sum of money (*fo.* 275) received from the grantees. Witnesses, William de Hunschelf, Robert de Ospring, John de Westhorp, John son of Alexander, and others. Dated at Peniston, the morrow of St. Andrew Apostle, 1310.

(477) Grant by Robert son of Thomas de Heselheved to Thomas de Cotingam, his heirs and assigns, of the property named in the preceding deed.[2] (*Fo.* 275*d*) To have and to hold, with the wood, etc., as in the last deed, to the grantee, his heirs and assigns, from the lord of the fee, by the services due and accustomed, freely, quietly, etc., with all liberties, etc., (as before), with free entry and exit through the middle of the land of Henry son of John son of Agnes de Ospring at all times of the year without hindrance by Henry or his heirs. Baldwin del Hill [and] Thomas de Heselheved were enfeoffed by the gift and feoffment of the said Henry, and after the death of Baldwin and Thomas the property descended to Robert son and heir of Thomas de Heselheved by hereditary right

[1] "Ospring" [*sic*] written in the margin.
[2] "Betoncrofte" is not described as held by Matthew Faber in this deed. "Stonicnoll" is called "Stonnyknoll."

fo. 276

INITIAL LETTER N (Deed 478).

(*Fo.* 276) Witnesses,[1] Robert de Secleye, John of the same, John son of Clesey the clerk, Richard son of the smith, John son of Roger, Gilbert Flecher, John son of Nalissone. Dated at Ospring, Tuesday after the feast of St. Ambrose bishop, 1342.

(478) Release and quitclaim by Aneta who was the wife of Richard Biyondbrok of Thurgoland, and John her son, to Thomas de Cotingham of Monkbretton, of all right and claim in all that land, meadow, and wood, with the appurtenances, which is called Brode-rode, Lonynges, and Stonyknoll, in Oxspring, or in any rent issuing from the said land. (*Fo.* 276*d*) Witnesses, Robert de Hesilheved, Richard de Oxspring, John Proctur of Peniston, and others. Dated at Oxspring, Wednesday, 22 May, 1359.

(479) Release and quitclaim by Nicholas de Wortelay, knight, to Thomas de Cotingham of Monkbretton and his heirs or assigns, of all right and claim in all those tenements, with the appurtenances, in Oxspring, which he (Thomas) had by the grant (*fo.* 277) of Robert de Hesilheved or in any rent issuing therefrom. Witnesses, Robert de Hesilheved, Richard de Oxspring, John Proctur of Peniston, and others. Dated at Oxspring, Wednesday, 22 May, 1359.

(480) Grant by Thomas le Renderour of Cotingham of Monk-bretton, to the prior and convent of Monkbretton and their successors of a yearly rent of 14*s.*, with the appurtenances, in Cutheworth, (*fo.* 277*d*)[2] Peniston, Oxspring, and Thurleston, namely a rent of 2*s.* 3*d.* yearly receivable from a messuage and a bovate of land in Peniston and Thurleston which is called Danngerous oxgang, and 5*d.* rent issuing from Southerode which was formerly Henry Wlff's, together with the fealties and all other services of William son of Richard de Oxspring, who previously held the said tenements to himself and the heirs of his body from the present grantor and his heirs; 4*s.* rent, with the appurtenances, in Oxspring in the parish of Peniston, receivable yearly from the Broderodes, Lonynges, and Stoniknoll, and from the meadow and woods adjacent, with the fealties and other services of Richard Byyonthebroke and his heirs, who hold these tenements by the demise of Robert son of Elias de Oxspring and Alice his wife, who held them previously from the present grantor to themselves and the heirs of his body; 7*s.* 9*d.* rent, with the appurtenances, in Coithworth, receivable from half a bovate of land and meadow called Sarle oxgang, and from half a bovate of land and meadow (*fo.* 278) formerly John Bell's, and from two acres of land and meadow formerly John Pull's in Cutheworth, and from an acre of land lying on Le Heghrode formerly John Tay-lor's, and from three and a half roods of land on Le Freneleghes formerly Thomas Bayard's, and from an acre of land and meadow formerly Adam's, son of Jordan, in Cutheworth, which tenements Robert Scot of Cutheworth, baxter, and Dionisia his wife previously

---

[1] The attestation clause commences "hiis testibus," but the Christian names are all in the nominative.

[2] Headed "Oxspryng Penyston Thurleston and Cudworthe."

held from the present grantor, to them and the heirs of his body,
together with the fealties and all other services of the said Robert
and Dionisia, and their heirs.   To have and to hold the said yearly
rent, with the appurtenances, to the said prior and convent and
their successors, with the fealties and all other services of the said
William, John, Robert, Alice, Robert, and Dionisia and their heirs,
well and in peace, from the chief lords of the fee, by the services
due and accustomed.   Witnesses, Thomas Bosevil, John de Barneburgh, (*fo.* 278*d*)[1] Thomas Bell, Richard son of Richard de Bretton,
William de Oxspring, William de Thurleston, and others.   Dated
at Monkbretton, 10 May, 45 Edw. III (1371).

Wakefeld.[2]

(481)   Grant by William Okes of Wakefeld, Thomas Holm and
Agnes Abba, lately wife of Robert Abba of Wakefeld, to Robert
Mason of Wakefeld, his heirs and assigns, of a tenement, with the
appurtenances, in Wakefeld, as it lies in a certain street of that vill
called Kirkgate, between the tenements of William Saltmerssh and
Henry Tayllour on the north and the tenement of Richard Hodes-
well on the south, which tenement, with the appurtenances, the
grantors lately had, among other things, by the gift and feoffment
of Nicholas Chapman, vicar of Corryngham in the county of Lincoln.   To have and to hold to the grantee, his heirs and assigns,
from the chief lords of the fee, by the services due and (*fo.* 279)
accustomed.   Witnesses, William Gairgrave, Thomas Beaumont,
Robert Hill, Robert Gryce, Robert Baroclogh, and others.   Dated
at Wakefield, 9 December, 35 Hen. VI (1456).

(482)   Grant by William Mason, chaplain, to Gerard Lascy,
gentleman, Thomas Oxspring, William Wadeluff, and Thomas Wodward, of all that his messuage, with the orchard and garden to the
same adjoining, with the appurtenances, in the vill of Wakefeld,
situated in a certain street there called Kirkgate, and in which John
Nante now dwells; which messuage, with the orchard and garden,
descended to the grantor by hereditary right after the death of
Robert Mason, his father.   To have and to hold to the grantees,
their heirs and assigns, for ever, from (*fo.* 279*d*) the chief lords of
that fee, by the services due and accustomed.   Warranty.   Appointment of Thomas Grene and William Scamond to deliver seisin.
Witnesses, John Chaloner, William Amyas, Brian Bradford, Thomas
Lister, Richard Pek, then bailiff of Wakefield, and many others.
Dated at Wakefield, 26 October, 20 Hen. VII (1504).

(*Fo.* 280) (483)   Release and quitclaim by William Mason, chaplain,
to the same grantees, of all right, title, etc., of and in the property
named in the previous deed.   Dated 6 November, (*fo.* 280*d*)[3]
20 Hen. VII (1504).

[1] Headed " Wakeffeld."

[2] " Wakefeld Masonthyng " written opposite in margin.

[3] Headed " Wakeffelde."   The heading " Wakefeld," with slight variations
in the spelling, continues to *fo.* 287*d*.

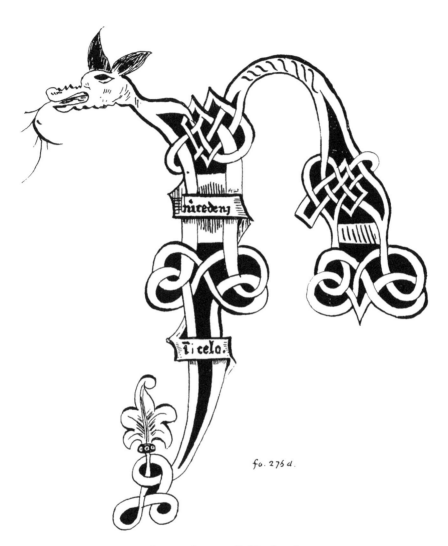

fo. 276 d.

INITIAL LETTER N (Deed 479).

(484) Release and quitclaim by Robert Taylyour of Sawlay kinsman and heir of William Mason, chaplain, and Thomas Taylyour, son and heir of the said Robert, to Thomas Oxspring, gentleman, of all right, title, and claim of and in a messuage, with orchard and garden, with the appurtenances, in the vill of Wakefeld in a certain street called Kyrkegate. (*Fo.* 281) Witnesses, Robert Roklay of Belynley, gentleman, William Gurry of Rotherham, Thomas Chamber of the same, and many others. Dated at Wakefeld, 28 June, 2 Hen. VIII (1510).

(485) Release and quitclaim by Thomas Oxspring, gentleman, to Thomas, prior of Monkbretton, and the convent there, and their successors for ever, of all right, title, estate, etc., which he had or has together with Gerard Lascy, William (*fo.* 281*d*) Wadeluff, and Thomas Wodeward, now deceased, by the grant of William Mason, chaplain, of and in a messuage, orchard, and garden, with the appurtenances, in Wakfeld, situated in a certain street there called Kirkgate, in which John Nante now dwells. Dated 7 February, 21 Hen. VII (1505–6).

(*Fo.* 282)[1] (486) Grant by Joan Spicer of Wakefeld, in her widowhood, to John del Rodes of the same, her son, of two tenements, with a croft adjoining one of them, and the appurtenances, in Wakefeld, as they are situated in the street called Westgate; whereof one lies between the tenement of Robert Bull on the east and the tenement of Joan Wawan on the west, and the other lies between the tenement of Magota Overhall and a certain waste plot. To have and to hold to the grantee, his heirs and assigns, freely, quietly, etc., for ever, from the chief lords of that fee, by the services due and accustomed. Witnesses, John de Kent, the bailiff, Robert Bron, Robert Bull, Simon Catney, William de Erdeslawe, and others. Dated 4 January, 11 Hen. IV (1409–10).

(*Fo.* 282*d*) (487) Grant by John Rodes of Wakfeld to Thurstan Banastre, William Bradford, and Thomas Dodworth, of two messuages with the crofts adjoining, in the vill of Wakefeld, in a certain street called Westgate, whereof one messuage, with the garden and croft adjoining, lies between the tenement of William Gairegrave on the east and the tenement of Robert Wowan on the west, and the other messuage, with the garden adjoining, lies between the tenements of John Flocton on either side, with the appurtenances. To have and to hold to the grantees, their heirs and assigns, for ever, from the chief lords of that fee, by the services due and accustomed. Witnesses, John Chaloner, Thomas Symkynson, Roger Crolande, Robert Wowan, William Spyve, (*fo.* 283) and others. Dated at Wakefeld, 7 May, 25 Hen. VI (1447).

(488) Feoffment by Thurstan Banastre and William Bradford to Richard Ledes, prior of Monkbretton, of two messuages, with the gardens and croft adjacent, in the vill of Wakefeld, in a certain street

---

[1] " Rodes thyng " written opposite in the margin.

called Westgate, whereof one messuage with the garden and croft adjacent lies between the tenement of Robert Gairegrave on the east and the tenement of Thomas Wowan on the west, and the other messuage with the garden adjacent lies between the tenements late of Robert[1] on either side; which jointly with Thomas Dodworth, now deceased, they (the grantors) had by the gift and feoffment of John Roydes of Wakefeld, with the appurtenances.   To have and to hold to the grantee and his successors for ever, from the chief lords of that fee, by the services due (*fo. 283d*) and accustomed. Witnesses, Christopher Horbury, Robert Chaloner, Thomas Wowan, and others.   Dated at Wakefeld, 20 February, 7 Edw. IV (1467–8).

(489)   Release and quitclaim by John Rodehouse and Joan his wife to Richard Ledes, prior of Monkbretton, and his successors, of all right and claim of and in all those messuages, lands, and tenements, with the appurtenances, which were lately John Rodes, of Wakefeld.   Dated 20 November, 14 Edw. IV (1474).

(*Fo.* 284) (490)   Release and quitclaim by Alice Turnor, kinswoman and heir of John Rodes late of Wakefeld, to Richard Ledys, prior of Monkbretton, and his successors, of all right and claim of and in all those messuages, lands, and tenements, with the appurtenances, which lately were of the said John Rodes.   Dated as in the previous deed.

(*Fo.* 284d) (491)   Release and quitclaim by Joan Yongsmyth, widow, and John Yongsmyth, to the prior and his successors, of all right and claim of and in the same properties.   Same date.

(492)   Release and quitclaim by John Turton and Alice his wife (*fo.* 285) to the same prior and his successors, of all right and claim of and in the same properties.   Same date.

(493)   Release and quitclaim by Oliver Lokwod, son and heir of Thomas Lokwod, (*fo.* 285d) to the prior and convent of Monkbretton and their successors for ever, of all right, title, claim, etc., of and in a tenement, with the buildings thereon, with the garden and croft adjoining, together with a certain selion of meadow adjacent, at the end of the said croft; in which tenement Robert Baroclogh now dwells.   Which tenement, with the said appurtenances, Thomas his (Oliver's) father (with others now deceased) had by the gift and feoffment of John Rodes of Wakefeld.   Dated 6 February, 13 Edw. IV (1473–4).

(*Fo.* 286) (494)   In the Court[2] held at Wakefeld, 13 October, 31 Hen. VI (1452).   Whereas lately at a Court held at Wakefeld, 6 October, 26 Hen. VI (1447), etc., it was presented by William Bolt and his fellows, tenants of the lord, in the said Court sworn, etc., that John Rodes of Wakefeld acquired from divers tenants twenty-five

---

[1] No surname given.

[2] The usual descriptive heading in red is wanting in the case of this copy of court roll.

acres of land and meadow lying separately within the reeveship of Thornes, Sandall and Alverthorp, and a parcel of land lately taken from the lord's waste in the Bredebothes, formerly in the tenure of John Carlehill and Alice his wife, with the appurtenances, in the reeveship of Wakefeld, which said land, meadow, and parcel of land, with the appurtenances, the said John Rodes held and occu- pied and took the profit therefrom for twelve complete years without making a fine with the lord or licence of the Court, etc., and against the custom of the manor, etc., in contempt of the lord, etc., for which cause the said properties, upon proclamation (*fo.* 286*d*) publicly and solemnly made in three Courts as the custom of the manor requires, were seized into the hands of the lord, etc. At this Court before John Seyvill, knight, steward of the lord of Wakefeld, John Vyncent receiver there, and other officials, came Thomas Dodworth, William Bradford, and Thomas Beaumont in full Court, and took from the lord the aforesaid properties, with the appurten- ances, which were granted to them, to hold to them, their heirs and assigns, for ever, by the services according to the custom of the manor, etc., and they give the lord as fine for entry 6*s.* 8*d.*

(495) John Rodes and Agnes his wife, present in Court in person, Agnes having been examined, they released and quitclaimed to the said Thomas, William, and Thomas, their heirs and assigns, all right and claim in the said properties. (*Fo.* 287) And the said Thomas, William, and Thomas give the lord as fine for the enrolment of that quitclaim, 6*d.*

(496) At the Court held at Wakefeld, 13 October, 31 Hen. VI (1452), John Rodes and Agnes his wife were present in Court in person, and Agnes having been examined, they surrendered into the hands of the lord a small tenement situated between the market cross and the Bredebothes, which was lately Joan Spiser's, with the appurtenances, in the reeveship of Wakefeld, to the use of Tho- mas Dodworth, William Bradford and Thomas Beaumont, and their heirs, for ever; which was granted to the said Thomas, William, and Thomas, to hold to them, their heirs and assigns, for ever, by the services according to the custom of the manor, etc. And they give the lord for fine on entry 6*d.*

(*Fo.* 287*d*) (497) At the Court held at Wakefeld, 18 December, 12 Edw. IV (1472). William Bradford, present in Court in person, surrendered into the hands of the lord the properties as described in the last document but two, which properties were late in the tenure and occupation of John Rodes, late of Wakefeld, to the use of Thomas Metheley, esquire, Richard Snytale, John Lake, Robert Baracloghe, John Sparke of Notton, and John Chaloner, son of Robert Chaloner, and their heirs, for ever; to whom the properties were granted, to hold to them and their heirs for ever, by the services according to the custom of the manor. And they give the lord as fine for entry 5*s.*, by the pledge of Robert Chaloner.

(*Fo.* 288) (498) At the Court held at Wakefeld, 31 January, 2 Hen. VIII (1510–11). John Chaloner, by George Hobson, a tenant, sworn, surrendered into the hands of the lord the same properties, late in the tenure and occupation of John Rodes, late of Wakefeld, which the said John Chaloner had, jointly with Thomas Methelay, esquire, etc., (as in the previous document), now deceased, by the surrender of William Bradford, to the use of Richard Lyster, William Grene, Robert Chaloner, Brian Bradford, junior, Thomas Amyas, Thomas Grene, Thomas Oxsprynge, Charles Jakson, and John Kyrkeby; to whom the properties were granted, to hold to them and their heirs for ever, by the services according to the custom of the manor. And they give the lord as fine for entry 6s.

(*Fo.* 288*d*)   *Ardyslaw*.[1]

(499) Grant by Adam son of Waltheff de Ardeslaw to God and Saint Mary Magdelene of Bretton and the monks there, for the soul of Adam son of Gamel, and for his own soul and those of all his ancestors, of half a bovate of land in Herdeslau, with all the appurtenances, which Fulk son of Gamel held from him (the grantor). To hold and possess in pure and perpetual alms. Witnesses, Roger de Montebegon, William son of Adam, William de Notton, and many others.

(*Fo.* 290)[2] (500) Grant by Adam, prior of Bretton. and the convent thereof to Hugh de Muhaud and his heirs by Ysond his wife, for his homage and service, of half a bovate of land, with all the appurtenances, in Herdeslaue within and without the vill. To hold from the grantors, freely and quietly, for 12*d*. payable to them yearly, for all service to them, namely that half bovate which Fulk held from Adam son of Waltheff, who gave it to the grantors as his charter which they have witnesses. Warranty so far as the charter of their donor can warrant to them. Witnesses, Peter Wadeworthe, John Tonetun, then bailiff of Westithing, Hugh de Elang, and many others.

(*Fo.* 290*d*)[3] (501) To all seeing or hearing this writing indentate, Thomas, prior of the monastery of Saint Mary Magdelene of Britton Monachorum and the convent thereof, greeting. Whereas a certain William de Chaumbor of Swillyngton, by his charter dated in the feast of Saint Leonard Abbot, 10 Hen. IV (1408), among other lands and tenements gave to John de Holm, chaplain, half a bovate of land, with the appurtenances, in Erdeslau, called Le Westrod, lying between the land of John Manyngham on the east and a certain lane leading to the Forms' wood on the west, and abutting at one head on the highway to Wakefeld; to have and to hold to the grantee and his heirs, from the chief lords of the fee, by the services due and accustomed, and undertook for himself and his heirs to warrant:

---

[1] Ardsley, near Barnsley. In the margin " Ardeslau " is written.
[2] Mispaged.
[3] Headed " Ardyslaw."

which half bovate a certain Adam, formerly prior of Birton, predecessor of the present prior, and the convent, by their charter granted (*fo.* 291) to a certain Hugh de Mauhaud and his heirs by Ysond, his wife, for his homage and service, to hold from the said late prior and convent and their successors, freely and quietly, for 12*d.* yearly. We for ourselves and our successors ratify, approve, and confirm the said grant as far as in us is, to the said John de Holm and his heirs, for the said yearly rent of 12*d.* to be paid to us and our successors. Power of distraint in case such rent is in arrear. (*Fo.* 291*d*)[1] Seals of the prior and convent and of the said John to the alternate parts of this indenture. Given in the Chapter House of the said monastery, 20 November, 1414.

(*Royston.*)

(502) Grant[2] by Thomas Tirel to God and the church of St. Mary Magdelene of Bretton and the monks there, of all the right and service which he had or might have from the messuage, with the appurtenances, which belonged to John Tyrel, his father, with the orchard in the vill of Roreston, lying beside the churchyard of the said vill in pure and perpetual alms. To hold and to have both in homages and in the rents, services, and issues, belonging to the said messuage, freely, quietly, etc. (*Fo.* 292) Witnesses, Sir Eudo de Lungeleis,[3] Simon de Norton, then bailiff of Staincros, John Rockeley, William de Bretton, and many others.

(503) Grant by William son of Thomas de Roreston, in pure and perpetual alms, to Thomas vicar of the church of St. John Baptist of Roreston, and all his successors, of a rood of land, with the appurtenances, from his (the grantor's) land which lies between Milnegate and the land of the church of Roreston. To hold and to have, freely, quietly, etc. Given in the church of Saint John Baptist of Roreston, 5th kal. August, 1240, in the presence (*fo.* 292*d*) of Sir Gilbert Candide Case,[4] who dedicated the said church on the same day and in witness placed his seal, together with the grantor's seal, to this writing. Witnesses, Sir Roger de Notton, Sir John de Schafton, knights, Richard Brasard, and others.

(504) Grant by William son of Thomas de Roreston, in pure and perpetual alms, to God and the vicarage of the church of Saint John Baptist of Roreston, of all his toft and croft which lie between the land of the said church and the road called Milnegate in Roreston, with all the appurtenances. To have and to hold freely, quietly, etc. Witnesses, Sir John de Hodode,[5] knight, Richard Brasard, Adam de Cutheworth, John son of Felix de Roreston, and others.

---

[1] This page is headed " Ruston," which heading (or " Roston ") continues on the dorses to *fo.* 296*d*.

[2] " Roreston " written in the margin opposite. The vill is Royston.

[3] *Sic*, for Lungevilers.

[4] In the margin, in a later hand, " Bishopp of Whitherne in Scotland."

[5] *Sic;* meant for " Hoderode."

(Fo. 293) (505) Grant[1] by Robert Monk of Swath to Thomas Cartwryght of Barneslay, his heirs and assigns, of a certain meadow, with the appurtenances, in Roston, called Le Wetenge, as it lies in length and breadth between the meadow of the prior of Monkbretton on the south side and the land called Le Kyrkhill on the north side and abuts at one head on Pedyrthwath towards the east and at the other head on the road to the church of Roston towards the west. To have and to hold to the grantee, his heirs and assigns, freely, quietly, etc., from the chief lords of those fees, by the services due and accustomed. *(Fo. 293d)* Witnesses, John Wylkynson of Roston, John Calthorne of the same, Robert Grafar of Barneslay, and others. Dated at Roston, Monday before the feast of All Saints, 11 Hen. IV (1409).

(506) Grant by Thomas Cartewright of Barnesley to William Ravensfold of Carlton, his heirs and assigns, of the same meadow (described as in the previous deed) which he (Thomas) lately had by the grant of Robert Monke of Swath. To have and to hold, with the appurtenances, to the grantee, his heirs and assigns, freely, quietly, etc., from the chief lords, etc., (as in the previous deed). *(Fo. 294)* Witnesses, Robert Gravar of Barnesley, John Bretton, Richard Yongsmygh of Carleton, and others. Dated at Ruston, the eve of All Saints, 14 Hen. VI (1435).

(507) Appointment by Thomas Cartewright of Barnesley of Richard Yongsmyth of Carleton as his attorney, to deliver seisin to William Ravenfeld of Carleton of a certain meadow in Ruston called Le Wetheng, with the appurtenances, according to the form and effect of a certain charter by him (Thomas) to the said William made. Dated at Ruston as in the previous deed.

(Fo. 294d) (508) Grant by William Ravenfeld of Carleton to Thomas Grasson of Wranbroke, his heirs and assigns, of the same meadow,[2] which he lately had by the gift and feoffment of Thomas Cartewryght of Barnesley. To have and to hold, with the appurtenances, to the grantee, his heirs and assigns, from the chief lords of that fee, by the services due and accustomed, for ever. Witnesses, John Oxspring, John Bretton, Richard *(fo. 295)* Yongsmyth, John Whytley, John Whyte of Cotheworth, and others. Dated at Ruston, Sunday after Martinmas, 16 Hen. VI (1437).

(509) Grant by Thomas Grasson of Wrangbrok to William Smyth, chaplain, and William Grubbar of Monkbretton, their heirs and assigns, of the same meadow called Weteenge, which he had by the gift and feoffment of William Ravenfeld of Carleton. To have and to hold, with the appurtenances, etc., as in the previous deed. *(Fo. 295d)* Witnesses, Thomas Oxspring of Cudworth, John Wilkynson, John Cusworth, William Calthorn, John Robynson, and others. Dated at Ruston, the feast of Saint Gregory Pope, 20 Hen. VI (1441-2).

[1] " Weteyng " written opposite in the margin.
[2] In this deed the eastern boundary is called " Pedyrthwaye."

(510) Appointment by Thomas Grasson of Wrangbroke of Thomas Pogson of Carleton as his attorney, to deliver seisin of the same meadow, with the appurtenances, to William Smyth and William Grubbar. Dated at Ruston, same date as in last deed.

(511) Grant[1] by William Smyth, chaplain, and William Grubbar of Monkbretton, to Richard, prior, and the convent of the house and the church of Saint Mary Magdalene of Monkbretton and their successors for ever, of the same meadow, (described as before), with the appurtenances, which the grantors had by the gift and feoffment of Thomas Grasson of Wrangbruk. To have and to hold to the grantees and their successors for ever, from the chief lords, etc., as before. Witnesses,[2] Nicholas Worley, Thomas Doddesworth, Richard Birton, and others. Dated at Ruston, 12 October, 22 Hen. VI (1443).

Abboldhagh.[3]

(512) Grant by William Foster of Notton to Richard Peke and John Doyn, chaplain, of a parcel of land containing four acres, with the appurtenances, in Abboldhagh, beside the land of the prior of Monkbretton, called Parson flate in the west and the lane leading from Abboldhagh to Spetill crosse on the north and the land of the lord Darcy called Kymancroft on the east and the land of the same lord called Lawdogrode on the south. To have and to hold, with the appurtenances, to the grantees, their heirs and assigns, for ever, from the chief lords of that fee, by the services due and accustomed. (Fo. 297) Witnesses, Thomas Wakefeld, John Wilkynson, John Cusworth, and many others. Dated at Notton, Wednesday the feast of Saint Katherine virgin, 23 Hen. VI (1444).

(513) Grant by Richard Peke and John Doyn, chaplain, to Richard, prior of Monkbretton, and the convent thereof and their successors, of the same parcel of land, described as in the previous deed,[4] which they (the grantors) lately had by the gift and feoffment of William Foster of Notton. To have and to hold, with the appurtenances, to the grantees (fo.297d)[5] and their successors for ever, from the chief lords, etc., as before. Witnesses, William Rilston, John Staynton, Richard Birton, John Foster, Richard Wilde, and many others. Dated at Notton, the feast of Saint Matthias Apostle, 23 Hen. VI (1444–5).

Notton.

(514) Grant[6] by Robert son of Lefwin to Assulf de Notton, of two bovates of land in Notton, namely the bovate which was Ste-

---

[1] The next folio, which is not numbered, commences here.

[2] The dorse of the unnumbered leaf commences here.

[3] " Abboldhagh " written opposite in the margin, i.e. " Appleday," in the township of Notton, which Mr. Hunter remarks is more properly " Applehay" (South Yorkshire, ii, 392).

[4] " Kydmancroft " in this deed instead of " Kymancroft."

[5] Headed " Notton," which heading continues to fo. 300d.

[6] " Notton " written in the margin opposite.

phen's and the bovate and the homage of Swane son of Roskel, for his service and homage, to him and his heirs, to hold from the grantor and his heirs in fee and inheritance, freely and quietly, for the service of the forty-eighth part of a knight. Witnesses, the prior of Saint Oswald's, Hugh dean of (*fo.* 298) Silkeston, Peter the clerk of Wakefeld, Adam the clerk of Sanddale, Paulinus his brother, and many others.

(515) Grant or confirmation by Gilbert de Notton to John his son of the donation which Robert son of Lefwin made to Assulf de Notton as the charter of the said Robert witnesses, namely two bovates of land in Notton, the bovate which was Stephen's, and the bovate and homage of Swane son of Roskel; for his (John's) homage and service. To hold from Gilbert and his heirs, freely and quietly, in fee and inheritance, by the service of the forty-eighth part of a knight. Witnesses, John de Birchine, Roger his brother, Peter de Birchethait, Robert his brother, John Thirel, and many others.

(516) Grant and quitclaim by Arnald Pigaze to God and St. Mary Magdalene of Bretton and the monks (*fo.* 298*d*) there, of Thomas son of Gamel of Notton, with all his issue, for ever. For this quitclaim Arnald has received 28*s.* from the monks. Witnesses, John Tyrel, Walter son of Barnard, Robert Bretton, Hugh de Bergh, and others.

(517) Grant by brother Roger, prior (*minister humilis*) of Bretton, and the convent thereof, to John Page and his heirs, for his homage and service, of all that land in the territory and vill of Notton, with the buildings, which Warin the chaplain formerly held from them (the grantors) in his lifetime, and which they had by the grant of Sir Gilbert de Notton, with all the appurtenances, saving to the grantors a place on the toft to build a grange at their will, with free entry and egress. To hold and to have to the grantee and his heirs, freely, quietly, etc., with all liberties and free commons, in wood, in plain, in pastures, and with all other easements belonging to the said land, within and without the vill of Notton. (*Fo.* 299) Rendering yearly to the church of the grantors 9*s.* of silver for all services and demands. Warranty so far as the charter of their donor can warrant to the grantors. The grantee and his heirs may not sell, give, alienate, or place the land in Jewry, without the grantor's consent. Witnesses, Robert de Stapilton, John de Hoderode, Richard Brasard, William de Roreston, Adam de Pul, Benedict de Cutheword, and others.

(518) Grant by Gilbert de Notton to God and St. Mary Magdalene of Bretton and the monks there, of eighteen acres of land in Notton, those namely which the same monks held from him at term for twenty years; with free common as belongs to two bovates of land in the same vill (*fo.* 299*d*) outside his hedge, for the souls of himself and his wife and Robert his brother and Reginald his (Gilbert's) son and his ancestors and heirs, in pure and perpetual alms. Witnesses, German de Tornehill, John Tirel, Richard the chaplain of Notton, William son of Adam, and others.

(519) Grant by Gilbert de Notton to God and the church of St. Mary Magdalene of Bretton and the monks there, in pure and perpetual alms, of a bovate of land in the vill of Notton, with all the appurtenances, without retention, namely that bovate which Margery wife of Asolf held; and by way of addition he, Gilbert, has given the monks five roods of land in the territory of the same vill of Notton, which Rainald Brian held, which abut on the dam of Adbaldehac. To hold, have, and possess freely, quietly, etc., in wood, in plain, in meadows, pastures, and in all other easements, (*fo.* 300) liberties, and commons to the said vill belonging; saving only to him (Gilbert) and his heirs the wood of his hedge of Notton. Witnesses, Henry de Tancresleia, Robert de Deneby, William Bretton, William parson of Peningeston, and others.

(520) Grant by brother William prior of Bretton, and the convent there, to Hugh the forester of Notton and his heirs or assigns, for his homage and service, of all that bovate of land together with the messuage and with free common of two bovates in the vill of Notton, namely all that bovate which Gilbert de Notton gave to the house of blessed Mary Magdalene of Bretton, in pure (*fo.* 300*d*) and perpetual alms. To hold and to have from the said house to him and his heirs or assigns, freely, quietly, etc., with all appurtenances, easements, and liberties to the said land and common belonging, within the bounds of Notton and without; rendering thence yearly to the said house half-a-pound of white incense on the day of St. Mary Magdalene for all services, etc. Warranty so far as the charter of their donor can warrant to the grantors. Witnesses, Sir Nicholas de Conriis, Sir Roger the chaplain of Notton, Henry de Rokelay, Henry de Byri, and many others.

(521) Whereas the prior and convent of Monkbretton demanded from William de Notton a certain yearly rent of a pound of white incense for a messuage, a bovate and an acre and a half of land, which he holds from them in Notton, and William often sought respite in payment of that rent until (*fo.* 302)[1] he should inspect his charters and writings touching the tenements, and should measure them, and because at the time of the making of these presents he has fully examined his estate in the said tenements and the muniments both his own and the prior's and convent's, and admits the said tenements to be only in his seisin as in his ancestors', he binds himself and his heirs and the said tenements by these presents to pay in future to the prior and convent and their successors yearly from the said tenements half-a-pound of white incense on the day of St. Mary Magdalene, beyond that half-pound of which they were previously seised; so that from now there be taken a pound yearly from the said tenements. Power of distraint, and the prior and convent disclaim the right to any other rent except the pound of white incense. Seals of the parties to the alternate parts of this agreement. Dated at Monkbretton, 1 April, 22 Edw. III (1348).

---

[1] *Sic* in the MS.

(Fo. 302d)   *Dartton, Mapylwell.*[1]

(522) Grant by Gilbert[2] de Notton to God and St. Mary
Magdalene of Bretton and the monks there, of common pasture for
their own demesne animals in his land of Dertona and Mapelwella, in
pure and perpetual alms, free and quit of all secular service, for the
health of his soul and the souls of his father and mother and Juliana
his wife and Reginald his son, and the souls of his ancestors and
heirs. Witnesses, Jeremia de Tornil, John Tyrel, William son of
Adam, Henry the clerk of Trafford, and many others.

(523) Grant by Godfrey de Staynton[3] to God and blessed Mary
Magdalene of Monkbretton and the monks there, of common pasture
with their own demesne animals in Derton, as much as belongs to
him, with free entry and egress, without hindrance by him or his
heirs. To have and to hold to the monks and their successors, in
(fo. 303) free, pure and perpetual alms, quit of all exaction and
secular service. Witnesses, Henry de Sothill, John de Turribus,
Robert Barneby, Henry Birthwaitt, Richard de Riall, and others.

(524) To all seeing or hearing this writing, Godfrey de Staynton
greeting. Know that I have inspected the charter of Gilbert de
Notton made to God and blessed Mary Magdalene of Monkbretton
and the monks there, of common pasture in the lands of the said
Gilbert in Derton for the demesne animals of the said monks, in
pure and perpetual alms, without any exaction, wherefore I grant
for me and my heirs or assigns that those monks and their successors
may have common pasture in the said vill of Darton with their
own demesne animals, as in the charter of Gilbert to the monks
(fo. 303d) is more fully contained, with free entry and egress; so
that neither he nor his heirs nor any one in their name shall hereafter
raise hindrance or impediment against the monks, touching the said
common pasture. Witnesses, Henry de Sutyle, John de Turribus,
Robert de Barneby, Henry de Birthwath, and others.

(525) Grant by Henry son of Sir John de Sutyle to God and
blessed Mary Magdalene of Monkbretton and the monks there, of
common pasture with their own demesne animals in Derton, as
much as belongs to him, with free entry and egress, without hindrance
by him or his heirs. To have and to hold to the monks and their
successors in free, pure, and perpetual alms, quit of all exaction and
secular service. *(Fo. 304)* Witnesses, John de Turribus, Godfrey
de Staynton, and others.

(526) Charter by Henry son of Sir John de Sutyle of inspeximus
and confirmation of Gilbert de Notton's grant to the monks, of common pasture in the lands of the said Gilbert in Derton for their own
demesne animals, in free, pure and perpetual alms, without any

[1] This heading continues to the dorse of *fo.* 304. In the margin of the
present page, " de Mapilwell and de Derton " is written.
[2] " Gelb'tus."
[3] " Staynston " in the text, " Staynton " in the heading.

exaction. (*Fo.* 304*d*) Witnesses, John de Turribus, Godfrey de Staynton, Robert de Barneby, Henry de Birthwayt, Richard de Riall, and others.

(527)   Exemplification[1] of a process of De Banco of 20 Edw. IV (1480), Easter term, Roll 316.   Ebor: James Strangwayes of Harlesay, knight, William Ourome of Notton, " laborer," William Spark of Notton, " laborer," and Thomas Benkes of Notton, " yoman," (all in the County of York), were summoned to answer to Richard, prior of the monastery of blessed Mary Magdalene of Monkbretton, as to why they took and detained his animals.   The prior, by Thomas Lyster, his attorney, complains that the defendants on Thursday after the feast of St. John Evangelist, 19 Edw. IV (1479), in the vill of Derton, in a place called Sheperdthorn, took his animals, namely 360 sheep, and unjustly detained them, etc., whence he says that he is damaged to the value of £20.

The defendants, by Richard Beilby, their attorney, come and defend, and say that the place called Sheperdthorn is in the vill of Notton, and not in Derton.   And the bailiffs of James and the other defendants admit the taking and justify, because they allege that James at that time and before was seised in demesne as of fee of a great moor in Notton called Notton more, containing five hundred acres of land, whereof the aforesaid place called Sheperdthorn is parcel, and that the sheep at the time they were taken were in the same place feeding on and treading down the grass there growing, and doing damage there.   The prior repeats that Sheperdthorn is in Derton, and begs that this be enquired of by the country, and the defendants ask the same.   The Sheriff is therefore directed to summon a jury to be present in fifteen days of Trinity.   Afterwards was respited to Michaelmas term, when the prior by his aforesaid attorney came and said that the defendant James (Strangwayes) was dead, therefore no further process against him.   The defendants solemnly summoned came not.   The jury say on their oath that the within-named place called Sheperdthorn is within the vill of Derton and not within the vill of Notton, as the prior alleged; and they assess his damages by reason of the taking and unjust detention, as above, beyond his expenses and costs at 8 marks, and for those expenses and costs at 4 marks.   Therefore it is adjudged that the prior recover against William Ourome, William Spark, and Thomas Benkes his damages of 12 marks as assessed by the jury.   And William, William and Thomas are in mercy, etc.[2]

(*Fo.* 306*d*) (528) Judgment of the Commissary General of the Official of the Court of York, *sede vacante*, in a cause respecting the tithes of trees and cut wood of Nottonhawe raised and pending in the said Court, a definite sentence as follows being pronounced the 29th November, 1352.   Having heard the cause respecting the tithes of trees and cut wood of Nottonhawe between the religious men, the

---

[1] This item extends to the middle of *fo.* 306*d*.

[2] The exemplification sealed at Westminster, 15 October, 20 Edw. VI.

K

prior and convent of the monastery of Bretton, by John de Roucliff, their proctor, (*fo.* 307) on the one part, and Henry Halyday of Wakefeld, by John Stanton, his proctor, on the other part, the proctor of the prior and convent alleging that Henry withheld tithes of trees and wood felled of Nottonhawe within the bounds of the parish of Roreston, the church of which is held for the proper uses of their monastery, estimated at £4 4s.

Sentence is pronounced in favour of the prior and convent and Henry to be compelled to pay the tithe and costs.

(*Fo.* 308) Dated at York, the day and year aforesaid.

Morehowse.

(529) Grant[1] by Adam Fullo, with the goodwill of Scherithe his wife, to God and St. Mary Magdalene of Bretton and the monks there, of five acres and a rood of arable land in the territory of Wolley at Morehosses in a place called Hallestedes, and two acres of meadow in the meadow which was Adam le Peitevin's beside the meadow of William son of Hugh. To hold and to have in pure and perpetual alms, freely, quietly, etc., with all appurtenances, liberties and easements, and with a moiety of all the common which belongs to all his (Adam's) land in the territory of Wolley. Witnesses, Thomas de (*fo.* 308*d*) Burgo, Eudo de Lungvilers, Henry de Tankerley, and others.

(530) Confirmation by Scherith daughter of Adam le Peitevin, to God and St. Mary Magdalene of Bretton and the monks there, in pure and perpetual alms, of the land and meadow named in the preceding deed, described as before. To hold, etc., as before, with the moiety of common, etc., as the charter of Adam Fullo, her husband, which the monks have, with her consent and goodwill witnesses. She has sworn on oath that never in her life will she dispute this gift, but she (*fo.* 309) and her heirs will warrant to the monks. Witnesses as in the last deed, with the addition of John de Rockley.

Wolley.[2]

(531) Grant by William de Staynton, prior of the monastery of Bretton Monachorum, and the convent thereof, to Thomas son of Thomas de Staynton of Wollay, of a plot of their (the grantor's) garden lying on the east side of their grange in Wollay, which plot lies on the west side of the messuage which the said Thomas son of Thomas has by the gift of his said father, and abuts on the common pasture of the vill of Wollay towards the north, and on the grantor's croft towards the south, and the said plot contains from the said croft as far as the said pasture forty-five ells only, and in width from the said messuage of Thomas as far as the remainder of the said garden fifteen ells only. To have and to hold to the grantee and the heirs of his body from the grantors and their successors, by

---

[1] " Morehose de Wolley " written opposite in the margin. See Hunter (*South Yorkshire*, ii, 384) as to " Wolley Moorhouse."

[2] Written in the margin opposite.

the service of 6*d*. yearly. (*Fo.* 309*d*)[1] Seals of the parties to the alternate parts of this indenture. Witnesses, Thomas de Staynton, William de Notton, Robert de Staynton, and others.

(532) Grant by William son of William to John de Lisoris and his heirs by his wife, for his homage and service, of all the land which Holfrid[2] held, and as much of his (William's) other land towards Schelintorp beside his park, namely from Holfrid's land as far as the water towards Schelintorp and from the land of Henry son of Leuevett so by the water as far as his (William's) park and by the bound between Hamelis and Schelintorp, to wit, eighty acres of land. To hold from the grantor and his heirs, in fee and inheritance, freely, quietly, etc., in wood and plain, etc., and in all liberties, commons, and easements to the vill of Emmelay belonging, except the grantor's park. (*Fo.* 310) John and his heirs by his wife shall have the liberty of giving the twentieth measure of their corn as multure, namely of the corn which they wish to grind at the grantor's mill, and shall grind their barley (*bres*)[3] at the grantor's mill when they choose and shall give no multure therefrom. Rendering yearly to the grantor and his heirs 4*s*. for all service. Witnesses, Richard de Wambwel, Richard de Schelton, Hugh de Bilam, and others.

(533) Grant by John Thomson of Wollay to Richard Wryd, chaplain, of that messuage, with garden adjoining and all the appurtenances, as it lies in the vill of Wollay, between the messuage of William de Rylleston on one side and the messuage of John de Whetlay on the other side, which he (the grantor) lately had by the gift of John Thomson, his father. To have and to hold (*fo.* 310*d*) to the grantee, his heirs and assigns, from the chief lords of that fee, by the services due and accustomed, freely, quietly, etc., for ever. Witnesses, Thomas de Whetlay, William Barnesyr, John Alkoc, and others. Dated at Wollay, Sunday after the feast of Saint Leonard, 1411.

(534) Grant by Richard Wryd, chaplain, to William Boswyll, son of John Boswyll of Erdesley, of a messuage with garden adjoining, and all the appurtenances, as it lies in the vill of Wolley between the messuage of William de Reliston (Rilston) on one side and the messuage of John Whetley on the other. (*Fo.* 310) [*sic*] To have and to hold to the grantee, his heirs and assigns, the messuage and garden which the grantor had by the grant of John Wollay of Wollay, from the chief lord of that fee, by the services due and accustomed, freely, quietly, etc., for ever. Witnesses, Thomas de Whetley, William Barnsyr, John Talyor, and others. Dated at Wollay, the feast of Saint Barnabas Apostle, 13 Hen. IV (1412).

(535) Grant by William Boswell to Richard Ryschworth and Alice his wife and the heirs of their bodies lawfully begotten, of a

---

[1] Headed " Wolley," which heading continues to *fo.* 313*d*.

[2] Holfridus.

[3] " bres," brace: a species of grain from which beer is made (Ducange).

messuage, with the appurtenances, in Wolley, situate between the messuage of John Wheteley on the south side (*fo.* 310*d*) and the messuage of William Rylleston on the north side, which messuage he (the grantor) formerly had jointly with Richard Wryde, chaplain, by the gift and feoffment of John Wolley. To have and to hold to the grantees and their heirs (as before), from the chief lords of the fee, by the services due and accustomed. If Richard and Alice should die without such heir, remainder to the right heirs of the said John Wolley, for ever. Witnesses, John Woderofe, esquire, William Wheteley, Laurence Staynton, and others. Dated at Wolley, the feast of Saint Bartholomew Apostle, 32 Hen. VI (1454).

(536) Appointment by William Bosvyll of William Whetelay as his attorney, to deliver seisin to Richard Rysshworth and Alice his wife of a messuage (*fo.* 311) with garden adjoining, and three acres of land, with the appurtenances, in Wollay, according to the form and effect of a certain charter by him (William) made. Dated 3 October, 33 Hen. VI (1454).

(537) Release and quitclaim by William Thomlynson, senior, and William Thomlynson, junior, to Richard Rysshworth and Alice his wife and their heirs, of all right and claim in a messuage with garden adjoining, as it lies between the messuage of John Wheteley on one side and the messuage of William Rilleston on the other, and in three acres of land, with the appurtenances, in Wolley, which formerly were the said[1] John's. (*Fo.* 311*d*) Dated at Wolley, 5 October, 33 Hen. VI (1454).

(538) Grant by Alice Ryssheworth, in her widowhood, to Henry Stafford, clerk, and Richard Galberd, chaplain, of all and singular the messuages, lands, and tenements, with the appurtenances, in Wolley, which she lately held and had jointly with Richard Ryssheworth, her late husband, by the grant and feoffment of William Boswell. To have and to hold to the grantees and their assigns, for ever, from the chief lords of that fee, by the services due and accustomed. (*Fo.* 312) Appointment of William Cay, chaplain, and Godfrey Thomasson, as her attorneys to deliver seisin. Witnesses, John Savile, knight, Percival Amyas, Thomas Blakker, and others. Dated 15 May, 11 Edw. IV (1471).

(*Fo.* 312*d*) (539) Release and quitclaim by Henry Stafford, clerk, and Richard Galbard, chaplain, to the prior of the monastery of blessed Mary Magdalene of Monkbretton and the convent thereof and their successors, for ever, of all right, title, claim, etc., of and in a messuage, with garden adjoining, as it lies between the messuage of John Whetelay, and the messuage of William Rilleston, and in three acres of land, with the appurtenances, in Wolley, which they (the grantors) had by the grant of Alice Ryssheworth, widow, for-

---

[1] The word " dicti " is interlined in red ink, apparently by the writer of the red headings. There is no record in the preceding deeds of the property having been John Wheteley's, and possibly the real wording of the deed was " que quondam fuerent Johannis Wolley."

merly wife of Richard Rissheworth. Dated 10 October, 11 Edw. IV (1471).

(*Fo.* 313) (540) Grant[1] by William Thomlynson of Wolley, and Isabella his wife, to Richard Ledes, prior of the monastery of blessed Mary Magdalene of Monkbretton, of a yearly rent of 6s. 8d. receivable from a tenement, two crofts, and forty acres of land and meadow lying separately in the vill and fields of Wolley, the tenement and two crofts lying in Wolley between the tenement of James Strangways, knight, on the east and the tenement of Robert Rilleston on the west and abutting on the highway towards the south and on the land of Thomas Boswyll and John Wentworth towards the north. To have and receive the said rent to the grantee and his successors, for ever. (*Fo.* 313d) Power of distraint if rent is in arrear for forty days. Witnesses, William Oxsping [*sic*], John Ruston, and others. Dated at Wolley, 5 July, 4 Edw. IV (1464).

(541) To all faithful of Christ, etc., Robert Thomlynson, (*fo.* 314) son and heir of William Thomlynson and Isabella his wife, of Wolley, greeting. Whereas the said William and Isabella, by their charter indentate, dated 5 July, ... Edw. IV,[2] granted to Richard Ledes, prior of blessed Mary Magdalene of Monkbretton, and his successors, a yearly rent of 6s. 8d. receivable from, etc., (the property described as in the last deed, with the same boundaries), to have and to receive to the said prior and his successors for ever, as in the same writing is more fully contained. Know that I the said Robert have seen, read, and examined the said writing, and have ratified, approved, and as much as in me is, in all things confirmed (*fo.* 314d)[3] it by these presents. Witnesses, James Haryngton, knight, Thomas Metheley, William Merton, esquires, and others. Dated at Monkbretton, 25 November, in the 7th year of the said King (1467).

Est Markam.

(542) Grant[4] by Nicholas Legat and Dionisia his wife to God and Saint Mary Magdalene of Bretton and the monks there, of all their (the grantor's) land which they had in the vill and territory of Est Markam, with all the appurtenances, as well in demesnes and villeins and free men as in rents and other things belonging to the land, namely a bovate of land which Roger son of Robert held, with the appurtenances, and half a bovate which Robert son of Gilbert held, and half a bovate which Giliana the widow held, and half a bovate which William Dogett held, and half a bovate which Arnebo the widow held, and half a bovate which William son of Robert held, (*fo.* 315) and a toft and forty-four acres of land in demesne, and a toft which Richard son of Robert held, and a toft

---

[1] " Thomlynson " written opposite in the margin.

[2] The scribe omitted the year; no doubt the charter in question was the previous one copied.

[3] Headed " Markam."

[4] " Est Markam " written in the margin opposite. The vill is East Markham, Nottinghamshire.

which William Belami held, and a toft which Willam By-the-beck (*juxta le bec*) held, and a toft which Edus the widow held, and the third part of a toft with one acre which Richard Crane held, and the homage and service of Richard St. Quintin (*de Sancto Quintino*) and his heirs, namely for one toft 2s. yearly, and the homage and service of Richard de Markam and his heirs, namely 4d. yearly, and the homage and service of Roger son of Hugh and his heirs, namely for two acres 8d. yearly, and the homage and service of Emma daughter of Ralph de Wath and her heirs, namely for one bovate of land one pair of gloves yearly, and the homage and service of Ydonia de Rodes and her heirs, for one bovate of land a pound of cummin yearly. All the aforesaid the monks shall hold and possess in perpetual alms, freely, quietly, etc., in wood, in plain, etc., and in all liberties (*fo.* 315d) and easements and commons of the said vill of Markam to the said land belonging, doing service to the chief lords of the fee as belongs to the said holding. Warranty, as perpetual alms. Witnesses, Sir Robert de Lessingeton, then Justice of the King, Sir John his brother, Robert de Ripperes, Sir William de Sandeby, Roger de Cressy, Richard St. Quintin (*Sancto Quintino*), and very many others. (Monkbretton Chart., Lansdowne MS. 405, fo. 42.)

(543)   Acknowledgment by Nicholas Legat that he has received from the prior and monks of Bretton 40 marks of silver, in which by their charter they were held bound to him and Dionisia de Lasceles, formerly his wife, for the land of Marcaham. He has also remitted and quitclaimed to the said prior and monks all debts in which they were liable to him, and all agreements, actions, disputes, and complaints which he had or might have against them in any way, (*fo.* 316)[1] saving to him his 10s. and his corrody. Moreover he has confessed himself well and fully satisfied for the said 40 marks and all other debts and demands, to wit, in the presence of Sir John de Hoderode, Adam Geffard, Gregory de Batelay, Alexander brother of the prior, Thomas Haliday, and others; and he will without delay or fraud or cavilling restore to them their instrument which he has respecting the 40 marks, before the feast of Saint Mary Magdalene, 1243, and if he should fail to do this, he will quitclaim to the prior and monks his corrody, with the 10s., in which they are liable to him. This discharge was made and this writing sealed with his (Nicholas') seal on the morrow of Saint Barnabas Apostle, 1243.

(544)   Grant by Dionisia daughter of Ranulf de Novo Mercato to Letitia (*fo.* 316d) Chev'curt, her mother, for her homage and service, of half a bovate of land, with the appurtenances, in the territory of Marcham, namely that half bovate which she (the grantor) had by the gift of Albreda St. Quintin, which Godfrey previously held from Albreda. To have and to hold to the grantee, her heirs or assigns, freely, quietly, etc., rendering two white gloves for all services. Witnesses, Sir Malveysins de Herresy, Walter de Wluesweit, Thomas St. Quintin, Robert de Derley, Simon de March, and many others.

---

[1] The heading is " Est Markam," which continues on the dorses to *fo.* 325d.

(545) Surrender by William Amyas to the prior and convent of Monkbretton of all his estate and whatsoever he had in the tenements of the said prior and convent in Estmarcham, and he has also remitted (*fo.* 317) and quitclaimed to them and their successors all manner of actions which he had or could have against them, by reason of any contract, obligation, demise, grant, or agreement, from the beginning of the world to this day. Witnesses, Sir William Scott, William de Notton, John de Marcham, and others. Dated at Notingham, the feast of the Nativity of the blessed Virgin Mary, 1343.

(546) These are the lands of the prior and convent of Monkbretton lying separately in the vill, fields, and territory of Estmarkham. And in whatsoever places the said lands lie, they lie altogether in the carucate of Linham.

First, at Lytylwode nine and a half roods; at Gromondland three quadrants[1]; at the Stonepittes, seven and a half roods; at the Kyrkzerdbrygge one acre; at Pesewell three and a half roods; Helywellbalke two acres and half a rood; at Sperwelbalke two acres one rood; (*fo.* 317*d*) in Langledale three acres one rood and a quadrant; betwene ye bekkes half an acre and half a rood; at Thyrlwelstygh three and a half roods; at Kyschywonge half an acre; Postegate two acres and half a rood; at the Wandole three roods; at the Strete seven and a half roods; at the Schortbutts half an acre and half a rood; at Markham town ende three and a half roods; at Markham Closes one acre; at Skotgate an acre and half a rood; at the Southpole five and a half roods; at the Northpole seven roods; at Clyfegate three and a half roods; in the same one and a half roods; at Brauncehage two acres one and a half roods; at Setcoppe seven roods; Harehill one acre three roods; on the Clyffe one acre three and a half roods; in the same one acre three and a half roods; at Northdole two acres one and a half roods; at the Morewell one acre three roods; at Mykylwodegate one acre three roods; in the lee two acres one rood; at Crookdoles one acre three and a half roods; at Etongate one acre one and a half roods; at Askhamhill one acre one and a half roods; at Akerzerde one rood three and a half quadrants; at Schitenerse an acre and half a rood; at the Grippe three and a half roods; in the Overlongdole two acres one and a half roods; in the Nethyrlongdole four acres three and a half roods; at the Lydegate half an acre three quadrants; at the Haghdole three roods one quadrant; (*fo.* 318) in the same one acre one and a half roods; at Stokyng one acre one and a half roods; at Wadelandes two acres one and a half roods; the Waghes half a rood; at the Longwaghes one acre and half a rood; at Grenecrofte one acre three

---

[1] The contraction here and elsewhere is " q^u," but in one place it is expanded to "quadrant'," and may therefore represent "quadrantata." The " quadrantata terre " was a measure of land which appears to have varied in different localities, but was generally a quarter-of-an-acre. The word is more probably intended for quarentena—a furlong—or furrow long—or 40 rods long (1 rood = 1 quarentena × 1 rod). A quarentena here would be a furlong of narrower width; see Seebohm's *English Village Community.*

roods; in the Longbreke three acres and half a rood; in the Estbreke five roods three quadrants; at Morgates three and a half roods; at the Marketstygh three and a half roods; at Bradgatedyke three quadrants; in the same half an acre; in Estfeld at Bradgatedyke one and a half roods; at the Threthornes half an acre; at the Mydylstele half an acre; in the same one and a half roods; at the Halwongend one rood; in Estfeld beside the land of Thomas Swan one acre; in the same beside the Vicar's land one and a half acres; in Longwathcroft one and a half roods; in Gybcroft one and a half acres; in Elwertofte half an acre; at the bekkes one and a half roods; in Elwertofte half an acre; in the same three roods; at the bekkes one and a half roods.

Total of acres eighty-five, quadrant and a half.[1]

(547)   These are the lands from which rent of assize is taken, called Bobet[2] rente in the fields of Est Markham aforesaid.

First, at Stonpittes half an acre; at Heliwelbalk half an acre; at the Wilestub half a rood; at the Twobekks three quadrants; at Prestgate one rood; at Markhamcleffes one rood; at the Wrynke half an acre; in the Mydildole half an acre; at (fo. 318d) Morewell half an acre; in ye lee half an acre and half a rood; at Clyfegate one rood; at Askhainhill one and a half roods; at the Gryppe one rood; in ye Nethyrlongdole three and a half roods; at the Haghdoles one rood; at the Lydratte three quadrants; in the Stokyng one and a half roods; at the Thernes one and a half roods; at the Neteherst one and a half roods; in the Estbreke three quadrants; at Moregate one rood; at the Marketstygh one rood; at the Threthornes one rood; in Estfeld one selion containing three quadrants, late Robert Abbotte's; in the same at dame Agnes Wyloghes a selion and a half, late John Hamonde's containing half an acre; in the same one rood, late John Attekyrkzatte's; at the dykes five selions containing five roods, late of William Lawes, chaplain. And all the said lands lie in the carucate of Lintham in all places in the fourth bovate.

(548)   Meadows with free pastures of the said prior and convent.

First, at the Holmes nine yardlands, five of full and four of medium[3]; in the Nabbe nine yardlands, five of full and four of medium; in Akerdoles four yardlands and four feet; under the Clyfe at the Spynkwiloges nine yardlands, five of full and four of medium; (fo. 319) in the Northhome five bovates, three of full and two of medium; in Bartylcroft nine yardlands, five of full and four of medium; in the Oldemore nine yardlands, five of full and four of medium; in the Bryherste nine yardlands, five of full and four of medium; in the Fuldole nine yardlands, five of full and four

---

[1] I cannot make the items agree with this total.

[2] This should probably be " Dobet," which name appears repeatedly later.

[3] " ix virgat', v de plen' et iiij de mediocr'."   I cannot explain the expression, which occurs frequently, unless it refers to the quality of the land.

of medium; in the Carr two bovates of full and half a bovate as far as the half of the meadow; in the same two bovates of medium at the Kyrke Swath to Brayton Dyke. And all these meadows, with the free pastures aforewritten, lie always in the carucate of Lynham as above said.

(549) These are the lands of the prior and convent of Monkbretton, lying separately in the territory of Estmarkham in the second carucate called the Lyneham as is proved by Augustine Porter, Robert Porter, Roger Hyghlay, George Porter, Robert Bekks, Thomas Billiold, and Thomas Ledbeter, to wit, the 20th day of October, 5 Hen. VIII (1513).

(*Fo.* 319*d*) First, one toft lies at Hallyatte between the messuage of John Markham on the south and the messuage of Augustine Porter on the north and abuts on the King's highway to the west and the land of John Thopclyffe, esquire, to the east; one toft lies there between the messuage of Augustine Porter on the south and the messuage of John Topclyffe, esquire, on the north and abuts on the highway to the west and the land of John Topclyffe to the east. Another toft lies there beside the churchyard between the King's highway on the south and the messuage of Augustine Porter on the north and abuts on the common highway to the west and the Rattanrawe to the east. Another toft lies there at the west end of the vill between the messuage of John Topclyffe, esquire, on the east and the Frankyshall on the west, and abuts on the highway to the south and the land of the same prior and convent to the north. And another toft lies between the messuage of Robert Bellamye on the east and the land of the heirs of Sañdes on the west and abuts on the Overgate to the south and on Overlongdoles to the north.

(*Fo.* 320)   *Southfeylde.*

(550) First, in the Southunderwood lie two selions containing three roods of land, two selions from the east bound,[1] and other two selions containing an acre of land lie there beside the west bound; and one selion lies there containing half an acre of land, four selions from the west bound; Gromellande lies in one selion containing three quadrants beside the west bound; Stonepyttes two selions lie containing three roods of land, two selions from the eastern bound, etc.; two other selions lie there containing an acre beside the west bound, and one selion lies there containing half an acre of land, four lands from the west bound and parcel of Dobett rent; Kyrkyerdbygg five selions lying together containing one acre, whereof three are full and two of medium; Peysswell two selions lie there containing a rood and a half, two selions from the east bound, etc., and two selions lie there containing half an acre of land beside the west; one selion lies there containing a rood of land, four selions from the west bound, and parcel of the rent of Dobbet;

---

[1] The wording is " p duos selion' de meta orient'," which I take to mean that the two selions in Southunderwood were separated by two other selions from the eastern boundary of the South Field.

Heliwaellbalke one selion lies there containing three roods of land, two selions from the east bound; two selions lie there containing an acre and half a rood of land beside the west bound; one selion lies there containing half an acre of land, four selions from the west bound, and parcel of the rent of Dobett.

(Fo. 320d)   *Conynggarthe syde beside Tobekk.*

(551)   There lie there two selions containing a rood and a half, two selions from the east bound; two selions containing half an acre of land beside the Westbalke; one rood lies there, four selions from the west bound (Dobett); two selions lie in the Sperwelbalke containing three roods, two selions from the east bound; and two selions lie there containing an acre of land beside the Westbalke; and a fourth selion lies there containing half an acre parcel (of) Dobett; two selions containing a rood lie between the Bekks, two selions from the east bound; two selions lie there containing a rood and a half beside the Westbalke; three quadrants, four selions from the bound, parcel (of) Dobett; two selions lie there containing five roods of land, two selions from the east bound; two selions lie there containing an acre and a half beside the Westbalke; one selion lies there, four selions from the west bound, and contains three roods of land; one selion lies there containing half an acre of land in the Rushywong beside the Westbalke; one selion containing three roods of land lies in the Streytfurlang, two from the east bound; one selion lies there containing three and a half roods beside the Westbalke and a fourth selion one and a half roods; two selions containing one rood lie *(fo. 321)* in the Shortbutts, two selions from the south bound; two selions containing one and a half roods beside Le Northbalke, one selion containing three quadrants lies there, four selions from the north bound; one selion containing one and a half roods lies at the end of the vill of Markham, two selions from the south bound; two selions lie there containing half an acre beside the Northbalke; one rood lies there, four selions from the south bound, Dobett; one and a half roods lie in the Markham Cleiffes, two selions from the south bound; two selions lie there containing half an acre of land beside the Northbalke; one rood lies there, four selions from the north bound, parcel of the rent of Dobett; three roods lie in one selion in the Wandoles beside the Westbalke; one selion containing three and a half roods lies in the Preistgate, two selions from the east bound; two selions containing one acre lie there beside the Balke; one rood there, four selions from the Westbalke, parcel of the rent of Dobett; half an acre and half a rood of land lie in the Southpoll, two selions from the east bound; two selions lie there containing three roods beside the Westbalke; one and a half roods lie there, four selions from the Westbalke; three roods of land lie there and abut on the land of Thomas Cressy towards the north; one selion lies in the Cleyffeld containing half an acre and half a rood in the Northpole, two selions from the east bound; two selions lie there containing three roods of land *(fo. 321d)* beside the Westbalke; one selion lies there containing one and a half roods of land, a selion from

the west bound; one selion containing one and a half roods lies on Clyffgate, two selions from the east bound; two selions lie there containing half an acre of land beside the west bound; one selion lies there containing a rood of land, four selions from the west bound, parcel of the rent of Dobett; one selion lies on Scotgate containing half an acre, two selions from the east bound; a selion and a half containing half an acre and half a rood of land beside the bound; a selion and a half containing one and a half roods of land lie on Clyffgate beside the west bound; two selions containing three and a half roods of land lie in the Branshaw, two selions from the south bound; two selions containing an acre of land beside the bound on the north side; one selion lies there containing half an acre of land, four selions from the north bound; two selions lie in the Setcoppe containing half an acre and half a rood of land, two selions from the south bound; two selions containing three roods of land beside the north bound; one selion containing one and a half roods, four selions from the north bound; two selions containing half an acre and half a rood of land lie on the Harkhill, two selions from the east bound; two selions containing three roods lie beside the west bound; one selion lies there containing one and a half roods, four (*fo.* 322) selions from the west bound; one selion containing three and a half roods lies on Subclyffe, two selions from the south bound; two selions containing an acre lie beside the bound on the north side; one selion lies there containing half an acre, four selions from the north bound, parcel of the rent of Dobett; two selions containing three and a half roods lie there, two selions from the south bound; two selions containing an acre lie beside the north bound; one selion containing half an acre, the fourth selion from the north bound, parcel of Dobett; one selion containing three and a half roods lies in the Northdolez, two selions from the south bound; two selions containing an acre lie beside the north bound; one selion containing half an acre lies there, the fourth selion from the north bound, parcel of Dobett; one selion containing three roods lies above the Morewell, two selions from the south bound; two selions containing one acre lie, there beside the north bound; one selion lies there containing half an acre, four selions from the north bound, parcel of the rent of Dobett; two selions containing half an acre and half a rood lie on Mekyllowodgate, two selions from the east bound; two selions containing three roods of land lie there beside the west bound; one selion containing a rood and a half lies the fourth selion from the west bound; two selions containing one acre lie on the . . . . . . ,[1] the second selion from the east bound; two selions containing five roods beside the west bound; one selion containing half an acre and half a rood lies the fourth selion from the west bound, parcel of the rent of Dobett; (*fo.* 322*d*) one selion containing one acre lying in the Crokyd-dolez, five selions from the east bound; two selions containing three roods beside the west bound; one selion containing one and a half roods lying there, four selions from the west bound; one selion containing an acre and half a rood lying at Hettongate, two selions from

---

[1] Apparently a word omitted.

the east bound; two selions containing three roods beside the bound towards the west; one selion lying there containing one and a half roods, four selions from the west bound, parcel of the rent of Dobett; one selion containing half an acre and half a rood lying on Askham-hyll, two selions from the east bound; two selions containing three roods lying there beside the west bound; one selion containing one and a half roods lying there, four selions from the west bound, parcel of the rent of Dobett; two selions containing one and a half roods ly-ing on Shytynhers, two selions from the south bound; two selions there containing half an acre beside the north bound; one selion lies there containing one rood, the fourth selion from the north bound; a rood and a half lie in the Gryppe, two selions from the east bound; two selions containing half an acre and half a rood lie beside the east bound, and one selion lies there [containing] one rood, four selions from the west bound, parcel of the rent of Dobett.   And there lie in the Akeryerd one rood and a half and three quadrants.

(Fo. 323)   *In the Brekkffelde.*

(552)   One selion lies in Overlongdolez containing three and a half roods, two selions from the east bound; two selions containing one acre lie beside the west bound; one selion containing half an acre lies there, four selions from the west bound.   And there lie in Netherlongdolez two selions containing two acres, two selions from the east bound; two selions containing two and a half acres lie beside the west bound; one selion containing five roods of land, whereof one part contains one and a half roods and the other two parts contain three and a half roods, parcel of Dobett, and lie there four selions from the west bound.   And there lies at the Legiate one selion con-taining one and a half roods, two selions from the east bound; two selions containing half an acre lie beside the west bound; one selion lies there containing one rood, four selions from the west bound, parcel of Dobett; two selions containing half an acre and half a rood lie at Stokyng, two selions from the south bound; two selions containing three roods of land beside the north bound; one selion containing one and a half roods lies there, four selions from the north bound, parcel of the rent of Dobett; one selion containing one and a half roods lies at Haghedolez, two selions from the south bound; two selions containing half an acre lie beside the north bound; one selion containing one rood lies there, four selions from the north bound, parcel of the rent of Dobett; (*fo. 323d*) and there lie two selions con-taining three roods of land at the Wadlands lying two selions from the south bound; two selions containing one acre lie beside the north [bound], one selion containing half an acre lies the fourth selion from the north bound; two selions containing half an acre and half a rood of land lies at Fernys, two selions from the south bound; two selions containing three roods lie beside the north bound; and in Shorteways half a rood lies; and one selion containing one and a half roods there, four selions from the north bound, parcel of the rent of Dobett; and two selions lie containing one and a half roods on Longways, two selions from the east bound; two selions containing

half an acre beside the west bound; one selion containing one rood lies the fourth selion from the west bound; one selion containing half an acre and half a rood lies in Estbreks, the third selion from the east bound; two selions containing three roods lie beside . . . ;[1] one selion containing one and a half roods lies four selions from the west bound, parcel of the rent of Dobett; two selions containing three roods of land lie on the Longbreks, two selions from the east bound; two selions containing six roods lie beside the west bound; one selion lies there containing three roods, the fourth selion from the west bound; and there lies one selion containing half an acre and half a rood at the Grencrofte, the third selion from the east bound; and two selions containing three roods lie beside the west bound; and one selion containing one and a half roods lies the fourth selion from the west bound; (*fo.* 324) and two selions containing one and a half roods lie at the Moregats, two selions from the east bound; two selions containing half an acre lie beside the west bound; one selion containing a rood lies the fourth selion from the west bound; one selion containing one and a half roods lies at Marketstyghe, two selions from the bound on the east side; two selions containing half an acre lie there beside the bound on the west side; one selion containing one rood, four selions from the west bound.

(553) Meadows with free pastures of the said prior and convent of the same place in Estmarkam.

First, at the Holmes lie nine virgates of meadow, whereof five are full and four are medium; in the same place, in the Nabbe nine virgates, whereof five are full and four medium; in the Cardoles lie four virgates and four feet; below Le Clyffe at Spynkwyloghes nine virgates of meadow, whereof five are full and four medium ; in the Northholome lie five bovates, whereof three are full and two medium; in the Bartilcrofte lie nine virgates, whereof (*fo.* 324*d*) five are full and four medium; in the Oldmore lie nine virgates, whereof five are full and four medium; in the Dryhyrste lie nine virgates, whereof five are full and four medium; in the Fuldole lie nine virgates, whereof five are full and four medium; in the Carr' lie two bovates full and half a bovate towards the middle of the meadow; in the same two bovates medium at the Kyrkeswathe, towards Braton Dyke.

And be it noted that all these meadows, with the free pastures aforewritten, lie altogether in a carucate of Lynham.

Also in See Crofte lie five virgates, whereof three are full beside the Westestone, and two medium by two virgates from the Eststone.

First, a toft lying at Hallyate, between the messuage of John Markham on the south and the messuage of Augustine Porter on the north, and abutting on the King's highway to the west and the land of John Topclyffe, esquire, to the east.

One toft lying there between the messuage of Augustine (*fo.* 325) Porter on the south and the messuage of John Topclyff, esquire, on the north, and abutting on the highway to the west and the land of John Topclyffe to the east.

---

[1] Apparently a word omitted.

Another toft lies there beside the churchyard between the King's highway on the south and the messuage of Augustine Porter on the north, and abuts on the common way to the west and the Rattanrawe to the east.

Another toft lies there at the west end of the vill between the messuage of John Topclyffe, esquire, on the east and the Frankysshall on the west, and abuts on the highway to the south and the land of the same prior and convent to the north.

Another toft lies between the messuage of Robert Bellamye on the east and the land of the heirs of Sandes on the west, and abuts on the Overgate to the south and on Overlondoles to the north.

The Holmes.

(554)   One half acre of land lies there beside the common bound on the north.

Half an acre and half a rood of land lie there, and abut on Bradgatedyke to the north, and beside the common bound on the east. And two selions of land containing half an acre lie there and abut on Whakesendyke to the south and the land of Robert Thorney on the east.

(*Fo.* 325*d*)   *Estfeylde.*

(555)   An acre and a half of land lie there between the land of the vicarage of Markham aforesaid on either side and abut on the King's highway to the west; in the Meddulsteyks half an acre, and in the same place a rood and a half; in the Howlewongende a rood; also there lies there one acre beside the land of Thomas Swan; also there lies in Lang Wathcrofte a rood and a half; also in Gybcrofte an acre and a half; also in Elwartofte half an acre; at the Bekks a rood and a half.

(556)   Free tenants now in Estmarkham, belonging to the aforesaid prior and the convent of the same place, as appears below:

First, John Markham holds a toft in Rattonraw and half a bovate of land and renders yearly. . . . . . 7s. 7d.

The same John holds two tofts in his garden beside Linanlans and renders yearly . . . . . 15d.

The same John holds a messuage and a bovate of land, formerly William Patte's, and renders yearly a pair of gloves or . . . . 1d.

John Bee holds a cottage and toft, with a little toft contained in the same toft, and renders yearly . . . 2s.2½d.

(*Fo.* 326) Joan Porter holds a toft and renders yearly . 12d.

The said Joan holds a rood of land at the Halewelbalke and renders yearly . . . . 1d.

Robert Bekks holds a toft beside his messuage and renders yearly . . . . 2s.

The same Robert holds one [1] lying at Priestgats at the Northende and renders yearly . . . . . 1d.

---

[1] A word omitted in the MS.

The heirs of Robert Boswell hold half a rood of land at
Stonepytts and render yearly . . . . . 2d.
The said heirs hold half an acre at Morewell and render
yearly . . . . 2d.
The said heirs hold a rood and a half at Ashamhill and
render yearly . . . . 1½d.
The said heirs hold a rood and a half at the Nethyrhirste
and render yearly . . . . 1½d.
Thomas . . . . . .[1] holds a rood and a half and renders
yearly . . . . 1½d.
Thomas . . . . . . holds a rood and a half at Estbrokk
and renders yearly . . . . 1d.
Thomas . . . . . . holds a rood and a half at the Dalestyg-
hend and renders yearly . . . . . . 1d.
These are the names of the carucates in Estmarkham, namely
Belyalde, Lyncham, Cressy, Castryke, Burdon, and Sawndbye.

(Fo. 326d)[2]   Bekcton.

(557) Confirmation by Nicholas Legat of Houdernesse and
Dionisia de Lasceles his wife to God and the church of Saint Mary
Magdalene of Bretton and the monks there, of all the land, with the
appurtenances, without retention, which they (Nicholas and Dionisia)
had in the vill and territory of Becton, or which they or their heirs
may have by hereditary right, both in demesnes and free men and
in villeins, mills, rents, wardships, reliefs, escheats, and in all other
services and customs to them or their heirs belonging or which
might belong from the said land.   To hold and to have, in perpetual
alms, freely, quietly, etc., in wood, in plain, etc., and in all other liberties, easements, and commons to the said vill of Becton belonging,
doing thence all services belonging to the chief lords of the same fee.
(Fo. 327) Witnesses, Sir William de Chauworth, Walter clerk of the
Countess of Eou, and many others.
                    (Monkbretton Chart., Lansdowne MS. 405, fo. 13.)

(558) Confirmation by Nicholas Legat of Houdernesse, to the
same church and monks, of the donation which Dionisia his wife
gave the same monks and confirmed by her charter, namely of all
her land, without retention, which she had or might have by hereditary right in the vill of Becton, in perpetual alms.   (Fo. 327d) Warranty by Nicholas during the life of Dionisia.   Witnesses as in the
previous deed.[3]

(559) Grant by Dionisia de Lasceles to God and Saint Mary
Magdalene of Bretton and the monks there, of all her land, with the
appurtenances, without retention, which she had in the vill and
territory of Becton, or which she or her heirs could have by hereditary right, both in demesnes and free men, etc., (as in the last deed

---

[1] No surname given here or in the following items.

[2] Headed " Bekcton," which heading with variations to " Bekton " and
" Beghton " continues to the end.   The vill is Beighton, in Derbyshire.

[3] The first is here and in the two following deeds called " Chaworth."

but one). To hold and to have, etc., (as in the same deed), doing thence all services, etc., (as in the same deed). (*Fo.* 328) Same witnesses. (Monkbretton Chart., Lansdowne MS. 405, fo. 13*d*.)

(560) Confirmation by Dionisia de Lasceles, in widowhood, to the same donees of the same property. To have and to hold to the monks and their successors, in pure and perpetual alms, freely, quietly, etc., (*fo.* 328*d*) in wood, in plain, etc., and in all other liberties and easements to the vill of Becton belonging. The same witnesses.

(561) Agreement and equal partition, by the view of lawful men and by lot, between Nicholas Legat and Dionisia his wife of the one part, Nichola daughter of Ranulf de Novo Mercato of the other part, and Thomas de Ponte and Juliana his wife of the third part, respecting the lands and rents, with the appurtenances, in Becton, Karleton, and Lindric, which were of Ranulf de Novo Mercato, whose heirs they are, to wit, that Nicholas Legat and Dionisia his wife hold themselves satisfied for their share, as is contained in a charter chirographate of so much rent in Becton, in (*fo.* 329) free men and in villeins, namely from Richard the forester 5*s.* 11*d.*, from John de Hacantorp 9*s.* and three hens, from Roger del Pec 15*d.*, from Roger the clerk 6*d.*, from Robert the smith 18*d.*, from Robert Bastard a pound of cummin or a penny, from Jordan son of Simon 5*d.*, from Alice the widow 10*d.*, from Gena 4*s.*, from Roger the smith 34*d.*, from William son of Tholiff 32*d.*, from Ralph the tentmaker 6*d.*, from the bovate of land which Nicholas son of Walter holds from Thomas de Ponte and Juliana his wife 2*s.* 10*d.* only. And to the said Thomas and Juliana his wife all the residue, with the homages and services and issues, in Karleton, from Matthew the chaplain 1*d.*, from William At-bridge 2*d.*, from William the fullur 2*d.*, in Lindric from Moses 5*d.*; similarly with their share in Becton in demesne, in meadow, in wood, in park, in the mills; and with the third part of the arable land in Lindric which belongs to them. And Nichola daughter of Ranulf de Novo Mercato holds herself satisfied for her share in Becton, from Thomas Ger' 5*s.*, from William son of John 6*d.*, from Wist 22*d.*, from Hugh de Waltertorp 4*s.*, from Thomas the dispenser 18*d.*, from Ranulf Hyph' 2*s.* 6*d.*; in Karleton, from Thomas son of Hugh 16*d.*, from William At-bridge 2*d.*, from William de fullur [*sic*] 2*d.*; in Lindric, from Moses 5*d.*; similarly with her third share in demesnes, meadows, woods, parks, mills, both in Becton and Karleton and Lindric, Thomas Bridge and Juliana his wife hold themselves satisfied for their share in Karleton, from William At-bridge 2*d.*; from William le fullur 2*d.*; (*fo.* 329*d*) in Lindric, from Moses 5*d.*; in Becton, from Dode 1*d.*, from Michael 1*d.*; similarly with their third share in Becton in demesne, in meadow, in wood, in park, in mills, with their appurtenances; and of two parts in Karleton, in demesnes, meadows and parks, and with all the capital messuage, and two parts of the Court. And in Lindric, with two parts of the wood and the third part of the arable land. And to the firm observance of this agreement, the parties swore on the holy things and to these writings chirographate set their seals. Witnesses,

Matthew the chaplain of Wallandwell, Robert de Furneis, Walter the clerk of Tikehull, Thomas de St. Quintin, Robert Bastard, and many others.   (Monkbretton Chart., Lansdowne MS. 405, fo. 13.)

(562) Grant by Letitia,[1] formerly wife of Ranulf de Novo Mercato, in her free widowhood, to Thomas Gere and his heirs or assigns, for his homage and service, of a bovate of land, with the appurtenances, in the territory of Becton, which Ranulf Gere formerly held, and two tofts in the vill of Becton which Fabian and Mirihild held, and a toft beside the bridge which William Gere formerly (fo. 340)[2] held. To have and to hold to the grantee and his heirs or assigns, from the grantor, her heirs or assigns, freely, quietly, etc., with all appurtenances, within and without the vill, rendering to them yearly for all secular service, etc., save the forinsec service of the King, 5s. sterling. Witnesses, Sir Geoffrey de Musters, Sir Geoffrey de Stoks, John the parson of Ekinton, Adam de Horbyri, and many others.

(563) Confirmation of the preceding grant, by Ranulf de Novo Mercato, (fo. 340d) son of Letitia the donor, under the same conditions and rent. Same witnesses, with the exception of Adam de Horbyri.

(564) Grant by Nichola de Novoforo, in her lawful and free power, to Thomas (fo. 341) Gere of Becton, his heirs or assigns, of all her demesne arable land within and without the vill of Becton, namely within the bounds of the fields of Becton, excepting her free and other tenants, and excepting her share in the great wood of Becton, and excepting the land in the same wood, namely in Westwode, and except the land which falls to her after the death of Amabel, wife of her brother; and also the meadow and all her share of the mill, with the suit of her men and all her share in the park, and the tower of the former castle, with free and due entry and egress to and from the same, for vehicles and cattle. To hold and to have from the grantor and her heirs to the said Thomas Gere and his heirs or assigns, freely, quietly, etc., in roads, in waters, in lanes, etc., with all appurtenances, easements, and liberties to the said land belonging; rendering to her and her heirs a pound of cummin yearly for all secular service and exaction. For this grant Thomas has given her 11 marks of silver as a fine. (Fo. 341d) Witnesses, Sir Robert de Furneys, John and John, parsons of Ekynton, Ralph Britone, Robert de Winerton, and many others.

(565) Grant and surrender by Roger, prior of Bretton, and the convent thereof, to William son of John de Becton and his heirs, for his homage and service, of half a bovate of land, with the appurtenances, which William son of Thor sometime held in Becton, and a bovate and the third part of a bovate of land, with the appurtenances,

---

[1] The red heading has " carta Juliane ux' Ranulfi," etc. The name " Letitia " is confirmed by the next deed.

[2] Should be 330: the mistake is continued to the end.

L

which Roger Pek and Juliana his wife, and Richard the clerk of Becton, and Michael de . . . . . .[1] sometime held from them (the grantors) in the same vill, which he (the grantee) claimed against them (the grantors) by writ of right.   To have and to hold to the grantee, his heirs or assigns, from the grantors and their successors, freely, quietly, etc., in fee and inheritance, rendering to them yearly 12*d*., for all secular service, save forinsec (*fo.* 342) service, as belongs to so much land.   For this grant and surrender the grantee has quit-claimed, for himself and his heirs, to the grantors and their successors, the homage and all the services of John de Hacuntorp and his heirs, which he claimed from the said John by the King's writ, and all right and claim in their (the monks') fee in Becton.   The monks and their successors will warrant to William and his heirs, so far as the charters of their donors can warrant to them.   Witnesses, John, rector of a mediety of the church of Becton, Alexander Boffin, Thomas son of Nicholas de Hacuntorp, and others.   Seals of the parties to either part of this chirograph, with the witnesses aforesaid.

(Monkbretton Chart., Lansdowne MS. 405, fo. 15d.)

(566)   Grant by brother Roger, prior (*humilis minister*) of Bretton, and the convent of the same place, (*fo.* 342*d*) to Richard son of William de Becton and his heirs, for his homage and service of a toft with the buildings, and all the appurtenances, in Becton; that toft namely which Roger the clerk formerly held from them. To have and to hold to the grantee, his heirs and assigns, except Religious and Jews and the chief lord, from the grantors and their successors, freely, quietly, etc., in fee and inheritance, rendering yearly to their church of Bretton 6*d*. for all service and demand. Seals of the parties to this chirograph.   Witnesses, Sir Robert de Furnes, John, parson of Ekynton, and many others.

(Monkbretton Chart., Lansdowne MS. 405, fo. 15.)

(*Fo.* 343)   (567)   Agreement made between William Wambays of the one part, and the prior and monks of Bretton of the other part. William has demised and granted for the lifetime of his wife, to the same prior and monks, all her land within and without the vill of Becton, which he had of the dowry of Amabel his wife, as well in demesnes and rents as in free men and villeins, and all other liberties and free commons and escheats and wardships belonging to the said land.   To hold and to have, freely, quietly, etc., rendering to William yearly 34*s*. 8*d*., which he shall receive from the prior's and monks' ferm of Tunstal, for his wife's life.   William may distrain the monks' land of Tunstal only for the ferm if it should be wanting at any time, but he may not demand anything else from the said land of Tunstal beyond his ferm, and that only in the lifetime of his wife; and he is to warrant the aforesaid land to the monks during her life so long as he receives the ferm.   Witnesses, Sir Robert de Furneys, Thomas de Lincoln, and many others.

[1] A blank of about half-an-inch in the MS.   " Swotal " in Lansdowne MS. 405, fo. 15*d*.

(*Fo.* 343*d*) (568) Grant by the lady Nichola de Hicilton to God and the church of Saint Mary Magdalene of Bretton and the monks there, of all her share, which fell or might fall to her or her heirs by inheritance, of the park of Becton, namely the wood and plain on the land and beneath, with all appurtenances of the dower of Amabel, formerly wife of Ralph de Novo Mercato, in pure and perpetual alms.   To hold and to have to the grantees or their assigns, freely, quietly, etc., with all easements on the land and beneath it, and liberties and commons thereto belonging.   For this grant the monks have given her 10*s.* of silver.   (*Fo.* 344) Witnesses, Robert de Furneys, Jordan de Cretun, John de Hacuntorp, and many others.

(Monkbretton Chart., Lansdowne MS. 405, fo. 14.)

(569)   Grant by the lady Nichola, daughter of Randulf de Novo Mercato, to God and the church of Saint Mary Magdalene of Bretton and the monks there, of all her share of all the dower of Amabel, formerly wife of Randulf the grantor's brother, in the vill of Becton, with all appurtenances, without retention, whereof she and her sisters dowered [her] after the death of their said brother, as well in demesnes, free men, and villeins, as in the mills and other things to the said dower belonging, or which might hereafter belong.   To hold and have, in perpetual alms, freely, quietly, etc., in wood, in plain, etc., and with all other liberties and easements and free common, within and without the vill of Becton, belonging to the said land, (*fo.* 344*d*) doing the King's forinsec service and the service at Blyth and Tikehill and Eckington as belongs to the said land. Warranty in perpetual alms.   Witnesses; Sir Robert de Furneis, Robert de Wenerton, Hugh de Duomantun then bailiff of that fief, Richard the clerk of Becton, and many others.

(570)   Grant by Thomas de Lincoln and Juliana his wife to God and the church of Saint Mary Magdalene of Bretton and the monks there, of all their share of the park of Becton, which may fall to them or their heirs in any way, namely the wood and plain on the land and beneath, with all the appurtenances, in pure and perpetual alms.   To hold and to have to the grantees or their assigns, freely, quietly, etc., with all easements on the land and beneath it, and liberties and commons thereto belonging.   Moreover they have granted to the same monks and their successors a certain rent of a pound of cummin which they (the grantors) were accustomed to receive (*fo.* 345) from Thomas son of Ralph Gere at the feast of Saint Thomas Apostle, and all other things falling to them or their heirs in any way in the soke of Becton by hereditary right.   This grant they have made for their souls, and the souls of their fathers and mothers and ancestors and successors, free and quit of all secular service and demand. Witnesses, Robert de Furneys, Jordan de Treton, and many others.

(571) Grant by Thomas de Lincoln in Karleton and Juliana his wife (*fo.* 345*d*) to the same grantees, of all their share of all the wood of Becton which is called Westwode, with the appurtenances, as well beneath as upon the land, which falls to them by inheritance

after the death of Ranulf de Novo Mercato. Moreover they have given the same church all their share of all the dower of Amabel, formerly wife of Randulf de Novo Mercato, brother of Juliana, in the vill of Becton, with all appurtenances, without retention, whereof they (the grantors) and the sisters of Juliana dowered Amabel after the death of the said Randulf de Novo Mercato, both in woods, demesnes, houses, villeins, and all services of free men, and in natives and their lands, in mills, meadows, pastures, meadows, and all other places belonging to the said dower, and in all other things which may fall to them in the soke of Becton by reason of the said dower and by reason of the said wood in Westwode. To hold and to have in perpetual alms, freely, quietly, etc., with all appurtenances, etc., within the vill of Becton and without; doing foreign service and the service, to the chief lords, as belongs to the said land. (*Fo.* 346) Witnesses, Sir Robert Furneys, Hugh Dokemanton, and many others. (Monkbretton Chart., Lansdowne MS. 405, fo. 14.)

(572) Grant by Humphrey Laceles to the monks of Bretton of his body at his death, for burial with them. Moreover he has given to God and Saint Mary Magdalene of Bretton and the said monks, Geoffrey the son of Gamel, with all the land which he held from him (Humphrey), namely four acres, in pure and perpetual alms, for the souls of himself and his wife and his ancestors and heirs. Witnesses, John the chaplain, Jordan de Hec', and others.

(573) Grant and surrender by William Maundrel of Behgton (*fo.* 346*d*) to the prior and convent of Bretton, and the monks there, his chief lords, and their successors, of all right and claim in a rent of 12*d.* issuing from two tofts in the vill of Behgton, which John Ruiffin and Alice le Borkeman hold in the same vill, and of which rent he (William) was intermediary between the said prior and convent and the holders of the said tofts. To hold and to have the said rent to the prior and convent and their successors for ever, freely, quietly, etc., with all the appurtenances. Witnesses, John de Hakinthorpe, Gilbert de Somernsby, William Gere, and others.

(574) Grant by Emma de Stockewell, prioress of Wallandwells, and the convent thereof, to brother William, prior of Monkbretton, and the convent thereof and their successors, of the yearly rent of 5*s.* respecting which there had lately been dissension between them; to be received each year (*fo.* 347) at Martinmas without dispute by the grantors. If the grantors or their successors should be in arrear with the payment of the said rent at any time, they charge all their lands, rents, meadows, and all their other holdings which they have in lordship or demesne in the vill of Behgton, into whosesoever hands they shall have come, to be distrained by the said grantees and their successors, until satisfaction of the rent and arrears is made. Witnesses, Sir Richard de Furneis, knight, Adam de Cateby, Thomas de Schefeud, etc. Dated at Roderham, Monday after the Sunday on which *Quasi modo geniti* is sung, 25 Edw. I. (Monkbretton Chart., Lansdowne MS. 405, fo. 14*d*.)

(575) Indenture made between John Gaynesburgh, prior of the monastery of Blyth, and the convent thereof of the one part, and Thomas Dowdale, prior of the church of the blessed Mary Magdalene of Bretton, and the monks and convent there (*fo.* 347*d*) of the other part, witnessing that whereas the said prior and convent of the church of the blessed Mary Magdalene have and freely hold all the lands and tenements, rents, and services, with the appurtenances, in Beghton in the county of Derby, which were formerly of Nicholas Legat and Dionisia his wife, and which by estimation contain the third part of the lordship of Beghton, from the said prior and convent of Blyth and their successors, by the rent and service of 5*s.* 2½*d.* yearly, nevertheless, that the said rent is now much in arrear and not paid. Be it known that the prior and convent of Blyth for themselves and their successors, as much as in them is, have ratified and confirmed the estate which the prior and convent of the church of the blessed Mary Magdalene have or possess in the said lands, tenements, rents and services, with the appurtenances, in Beghton, and have remitted the arrears of rent. To have and to hold from the prior and convent of Blyth and their successors, by the rent and service aforesaid, for all services. (*Fo.* 348) Power of distraint if the rent is in arrear at any time. The prior of Monkbretton to pay to the prior of Blyth 2*s.* 7*d.* in part payment of the rent for the term of Martinmas last past. Respective seals of the two houses to the two parts of this indenture. Dated 6 April, 2 Hen. VI, 1424.

(576) Grant by William de Staynton of Hakynthorp to Thomas Belle of Cotheworth and Thomas de Cotyngham, renderer, and their heirs or assigns, of a yearly rent, with the service of the same rent of 6*s.* 8*d.*, which John Puppan and Matilda his wife and Richard (*fo.* 348*d*) son of Hugh de Hakinthorp are liable to pay him (William) for two bovates of land called Fraunke Burgeysffyld in the territory of Hakinthorp within the fee of Beghton. He has also given and confirmed to the same grantees and their heirs or assigns the rent and service of 5*s.* and 22*d.* which the heir of William Cotyngham and John Wyott are liable to pay him for two messuages and a bovate and a half of land within the vill of Beghton. To have and to hold with all services, homages, wardships, reliefs, marriages, and escheats of the said tenants, to the grantees, their heirs or assigns, freely, etc., from the chief lord of that fee, by the services due and accustomed. Witnesses, William de Plumlay, William Dolfyn, Robert de Peke, and others. Dated at Hakinthorpe, Sunday after the feast of Saint Benedict, 43 Edw. III (1369).

(*Fo.* 349) (577) Release and quitclaim by Thomas Belle of Cudworth and Thomas Cotyngham, renderer, to the prior of the monastery of the blessed Mary Magdalene of Monkbretton and the convent there and their successors for ever, of all right, title, and claim of and in a yearly rent of 6*s.* 8*d.* which John Puppan and Matilda his wife and Richard son of Hugh de Hakinthorpe were accustomed to pay them (Thomas and Thomas), for two bovates of land which are called Fraunkeburgeysfeld in the territory of Hakinthorp within the fee of

Beghton; and of and in another yearly rent of 5s. and 22d. which the heirs of William de Cotingham and John Wyott were accustomed to pay them for two messuages and a bovate and a half of land within the vill of Beghton, with all services appertaining to the same rents which they (Thomas and Thomas) had by the grant of William Staynton. (*Fo.* 349d) Dated at Monkbretton, 4 September, 45 Edw. III (1371).

(578) Surrender and quitclaim by John Chernoke of Ekington, esquire, to the prior and convent of Monkbretton and their successors, of all the rent and all his right and claim in 13s. 6d., with the appurtenances, in Beghton, which rent he was accustomed to receive from the underwritten, to the use and profit of the said prior and convent; (*fo.* 350) namely from John del Kyrke for a messuage and a bovate of land in Beghton 5s.; from the heirs of John Wyot for a moiety of a messuage and of a bovate of land in Swotall 22d.; from Simon atte Wodd and John Davy for a bovate of land in Fraunkbergeffeld in Hawkynthorp, 6s. 8d., namely from the said Simon for his part 5s., from the said John Davy for his part 20d. Witnesses, Master Robert Laghton, James Cresacre, John Frankys, John Auty, Adam Bate, and others. Dated 20 May, 1 Hen. V (1413).

(579) Demise by John Birthwayt, prior of the monastery of Monkbretton, and the convent thereof, (*fo.* 350d) to William de Staynton and Agnes his wife, for their lives and the life of the survivor of them, of all their (the prior's and convent's) part of their manor of Beghton, with the appurtenances, and with all lands and tenements, meadows, woods, rents, services of tenants, courts, wardships, reliefs, escheats, with all their part and the suit which belongs to them of the mill of Beghton.   To hold and to have to the grantees (as before) from the prior and convent and their successors, rendering to them yearly 2s. 8d. sterling, and rendering, for the grantors, to the lord of Ekynton 3s. 4d. yearly, and doing suit of the Court of the said lord of Ekynton, and all other burdens and services from the said tenements due and accustomed, and also doing attendances at the Wapentake and the great tourns of Cestrefeld,[1] and frankpledge and other burdens against the King's escheator and others his ministers, for the grantors and their successors, and rendering for them to the prior and convent of Blyth 5s. 2½d. yearly at Martinmas for all other services.   The grantors will warrant to the grantees and the survivor of them, and the grantees and their executors (*fo.* 351) shall restore all the said tenements and share of the mill, with the other appurtenances, in as good state as they received them, at the end of their lives.   Power of distraint if rent is in arrear, and if in arrear for six weeks power of re-entry.   Seals of the parties to the alternate parts of this indenture.   Dated in the chapter house of Monkbretton, Thursday after the feast of Saint Andrew Apostle, 1350.

[1] Chesterfield.

(*Fo.* 351*d*) (580) Surrender by Agnes de Hakelthorp, formerly wife of William de Staynton, to the prior and convent of Monkbretton, of all lands and tenements, rents and services, which she had in Beghton, Hakelthorp, and all their hamlets and parcels, which she and William de Staynton, formerly her husband, had by the grant of the predecessor of the present prior and convent for term of life, and she consents to pay to the prior and convent 14*s.* from the tenements which were John de Hakelthorp's, her first husband, in Hakilthorp, as they were held from the prior and convent. In consideration of which the prior and convent will pay to Agnes 7 marks of silver yearly at Beghton; if such rent is in arrear, it shall be lawful for her to distrain in all the lands and tenements of the prior and convent in Beghton and Hakelthorp, and the prior and convent pay her a penny in the name of seisin. (*Fo.* 352) Seals of the parties to the alternate parts of this indenture. Dated on Wednesday the morrow of Saint John ante portam Latinam, 5 Ric. II (May 7, 1382).

THE CHARTULARY OF MONKBRETTON PRIORY.

Lansdowne MS. CCCCV.

In this volume are inscribed or transcribed all the charters, feoffments, confirmations, and quitclaims of whatever condition which belong to the house of St. Mary Magdalene of Bretton and to the prior and convent of that place of the Order of St. Benedict, in the diocese of York, serving God there, by whatever title they hold possession.

In primis of the Wapentake of Staincross.

Charter of John son of Hugh de Brecton, and charter of John Heyron.

Charter of the Earl of Lancaster.

[*The rest of the folio so faded as to be illegible.*]

(*Fo.* 3*d*) (1) Grant by Adam son of Swane to God and St. Mary Magdalene of Lunda, as No. 6, W. MS.,[1] but only Alexander and Richard are given as witnesses.

(2) Grant by Adam son of Swane to God and St. Mary Magdalene of Lunda of all the tithe of wild colts throughout the whole of his lordship wherever there may be herds of mares. He also granted to them the whole rent which Ravan de Halcton was accustomed to render to Swane son of Eilric, which Robert son of Ravan rendered to the grantor on the death of his father. As No. 247, W. MS.

(3) Confirmation by Roger de Montbegon, as No. 9, W. MS., ending at "his ancestors and heirs free." [*The following page with list of witnesses has disappeared.*]

Wrangebroc.

(*Fo.* 4) (4) Grant by Roger de Montbegun, as No. 15, W. MS., only witness William the priest.

(5) Grant by Henry son of Swane of 8s. a year rent for two bovates in Warangebroc which Elias son of Hugh held of him. Witness, Rainer Fleming.

(6) Grant by Robert son of Roger de Warangebroc of two acres of land in Warangebroc, held in perpetuity of him and his heirs, and all the land between the house of the monks and that of Ralph son of Gamell, paying annually 12*d*. Witness, Hugh, dean of Silkeston.

---

[1] Woolley Manuscript.

(7) Grant by Hugh son of Roger de Warangebroc of half an acre of land in Wrangebroc, namely that which lies between the acre and a half that belonged to his brother Robert, and those lands as far as Undefurlang and of those lands which he had in Cheveril riding, paying a rent of 1*d.* at Christmas. Witness, William son of Adam.

(8) Confirmation of the above grant. The same witness.

(*Fo.* 4*d*) (9) Confirmation by Adam son of Robert de Wrangebroc to God and St. Mary Magdalene of Bretton of two acres in Wrangebroc and all the land which Robert his father gave to the monks, between their house and the house of Ralph son of Gamell, from the water as far as middilfurlong for one acre and a half, and in haulandes moderles halwacker in length and breadth half an acre; and one and a half acres next le Rig super hulin, and in hulin one and a half acres to flaskedales, and one and a half acres in unddirfurlang ad pipidalis in length and breadth as it lies between Cliffurlang and brocfurlang; also the land in Cheverilriding, paying 12*d.* yearly. Witness, Walter Danever.

(10) Confirmation by Adam son of Robert de Wrangebrok of the above grant. Witness, Hugh son of Roger.

(*Fo.* 5) (11) Confirmation by Adam son of Robert de Wrangebrok of the above two acres. Witness, Hugh son of Roger de Wrangebroc.

(*Fo.* 5*d*) (12) Grant by Adam son of Robert of half an acre in the field of Wrangebroc near Watlingstret in Uverfurllanges de Hulin. Witness, John Tyrel.

(13) Grant by Adam son of Robert de Wrangebroc for one horse which they (the monks) have given for two acres in Wrangebroc, one acre on Hulin as it lies by the spring Ulsebern and one acre at Haverlandes next the land of Reiner on the north side. Witness, Thomas de Hortenston.

(14) Grant by Adam son of Robert de Wrangebroc of all his part of Cheverilriding and of one acre next le rig on hulin. Witness, Gilbert de Notton.

(*Fo.* 6) (15) Grant by Adam son of Robert de Wrangebroc of two acres in Wrangebroc and half an acre lying on the east side of the chapel, and half an acre between Morcotes and southfurlang and one acre between the land of the monastery and that of Ralph son of Gamell. Witness, Ralph son of Gamell.

(16) Grant by Adam de Wrangebroc of one rood of land in Wrangebroc next the cultured land of the monks, out of that acre which lies on the Hulin between the lands of the monks and of Henry Nalor. Witness, Gilbert de Notton.

(17) Confirmation of the above grant by Adam son of Robert de Wrangebroc. Witness, Morice de Haskerne.

(18)   Grant by Adam son of Robert de Wrangebrok, as No. 309, W. MS.

(19)   Grant by the same Adam of ten acres in Wrangebrok. Witness, Roger de Montbegon.

(*Fo.* 7) (20) Grant by the same Adam of two parts of the whole of Ravenscroft on the north as far as the stream, paying yearly 2*s.* Witness, Gilbert de Notton.

(21)   Confirmation by the same of the above grant. Witness, Adam de Ranavill.

(22)   Grant by the same Adam of all his land in Ravenescroft, as No. 307, W. MS.

(*Fo.* 7*d*) (23) Confirmation by Maurice de Haskerne of all his land in Wrangebroc, held of Adam son of Robert de Wrangebroc in fealty. Witness, Gilbert de Notton.

(24)   Grant by Maurice de Askarne of Ravenscroft with its appurtenances in Wrangebroc, and all the lands which Adam son of Robert de Wrangebroc held of him. Witness, John Tyrel.

(25)   Grant by the same Maurice, as No. 308, W. MS.

(*Fo.* 8) (26) Confirmation by John Franceys and Margaret his wife, daughter of Adam son of Robert de Wrangbroc, of all the lands and possessions which Adam, father of Margaret, gave to the monks of Bretton. Witness, Robert de Torp.

(27)   Confirmation by John son of John Franceys of Wrangebroc of all the lands and possessions which his ancestors and progenitors gave to the monks, and which were of the gift of Robert grandfather of his mother, Margaret de Wrangebroc, or his grandfather Roger, or any other of his ancestors. Witness, Alan son of John Smytheton.

(*Fo.* 8*d*) (28) Quitclaim by Peter de Hornecastel, as No. 313, W. MS.

(29)   Confirmation by Gervase Pulann, as No. 314, W. MS.

(30)   Grant by Gervase Pulain of Wrangebroc of one rood of land in Wrangebroc, namely that which is by the gate of the monastery, and which extends as far as the road, and half an acre in the same vill next Osegote Raven extending to the hill as far as Haulandes. Witness, William son of Adam.

(31)   Grant by the same Gervase of one and a half acres in Wrangebroc, and two roods in Haulandes, and three roods next the street of Ravenscroft to the west, and one rood by the gate of the monastery. Witness, Simon, clerk of Wyrkesburg.

(*Fo.* 9) (32) Grant by Gervase Pulain of Wrangebroc of one rood in Wrangebroc, that which is by the gate of the monks and stretches from the waters as far as the road. Witness, Richard Pulain.

(33) Grant by Adam son of Gervase Pulayn of all the land in Wrangebroc which he holds of the monks of Bretton; also he confirmed to them one rood in the same territory, namely that which Simon Pulayn gave between his toft and that which he (Adam) held of the monks. Witness, Sir Henry de Walensis.

(34) Grant by Richard Pulayn of six and a half roods in Wrangebroc, two and a half roods on the moor, and one rood in Midelfurlang, and three roods between the highroad in Ravenscroft, and half a rood next the gate of the monastery. Witness, Gervase Pulain.

(*Fo.* 9*d*) (35) Grant by Benedict son of Simon Polain of Wrangebroc of three roods of arable land in the territory of Wrangebroc, lying in the Brokifurlang between the land of the monks, one head abutting on the brook, the other head on Somlandegate towards the south. Witness, John son of John Byset.

(36) Grant by Adam son of Godfrey of half an acre in Wrangebroc lying between the stream and Midilfurlang. Witness, Gilbert de Notton.

(37) Confirmation by Adam son of Robert de Wrangebroc of the grant of Adam son of Godfrey (as above). Witness, Gilbert de Notton.

(*Fo.* 10) (38) Grant by William son of Gamell de Wrangebroc of one rood in Langpittes which is next the cultured land of the monks at the mill which Ralph holds of him (William) in Wrangebroc. Wit·ness, Adam son of Ralph Gamell.

Schelebroc.

(39) Grant by William son of Gamell de Wrangebroc of half an acre of land in langpittes which lies within the lands of the monks. Witness, William son of Adam.

Wrangbroc (*inserted in later writing*).

(40) Grant by William son of Gamell de Wrangebroc, as No. 310, W. MS.

(*Fo.* 10*d*) (41) Grant by the same William, as No. 311, W. MS.

(42) Grant by Sibilia daughter of Adam Burnel of Elmissale of half an acre near the market of Wrangebroc for the light of the altar of the blessed Mary at Breton, namely that half acre which Adam de Bechale held of her (Sibilia) lying between the cultured land of the monks on the west and the land of John Wirre and abutting on the land of Adam son of Reiner de Wrangebroc. Witness, John de Curtenay.

(43) Grant by Henry Nalor of half an acre in the territory of Wrangebroc, namely that half acre which is at the head of the toft of the monks' land in Midilfurlang, which is in the occupation of Agnes widow of Robert de Wrangebroc. Witness, Thomas de Torneton.

(44) Quitclaim by Richard Jubbe and Adam his brother of all claims in Meneland in Wrangebroc, namely two and a half acres, also in one rood in Langpittes.   Witness, William de Nevill.

(*Fo.* II) (45) Confirmation by William Maulunel and Sibill his wife of half an acre near the market of Wrangebroc for the light of the altar of the blessed Mary at Bretton, namely that half acre which Adam de Bechale held of them, abutting on the land of Adam son of Reiner de Wrangebroc.   Witness, John de Curtenay.

(46) Grant by Adam Jub of Wrangebroc of one rood of land in Wrangebroc at Langpittes.   Witness, Hyerome the priest.

(47) Grant by Adam son of William the forester of Wrangbroc of one acre of arable land in Wrangebroc, and half an acre next the brook, between the land of the monks and the head of the brook, abutting on the land of the same Adam, and another half acre which lies south of the brook with one head on Somlandgate.   Witness, John Byset.

(*Fo.* IId) (48) Grant by brother Roger, prior of the monastery of Bretton, to Simon Pulayn of Wrangebroc for his homage and service, of that toft and buildings which Adam Pulan holds of the monastery in Wrangebroc, lying between the house of the said Simon and the house of Adam son of Reiner, paying 3s. rent for all services and demands.   Witness, Robert Pincerna.

Manestorp.

(49) Grant by Adam de Burgo of one bovate in Manestorp, namely that which he held.   Witness, John de Rockeley.

(*Fo.* 12) (50) Confirmation by Henry de Burgo of one bovate in Manestorp, which Adam his brother gave to the monks.   Witness, Robert son of Adam.

[*In another handwriting.*]

(51) Confirmation by Adam son of Roger de Wrangbrok, as No. 312, W. MS.

de Wath.

(*Fo.* 12d) (52) Grant by William, prior of Bretton, to Henry son of Randolph de Wad and his wife Christian daughter of Robert le Fraunceis, of one acre of land in Wad, which Thomas the presbyter holds of the priory with the adjoining toft, paying a rent of 6d. free of all services and exactions.   Witnesses, Rainer Fleming, William, Adam and Thomas his sons.

Becton.

(*Fo.* 13) (53) Confirmation by Nicholas Legat of Houdernesse and Dionisia de Lasceles his wife, as No. 561, W. MS.

(*Fo.* 13d) (54) Grant by Dionisia de Lasceles, as No. 559, W. MS.

(55) Grant by Nichola de Novo Mercato, as No. 569, W. MS.

(*Fo.* 14) (56) Grant by Nichola de Hykylton, as No. 568, W. MS.

(57)   Grant by Thomas de Lincoln, as No. 571, W. MS.

(*Fo.* 14*d*) (58) Grant by Emma de Stockewell, as No.574, W. MS., with additional witnesses, John le Vavasour, John de Doncaster, Stephen Here, William Mondrel, and John Bovett.

(*Fo.* 15) (59) Quitclaim by Nicholas de Becton to Thomas the chaplain, for 12*s.* of silver, of the land which he holds in the vill of Becton.   Witness, Sir Geoffrey of the monastery.

(60)   Grant by Agnes de Churton to Roger the clerk of Becton of the toft and buildings which she had of Thomas the chaplain. Witness, John the priest.

(61)   Grant by Roger the clerk of Becton to the prior of St. Mary Magdalene of Bretton of his toft and buildings in Becton.   Witness, Sir Robert de Furneis.

(*Fo.* 15*d*) (62) Grant by Roger, prior of Bretton, to Richard son of William de Becton, as No. 566, W. MS.

(63)   Grant by Roger, prior of Bretton, to William son of John de Becton, as No. 565, W. MS.

Athewik.

(*Fo.* 16) (64) Grant by Thomas son of William, as No. 297, W. MS.

Scauceby.

(65)   Grant by Hugh son of Alexander de Scauceby of the homage and service of Brian de Scauceby and his heirs and all the lands in Scauceby[1] which he held of him, paying 5*s.* 1*d.* yearly. Witness, William de Bileham.

(66)   Grant by John de Bectun and Juliana daughter of Hugh Breton of Scauceby of one piece of arable land in the field of Scauceby lying between the land of Henry Doynel and the land of Henry de Scauceby, abutting on the cliff of Mar, and the remaining head on the lands which lie next the road to Broddesworth.   Witness, William de Bilham.

(*Fo.* 16*d*) (67) Confirmation by Gilian daughter of Hugh Breton of Scauceby of all the lands in the market of Scauceby which Hugh her father gave to the monks.   Witness, Hugh de Laggethwait.

(68)   Confirmation by Hugh son of Alexander de Scauceby of all the lands with their appurtenances in the fields of Scauceby which Hugh de Bretton gave to the monks.   Witness, Sir William de Middeton, then bailiff.

(69)   Grant by Roger, prior of Bretton, to William son of Elias de Scauceby of one piece of cultured ground in the field north of Scauceby called Godwin flat between the lands which were Henry Doynel's and the land of Henry de Scauceby.   Witness, William de Langethwait.

[1] Scawsby, near Brodsworth,

(Fo. 17) (70) Grant by Hugh de Bretton of Scauceby of six acres and one rood of land in the field of Scauceby lying in different places; and seven and a half acres in the north field between the lands of William son of Reynulf and of Hugh son of Stephen, one head abutting upon the King's highway, and the other upon the toft which Reginald White holds of the Hospital of St. John; and three roods between the lands of Richard de Scauceby and William de Belam; and two acres in the Westfield between the lands of Robert son of Linota and Hugh son of Stephen, one head abutting upon the said highway and the other upon the croft which Umfridus de Bentelay holds; half an acre lies in the Southfield between the lands of the said Richard and the said William son of Reynulf, and half an acre lies in the same field between the lands of Henry son of Elias and of the said Richard, one head against the land of the said Henry and one on the field of Cusceworth, and one acre in the same field between the lands of William son of Reinulf and of William de Adwik. Witness, Henry de Langethwait.

(Fo. 17d) (71) Grant by Hugh Breton of Scauceby of one cultivated land in the field north of Scauceby called Godewiflat between the land of Henry Doynel and Henry de Scauceby. Witness, Sir Thomas son of William.

(72) Confirmation by John son of Odo de Riton and Gilian his wife of all their lands in the territory of Scauceby without any retention, which lands Hugh father of Gilian conveyed to them. Witness, Hugh de Langethwait.

(73) Grant by Roger, prior of Bretton, and the convent of that place, with the assent of the whole of their chaplains, to Robert Clerk, son of Richard junior, of Scauceby, of six acres and one rood of land in the field of Scauceby for a payment of 6d. yearly. Witness, William de Langethwayt.

Halgeton.
(Fo. 18) (74) Grant by Jordan de Insula, as No. 232, W. MS., where Jordan is styled Jordan de Halton.

Adwick.
(75) Grant by Ralph Haket, as No. 298, W. MS.

Tykil.
(Fo. 18d) (76) Grant by Ralph Haket of 5s. 4d. rents in the town of Tykyl received annually from Walter de Wolverhampton and his heirs. Witness, Geoffrey de Breton.

(77) Quitclaim by John de Collay and Agnes his wife, Walter de Kyrkeby and Matilda his wife, of the lands which were Reyner de la Leye's. At the Court at Newhall, Tuesday before the feast of the Annunciation, 1251. Witness, William de Thornhill.

Mekesburg.

(*Fo.* 19) (78) Grant by Roger de Montbegon of all his land in Mekesburg, with his body, and also the mediety of the church of Mekesburg with all its appurtenances. Witness, Richard de Vesci.

(79) Confirmation by Clemencia de Lungvillers of the above grant, for her soul and for that of her brother, Sir Roger de Montbegon. Witness, Richard de Vesci.

(80) Confirmation by Eudo de Lungvillers, with the consent of Clemencia his wife, of the donation which Roger de Montbegon made as above. Witness, Richard de Vescy.

(*Fo.* 19*d*) (81) Confirmation by Geoffrey de Nevill, with the consent of Mabel his wife, of the above donation of Roger de Montbegon. Witness, Hugh de Meus.

(82) Confirmation by the lady Mabel de Novavilla, daughter of William de Mara, of the above donation. Witness, John de Hoderode.

(*Fo.* 20) (83) Grant by Richard son of Mathew de Monte Acuto of Mekesburg of one half acre of land with appurtenances lying in Mekesburg, namely one rood in Whetecroft, which lies between the grantor's land and that of the monks, and one rood in Riecroft, lying between the same lands. Witness, Ralph de Rupe.

(84) Grant by Richard de Monte Acuto of one acre of land in Mekesburg, namely one rood lying on Riecroft between the land of the prior and the land of John de Addewic, and one rood lying on the north between the land of the prior and the said John, and one rood lying in Corland between the land of the said prior and the land of John de Adwic, and one rood lying next Gategraynes between the lands of the prior and the said John. Witness, Ralph de Rupe.

(85) Grant by Richard de Monte Acuto of one and a half acres in Mekesburg, one half acre lying upon Riecroft between the lands of the prior and of John de Addewic, another half acre upon Wethecroft between the lands of the prior and of John de Addewic, one rood lies on the north between Richard's land and the prior's, and one rood lies in Gorland, also he gave one rood next Gategraynes. Witness, Ralph de Rupe.

(*Fo.* 20*d*) (86) Confirmation by Juliana daughter of Matthew de Monte Acuto of one acre in Mekesburg, namely one rood in Westcroft between the lands of John Ravensfeud and of William son of John, and one rood on le Clay between the lands of the said John and William, and one rood on Brerihil between the same lands, and one rood beneath le Rages between the same lands. Witness, Master Ralph, priest.

(87)   Quitclaim by William son of Rainer de Storthes of all his right and claim in one bovate of land in Mekesburg, namely that bovate which he held of the monks of Monkbretton.   Witness, Peter de Waddeworth.

(88)   Quitclaim by William Buskeevid of all his right in one bovate of land which he held of the prior in Mekesburg, namely that bovate which William son of Rainer de Storthes held of him in the said town, and he gives this in pure and perpetual alms to the monks. Witness, Henry de Selton.

(*Fo.* 21) (89) Grant by Eustace Bacun of Mecesburg of one acre of land in Mecesburg, and one toft in the same town, and half an acre which lies between the lands of William Bule and Thomas de la Bayil, and half an acre on the clay between the lands of the said William Bule and Thomas le Bayle, and a toft which lies next the house of William the priest and the land which Walter Pudding holds.   Witness. Roger de Montbegon.

(90)   Grant by Mathew de Breton of one toft in Mekesburg, which Richard Faber formerly held of Mathew de Scepelay, paying to him and his heirs 12*d.* yearly.   Witness, Sir Robert de Furneis.

(*Fo. 21d*) (91) Quitclaim by John le Vavasour, lord of Denby, of all his right and claim to an annual rent of 12*d.* for a certain toft with its appurtenances lying in Mekesburg between the lands of the prior and Robert Walgrin.   Witness, Richard de Estfeld.

(92)   Grant by Susanna daughter of Hugh de Addewic to Lambert le Colevil of Mekesburg, for 20*s.* of silver which he has paid in hand, of one messuage in the town of Mekesburg, which formerly belonged to Richard Togod, and then to Mabel daughter of the said Richard, paying to Susanna 4*s.* of silver yearly.   Witness, William de Suniton.

(*Fo.* 22) (93) Quitclaim by Mabel Togod of Mekesburg of the above grant.   Witness, Sir William de Thornil.

(94)   Grant by Adam, prior of Monkbretton, to Ralph son of William, reeve (*prepositus*) of Mekesburg, of the homage and service of two bovates of land in Mekesburg, namely those two bovates which William, father of the said Ralph, held on the day of his death, paying yearly 10*s.* of silver. Witness, Henry de Tankersley.

(*Fo. 22d*) (95) Quitclaim by Robert de Raynebergh of all claim to one toft with buildings and in three bovates of land with the appurtenances in Mekesburg which Ralph Walgrym and Roger his son hold of the prior and convent.   Given at York, Friday next after the feast of St. John Baptist, 1298.

Cuthworth.

(96)   Grant by Robert son of Adam to Peter Dercar of Cuthworth of certain land in the length of his garden, from the west angle of his garden to the road, paying yearly one penny at Christmas.

(97)   Quitclaim by Agnes de Cuthworth formerly wife of William de Scepelay, of that part of a bovate of land in Cuthworth, which was formerly William de Scepelay's, her husband.   For which grant the monks have given her 4s.

(98)   Quitclaim by Hugh son of Hugh de Scepelay of Cuthworth to William the miller of Cuthworth of a mediety of all his lands in Cuthworth except his own messuage, paying 3s. yearly.

(Fo. 23) (99)   Grant by John son of Robert de le Kerr to Peter de Salton of one acre in Cuthworth in Wellfield in the croft of the said Peter, half an acre next the house of Robert Gretheved, one rood on the south, and one rood of land in Langelands, paying 4d. yearly.

(100)   Grant by William son of John son of Osan de Cuthworth to Henry son of William Spark of the same place of the homage and service of one toft in Cuthworth lying between the tofts of John son of Osan, and of Thomas Tyrel, to hold of the house of St. Mary Magdalene of Bretton in fealty, paying yearly to the monastery on the day of St. Oswald 12d. in silver.

Newhale.

(Fo. 23d) (101)   Grant by William, prior of Bretton, to Henry de Bosco of one assart of land called Arundesderrode in Newhale near Wath lying between an assart of William Mos of hutlane and abutting on the one head on the Syke and on the other on Kobergh, paying yearly 2s. in silver.   Witnesses, Alan Bacun, Peter de Wath, Henry de Laley, John de la Abdi, John de Areyelton, chaplain, Simon Brun, and many others.

(Fo. 24) (102)   Grant by Adam son of Swane, as No. 6, W. MS.

(103)   Grant by Robert Talun, son of Siward de Neville, of four acres and one rood of land in the field of Newhall and the toft of Robert Mercher, one acre and another acre which Rayner Sarcautt was in possession of, and one acre in Hallerode.   Witness, Rayner Fleming.

(104)   Confirmation by Thomas son of Siward Child of Newhal of four acres in Newhal and one acre of land next the culture of Ralph at the head of the vill adjoining the stream, and one acre called Chapmancroft, which lies between Abedi and the land which Robert his brother gave to the monks, one acre next the highroad at Rodirham, part of an acre in Hallerode and one acre in Braywhait next Spitiland.   Witness, Hugh son of Alan.

(Fo. 24d) (105)   Grant by Roger de Swinesheveht of all his lands in the territory of Newhall between the lands of Roger de Echekeliffeud and those which were Astun de Mertton's, abutting on the croft of Henry on the east, and on the fields of Scute on the west. Witness, Elias de Witekyrke then bailiff of Westrithig.

(106)   Grant by Robert Testard of all his lands and woods between the rivulet of Heselwell and the assart of Peter de Newhall's. Witness, William Fleming,

M

(107) Grant by Robert Testard of Meuton of half an acre in Neuhale and of one rood of land stretching to the stream, and one rood between the land which was Henry's and the stream. Witness, Thomas the priest.

(*Fo.* 25) (108) Quitclaim by Roger son of Siward de Newhall of all his right in the lands which were his father's, in perpetuity. Witness, John de Rokelay.

(109) Confirmation by Hugh the deacon son of Alan the clerk of Merton of two roods of land lying separately, namely one rood between the land of Henry and the stream next the culture of the monks, the other by the road ascending to Newhalle as far as the stream next the culture of the monks. Witness, G. de Notton.

(110) Quitclaim by Roger de Swinesheved of all his right and claim in the pool of Newhall. Witness, John de Hoderode.

(111) Grant by Robert Talun, son of Siward Child, of two acres in the territory of Newhall, and one acre of arable land in Hallerode on the road which leads to Roderam, and one acre in the wood of Hallerode which lies outside the arable land, also all the services of Thomas his brother and his wife and their heirs. Witness, William Fleming.

(*Fo.* 25*d*) (112) Grant by Elias Sorel of one toft which was Robert's next the cold spring (*frigidam fontem*), also an acre and a half on the east next the land of the prior. Witness, William son of Adam.

(113) Grant by Robert Talun of Newale of two acres in New-halle, namely half an acre under the mount as far as Holleg next the land of Thomas his brother, half an acre under the mount next that of Richard his son, half an acre in Braithwait between Thomas' land and the hospital (*hospitale*), and half an acre in Hallerode be-tween the land of the said Thomas and Reiner de Dalton, and a messuage with garden between his hall (*curiam*) and the highroad. Witness, William Fleming.

Bramton.

(114) Quitclaim by William de Mundister of the tenement which he held of the monastery in Bramton in the tenancy of William son of Peter and his heirs in Bramton, and of Hugh son of William de Bramton and Amilia daughter of Alan and their heirs, with the homage and rents and all other services pertaining to the said tene-ment. Witness, Ralph de Rupe.

(*Fo.* 26) (115) Confirmation by Roger son of Robert de Berch of that assart which was William de Mundister's, which lies between the assart of Henry Palefrai and that of Edric. Witness, William Fleming.

Melton.

(116) Confirmation by Roger de Swineshevet of all his land in Melton between the lands of Henry Henridic and the stream. Wit-ness, Rainer Fleming.

(117)   Confirmation by Hugh son of Richard de Bramton son of the priest of all his land in the territory of Melton between Henridic and the stream, in length and breadth by the territory of the monastery as far as the road which leads to the house of the monks and as far as the said stream.   Witness, Rainer Fleming.

(*Fo. 26d*)   *Bramton.*

(118)   Confirmation by Juliana daughter of Roger de Swinesheved of Bramton, in her widowhood, of six acres of land in Bramton with a toft, namely three acres of land and one acre of pasture between the assart of Roger de Bosco and Scinnereker, and one acre of land under West Pithil between the lands of Thomas de Ecliffeld and William son of Lews, and half an acre of land under le Dikes, one head abutting against the toft of Thomas Pulain and the other under Croshil.   And half an acre in Sandfeld which lies between Wambwell and Wath between the lands of Roger le Paumer and John Faber.   Witness, Thomas son of William.

(119)   Quitclaim by Peter Blanche and Emma his wife of all right and claim to that bovate of land in Bramton which Roger son of Ailric holds, for which quitclaim the monks have given them half a mark of silver.   Witness, William son of Adam.

(120)   Grant by Alice de Winton in her widowhood of the services of Jollan de Bramton and his heirs in return for 2s. of silver yearly, and of all her right and claim which she had in the land which the said Jollan held in Bramton.   Witness, Ralph de Rupe.

(*Fo. 27*) (121) Grant by Jollan de Bramton of one acre in Brecton, namely half an acre in the field of Onukebek, as it lies between the lands of Elis de Bramton, abutting against the road leading to Wambwell near Wath, and on the west against the land of the said Elis, and half an acre in the field by Wambwelle between the lands of the said Elis and of Henry son of Adam.   Witness, Adam de Rupe.

(122)   Quitclaim by Alexander son of Walter de Acilum of one and a half acres of arable land in Bramton of the fealty of the prior which lies between the lands of William le Westys and Yvo de Methelton, one head lying on Langforland, and the other on the road which leads to Wath.   Given at the priory of Bretton, St. Mark the Evangelist's day, 1255.   Witness, Richard de Tankersley.

(123)   Grant by Roger de Berg of the homage and service of Thomas Pulain and his heirs, namely 26d. yearly, for two bovates of land in Bramton which the aforesaid Thomas holds of Roger with all escheats, reliefs, wards, and everything else pertaining to the said bovates.   Also he has given to the monks one bovate of land in Bramton which Robert the miller held of him.   Witness, Randulph de Wambwell.

(124)   Grant by Roger de Berg son of Robert de Berg, of one bovate of land which Roger son of Duranus holds.   Witness, Robert de Berg.

(Fo. 28)   *Melton.*

(125)   Quitclaim by Amilia de Gobderode of all her land with the buildings in Mepelton in Bramton, except two roods which William de Tornil held of her.   Witness, Roger de Berg.

Wath.

(126)   Grant by Richard son of Hulkell of one acre of land in Wath which was Ralph Geke's, namely half an acre in the whole toft as it lies, and half an acre in Bramtonfurlang.   Witness, Reiner Fleming.

(127)   Confirmation by Richard son of Ulkel de Wath of one acre of land in Wath which was Ralph Geke's, and half an acre at Bramton.   Witness, Reiner Fleming.

(Fo. 28d) (128) Grant by Hugh de Wath, forester, of the whole of his portion in Netherholme, which lies next the portion of Thomas son of Hugh Lot, one head of which extends to the river of Dirne, and the other head to Shelebec.   Witness, William son of Ralph.

Winteworth.

(129)   Grant by John son of Aisolf, as No. 361, W. MS.

(130)   Confirmation by William de Winteworth, son of Hugh son of Henry de Winteworth, of eleven acres in Winteworth, namely one acre at the head of the said vill on the east, and one acre in Langfurlanges and half an acre opposite the mill, half an acre opposite the road of Wath, and the other acres in the field as they lie, with all commons and easements of the said vill.   Witness, John Tyrel.

(Fo. 29) (131) Grant by Ralph de Montagu of his toft in Winteworthe against the garden of the chapel of the said vill, also one rood of land.   Witness, Reginald, chaplain of Gresebroc.

(132)   Confirmation by Hugh son of Henry de Winteworth, as No. 365, W. MS.

(133)   Quitclaim by Robert de White of land below Hoberg which Hugh the factor of Kalthorn claimed of him, which was given in exchange for two bovates in Bramton which were William and Siward's, the sons of Offi.   Witness, William de Nosmarche.

(134)   Grant by Hugh de Brito of one and a half roods of land against the garden of the chapel of Winteworth.   Witness, T. Barbot.

(Fo. 29d)   *Coldelawe.*

(135)   Quitclaim by Geoffrey son of Roger de Coaldelawe of all his land held of the monastery of Bretton in Caoldelawe.   Witness, Robert de Virkereslay.

(136)   Grant by John de Holand of the whole of his lands in Bramton and Caldelau.   Witness, Thomas de Burg.

Rainberg.

(137) Grant by Thomas son of Thomas de Burgo and Sara de Neville of the services of Alexander Walegrin and his heirs, and whatever pertains to him of the fealty of Rainberg. Witness, Roger de Montebegon.

Alwarthawatt.

(138) Agreement between the prior and convent of Bretton on the one part and John de Novoforo on the other part in the year 1239, in a suit regarding the manor of Alwarthuatt before Sir Pico de Lasceles, Robert de Cokefeld, Gerard Salvein, William Constable, justices. It has been decided that the said John shall hold in heredity the said manor of the prior and convent, paying them yearly 5 marks of silver, saving forinsec service which pertains to half a bovate of land which the said John holds in hand, where thirteen carucates make one knight's fee, as is contained in charters which the prior and convent have in their possession. It shall be lawful if the said John or his heirs cease payments for the prior and convent to distrain. If the said prior and convent neglect to provide a priest to say mass for the soul of Henry de Novoforo, John's uncle, it shall be lawful for the said John and his heirs to compel the said prior and convent to find a competent priest or monk. Both parties have sworn to carry out the agreement and have affixed their seals thereto. Witness, Sir Pico de Lasceles.

[*Three first lines of a charter of Roger, prior of Bretton, ending* "by this present charter," *and not continued on the next folio.*]

[*In different handwriting.*]

(*Fo.* 30*d*) (139) Grant by Henry de Novo Mercato of Alvardethwait of all his manor of Alwardethuait in Holand with woods, etc.; also his tenement in Holand in the holding of Ralph son of Jordan de Akithorp, and half a bovate which Jordan held in Holand, paying yearly 13*d.* for all services and secular exactions. Also he gives to the monks of Bretton the services of Richard Faber of Holand and his heirs, namely 12*d.* yearly with 1 lb. of cummin, and the services of Richard de Bosco of Holand and his heirs, namely 2*s.* yearly, and in the wood of Wambwelle 2*s.* 6*d.* yearly; paying yearly to Stephen de Harelay and his heirs 26*d.* Witnesses, Adam de Novo Mercato, John his son.

Winteworth.

[*In the same writing as fo.* 30.]

(*Fo.* 31) (140) Grant by Roger, prior of Bretton, to Adam de Roderam, chaplain, and his assigns, of all that toft in Winteworth next the garden of the chapel, the gift of Hugh de Breton and Ralph de Montagu, with all liberties in the vill of Winteworth. Witness, William son of Hugo.

(141) Agreement between Roger, prior of Bretton, and William son of William de Winteworth, as No. 363, W. MS.

(142) Final accord in the court of the prior at Newhale between the prior and Richard son of William Hoienus with regard to those

lands between Corteworde (Cudworth) and the lands of the said Richard, which he is to have freely and quietly for ever; paying to the monks 28*d*.   And for this agreement he has paid to the monks half a mark of silver.   Witness, Gilbert de Christum.

Bramton.

(*Fo.* 31*d*) (143) Grant by Roger, prior of Bretton, to Gilbert the baker for his homage and service of one toft in Bramton and three roods, lying near the toft of Aldith, widow.   Also six acres of land in the fields of Bramton; four acres in the assart between the moor of Melthelt and Kynarker; one acre on the west Pithill next the land of Thomas de Ecliffeld, half an acre on Dyccleuys extending to the garden of Thomas Polain; half an acre touching the road to Wambwell, lying next the land of Hugh son of Roger Palmar; paying yearly 4*d*. of silver.   Witness, William son of Ralph.

(144) Confirmation by Roger, prior of Bretton, to William Beltam for his homage and service of one acre of land with part of the territory of Bramton which lies in Corteworth next the spring of Heselwell; paying yearly 12*d*.   Witness, John de Hoderode.

(*Fo.* 32) (145) Grant by Roger, prior of Bretton, by the counsel and assent of the whole of the chaplains, to Thomas son of Robert de Hulvethayt, for his homage and service, of one bovate in Bramton which Roger Hare formerly held of the priory; paying yearly 5*s*.   Witness, Roger son of Roger de Swinheved.

(146) Grant by Roger, prior of Bretton, to Roger son of Robert de Wluethait for his homage and service of one assart in Bramton called Mundister Rode lying between the assarts of Roger de Berch and Henry de Palefrai, extending to the wood of Hoberg as far as Siket; paying 3*s*. yearly.   Witness, Roger de Berg.

Newhale.

(147) On the morrow of Hilary 1246-7, in the great church of Southwell, before the dean of Retforth, as deputy of the dean and chancellor of Oxford, a cause was heard between Master Robert de Herst, rector of Wath, who appeared in person, and the prior of Bretton, as to a claim for tithe of hay to the church of Wat from the meadow at Neuhal in Henricroft, and out of the land they have newly ploughed in the same meadow, and of a windmill and a water-mill at Neuhal.   It was decided that the priory should pay every year in lieu of the said tithes, 12*d*. at Whitsuntide, during the life of the said Robert.

Bramton.

(*Fo.* 32*d*) (148) Grant by Adam, prior of Bretton, to Thomas son of Richard Pulain for his homage and service of a bovate of land in the territory of Bramton, namely that bovate of land with the toft and croft which Walthef de Bramton held of the priory.   To hold freely with all liberties and easements in the said vill to so much land belonging, for a yearly rent of 5*s*., half at Whitsuntide and half at Martinmas.   Witness, W. le Fleming.

Abbedi.

(149)   Grant by Adam, prior of Bretton, to Robert son of William de Abbedi for his homage and service of all that land which William, Robert's father, held of the monks in Abbedi in Bramton; paying yearly 5s.   Witness, Gilbert de Notton.

Newhale.

(*Fo.* 33)   (150)   Grant by Adam, prior of Bretton, to Robert de Lehabedi of one toft and curtilage in the vill of Newhall which Alexander Shepherd formerly held of the priory; paying yearly 15d.   Witness, Roger de Hern.

(151)   Grant by Adam, prior of Bretton, to William son of Nigel de Sprotteburg for his homage and service of all that pasture which Hugh de Wath, forester, gave to the prior lying in Netherholme in the fields of Wath, against the pasture of Thomas son of Hugh Lot; paying half a pound of incense yearly.   Witness, Reiner, priest of Barneborough.

(*Fo.* 33*d*)   *Boelton.*

(152)   Grant by Reiner Malet of four bovates in Boelton, namely those which Thomas de Boelton holds.   Witness, William son of William.

(153)   Confirmation by Robert de Mikelbring of four bovates in Boelton, which his uncle Reiner Malet gave to the monastery of Bretton by grant.   Witness, Henry de Novo Mercato.

(154)   Grant by Reiner Malet of Boelton of the mediety of his mill at Boelton and one toft in the same vill which Richard de Addewic and Eelias Pol hold; also fifteen acres of land and four acres of meadow in the territory of the vill of Boelton, namely one acre in Lothfford between the lands of William son of Adam and Roger de Wanto, one acre in Watirssakis between the land which Richard de Fonte held and the land of William son of Mauger; one acre on Hertewellhil between the lands of Alexander the tanner and Ralph the miller; one acre at Standik between the lands of William son of Robert and Alexander the bailiff; and one acre outside the vill of Welton on the west between the lands of Robert the priest and John son of Roger, and three acres at the head of his garden between the lands of William son of Adam and Roger de Wauld; and three roods of land between the lands of Richard the clerk and John Kempe; and one acre on the moor between the lands of William son of Baldwin and John son of Roger, and one half acre on the moor between the land of Adam the miller and William son of Robert; one acre on the west next the road which leads to Thirnescoh between the lands of Walter son of John and of Matilda de Balne; and one acre at the chapel on the west between the lands of Robert the bailiff and Adam son of Sibil; one acre at the spring of Mauger between the lands of William son of Mauger and William son of Richard; one acre on Longebuttelandes between the lands of Roger de Wauld and Roger son of Adam; one acre at Noutecarlewell

on the west between the lands of Roger de Wald and Matilda de
Balne; two acres of pasture between the great stream and le Pul;
one acre between the pastures of William son of Adam and Adam son
of Hugh; one acre between the pastures of Matilda de Balne and
William son of Baldwin; two acres of pasture between le Pul and
the arable land next the pasture of Henry de Novo Mercato.   He
has given this to the monastery with his corpse for the light before
the altar of St. Mary the Virgin.   Witness, Henry de Novo Mercato.

(*Fo.* 34*d*) (155) Confirmation by Robert de Mikelbring of the above
grant.   Witness, Henry de Novo Mercato.

(156)   Grant by Adam, prior of Bretton, to Thomas de Boelton
of four bovates in the vill of Boelton for his homage and service
which Reiner Malet gave to the church of St. Mary Magdalene in
Bretton, paying yearly 12*d*.   Witness, Henry de Novo Mercato.

(*Fo.* 35) (157) Grant by Adam, prior of Bretton, to Robert son of
Hugh de Mickelbring for his homage and service of the mediety of
the mill of Boelton which Reiner Malet gave to the church, and one
toft in the same vill which Richard de Addewic and Elias Pol hold;
also ten acres in the said vill, and four acres in scattered lots as contained in the grant of the said Reiner, paying yearly 2*s*.   Witness,
Henry de Novo Mercato.

Newhall.

(158)   Quitclaim by Adam de Brerthwysil of ten acres in Newhale, namely two acres lying between the lands of John de la Skyres
and le Schyresflat; three acres between the lands of Sir Peter de
Testa; one acre lying between the lands of the same Sir Peter and
Tendmancrosse, which extends on one head to Colismore and on the
other to Henricroft; five acres between the land of the said Sir Peter
and the road to Newhall, one head extending to Colisbroke and the
other as far as Newhall.   Witnesses, Nicholas son of Tyte, Alan
Bacun of Wath, William de Wath, carpenter, Thomas son of Gilbert of the same, Robert Wyterit, and others.

(*Fo.* 35*d*) (159) Proceedings in the chapter at York on the vigil of
St. Thomas the Apostle in the cause pending between the hospital
of St. Peter of York and Bretton priory.   H. the monk appeared as
proctor for the priory, who, after much discussion, confessed that
his house was bound to pay to the said hospital for ever one thrave
every year upon every plough of theirs in the province of York,
wheresoever they might be; and thereupon the sentence binding
the prior and cellarer, by authority of the chapter of York, was
rescinded, and these proceedings were sealed with the chapter seal.

Two letters follow.   (1) The prior's letter to H., dean of York, and
the chapter constituting the abovesaid H., monk of their house, their
attorney in this matter.   (2) The same to R. the dean, R. the chancellor, and J. the sub-dean of Lincoln, informing them that the
priory owes the said payment to the hospital according to the
general custom of Eboracens schyre.

Hykelton.

(*Fo.* 36)   (160)   Grant by Randulf de Novo Mercato, as No. 267, W. MS.

(161)   Surrender and quitclaim by the lady Nichola de Hykelton, as No. 270, W. MS.

(162)   Grant by Nichola daughter of Randulf de Novo Mercato, as No. 272, W. MS.

(*Fo.* 36*d*)   (163)   Covenant by Thomas de Ponte of Lincoln and Juliana his wife on the one part and the lady Nichola daughter of Randulf de Novo Mercato on the other part.   Whereas the said Thomas and Juliana quitclaimed to the lady Nichola one bovate of land in Hekelton which they had of the gift of the aforesaid Nichola in frank marriage.   By this quitclaim they restore to the said Nichola all the land which came to her on the death of Randulf her brother by heredity, and all the third part of all the land which Randulf her brother had in Carleton and Lunda; that part which was for her sole use, except her part of the park, and except the part which fell to the lady Amabil wife of the said Randulf.   And if it should happen that the aforesaid Nichola, her heirs or assigns should make over the said lands to the said Thomas and Juliana she would warrant the said bovate at Hykelton to be held peaceably and quietly to the said Thomas and Juliana.   And if the said Thomas and Juliana make over the said lands of Carleton and Lunda to Nichola it shall be without any condition.

To this covenant Thomas and Juliana have affixed their seals in the presence of Juliana, and Nichola her seal in the presence of Thomas and Juliana.   Witness, Sir Ralph Salvein.

(*Fo.* 37)   (164)   Confirmation of the above covenant by Nichola de Hikilton, mentioning Juliana as her sister.   Witness, Robert Bastard.

(165)   Confirmation by Randulf de Hikelton, as No. 295, W. MS.

(*Fo.* 37*d*)   (166)   Grant by Adam, prior of Bretton, to Nicholas de Sutwell of three acres of land in Hickelton, namely the toft and croft which Waltheof the reeve holds which lie in that bovate which Swane holds, paying yearly 5*s.*   Witness, John de Rockelay.

(167)   Letters patent of John, rector of Hykelton, recording that the dispute between himself and the prior of Bretton was heard before Master William Passemer, official of his lordship of York, in the year of grace 1246, and was settled by the rector's remitting to them all claim for payment of small tithes in view of the privileges which they provided, by the advice of experienced persons who had duly considered the matter.   Witness, Sir Nicholas de Rotherfeld.

(*Fo.* 38)   (168)   Confirmation by William de Nosmarche of one bovate in Cateby which was Luke's.   Witness, Reginald, parson de Hikelton.

(169) Grant by William Fitz William. (*Only two lines and then repeated in full on fo. 38d, No. 172.*)

Cudworth.

(170) Confirmation by Richard, prior of the church of Monk-bretton, to Richard son of Nicholas Doynel of Codeworth of all the lands which he had of the gift of Peter de la Mor in Codeworth, paying yearly 2s. 6d.

Parva Halgton.

(171) Confirmation by Adam Fitz Swane of the homage and service of Robert son of Ravan of Parva Halghton with all rents, etc. Witnesses, Alexander and Richard, Adam's sons.

Milnehouses.

(Fo. 38d) (172) Grant by William Fitz-William, as No. 206, W. MS.

(173) Grant by John son of Richard de Batelay, as No. 205, W. MS.

(174) Grant by Thomas son of Isabel, as No. 207, W. MS.

(Fo. 39) (175) Confirmation by Robert son of Thomas son of Isabel de Horbiri, as No. 208, W. MS.

(176) Grant by Thomas son of William de Horebyri, as No. 210, W. MS.

(177) Grant by Sir Thomas de Horbyri, as No. 191, W. MS.

(Fo. 39d) (178) Confirmation by John de Batelay of the above grant. Witness, Sir Thomas FitzWilliam.

(Fo. 40) (179) Grant by Dionis de Eyvill of the service of Alan de Hille, miller, her native (*nativus*). Witness, John le Breton.

Hylle.

(180) Grant by Roger, prior of Bretton, to Ralph son of Richard Wace of all the land in le Hil, paying yearly 2s. Witness, Jordan de Insula. As No. 219, W. MS.

Smithelay.

(Fo. 40d) (181) Grant by Richard son of Richard de Wambwell for the safety of his soul and that of his wife of all the land which Richard Aldam held of him in Smitheley, paying yearly 4d. at the altar of St. Nicholas in St. Mary's chapel at Wambwell on St. Nicholas day, saving forinsec service to the King which pertains to one bovate of land, where twelve carucates make a knight's fee. Witness, Sir William FitzWilliam.

(182) Grant by Adam, prior of Bretton, to Master Thomas, " medico " of Scelton, of one bovate of land in Smithelei which Richard de Wambewel gave to him (the prior), paying 4s. yearly at the altar of St. Nicholas in the chapel of Wambwelle. Witness, William FitzWilliam. As No. 453, W. MS.

Dorweleys.

(183) Grant by Richard son of Richard de Wambwelle of one acre of land in Dorweleys next the land of William Stiward on the east. Witness, John de Rokelay.

(*Fo.* 41) [*Blank.*]

(*Fo.* 41*d*) *Markham.*

(184) From the roll of the justices of Schyrwode Forest in co. Nottingham:—These are the bounds which surround the King's demesne wood and the King's land of Kyngeschagh, beginning on the north at a ditch between Derlton and Kyngeschagh and stretching along the road which is to Donham and Tuxforde, and so far as the ditch which stretches to the duct (*ductum*) of Estmarkam, and so to the manor of Kyngeschagh where it began.

From the roll of the Sheriff of Nottingham:—John Bolyngbroke sues John Markham and Robert Cressy of Estmarkham for a plea of the seizing and detention of cattle. Sureties for prosecution, John Allerton and Hugh Went.

Alric–Swane–Adam { Matilda { Roger / Matilda–William–Matilda–Hugo / Clemencia–John–John–Margaret < John–John / Robert–Robert } Amabil–Sara–Thomas–Thomas–John–Philip }

Wapentake of Bersetlawe.

(*Fo.* 42) (185) *The last three lines of a deed, the folio bearing the substance of the deed having disappeared. The witness is* John, procurator of the mediety of Bretton.

Markham.

(186) Grant by Nicholas Legat and Dyonisia his wife, as No. 542, W. MS.

(*Fo.* 42*d*) (187) This is the final concord in the Court of our lord the King at Hotham, on Thursday next after the feast of St. Michael, Henry son of John, 20 (1236), in the presence of Robert de Lexington, Ralph de Fuller, and Warren Engayne, justices, between the prior of Bretton, plaintiff, and Nicholas Legat and Dionisia his wife, concerning forty-four acres and three and a half bovates of land and twelve tofts, and part of a toft, and 50*d.* of rents, one pound of cummin and one pair of gloves with their accoutrements in East Markham. It is awarded that the said Nicholas and Dionis recognise all the said lands to be the right of the said prior of the church of Bretton, and that the said prior holds it as of the gift of Nicholas and Dionis. And for this recognition the prior gives to Nicholas and Dionis 50 marks of silver.

(188) I, Nicholas Legat of Morlund owe to Justus son of Benedict the Jew, of Lincoln, 12 marks sterling, to wit, 2 marks at Martinmas, 24 Hen. III (1239), and 2 marks at the Whitsuntide following, and so 4 marks every year until the said 12 marks are

paid.   And if I do not pay what is due at the said terms I will give
him for every week during which I retain his money 2*d.* in the £1
interest, for which I pledge all my lands, rents and chattels.   Given
on the Friday after Holy Trinity, 23 Hen. III (1238).

(*Fo.* 43) (189) Quitclaim by Aron the Jew, son of Joscelyn of York,
to Nicholas Legat and Dionisia de Lassels, his wife, and the heirs and
assigns of Dionisia of a debt of 48 marks on the part of Dionisia de
Lassels and 12 marks of the debt of Randulf de Novo Mercato,
brother of Dionisia, which the said Nicholas Legat and Dionisia his
wife have paid to Aron on the day of Holy Cross in the autumn in
the year of grace 1240, in the presence of the justices sitting at the
time at the court in York, to wit, Gerard Sexton and his colleagues.
Aron for himself, his heirs and successors, agrees never to contest
the quitclaim, and affixes his seal to the deed.   Witness, the dean
of York.

(190)   Grant by Roger de Montbegon of four bovates in Tunstall
which Simon de Tunstall rents in Thorneholm.   Witness, Henry de
Milledene.

Holecumb.

(191)   Grant by Roger de Montbegon of his whole forest of
Holecumbe and the wood and plain within the underwritten divisions, and as much of his forest as extends towards Querendonam in
length and breadth and climbing up through the divisions of his
forest as far as Langschevet, and from Langschevet as far as Alledenehevet, and from Alledenehevet as far as Arkilleshou, and thence
through the middle of Arkilleshou as far as Pilegrimescrosschahe,
and thence by a descent as far as the road which leads through the
middle of Titleshou, following the aforesaid road as far as Titleshoubrok, and thence towards the west by following a lane, which is
called the lane cf thieves, as far as Salterbrigge, and from Salterbrigge as far as the road to Oskelleie, saving to me and my heirs
the hunting in these divisions.   And let it be known that the monks
shall have of the wood between Holcumbe and Titleshougate a
sufficiency for building and fuel for their herdsmen and for the reasonable sustentation of their herdsmen in winter.   Also all my pasture
and forest and a sufficiency of wood in the underwritten divisions,
Caldewellhevet as far as the water of Yrewell following Caldewellsic,
and following Yrewell as far as Titleshoubrok by an ascent through
Titleshoubrok as far as the road which leads through the middle of
Titleshou, then following the said road as far as Caldewellhevet.
Also three acres of meadow in Arkilleshou next Pilegrimescrosschahe,
and each year they shall be allowed to make fences around that
meadow and around the meadow at Haderleies as they wish.   Also
they shall be allowed to share everywhere with the men of Toting-
tune, saving however to them the common which they have been
accustomed to have from olden time, etc.   Witness, William son of
Adam.

(*Fo.* 43*d*) (192) York. Pleas at York before the justices of the Common Pleas (de Banco) in three weeks from Easter, 10 Edw. III (1336) [rot. 82].

William de Stainton demands against Geoffrey son of Henry son of Nicholas de Tunstal a messuage in Carleton as his right. Geoffrey comes and says that he is a villein of the prior of Monkbretton, and that he holds that tenement from the prior in villeinage, and that without the prior he cannot make answer. And he demands judgment on the writ. And William cannot deny this. Therefore it is considered that he shall take nothing by his writ, and the said Geoffrey shall go without a day etc.; and the said William is in mercy.

(*Fo.* 44) (193) Grant by Roger de Montebegon of the whole of Holecumbe, all the wood and plain in the divisions of Holcumbhevet, as far as the brow of Arkileshou to Aledenehevet and to Titeleshougate and from Titeleshougate as far as Caldewellhevet and from Caldewellhevet as far as Yrewel, and to the higher part of Holcumbe as far as his forest extends, saving to him and his heirs the hunting, for his soul and that of his wife and of his brother, John Malherbe. Witness, William son of William.

(194) Grant by Roger de Montebegon of all his pasture of Holecumbe, saving his beasts of chase and cattle and pasture for them in these bounds, from Holecumbe to the brow of Arkileshou hill, descending thence to the road running through Titelleshou towards the vill of Totington. The said cattle are not to go beyond these bounds. And if by chance they do wander further the priory will not take legal proceedings against him, but the cattle shall be freely given up to the monks' servants, if they be taken. But if his cattle, or those of other people, get into the said pasture the monks' servants shall impound them, and shall not release them until they have received satisfaction for unlawful entry. Witness, John Malherbe.

Akedene.

(*Fo.* 44*d*) (195) Grant by Roger de Notton of all the land which he held in the vill of Akedene. Witness, Peter de Byrkethwait.

(196) Confirmation by John son of Hugh de Helaund of the mediety of the vill of Akeden which Roger de Notton gave to the monastery by his charter. Witness, Peter de Rockelay.

(197) Quitclaim by Richard son of Hugh de Birtwathe of all his right and claim in the mediety of Akedene which Gilbert de Notton gave by his charter. Witness, Geoffrey de Rockelay.

(*Fo.* 45) (198) Confirmation by Sir Baldwin Theutonicus for his soul and the soul of Margaret his wife of all his right and claim in Akdene and in 12*d*. rents which Reginald de Akedene formerly held. Witness, Sir Adam de Byri.

(199) Final concord between the monks of Bretton and Reginald de Akedene concerning the lands which the prior holds of the gift

of Gilbert de Notton and those which Reginald holds in patrimony and by hereditary right. The prior has two cultures in the fields of Akedene, one culture on the east and the other lower down on the west, and one part towards the south. Reginald likewise has two cultures on high ground for the use of his house and one lower culture, also one culture called Finebothes, besides that land called Witheleis. There shall be held by the prior that portion on the south and Reginald shall have all the portion on the higher ground. Witness, John de Rockelay.

(*Fo.* 45*d*) (200) Confirmation by Prior Adam of Bretton to Adam de Alaveden, for his homage and service and for 8 marks of silver paid, of three bovates in the three divisions of Alkedene, namely those which Gilbert de Notton gave to the church of Bretton, paying yearly 3s. of silver. Witness, Geoffrey de Buckelay.

Middelton en lepecke.

(201) Grant by Waltheof son of Swane of eight acres of land and his chapel in the vill of Midelton. Witness, Adam FitzSwane.

Reddeburne.

(*Fo.* 46) (202) Confirmation by Alexander de Nevill of forty acres of land with two tofts in the vill and territory of Reddeburne, twenty acres in one part of the said vill and twenty acres in another part, all of which John de Paris holds, to be made over to the monastery in perpetuity on the day on which his body is buried. Witness, Sir Adam de Byrie.

(*Fo.* 46*d*) (203) An inspeximus, 8 ides March, 1306, of letters patent of archbishop Thomas (Corbridge), dated at Cawode, 7 ides Oct., 1300, delivering an ordinance in the dispute between Bretton priory, appropriators of Roreston church, and Robert de Holtham, the vicar. Since the monks are temporal lords of the greater part of the parish and can more easily collect the tithes than the vicar can, by their power compelling the parishioners to pay the same, the archbishop decrees that the priory shall henceforth have all the tithes that were apportioned to the vicar, to whom they shall pay, in lieu thereof, 25 marks a year. The vicar to have the right to retain all offerings on the altar, in case of non-payment of the annuity. If any impediment to payment is raised by the prior or any of the obedientiaries or any other of the monks or by any secular person in their behalf they shall under this ordinance incur suspension from entering the church.

In addition to the said annuity the vicar shall have a bovate of land in Roreston, tithe free, and the manse next the church in which his predecessors have been accustomed to live. And the vicar shall not be bound to do any service in the chapel of Chevet, nor to pay tithes on his cattle, whatever number he may have. And the vicar shall have the fees paid on espousals or weddings, and shall at his own expense find a suitable clerk to serve in the said church.

The priory shall find a priest to celebrate in the chapel of Wlvelay, in the parish of Roreston; all ordinary charges, viz. procurations and synodals, shall be provided by the priory; extraordinary charges to be borne by the priory and vicar in their proportions.

The Church of Roreston.

(204) The dean and chapter of York and Walter (Gray), archbishop of York. Know that we, moved by the poverty and honesty of our beloved sons the prior and convent of Bretton, and having inspected the charter of Geoffrey (Plantagenet), formerly archbishop of York, in connection with the church of Roreston, confirm that church for its proper uses, appropriating it to the prior and monks of Bretton, and ordain that there shall be a perpetual vicar, that he shall have the tithe of the corn of Roreston, Cudewrth and of Chivot, and all the altarage and the lesser tithes of the whole parish, except the lesser tithes belonging to the monks and those of their mill, also excepting the oblations of the chapel of St. Elen of Carlton, and of two bovates of land with their appurtenances in the vill of Carlton, and the tithes of hay of the whole parish of Roreston which remains in perpetuity to the monks. The vicar is to pay one mark of silver on St. Mary Magdalene's day to the monks, and bear all archiepiscopal and archidiaconal burdens due and customary. Witnesses, Thomas the precentor of York, Master Laurence de Lyncoln, canon of York, Robert Haget, canon of Hereford, Roger de Burton, our official, Mathew de Cantilupe, William de Vescy, Martin de Marisco, Odo de Richemund, John de Camsal, and Reginald de Stowa. Given at Cawod, 4 kal. April, 1234. Ratified at York, 1360. [*Gray's Register*, Surt. Soc., p. 59.]

Mekesburgh.

(*Fo.* 47*d*) (205) Confirmation by Geoffrey de Nova Villa of all that land in Mekesburgh which Alicia formerly wife of Roger de Montebegon gave to the prior and monks of Bretton, that they may possess it peacefully and quietly after the death of the said Alicia. Witnesses, Baldwin de Nauton, Richard de Alent', Simon de Hedon, John de . . . . . . , knights, William son of John, Colin de Gardin, Roger de Bergh, William son of Alan, William son of Barbe, and others.

Church of Roston and Carleton.

(*Fo.* 48) (206) Grant by Geoffrey de Nevill and Mabel his wife, as No. 11, W. MS.

Holand by Wentworth.

(207) Grant by Adam, prior of Bretton, to Ydonia, daughter of Adam son of Richard de Swinton, and her heirs for their homage and service of the territory of Holand which Adam her father gave to the monks, namely an assart called Clayrode, and an assart called Aylsi Ridings, and two acres in Harelay between the land of Henry de Novo Mercato and the land of Geoffrey de Alvarthayt, paying yearly 2s. Witnesses, Henry de Tankreslay, Hugh and Philip his brothers, Hugh de Estales, Stephen de Harelay, Peter de Alwarthwavt. William de Wynthword, William his son, etc.

(*Fo.* 48*d*) (208) Grant by Adam son of Richard de Swynton of the whole assart called Clairod and the assart called Aylsi Riding, which lie in Holand, two acres in Harelay between the land of Henry de Novo Mercato and the land of Geoffrey de Alwardethwait. Witnesses, Henry de Tancresley, John de Rocley, Roger de Berog, William de Wynteworde, Hugh de Tancresley, Philip his brother, Hugh de Estales, Stephen de Hareley, Peter de Alwardethwayt, etc.

Tonstall.

(209) Grant by Roger de Montbegon of four bovates in Tunestall with his corpse, namely those four bovates which remain in his hands in the lordship of Tunestall formerly Simon de Tunestall's, rented from the lord of Borhalm. Witnesses, Richard de Vescy, his brother, Richard Bĺanchard, William de Sotyll, Ralph Haket, Henry de Monckdene, Ralph de Rupe, John de Penigestone, and Martin de Thorp.

(210) Confirmation by Henry de Mounkdene of four bovates in Tunstall which Roger de Montebegon his predecessor gave with his corpse to the monks of Bretton. Witnesses, John de la Mare, Richard Blanchard, Henry de Tanckresley, Hugh de Cant, Ralph de Trehampton, William parson of Tanckersley, William son of Ralph, Robert his son, Gilbert de Staynton, Hugh de Tattresall, Martin de Thorp.

(*Fo.* 49) (211) Confirmation by William de Nevyll and Amabel his wife, as No. 12, W. MS., with additional witnesses, Thomas de Burg, Walter sòn of Ravenhill, Adam son of the same, Hugh de Flamwyll, William his brother, John their nephew, William de Wynnich, Hugh son of Alan, Robert de Turf, Adam de Cleipol, Beward son of Adam, Henry Bretun, Roland Bretun, Richard Phoine, Ranulf de Glanvyll.

Hep.

(212) Grant by Adam de Biry of part of Hep called Tumehalegesstik from the stream which flows through Blackwell as far as Meresache, also certain land in Guledene, and from Guledene to the stream of Rached, with their appurtenances in Hep. Witnesses, Roger de Montebegon, William son of Adam, Gilbert de Notton.

(*Fo.* 49*d*) (213) Grant by Adam de Byri, for the souls of himself, his wife and children, to the priory of Bretton of a certain portion of land in the territory of Hepworth, within these bounds:—from Maresachevet along a ditch to the moss, then crossing the moss as far as the Cauce, then following the causeway of Cauce as far as Guleden, and down Guleden to the great water of Rachet, and thence to Retingpolsnappe, and up through Retingpolsnappe by the bounds of the monks of Bretton [*blank*] side of Hafford Hulles to Mareschefet again; to hold in frankalmoign, with the common of pasture and easements belonging to the vill of Hepworth. Witnesses, Sir Roger de Midilton, Alexander de Pilkenton.

Wyrsburgh.

(214) Grant by Adam, prior of Bretton, as No. 382, W. MS.

(215)   Grant by brother R., humble minister (prior) of Bretton, as No. 388, W. MS.

(*Fo.* 50) (216)   Quitclaim by John son of Elias, parson of Edlington, to Simon de Rockeley of all the lands which Amabel his mother holds of William de Rockeley in Wirkesburgh.   For which Simon has given 2 marks of silver.

(217)   Surrender and quitclaim by Richard Grusci, as No. 389, W. MS.

(218)   Quitclaim by Juliana, late wife of Simon the dyer of Wirkisburg, of the whole of the land which Simon her husband held of the monks in Wirkesburg.

(*Fo.* 50*d*) (219)   Confirmation by Ralph son of Ralph de Wirkesburgh of 12*d*. yearly out of his capital toft in Wirkesburgh.

Wrangbrok.

(220)   Agreement made between Ralph Maunnel and the prior of Bretton, to wit, that Ralph demised to the priory all the service of his men of Warangebroc, to wit, a rent of 12*s.*, with all issues and escheats, for five years, for 30*s.* sterling which the monks paid him in hand.   This agreement was made at Whitsuntide next after the death of Queen Eleanor.

(221)   Quitclaim by Agnes wife of Robert de Warangebrok of all the lands which Adam her son sold to the prior and monks, namely one and a half acres next le Rig on the hulin, one and a half acres at Flaskedal, and one acre at Cheveril ridding, for the sum of 10*s.* which the monks have paid her.

(222)   Confirmation by Panneia de Rannetun of the agreement made between the prior of Bretton and her son Ralph Maunnel of his services and rents in Warangebroc for five years, after which time the prior shall return it to the said Ralph Maunnel without any exaction.

(*Fo.* 51) (223)   Quitclaim by Agnes daughter of Adam Warfald of her messuage at Ravinscroft for 1 mark of silver, also her portion of Cheviril ridding, and half an acre next le Rig.

(224)   Grant by Gervase Pulain of seven and a half acres in Wrangbrok, which he held of the monks, paying to them yearly 18*d*. to be held for a term of twenty years, if his wife Lecie shall live so long; two and a half acres to be held of the prior for the aforesaid term paying yearly 6*d*. to the prior, and if his said wife shall die within that time one acre and a half shall revert to the prior and monks and Gervase should hold the rest of the land for the remainder of the term.   For which he has paid to the monks 2 marks sterling, 1230.

(225)   Grant by Adam son of Robert de Wrangbrok to the church of St. Cuthbert of Wrangbrok of one half parcel of land abutting on the cemetery of the church of Wrangbrok.

N

(226)   Grant by Adam son of Robert de Wrangbrok of all his land in Wrangbrok, his capital messuage and all his lordship in the said vill, and a rent of 18*d.*, which the prior and Robert de Amessorte and Adam de Mesthorp and Reymund of Pontefract pay yearly. Dated at the feast of St. Martin, 1218.

(*Fo.* 51*d*) (227) Quitclaim by Eva widow of Maurice de Askerne of all her share of the rents of her land in Ravensecroft in Wrangebrok, which lies on one side of her lordship of Askerne, namely 12*d.* yearly.

(228) Confirmation by Adam son of Robert de Wrangebrok of all the covenants and agreements of Hugh husband of Agnes his (Adam's) mother, and those of Agnes his mother concerning the lands in Cheverilridding in the fields of Wrangbrok which have been demised to the prior of Bretton for a term of twelve years.   If his mother should die within the term he warrants the same to the prior for the remainder of the term.   Dated the day of St. Gregory, 1204.

(229)   Grant by Simon Pulain of Wrangebrok to Adam Pulain of Wrangbrok of one rood of land in Wrangbrok, namely that one which he held of Henry Disseth as it lies between his (Simon's) toft and the toft of Adam aforesaid.   For this grant the said Adam quitclaims to Simon all his right and claim to one acre of land in Wrangbrok.

(230)   Grant by Cecilia daughter of Simon Pulayn of Wrangbrok and Luciana and Dyonisia her daughters to Benedict her brother and Joan his wife of one rood of land in Wrangbrok between the lands of the prior of Bretton and the said Benedict at the head of the pool next the brook.

(*Fo.*52) (231) Grant by Richard Pulain of five acres of land in Wrangbrok which he holds of the prior and monks of Bretton.

(232)   Grant by Adam son of Robert de Wrangbrok to his brother Gilbert for his homage and service of one croft, and half an acre on Holme between the land of the monks and his land, paying yearly 6*d.* at Easter.

(233)   This is the agreement made on the feast of St. Martin, 1230, between the prior of Bretton and Arnald Faber of Helmesale, that the prior concedes to Arnald half a bovate of land in Wrangbrok for a term of three years, Arnald paying 2*s.* yearly.

(*Fo.* 52*d*) (234) Confirmation by Adam Pulain of Wrangbrok to Henry Bargain of the same of 3*s.* 6*d.* rents in Wrangebrok for two years, namely of Simon Pulain 6*d.*; of Robert son of Simon, 3*d.*; of Adam son of Rainer, 7*d.*; of Robert de Moreton, 18*d.*; of William Forestar, 6*d.*; of Adam son of Godfrey, 1*d.*; of the aforesaid Henry, 1*d.*; paying yearly to the prior of Bretton 3*s.* 6*d.* For which donation Henry has given 20*s.*

Bretton.

(235) Grant by Emma widow of Ranulph de Munckbretton to Robert de le Stones of the same of five roods of land lying in Mouncbretton, one of which lies on le Schelegrene, one next Gerston henges, one in Hathelwelmor, one on the Bromcliffe, the rest in Lethevetrode, paying to her and her heirs one rose on the feast of the Nativity of St. John Baptist. Given at the vill of Bretton at Easter, 22 Edw. fil. Hen. (1294).

(236) Grant by William, prior of Bretton, with the consent of the brethren of the monastery, to Aky of that land which belonged to the monks and the closes below Sepe Swane, to be held of St. Mary Magdalene in fealty free of all services for a rent of 7s. yearly.

(237) Confirmation by John son of German de Bretton to Margaret de Ricroft of one rood of land in Bretton, one half next Hesewellchath extending as far as Gertheston, the other half on Braincliffe, paying yearly 1d. in silver.

(*Fo.* 53) (238) Grant by Roger son of Roger de Erdeslay to his son Roger and his heirs of two acres and one rood of land in Bretton, namely those which were John's son of German de Bretton, which were confirmed in a charter by the said John, namely one rood of land in Grimildewell, and one rood in le Fal which extends as far as Gamelrodwell next the land of Edusa which commences at the Swine pit and descends as far as Birkenestawe; and one rood in le Brome, which commences at Rissinhenges and descends as far as Bradhenges, and one rood and a half in Lingehill next the land of Margaret de Riecroft, which commences at Birkenestawe and descends as far as the new assart, and one rood and a half in le Fal between the land of the prior and the land of Margerie de Riecroft, and one rood lies in Hungerhil in le Brom between the lands of Hugh son of Roger and the land of Edusa. Paying to John son of German de Bretton one halfpenny in silver at Pentecost.

(239) Grant by William son of Alice daughter of German to Margaret daughter of John Tirel and Constance daughter of Thomas the clerk of Carleton of three and a half acres of land in Bretton for 20s. paid in hand, namely, those three and a half acres which Adam his brother holds in the same vill, namely half an acre with messuage and garden adjacent between the lands of the prior of Bretton and of Adam son of Roger the baker (*Pistor*), holden of the fee of Adam de Holand, and one and a half roods in le Fal, and one rood and a half in Fal and one rood in Lingebil, and one acre in Haselwellerod, and one rood in Holealdefeld, and one rood on Hetherod, and one rood on Braincliffe, and one rood on Cuthworthsby, and one rood in Bram, paying 4d. yearly.

Akedene.

(*Fo.* 53*d*) (240) Grant by Gilbert de Notton to William son of Osbert de Marchisdene of all the lands which were Adam's son of Avard Birim in Akedene, paying 4s. yearly, and the said William gives 2 marks of silver as recognition.

(241)   Grant by Gilbert de Notton of all his land of Akedene, namely a full half of the whole of the vill of Akedene.

(242)   Grant by Michael de Akedene and Emma his wife of all their land which Reginald de Akedene gave them, for 8s. of silver. Dated within the octave of St. Michael, 1249.

(Fo. 54) (243) Grant by John son of Hugh de Monkebretton of all his land in Monkebretton without any retention, namely one messuage and garden, fourteen acres in adjacent parcels on a certain bovate, three and a half acres of land with a croft abutting on the said messuage, one acre on Bretton, three and a half acres part wood and part pasture in an assart called Calvecroft, and half an acre in Loesing, eight acres of land, and sixteen acres of wood and pasture in an assart called Westker.   Likewise . . . . . .[1] between lands of the prior on the north and of Hugh de Hord . . . . . .[1] ird son of Roger on the south, abutting on the west on the water of Dirne.   Witnesses, Sir Thomas de Burgo, Sir Nicholas de Wortelay, Sir Adam de Wennervile, knights, John de Staynton, Godfrey and Thomas his brothers, John de Thours, Thomas de Cailly, Gilbert de Notton, and others.

(244)   Grant by Robert the cellarer of Monkebretton to the monastery and to Sir Richard, prior of the monastery, of ten selions of land in Monkebretton in Oldefeld lying between Choksthorpe and Hekrod, of which one head abuts on part of Oldefeld and the other next Lund.   Witnesses, John de Staynton, Godfrey de Staynton, William de Notton, Robert de Pul, Thomas Belle, John Heyrun, William Heyrun, and others.

(245)   Grant by William Marshall of Monkebretton of one rood of land, namely the fourth part of an acre in Monkebretton, as it lies on Hokynhil next the lands of the prior.   Witnesses, John de Staynton, Godfrey his brother, Thomas de Cailly, Gilbert de Notton, Robert the cellarer of Monkebretton, Robert son of Alexander of the same, and others.

(246)   Grant by William Marshall of Monkebretton of an annual rent of 2s. in Monkebretton, payable by Richard son of Roger and his heirs, with the homage and service of the said Richard from half a bovate of land in the same vill.   Witnesses, John de Staynton, Godfrey his brother, Thomas de Caylly, Gilbert de Notton, Thomas Belle of Cotheworth, and John de Wodehall of the same.

(Fo. 54d) (247) Grant by Stephen de Bella Aqua of three acres of land in Boulton in Dirnesherth, with the advowson of the mediety of the church of that vill, which he had of the gift of John son of William de Ketelbergh of Doncastre.   Witnesses, Sir Nicholas de Worthelay, Sir Thomas de Burgo, Sir Adam de Wennervile, knights, John de Staynton, Godfrey his brother, John de Cresacre, and Gilbert de Notton.

---

[1] Letters obliterated by stain.

(248) Grant by Thomas Shepherd (*Bercarius*) of Bretton of two acres of land in Monkebretton, of which one and a half acres lie in his field, between the land of the prior abutting on his (Thomas's) garden on the east, and on Oldegore to the west, and half an acre of land lies at the head of the land on the west called Oldegore, next to le Wodeclif. Witnesses, Robert de Pul, Robert the cellarer, Robert son of Alexander, William Heyrun, John Heyrun, and others.

(249) Confirmation by Robert son of Thomas Barker of the above grant. Witnesses, John de Staynton, Godfrey and Thomas his brothers, Thomas de Caylly, Gilbert de Notton.

(250) Quitclaim by John de Wollai and Agnes his wife, Walter de Kirkeby and Matilda his wife, of all right and claim to those lands which were Reyner de la Leye's. The prior and convent have paid to them 10 silver marks in the presence of the whole court of New-halle. Friday the vigil of the Annunciation of the blessed Mary. A.D. 1251. Witnesses, William de Tornhill, Roger de Berg, William de Wynton, William de Wynteworth, Gilbert Dun, Henry Lot, Robert Walegrim, Reyner de Rodes, Hugh de Wylthorp, Robert de Bosco.

(251) Grant by William de Went, prior of Monkbretton to Robert Waryn of Byrlay in Beghton and to Marjorie his wife and the heirs of their bodies lawfully begotten of one messuage with three and a half bovates of land in Beghton called Byrlay, namely that messuage and three bovates of land which the said Robert holds of the priory, and the other half bovate which Adam de Birlay formerly held of the priory, paying yearly 12s. Witnesses, John Savage, John de Hakinthorpe, John le Marshall of Ekynton, Robert Bryan of the same, Thomas de Ouston, clerk. Dated the day after the feast of St. Lucy the virgin, 1324.

(*Fo.* 55) (252) Confirmation by Robert son of William of Skelbrok to God and the blessed Mary and the canons of Hampole of a rent of 12s. 4d. per annum in the vill of Wrangbroke, which Adam son of Rayner of the same pays as rent for one bovate of land in the same vill held of Robert. To be held by the said God and blessed Mary and canons of Hampole of Robert and his heirs and assigns for 40s. which they have given to him, paying yearly to the lord of the fee 3s.

(*Fo.* 55d) (253) Tithes of the prior of Monkebretton, spiritualities and temporalities. £7 4s. 2d.

From the church of Roreston,	tithe	.	£2
,, the vicar of the same,	,,	.	26s. 8d.
,, the church of Bolton,	,,	.	21s. 4d.
,, the temporalities of the same,	,,	.	56s. 2d.
,, the church of Hykylton, newly appropriated			16s.
,, the church of Darton,	tithe	.	46s. 8d.

Total £8 2s.

(254) Sums of the tithes of the several dioceses throughout the Kingdom of England.

Canterbury	. £886	17	7	Ely . .	. £676	9	11¼
Rochester	. 239	2	11	Excester .	. 494	5	2
Sychester	. 240	7	7	Hereford .	. 553	2	10
Winchester	. 1,214	8	1	Lincoln .	. 4,094	5	1
Salisbury	. 1,422	11	1¼				
London	. 1,085	7	7¼	In Wales—			
Wyrcester	. 735	18	3	St. Asaph .	. £127	8	8¼
Coventry and Lychefeld .	} 862	18	9	Bangor .	. 85	2	7
				Landaff .	. 207	6	5¼
Norwich	. 2,355	18	3	St. David's	. 273	0	10½
Bath and Wells	649	18	9				

(*Fo.* 56) (255) Grant by Roger le Chappeman of Cudworth giving to the blessed Virgin Mary a certain annual rent of 12*d.* in honour of the blessed Virgin Mary at the altar of the same in Roston in perpetuity; from a tenement held of him (Roger) in Cudworth by the heirs of Richard Peck, 5*d.*; from John Bell for a tenement, 4*d.*; from John Atthall for a tenement, 2*d.*; from John Camell, ½*d.*; from Adam le Chappman, ½*d.* Witnesses, Arthur Boswell, John de Pull, Richard Bayard, Thomas Bayard, Ric. Witteman, and others. Dated at Roston, 20 December, 1336.

(*Fo.* 56*d*) (256) [*in French*] A true charm for the cure of boils, cankers, etc., including a mass of the Holy Ghost, and the repetition of a formula—because God is and was and ever will be, because Christ died, etc., and because this is true and I firmly believe it, therefore you are protected from boils, etc. Dead are boils, etc.

(*Fo.* 57) (257) Bull of Pope [Clement IV] dated at Perugia, 3 kal. April, in his first year, being an exemplification on behalf of the subprior and convent of Bretton of the proceedings between them and Pontefract priory with respect to the election of a prior at Bretton. While the matter was before the pope, the prior of Pontefract with an armed force had gone to Bretton, and instituted Adam de Norhamton, a monk of Pontefract, as prior of Bretton. Bretton complained to Master Roston, chaplain, appointed to hear the matter by Pope Innocent IV, demanding the quashing of the institution and a declaration that Bretton was free from subjection to Pontefract in all things save the payment of a yearly pension of 1 mark. Pontefract replied by saying that Richard, proctor of Bretton, was not a true proctor, but by command of pope Alexander the said Roston admitted the plea, and called upon them to prove it, under a penalty of 60 marks and payment of the expenses of Bretton if they failed. He also ordered that any surplus of the goods of the monastery, after maintenance of the monks and their servants, should be sequestrated to persons to be appointed by pope Alexander, that the monks of Bretton who had been taken should be set at liberty; and forbade Adam, who was acting as prior of Bretton, to alienate any property of the monastery until the question should be settled. Pope Alexander appointed J. St. Nicholas, cardinal-deacon, to determine the matter in Rome, hearing witnesses, etc.   The plea of the Pontefract proctor that the matter had already been decided in England by judges appointed by the pope was not admitted, nor his objection to Guillemon, monk of Bretton, as their proctor.   Pope Urban then appointed another cardinal to hear the matter, together with the bishop of Ostia, and with them pope Clement thoroughly discussed it, in all its bearings, before he was elected pope.   The election of prior Adam was by these judges pronounced void, and he was ordered to return to Pontefract with such of the monks of that house as he had with him, taking none of the goods of Bretton with him; the monks who had been taken and the sequestrated goods to be returned to Bretton; any alienations made by Adam, after the decree of Master Roston, were pronounced void, and Bretton was declared to be free from Pontefract, except for the aforesaid pension of 1 mark. The prior of Pontefract ought to take part in the election of the prior of Bretton, according to a composition formerly made between the parties.   Pontefract was condemned to pay the aforesaid 60 marks for failure to prove and 100 marks expenses.   The pope confirms this sentence appealed against by Pontefract.

The Bull then recites the declaration of Bretton before Master Roston, and the proofs put in in support of it, viz. the foundation charter by one Adam; the charter of the priory of La Charité, giving liberty to elect a prior, the prior of Pontefract having the right to be present if he chooses; a writing showing that Simon, dean of York, and William, archdeacon of Nottingham, judges delegated by the pope, absolved Bretton from subjection to Pontefract, except for payment of the said pension; and that the prior of Pontefract ought to be present at the election of the prior of Bretton; another writing, setting forth an agreement between the two houses, that when a vacancy occurred at Monkbretton, the monks should send to announce the prior's death at Pontefract, and the prior of Pontefract should then without delay appoint a time to come over to Bretton for the election.

The Bull then restates in more detail the whole of the subsequent proceedings in the abovesaid judgment given in Rome, where it was arranged that, on the occasion of a vacancy, the prior of Pontefract and the subprior of Bretton should discuss the matter, and agree if possible, upon some suitable person belonging to either house, who should then be installed by the prior of Pontefract and received by Bretton, according to the statutes of the Cluniac order.   If they could not agree, which God forbid, they should summon to them three of the wiser sort of Pontefract and three of Bretton, and whoever should then be chosen, should be installed prior as above; but if still they could not agree, and there should be an equal number on either side, they should call upon the prior of Lenton (or his subprior, if he could not come) to give the casting vote.   On a vacancy at Bretton the subprior and cellarer to have custody of the house.   A prior, once instituted, cannot be removed except for disobedience incurring deposition according to the Benedictine rule, or in other cases laid down by the Lateran Council.

All the priors of Bretton have been elected according to the composition made, until the time of this Adam.

This sentence is pronounced at Rome, 6 Nov., 1263.

Then follows the account of the taxing of the costs.

(Lansdowne MS. 405.)

(*Fo.* 61*d*) (258) Letter of submission to William, archbishop of York,-by William de Riall, prior of Monckebretton, as a cause of a visitation to the house of Monckebrettone of the order of St. Benedict, second nones of January (4 January), 1280–1, in form as follows.

I, William de Riall, prior of Monckebretton, of the order of St. Benedict, for myself and my successors, make to you venerable father, lord William by the grace of God archbishop of York, primate of England, and to your successors and to your church of York, canonical obedience for myself and the whole house and convent at Monckebretton, and with the hand we make oath and promise for ourselves and successors to faithfully observe for ever what is here written . . . . .

We therefore, the prior and convent of the house of Munkbrettone by this memorable decree of the said father and in filial obedience, humbly complying reverently admit his corrections, and we will conform to them as far as possible in our Lord Jesus Christ.

In testimony whereof we, William, prior, and our whole convent, have subscribed this instrument, and have affixed the seal of the convent with the unanimous assent of our convent. Given in our chapter of Munkbrettone the day and year above written. [*Wickwane's Register*, Surtees Soc., p. 139.]

(*Fo.* 62) (259) Bull of Pope Innocent, as fo. 1 of W. MS. (p. 9).

(*Fo.* 62*d*) (260) Letters of Pope Urban III, as fo. 4 of W. MS. (p. 11).

(*Fo.* 63*d*) (261) Protection by Pope Honorius (III), as fo. 7*d* of W. MS. (p. 12).

(*Fo.* 64) (262) Bull of Pope Gregory (IX), dated at Perugia, 5 ides June, in his 9th year, confirming to Monkbretton the appropriation of the church of Roreston by the archbishop of York, with the consent of his chapter.

THE CHARTULARY OF MONKBRETTON PRIORY.

Dodsworth MS. VIII.

(*Fo.* 210*d*) (1) Quitclaim by Reginald son of Helias de Sothill, as W. MS. No. 458, fo. 264*d*, with additional witnesses, John de Birgh, Simon de Lungvillers, John Malherb, John Tirel, Ralph de Lamara, Robert Peitevin, and William de Lungvillers.

(*Fo.* 214) (2) Grant by Gilbert de Notton of all his land in Akedene, as Lansdowne MS. 405, fo. 53*d* (240), with witnesses, Roger de Montbegon, John Malherbe, Helias de Coniun, Thomas de Roristun, Adam de Pennelbiri, Hugh de Bretton, William son of Roger, Roger Cusin, and Henry Haliday.

(3) Grant by Sir Roger de Novo Mercato of his mediety of the advowson of the church of St. Andrew of Boulton in Dirnesherth which descended to him after the death of his brother John, Witnesses, Stephen de Bella Aqua, William de Miggeley, Godfrey de Staynton, William Shcot of Byrthwait, William de Notton, Richard le Ker of Boulton, John Ward of the same, Adam Belle of Balne, Robert son of Ralph de Halghton. Given at Monkbretton, Friday in the feast of St. Mathew the Apostle, 1390.

(*Fo.* 214*d*) (4) Grant by Alexander son of Alexander de Ledes of his mediety of the church of Bolton upon Dirne. Given at Monkbretton, Thursday before the feast of St. Cuthbert bishop, anno reg. Edward son of Edward, 14 (1320).

(5) Quitclaim of the above, Friday before the feast of the Annunciation, 1320. Witnesses, William de Miggeley, Edmund de Percy, Henry de Ledes, Hugh Pycorde, John Taillour of Cotheworth.

(*Fo.* 224) (6) Grant by Robert, prior of Monkbretton, at the instance of the noble lords, Thomas, earl of Derbie; George Stanley, lord Strange; and Edward Stanley, knight of the lordship of Brierley; to John Holme, bailiff of the lordship of Brierley, of the advowson and right of presentation of the vicarage of the church of Roreston for the next presentation. Dated 18 January, 1497–8.

(*Fo.* 229*d*) (7) Grant by Adam, prior of Bretton, to Nichola daughter of Sir Randulph de Novo Mercato, as W. MS. No. 269, fo.162*d*, with additional witnesses, Nicholas de Treton, Hugh, parson of Treton, Robert, parson of Heton, and Michael de Suton.

(*Fo*. 232) (8) Grant by Sir William Scot, knt., of the advowson of the church of Hykylton, which advowson he acquired of Roger Curson.   Witnesses, William de Notton, William his (Scot's) son, Robert de Staynton, John Tours, William de Staynton.   Dated at Cauwedon, 10 March, 25 Edw. III (1351–2).

(9)   Grant by Sir John Scot, knt., to Thomas de Cottyngham, le Renderour, and William de Peketon, of one acre of land in the fields of Hykelton, also the advowson of the church of Hikelton.   Witnesses, John de Wodefall, Thomas Bosewill, John de Staynton, John de Barneburgh, Nicholas de Barington, Thomas Bell.   Dated at Hikelton, Wednesday, 11 May, 30 Edw. III (1356).

(*Fo*. 243) (10) Grant by Robert son of Lefwin to Assulf de Nottun, as W. MS. No. 514, fo. 297*d*, with additional witnesses, Matthew son of Robert, Asward son of Jordan, Richard de Turstan, Henry his son, Osbert son of Hugh, Walter de Birchon, Adam his brother, Adam son of Asward, Simon son of Reginald, Robert son of Paul, and Alexander his brother.

(11)   Grant by Gilbert de Notton to John his son, as W. MS· No. 515, fo. 298, with additional witnesses after John Thirel, Ralph his brother, William de Peningestun, William son of Adam, Adam de Holand, John de Peningestun, Adam the clerk, and Matthew his brother.

(*Fo*. 243*d*) (12)   Grant and quitclaim by Arnald Pigaze, as W. MS. No. 516, fo. 298, with additional witnesses, Simon de Claitun, Peter son of Moses de Hoderode, Geoffrey, chaplain of Hoderode, John de Roreston, and Hugh de Bretton.

(*Fo*. 249) (13) Indenture between the prior of Monkbretton and William Dodworth and Thomas his son.   Whereas Thomas Cartwright of Barnsley holds a certain assart called Rawfroyde in Bargh of the prior by the rolls of the court of the priory, belonging to the chapel of St. Elen, for a term of thirty years, paying yearly 3*s*. 4*d*.   Should Thomas put an end to the lease the prior agrees to the reversion of the lease to William and Thomas his son, paying to the prior 3*s*. 4*d*. yearly, as Thomas Cartwright paid.   Given at Monkbretton in the chapter house of the prior and convent, 20 Nov., 1416.

(*Fo*. 249*d*) (14) Quitclaim by William Dodworth, son of Thomas Dodworth, to Richard, prior of Monkbretton, of his right and title to a parcel of land lying in Bargh called Rauf Roode.   Dated 16 June, 1 Ric. III (1484).

(*Fo*. 251) (15) Charter of G., prior of La Charité (of the Cluniac order in parts across the seas of the same order as the chief house), to Adam FitzSwane, founder of Bretton.
    The prior of La Charité returns thanks to the founder for his liberality; and ordains that the founder shall select such

brethren from the house at Pontefract or any others in England whom he may approve, for his new foundation; the prior of St. John of Pontefract, if requested by the community of Bretton, to enter into the chapter with the patron for the election of a prior. On the election of a prior by the common consent of the whole chapter the election to be assented to by the prior of La Charité.

(*Fo.* 251*d*) (16) In the year 1255, 6 ides May, letters of the pope Alexander IV were exhibited at London to commission R., dean and archdeacon of Lincoln, to enquire into the dispute between the subprior and monastery of Bretton and the prior and monastery of Pontefract touching the subjection of the former house to that of Pontefract, to inspect the charters, and to examine witnesses within the next two months, and to send to the pope a transcript of the evidences under his seal.

(*Fo.* 252) (17) Covenant made between the prior and convent of Bretton and Sir John de Novoforo in the year 1239, on the morrow of the translation of blessed Thomas the Martyr, at York, in the court before Sir Pico de Lasceles, Robert de Coke-feld, Gerard Salvein, William Constable, justices. The said John shall hold the manor of Alwardethwait of the prior and convent, paying to them yearly 5 silver marks, and the said John shall hold the manor as Henry de Novoforo, his uncle, held it. Saving forinsec service which pertains to half a bovate of land, which the said John holds, where thirteen carucates make one knight's fee, as is contained in the charters which the monks possess. And it shall be lawful if the said John or his heirs cease payments for the prior and convent to distrain. And if the prior and convent or their successors are negligent in praying for the soul of Henry de Novoforo, John's uncle, it shall be lawful for the said John to compel the prior and convent to find a competent priest or monk for this purpose. Each party has placed his seal to the deed of the other. Witnesses, Sir Pico de Lasceles, Sir Robert de Cokefeld, Sir Gerard Salvein, Sir William Cunestable, Sir Peter de Brus, Sir Robert de Deiwile, Marmaduke Darel, Thomas de Portinton, Nicholas Devias, Reiner de Wombewell, William de Steinton, Robert de Wodehose, Ralph de Rupe, etc.

(*Fo.* 253) (18) Confirmation by Thomas de Burgo, as W. MS. No. 13, fo. 12, with additional witnesses, Robert de Tours, Ralph de Midelton, William son of Roger.

(19) Confirmation by Thomas son of Thomas de Burgo and Sarra his wife of the above charter. Witnesses, Roger de Montebegon, William son of Adam, Philip de Burgh, Mathew de Sepeley, Robert de Tours, Hugh son of Alan, John son of the same, William de Winteworthe, Richard Pullo, Peter Chancellor.

(*Fo.* 254) (20) Confirmation by John Malherbe and his wife Matilda, daughter of Adam FitzSwane, to the church of St.

Mary of Rievaulx, of two acres of land in Wirkesburgh on the river Derne, opposite their houses in the territory of Stainburg, which they have of the gift of Adam son of Peter, to hold as Henry son of Swane gave to them. Also the land which they have in the Malherbe fee of the gift of Adam son of Orm. Also the land which William son of Godric gave them. Witnesses, Benedict of York, chaplain, Richard, chaplain, Ralph, chaplain of Wirkeburg, Dodo Bardulf, Robert de St. Martin, Robert de Vercorol, William de Agnellis, William Bigot, William son of Adam, Walter de Preston, John son of Axolf, Richard son of Ardinge. [*Cart. Rievallense*, Surtees Soc., p. 62, cvii.]

(*Fo.* 255) (21) Confirmation by the lady Mabel de Novavilla, daughter of William de Mora, in her widowhood, of all the lands and possessions which Geoffrey de Novavilla, her late husband, gave. Witnesses, John de Hoderode, steward of Pontefract, William son of John, John de Hoili, knight, John de Raddemere, Stephen de Sutkirbi, Adam de Brahm, William de Brerlay, Adam Cossard, etc.

(*Fo.* 255*d*) (22) Quitclaim by Margaret, widow of Geoffrey de Nevill, to Sir Nicholas de Leycester of certain rents in Addewyke, value 6*d*. Witnesses, Sir Hugh de Cressington, Sir Henry de Kielay, knights, Robert de Wickerlay, William de Thoneton, Ralph son of Nicholas de Addewyke, William de Louerd, and Nicholas de Tikhill. Dated at Lancaster, Tuesday on the morrow of St. Thomas the Martyr, 20 Edw. I (1292).

(*Fo.* 256*d*) (23) Grant by Roger de Montbegon of all his land in Mekesburg, as Lansdowne MS. 405, fo. 19 (78), with additional witnesses, Eudo de Lungvilers, Geoffrey Britone, William de Sothill, Richard Blanchard, John Delamare, John de Lungvilers, Henry de Munkedene, Gilbert de Haya, Ralph Haigh, Ralph de Rupe, and John de Peningeston.

(*Fo.* 260) (24) This is the final covenant in the octave of Trinity, 12 Edw. II (1318), between the prior of Monkbretton, plaintiff, and Godfrey de Stainton and Isabella his wife, deforciants, in the presence of William de Bereford, Gilbert de Roubirie, John de Wustede, John Bacun, and John de Mutford, justices, of one messuage, sixty-three acres of land, seven acres of meadow, thirty acres of wood in Akworth.

The said Godfrey and Isabella recognize the right of the prior and church of St. Mary Magdalene of Bretton, and they restore the above property in this Court, to hold to the prior and convent for ever. The monks are to celebrate for ever in their priory for the souls of the said Godfrey and Isabella, and for the soul of Adam de Castelford, formerly husband of Isabella. For this recognition the prior has given to Godfrey and Isabella 100 silver marks.

(*Fo.* 275) (25) Grant by William de Notton and Isabel his wife to John de Birthwait, prior of Monkbretton, of all their tenements in Fishelake which they hold of the King *in capite*, and for which the said William did fealty to the King, as is shown in the rolls of the chancellor of the said King in the 20th year of his reign.   To hold to the said prior and convent of the King for due services, for the founding of a chapel in the church of Wulveley to celebrate for the health of the King and Philippa, queen of England, also for the said William and Isabel and their children while they live and for their souls when they are dead.   And the prior and convent are to find a chaplain to celebrate there, also to provide vessels, books, vestments, bread and wine and everything required for the mass to be celebrated.   And the said chaplain shall celebrate divine service for the health and souls of the aforesaid in the chapel of Wulveley, as is usual in the diocese of York after the manner and form which the monks of the order of St. Benedict hold for the living and the dead. And if the prior and convent do not provide a service for fifteen days they shall be held liable to pay to the King 40s.   Witnesses, Hugh de Hastings, John Fitzwilliam, Adam de Everingham of Rokley, knight, Robert de Staynton, John son of the same Robert, and John son of Godfrey de Staynton.   Dated at Fishelake, 28 March, 27 Edw. III (1354).

Dodsworth MS. CLV.

Transcribed from the Chartulary of Monkbretton in the possession of Thomas
Holcroft of Vale Royal, 1614, and in that of Sir William Ayrmine, 1634.

(*Fo.* 61) (26) Grant by Adam de Holand of all the tenements which he held of the monks in the vill of Bretton, also the homage and services of Hugh son of John de Bretton and his heirs for one bovate of land which he held of him (Adam), also the homage and services of John son of Guarin and his heirs for two bovates of land held of him, also the homage and services of Hugh son of Hugh Shepherd and his heirs for one bovate, also the homage and services of Roger son of the baker for one toft.   He also confirmed to them the concession which Richard Pele made to them of two bovates of land which he held of Adam in Bretton, as the charter of the said Richard shows.   Witness, William de Bretton.

(*Fo.* 61d) (27) Grant by Adam de Holande of two bovates of land in Bretton, which were formerly Ketell's and Raney's; and he gave to them his assart called Stywardrode next Lund of Bretton.   Witness, John son of Aisolf.

(28) Grant by Adam son of Peter de Birkin of the fishpond which is in Royston and Carleton.

(29) Confirmation by Isabella de Sunnington of all her right in the aforesaid fishpond, and in another charter the same Isabella de Sunnington released all her right in the marsh (*marisco*) called Northpole between Roreston and Carleton, about which there was a contention between the monks and Isabella at the first assizes at York after the coronation of King Henry son of John, 1 Hen. III (1216).

(30)   Confirmation by William de Neville and Amabel his wife of the mediety of the church of Roreston.   Witness, lord Roger, archbishop of York.

(*Fo.* 62)   (31)   Appropriation of the church of Roreston.

Walter, by the grace of God, archbishop of York.   Having inspected certain charters of Geoffrey formerly archbishop of York, and of the chapter of York, concerning the church of Roreston, we confirm that church for its proper uses and ordain a perpetual vicar of that church who shall have all the tithes of corn of Royston, Cudworth and Chivett, and all the altarage, and all the small tithes of the whole parish, and all the lands pertaining to the church of Roreston shall belong in perpetuity to the vicar, except all the small tithes of the lands of the monks and the tithes of their mill, also the oblations of the chapel of St. Helen of Carleton, also two bovates of land in the vill of Carleton, and the tithes of hay in the parish of Roreston which belong to the monks.   The vicar is to pay each year 1 silver mark on St. Mary Magdalene's day to the monks, and he shall bear all other episcopal and archidiaconal dues.   Witnesses, Thomas, precentor of York, and others.   Cawod, 4 cal. April, 1234.

(32)   A.D. 1296.   Quitclaim by Robert de Holthorn, vicar of Rorestun, to the prior and convent of Bretton, of all right and claim in the tithes of corn in Cudworth.

(*Fo.* 62*d*)   (33)   Confirmation by Peter son of William de Rockeley of those bovates of land in Cudworth which Peter de Byrthwait gave to the monks.   Witness, Peter de Bosvyle.

(34)   Grant by Nicholas son of Adam de Horbury of all his right and services in half a carucate of land in Branscroft which Robert de Clayton held, paying 2*s*. annually.   Witness, Robert de Stapleton.

(*Fo.* 63)   (35)   The chantry within the chapel in the hall of Cudworth.

This is the final agreement between John Tyrell, parson of Roreston, and Claricia wife of Robert de Stapleton and William their son.   The said John, parson of Roreston, to give up to Claricia and William the chantry of their chapel within their hall of Cudworth, saving the right of mother church; the lady Claricia and William her son shall find the chapel with all necessary things, etc.; the parishioners of the mother church shall have no communion in the chapel, unless with the consent of the church; the aforesaid church of Roreston shall have all the oblations of the said chapel at the four annual feasts, Christmas day, the Purification, Easter and All Saints, and on the feast of the chapel.   For this agreement the said Claricia and William have given to the mother church of Roreston six acres of land of their lordship in the same vill, for which benefit the name of Robert de Stapleton has been placed in the martyrology of the church of Roreston, and his anniversary shall be held there annually. Witnesses, Adam son of Orm, Gilbert de Notton, Richard de Stapleton, Hugh de Stapleton his brother, Richard de Felkirk, Adam the chaplain, Hugh de Bretton.

(*Fo.* 64) (36) Confirmation by William de Bretton and Matilda his wife of a moiety of the land of William the smith of Swalohill and the service of the same, which Swane de Holande gave to the church of St. Mary Magdalene of Lunda. Witness, Symon, clerk of Barnislay.

(*Fo.* 65*d*) (37) Grant by Alan de Bretton of all his land in his lordship of Bretton which Robert de Athelwaldele holds, paying 16*d*. Witness, Robert de Bretton.

(38) Grant by John son of Adam de Deneby of three acres of land in Deneby in a place called Ebriches.

(39) Symon son of Mathew de Deneby confirmed the donation.

(40) Adam the prior and convent of Bretton granted to Simon son of Hugh de Deneby the aforesaid three acres in Deneby in Ebriches.

Dodsworth MS. CLIX.

Transcribed from the Chartulary of Monkbretton in the possession of Thomas Holcroft of Vale Royal, 1614, and in that of Sir William Ayrmine, 1634.

(*Fo.* 35*d*) (41) Charter of Adam FitzSwane of the gift of the monastery of St. Mary of Lund, Bretton, to the priory of St. John of Pontefract.

To the lord archbishop of York and all faithful sons of holy mother church. Notification that Adam FitzSwane has given to the church of St. John of Pontefract the place of St. Mary Magdalene of Lund, which he had founded out of his patrimony, for monks to serve God regularly for the souls of his father and mother, for his own health and that of his successors. For this benefaction a year's obit is to be done for him in the mother church of La Charité, and an obit for him in the house of Pontefract, also his anniversary there, and in all other houses of the order a trental, but in others as much as for a Cluniac monk. Adam, prior of that place, the acquirer and first founder, when he has departed from Pontefract, shall remain at Lund as custodian and prior as long as he shall live. After his decease the prior of Pontefract and the monks of that place with the counsel of Adam and his heirs shall elect a suitable successor in his place. And if by chance any brother of Pontefract comes to see the prior on business of his house he shall eat with him. For this he authorises the payment of 1 silver mark from the house of Lund to the church of St. John of Pontefract in recognition. Witnesses, Osbert, archdeacon; Ralph, dapifer; Ernald and Robert, chaplains; Thomas, dapifer of the monks,

(*Fo.* 36) (42) Decree as to the election of the prior of Bretton.

R., abbot of Burgo, and R., dean of Lincoln, have undertaken a mandate from pope Innocent to grant a hearing to Reiner, prior of Pontefract, and W[illiam], prior of Bretton. Roger de Montebegun appeared as advocate for Bretton. It was decreed that the monks of Bretton should inform the prior of Pontefract of the death of their prior without any delay, and on the third day he should come for the election of a prior. The prior of Pontefract shall install the new prior whom the convent of Bretton shall accept. During a vacancy the subprior and cellarer shall have the custody of the house. When appointed the prior of Bretton shall not be removed except for disobedience incurring deposition, according to the rule of St. Benedict. The prior and convent of Bretton shall observe all the customs of the Cluniac order faithfully. They shall pay 1 mark annually to Pontefract on the feast of SS. Peter and Paul.

(*Fo.* 39–43*d*) (43) Adjudication of the dispute between the houses of Pontefract and Munckbretton as to the election of the prior of Munckbretton, dated 1269; confirmed 1278, sealed 1289.

[A long charter printed in *Mon. Anglicanum*, v, 123.]

INDEX OF NAMES AND PLACES.

o

Barnburg, Barnburgh, Barnebur, Barneburg, Barneburgh, Barne-burghe, Barneburght, Barnebor-ough, 93, 97, 98; John de, 22, 23, 24, 28, 29, 31, 72, 150, 218; Reiner the priest of, 199; Richard de, 87

Barnesyr, Barnsyr, William, 163

Barnsley, Barneslay, Barnisley, Barn-yslay, Barnysley, 1, 20, 21, 22, 24, 25, 26, 34, 37, 41, 42, 43, 44, 54, 63, 68, 79, 95, 100, 101, 115, 130, 140, 156, 218; Simon the clerk of, 223; Barnesley brigge, 25; Barnysdale ryg, 107

Baroclogh, Robert, 150, 152

Bartilcrofte, Bartylcroft, 168, 173

Barton, Richard, 29

Basset, William, 59

Bassewell, Arthur de, 30

Bastard, Robert, 176, 177, 201

Bate, Adam, 68, 102, 182; Dionisia, 96; Richard, 96; Thomas, 32, 96, 97

Batelay, Bateley, Gregory de, 56, 128, 166; John de, 76; Richard de, 76, 202

Batet, William, 98

Bath and Wells, tithes of the diocese of, 214

Baty, Diota, 95; Thomas, 95

Baxter, Baxster, John, 113, 116; Ro-bert, 86, 137; Thomas, 96

Bayard, Baiard, Bayerd, Biard, By-ard, Avice, 30; Hugh, 87, 88; Oliver, 107; Richard, 1, 29, 30, 31, 33, 214; Thomas, 30, 31, 32, 149

Bayle, Bayil, Thomas, 192

Beatrice, daughter of Richard the carter, 81; William son of, 94

Beaumont, Thomas, 59, 61, 150, 153

Bebbeal More, 141

Bechale, Adam de, 187

Becton, Bekton, Beghton, Behgton, 4, 175, 176, 177, 178, 179, 180, 181, 182, 183, 188, 189, 195, 213; John de, 177, 189; John rector of, 178; Nicholas de, 189; Richard de, 178; Richard the clerk of, 178, 179; Roger the clerk of, 189; William de, 177, 178, 189

Bee, John, 174

Bek, Bekks, 170, 174; Robert, 169, 174; Thomas, 45

Belam, Henry de, 83

Belami, Bellamye, Robert, 169, 174; William, 166

Bell, Belle, Adam, 217; Avice, 83; Diota, 30; John, 32, 149, 214; Thomas, 29, 30, 31, 32, 33, 46, 47, 83, 150, 181, 212, 218; William, 33, 91, 95, 97

Bella Aqua, John de, 89; Stephen de, 88, 127, 212, 217; Thomas de, 88

Bellcrosse, Le, 35

Bellomonte, Lady Elizabeth, 130

Beltam, William, 198

Belynley, 151

Benedict, Justus son of, 203

Benerans, Robert de, 76

Benks, Benkes, Henry, 40; Thomas, 161

Bentley, Bentelay, 74; Umfridus de, 190

Berelay, Berley, 138; Thomas de, 49

Berford, Bereford, Alice, 27; Walter de, 27; William de, 220

Berlyng, Roger de, 79

Berntonroydes, 139

Bersetlawe, 203

Berwyke, John, 85

Bet, Best, Richard, 28, 42, 44, 70, 81

Beter, Becar, Richard, 40, 43

Betoncrofte, 148

Betwenyegates, 71

Beward, son of Adam, 208

Bigot, William, 220

Bilham, Bilam, Bilaham, Bileh', Bile-ham, Billam, Byllam, Elias de, 51; Helias, 55, 56; Henry de, 51; Hugh de, 124, 163; William de, 51

Billinglay, Billingley, Billynglay, Bil-lyngley, Byllinglay, Byllynglay, Byllyngley, 2, 29, 51, 52, 78, 79, 81, 86, 87, 88, 89, 102, 135; William de, 87; Hugh son of, 87

Billiold, Thomas, 169

Biri, Byri, Byrie, Adam de, 14, 205, 206, 208, 218; Henry de, 14, 16, 59, 102, 159

Birim, Adam, 211; Avard, 211

Birkenstawe, 211

Birkin, Birchine, Birchin, Birkine, Birkyne, Byrkyn, Adam de, 123; Edmund de, 39, 40; John de, 77, 123, 158; Peter de, 123, 221; Roger de, 158; Walter de, 218

Birthwait, Birckneith, Birchethait, Birkethwat, Birkethwait, Birk-tuait, Birthwat, Birtwaith, Birt-wathe, Byrthwat, vii, 54, 217; Adam de, 66, 122; Henry de, 30, 160, 161; Hugh de, 205; John de, 31, 74, 75, 110, 182; John de, prior of Monk-bretton, 31, 72, 75, 220; Peter de, 1, 18, 122, 124, 158, 205, 222; Robert de, 17, 103, 158

Bishops, Guido of Praeneste, 10; Hen-ry of Albano, 12; John of Albano, 10; Paul of Praeneste, 12; Peter of Porto and Sancta Rufino, 10; Theobald of Ostia and Velletri, 12

Coniun, Helias de, 217
Connesburgh, 118
Conriis, Sir Nicholas de, 159
Constable, William, 197, 219
Constablebutts, 21
Conteres, John, 53
Conynggarthe, 170
Cook, Coce, Cock, Coke, Adam, 56,
57; Agnes, 70; John, 27; Richard,
79
Cop, Copp, 119
Corbridge, Thomas, 206
Corland, 191
Cornelius, Gilbert son of, 80
Cornhil, German de, 123
Cortilingston, Sir Philip de, 99
Cossard, Adam, 123, 126, 220
Cotes, Matilda, 19; William, 19, 20
Cothewych, 121
Cotingham, Cotyngam, Cotyngham,
Cottyngham, Thomas le Rendereur,
22, 23, 27, 28, 30, 31, 32, 33, 110,
148, 149, 181, 218; William, 181,
182
Coventry and Lychefeld, tithes of the
diocese of, 214
Cowclose, 61
Cowper, John, 60, 81, 94
Coyntres, William, 58
Crane, Richard, 166
Cregeliston, Cregylston, Crigelstun,
Crigilston, Crigileston, Crygleston,
40, 41, 51, 52, 53, 124, 142, 127
Cresacre, Cresaker, James, 68, 182;
John, 96, 135, 136, 212; Percival,
119; Thomas, 55
Cressington, Hugh de, 220
Cressy, Crecy, 175; John, 111, 112,
113; Robert, 203; Roger, 166;
Thomas, 170; William, 3, 111, 113
Cretun, Cretona, Jordan de, 128, 179;
William de, 129
Crinocclyf, 55
Croc, Crock, Crok, Croke, Hugh, 79;
Richard, 51, 87; William, 46, 51,
55, 56, 73, 80, 83, 84, 127
Croco, Richard, 56
Croft, Thomas, 37
Crokrode, 123
Crokyddolez, 171
Crolande, Roger, 151
Crome, 64
Crookdoles, 167
Crosacre, 34, 35
Croshil, 195
Crosse Cliff Bank, 132
Crosseslake, 14
Croswelle, Crosswelle, 81, 82
Crumlandes, 55
Cublay, Coblay, Cubley, 4, 144, 145;
John, 144

Cudworth, Chudewrda, Codworth,
Coithworth, Corteworde, Cotheworth, Cotheworthe, Cothworth,
Coutworth, Cudeworthe, Cudewrth,
Cudewrda, Cudworthe, Cusceworth,
Cutheworthe, Cuthworth, 1, 4, 9,
11, 17, 18, 23, 24, 28, 29, 30–44, 46,
47, 48, 145, 149, 156, 181, 190, 193,
198, 202, 207, 212, 214, 217, 222;
Adam de, 32, 155; Agnes de, 32,
193; Benedict de, 158; Dionisia de,
33; John, 193; Jordan de, 32;
Osan, 193; Peter de, 33, 74; Peter
the shepherd of, 17; Robert de, 33;
Thomas, 32, 131; William, 193;
William the miller of, 193; Cud-
worth broke, 39; Cuthworthsby,
211; Ower Cudworth, 34
Cunegeshaccroftes, 17
Curs, Simon de, 15
Curson, Curzon, John, 84, 85; Nicho-
las, 85; Robert, 93; Roger, 55,
217; Thomas, 85
Curtenay, John de, 187
Cusin, Roger, 217
Cusworth, John, 37, 74, 147, 156, 157
Cutteler, James, 101

Dadderodes, Daderodis, 51, 52
Dalahay, Peter, 106
Dalefurlang, 93
Dalehades, 94
Dalestyghend, 175
Dalton, Reiner, 194; Thomas, 194
Dand londes, 62
Danngerous oxgang, 149
Darcy, Sir John, 54; Lord, 154
Darel, Marmaduke, 219
Darfeld, Darffeld, Darffelde, Darfield,
Derfeld, Derffeld, Derefeud, 2, 37,
46, 47, 48, 49, 50, 57, 59, 60, 64, 65,
66, 70, 71, 72, 73, 76, 77, 78, 79, 82,
84; church of, 64, 82; on Dern,
Dyrn, 73, 74, 75; Hugh, parson of,
56, 79; Mauger de, 70; Rainer the
clerk of, 15, 18; Reiner, parson of,
56; Richard, parson of, 72; Richard
de, 70; Swain de, 11; Sir William
de Quinton, rector of, 72
Darlay, Darley, Derlay, Derley, 60,
125, 126, 137; Adam de, 120, 127,
129, 138 ; Agnes de, 57; Henry de,
138; John, 108, 113, 114; Ralph
de, 120, 138; Richard de, 138;
Robert de, 41, 42, 108, 166; Simon
de, 129; William de, 121, 126, 138
Darlayclyff, Darleycliff, Derleyclyff,
3, 136, 139, 140
Darley Oxgang, 60
Darthingtonrode, 138
Darton, Dartton, Derton, Dertona, 4,

de, 88; Alexander de, 189; Brian
de, 189; Elias de, 189; Henry de,
189, 190; Hugh, 189; Joan, 100;
John, 100; Richard de, 190; Tho-
mas, 88
Scelton, Schelton, Selton, Henry de,
192; John de, 52,53, 56, 104; Rich-
ard de, 163; Thomas the physician
of, 142, 202
Schafton, Safton, 17, 29, 34, 35; Sir
John de, 155
Schaftonstye, 36
Schalebrok, 104
Scheffeld, Schefeud, Schessefeld,
Scheffefeld, Roger de, 45; Thomas
de, 73, 180
Schelegrene, 211
Schelintorp, 163
Schepenker, Le, 109
Schepeschank, Schepschank, Shepe-
shank, Hugh, 73; John, 141; Rich-
ard, 72; Roger, 73
Schepherd, Alice, 81, 82; Henry, 81;
John, 110; Richard, 81, 82; Wil-
liam, 82
Scherithe, 162
Schitenesse, 167
Schortbutts, 167
Schortelay, 29
Schortsetcop, 34
Schyresflat, 200
Schyrewode forest, 203
Scinnereker, 195
Sclephill, 106
Scolay, Alan de, 28; Thomas, 84
Scot, Scott, Shcot, Skott, Alice, 47,
52, 54, 58, 59; Dionisia, 149, 150;
Elizabeth, 47; Francis, 53; John,
46, 47, 50, 53, 55, 62, 146, 147, 218;
Nicholas, 53; Peter, 30; Robert,
149, 150; Thomas, 52; William,
55, 217, 218
Scotgate, 167, 171
Scute, 193
Seckerrode, Sekkeroyde, 138, 139
Secleye, John, 149; Robert, 149
See Crofte, 173
Selar, William de, 22
Selby, abbot of, 12
Selcoppe, Sedecop, 29, 167, 171
Selildroyde, 34
Sellesc, Henry de, 103
Sepe Swane, 211
Serebek, 45
Serlo, the clerk of Mirefeld, 15
Sexton, Gerard, 204
Shafton, Schafton, Safton, 17, 29, 34,
35; Alice, 83; Anote, 83; Hugh,
83; John, 155; Robert, 83
Shaw, Shaghe, Elizabeth, 86; Wil-
liam, 86

Shelebec, 196
Shellito, Richard, 86
Shelton, John, 87
Shepeley, Sepeley, Scepelay, Agnes
de, 193; Hugh, 193; Matthew de,
120, 192, 219; William de, 193
Shepeyngesike, 21
Shepherd, Alexander, 199; Henry,
31; Hugh, 221; Thomas, 148, 213;
William, 105; Alan son of Thomas
the, 148; Richard son of Henry the,
31
Shepherd thorn, 161
Shortbutts, 170
Shorteways, 172
Shostlyng, John, 18
Shrewsbury, George, 6th earl of, viii
Shyres, John, 137
Shytynhers, 172
Sibil, Adam son of, 199
Sicliglina, Adam de, 77
Sighroyde, 20
Sike, John, 97, 98
Sililsyke, 36
Siliroid, 36
Silkeston, Silkestona, Barnard, 13;
Hugh, dean of, 123, 158, 184; John
the chaplain, 18; Richard, 13
Silverwod, John, 70
Simon, parson of Tanceslaia, Tank-
reslei, 123, 124; the clerk, 123; of
Barnislay, 223; the dyer, 209;
son of Reginald, 218; Adam son of,
50, 51, 55, 56; John son of, 53, 128;
Jordan son of, 179
Sinedahalis, 9
Sisson, Thomas, 96
Siward son of Offi, 196
Sixhrode, Sixtrode, 19, 20
Skaraill, William, 22
Skargill, Skargyll, Skergill, William,
25, 36, 63
Skeknes, Skeknesse, Robert de, 14,
125
Skelbrok, Skelbroke, Schelebroc, 48,
50, 104, 105, 106, 107, 108, 187;
lord of, 106; Lynges of, 105; Ro-
bert, 213; William, 213
Skires, Skyres, John, 39, 40, 200;
Roger, 53
Slatebanke, 119; Slatebankesyke,119
Slephill, 104, 105, 107, 108, 109
Slethley, Robert de, 120
Slogrode, 66
Smalbrygfeld, Smallbrygfeld, 35, 36
Smalbryghyll, 35
Smaleby, 124
Smethehale, 123
Smith, Smyth, Smythe, Smeythe,
croft, 61, 110; John, 2, 96; Mar-
garet, 96, 141; Matthew, 21, 148;

J. WHITEHEAD AND SON LTD., PRINTERS, LEEDS.